D1295881

Ever since Plato, philosophers have faced one central question: What is the scope and nature of human knowledge? In this volume the distinguished philosopher Ernest Sosa has collected his essays on this subject written over a period of twenty-five years. All the major topics of contemporary epistemology are covered: the nature of propositional knowledge, externalism versus internalism, foundationalism versus coherentism, and the problem of the criterion. The resulting book is a valuable resource for scholars and can serve as a textbook for graduate seminars in epistemology.

Knowledge in perspective

Knowledge in perspective
Selected essays in epistemology

ERNEST SOSA

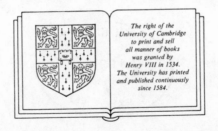

The right of the
University of Cambridge
to print and sell
all manner of books
was granted by
Henry VIII in 1534.
The University has printed
and published continuously
since 1584.

CAMBRIDGE UNIVERSITY PRESS

CAMBRIDGE

NEW YORK PORT CHESTER MELBOURNE SYDNEY

Published by the Press Syndicate of the University of Cambridge
The Pitt Building, Trumpington Street, Cambridge CB2 1RP
40 West 20th Street, New York, NY 10011, USA
10 Stamford Road, Oakleigh, Melbourne 3166, Australia

© Cambridge University Press 1991

First published 1991

Printed in the United States of America

Library of Congress Cataloging-in-Publication Data
Sosa, Ernest.
Knowledge in perspective: selected essays in epistemology /
Ernest Sosa.
p.   cm.
Includes bibliographical references.
ISBN 0–521–35628–8. – ISBN 0–521–39643–3 (pbk.)
1. Knowledge, Theory of.   I. Title.
BD161.S647   1991
121 – dc20   90–44708
CIP

British Library Cataloguing in Publication Data
Sosa, Ernest
Knowledge in perspective: selected essays in
epistemology.
1. Epistemology
I. Title
121

ISBN 0–521–35628–8 hardback
ISBN 0–521–39643–3 paperback

WIDENER UNIVERSITY
WOLFGRAM
LIBRARY
CHESTER, PA.
DISCARDED

To Sara, who likes knowledge in perspective

Contents

Sources and acknowledgments   ix

Introduction: back to basics   1

PART I. WHAT IS KNOWLEDGE, AND HOW IS IT POSSIBLE?

1   The analysis of "knowledge that p"   15
2   How do you know?   19
3   On our knowledge of matters of fact   35
4   Presuppositions of empirical knowledge   51

PART II. THEORIES OF JUSTIFICATION

5   Epistemology today: a perspective in retrospect   65
6   Nature unmirrored, epistemology naturalized   86
7   Theories of justification: old doctrines newly defended   108
8   Reliabilism and intellectual virtue   131

PART III. INTELLECTUAL VIRTUE AND EPISTEMIC PERSPECTIVE: A VIEW PRESENTED

9   The foundations of foundationalism   149
10   The raft and the pyramid: coherence versus foundations in the theory of knowledge   165
11   The coherence of virtue and the virtue of coherence   192
12   Testimony and coherence   215

PART IV. INTELLECTUAL VIRTUE IN PERSPECTIVE: THE VIEW DEVELOPED

13   Knowledge and intellectual virtue   225

14   Methodology and apt belief   245
15   Equilibrium in coherence?   257
16   Intellectual virtue in perspective   270

Index   295

Sources and acknowledgments

This collection falls into four parts: one on knowledge, one on justification, and two that present and develop a view called virtue perspectivism. These parts share a pattern: Early essays within each part make proposals that later essays develop and defend, and the parts themselves form a similar pattern.

Three of these collected essays appear here for the first time: (1) "Back to Basics" – the Introduction, which provides some historical and contemporary context; (2) "Testimony and Coherence" – which also appears elsewhere concurrently; and (3) "Reliabilism and Intellectual Virtue" – which compares the present view with externalist reliabilism. In addition, "Theories of Justification: Old Doctrines Newly Defended" contains a new discussion of coherentism. And the final essay, "Intellectual Virtue in Perspective," contains new material – Sections E through G – that develops virtue perspectivism and makes it more precise.

All of the previously published essays have been revised, either with substantive changes or with minor changes for stylistic coherence and to avoid repetition. Finally, two of the chapters – 7 and 16 – combine materials from two or more publications.

Sources are listed below. I thank the editors and publishers who gave their permission for articles to be reprinted here.

"Introduction: Back to Basics." Previously unpublished.

Chapter 1. "The Analysis of "Knowledge that p," *Analysis* 25 (1964): 1–8.

Chapter 2. "How Do You Know?" *American Philosophical Quarterly* 11 (1974): 113–22.

Chapter 3. "On Our Knowledge of Matters of Fact," *Mind* 83 (1974): 388–405.

Chapter 4. "Presuppositions of Empirical Knowledge," *Philosophical Papers* 15 (1986): 75–87.

Chapter 5. "Epistemology Today: A Perspective in Retrospect," *Philosophical Studies* 40 (1981): 309–32.

Chapter 6. "Nature Unmirrored, Epistemology Naturalized," *Synthese* 55 (1983): 49–72.

Chapter 7. "Theories of Justification: Old Doctrines Newly Defended." Drawn in part from previously unpublished material; in part from "'Circular' Coherence and 'Absurd' Foundations," in Ernest Lepore, ed., *A Companion to Inquiries into Truth and Interpretation* (Oxford: Blackwell, 1986); and in part from "Beyond Skepticism, to the Best of Our Knowledge," *Mind* 97 (1988): 153–89.

Chapter 8. "Reliabilism and Intellectual Virtue." Previously unpublished.

Chapter 9. "The Foundations of Foundationalism," *Nous* 14 (1980): 547–65.

Chapter 10. "The Raft and the Pyramid: Coherence Versus Foundations in the Theory of Knowledge," *Midwest Studies in Philosophy* 5 (1980): 3–25. © 1980 by the University of Minnesota.

Chapter 11. "The Coherence of Virtue and the Virtue of Coherence," *Synthese* 64 (1985): 3–28.

Chapter 12. "Testimony and Coherence," in B. K. Matilal and A. Chakrabarti, eds., *Knowing from Words* (Oxford: Oxford University Press, in press).

Chapter 13. "Knowledge and Intellectual Virtue," *The Monist* 68 (1985): 224–45.

Chapter 14. "Methodology and Apt Belief," *Synthese* 74 (1988): 415–26.

Chapter 15. "Equilibrium in Coherence?" in John Bender, ed., *The Current State of the Coherence Theory* (Dordrecht and Boston: Kluwer Academic Publishers, 1989).

Chapter 16. "Intellectual Virtue in Perspective." Drawn in part from "Knowledge in Context, Skepticism in Doubt," *Philosophical Perspectives 2: Epistemology* (1988): 139–57; and in part from "Beyond Skepticism, to the Best of Our Knowledge," *Mind* 97 (1988): 153–89.

Warm thanks also to Eleanor Thum, for manifold secretarial help; to Michael DiRamio for copy editing; and to John Gibbons and Robert Welshon for the index.

Much of this work was aided by the American Council of Learned Societies, the Canada Council, the National Science Foundation, and the National Endowment for the Humanities; and all of it, by Brown University. During the twenty-five years spanned by the collection, Brown provided me with ideal conditions, for which I am most grateful.

In *Recent Philosophers*,[1] the sequel to his classic *One Hundred Years of Philosophy*, John Passmore writes:

1 John Passmore, *Recent Philosophers* (LaSalle, Ill.: Open Court, 1985).

[Philosophy] is still in many ways the most striking example of that familiar aphorism, "the more things change, the more they remain the same." To be sure, there are novelties, questions raised which Plato would not have understood. Yet for all the greater sophistication of method, the use of technical tools deriving from logic and semantics, it is surprising how much philosophical effort is still devoted to trying to solve problems which Plato, or Descartes, or Hume, first saw as such.

A particular case will serve to illustrate two points, the familiarity of some of the issues and the novel manner in which discussion of them is now often carried on. One of the questions which greatly troubled Plato is how knowledge differs from belief. For a time it looked as if philosophers were happy to suppose that they had the answer, that knowledge is a kind of belief which has two peculiarities. First, it is true; secondly, the believer is fully justified in believing that it is true. In 1963 E. L. Gettier published a two-and-a-half page article in the journal *Analysis* which set out two counter-examples to this way of making the distinction. . . . Gettier's miniscule article generated some hundreds of replies, a clear sign that the old issues are by no means dead.[2]

What first gripped me in epistemology was this Gettier problem, then freshly published, which prompted the first chapter of the present volume.

The Gettier problem began to fill a gap in my schooling, which had included no course in epistemology. That gap was entirely filled soon after I arrived at Brown as a postdoctoral fellow in 1964, and I owe thanks for that above all to Roderick Chisholm – for that, for his seminars and writings, and for innumerable discussions. We often disagree on the answers, seldom disagree on the questions, and never disagree on the way to settle the matter – or, rather, I've long agreed with him.

My warm thanks, finally, go to friends and colleagues for helpful comments on one or another of these collected essays: to Felicia Ackerman, Robert Adams, William Alston, Anthony Anderson, Robert Audi, David Bennett, John Bennett, David and Jean Blumenfeld, Laurence Bonjour, Hector Castañeda, Earl Conee, Michael DePaul, John Gibbons, Alvin Goldman, John Greco, Gilbert Harman, Jaegwon Kim, Stephen Leeds, Keith Lehrer, Noah Lemos, David Martens, Michael Pendlebury, Martin Perlmutter, Alvin Plantinga, Philip Quinn, Nicholas Rescher, Jerome Shaffer, Robert Shope, David Sosa, Robert Swartz, and William Throop; and to James Van Cleve go special thanks for his comments on drafts of these essays over a span of nearly two decades.

2 *Ibid.*, pp. 13–14.

Introduction: back to basics

Foundationalism postulates foundations for knowledge. Here agree its two branches – the rationalist and the empiricist – even if they disagree in their respective foundations, and disagree on how to erect a superstructure.

For the rationalist, only rational intuition can give a secure foundation, and only deduction can build further knowledge on that foundation. Here the model of knowledge is the axiomatic system, with its self-evident axioms and its theorems derived through logical deduction. Rationalists, therefore, were the logicists, who tried to reduce all mathematics to self-evident axioms.

More ambitious yet, Descartes sketched in his *Meditations* a strategy for rationally founding all knowledge, not only mathematical knowledge. But his strategy required substantive commitments that turned out to be less than axiomatic – commitments of natural theology, for example.

The failure of rationalism is evident both in Descartes and in logicism.

For their part, empiricists accept not only foundations by rational intuition but also foundations by sensory experience. Equally unsuccessful, however, was their project of reducing all physical reality to sensory experience – whose apotheosis is Carnap's phenomenalism. Besides, as Hume showed, the future cannot be predicted deductively: The reasoning required outstrips logical deduction.

Empiricism thus becomes more liberal than rationalism in two respects: First, it accepts a broader foundation, provided not only by rational intuition but also by sensory experience; second, it admits not only deductive reasoning but also inductive reasoning.

Not even this liberalization suffices, however; we enjoy much knowledge not empirically buttressed by sensory experience, present or even recalled – almost everything one knows of history or geography or science, for example, as well as the names of friends and relatives, and a great diversity of knowledge about artifacts, about dishes and how they taste, about how people react, and so forth. None of that can be defended solely by induction on the basis of sensory experience present or recalled.

Consider also observational knowledge of immediate surroundings perceived without instruments. Not even this observational knowledge

1

can easily be explained merely by induction or deduction from what one knows by introspection of one's own sensory experience. Enumerative induction is not enough. That is clear. Nor is it clearly sufficient to use abductive inference – inference to the best explanation.

Accordingly, many have adopted an even more liberal empiricism, with a broader foundation that includes not only what we intuit rationally and what we know by introspection of our own sensory experience but also what we know by direct observation of our surroundings.

Let us pause, however, to consider in greater detail this broader foundation, in its three parts: the intuitive, the introspective, and the observational. What is a rational intuition? Is it a true belief, without inference, in something logically necessary? Not necessarily, for such a belief can arise and be sustained by guessing or by superstition or by brainwashing – and, in any of these cases, even if one believes something logically necessary, this does not imply that one knows what one believes. The question remains: What is a rational intuition?

With respect to the other two parts of the empiricist foundations there are similar questions: What is introspection? What is observation? Suppose a well-lit, white, triangular surface against a black background. From a favorable angle and distance, the observer sees the white triangle and knows two things. He knows, first, that his visual experience has a certain character: that of being visual experience *as if* he had a white triangle before his eyes. And he knows also that in fact he does have before him at a certain distance a white triangular surface. These are indeed paradigms of knowledge by introspection of one's own experience, and by observation of one's immediate surroundings.

Once again, suppose an observation of a white surface, well lit and ideally situated, against a black background. But suppose this time it is not a triangle but a dodecagon (with twelve equal sides). The observer sees the white dodecagon and has two thoughts. He thinks, first, that his visual experience has a certain character, that of being visual experience as if he saw a white dodecagon. And he thinks, further, that in fact he sees a white dodecagon a certain distance away. Although he is twice right, however, he is right only by chance, for he lacks the capacity to distinguish dodecagons with a high probability of success – indeed, he often confuses dodecagons with decagons. Therefore, not every observational belief constitutes foundational knowledge.

Summing up: Foundational empiricism postulates three ways for a belief to constitute foundational knowledge – rational intuition, introspection of one's own experience, and direct observation of one's environment. For rational intuition there is the problem that one can be right in accepting some necessary truth although one is only guessing – which

2

means, of course, that one does not know. The problem here for the foundationalist is this: We need an explanation of what distinguishes beliefs that constitute rational intuition from those that do not, when both are beliefs in propositions true with apodictic necessity. Simplicity alone will not yield our distinction, moreover, because people differ widely in the relevant capacities, and some mathematicians are capable of rather complex intuitions (as was, e.g., the amazing Ramanujan).

Besides, neither introspection nor observation is always a trustworthy source of fundamental knowledge. As we saw with our dodecagon, a belief can be introspective or observational without constituting knowledge or a foundation for further knowledge. Once more the foundationalist needs to explain the difference between, on one hand, introspective or observational beliefs that constitute knowledge and, on the other, beliefs that are not knowledge, despite being introspective or observational.

Just how widely people differ in the relevant capacities – intuition, introspection, or observation – may be seen in a case described by the neurologist Oliver Sacks, a case of identical twins, John and Michael, idiots savants with a measured IQ of 60. Sacks described his first encounter with the twins as follows:

A box of matches on their table fell, and discharged its contents on the floor: "111" they both cried simultaneously; and then, in a murmur, John said "37." Michael repeated this, John said it a third time and stopped. I counted the matches – it took me some time – and there were 111.

"How could you count the matches so quickly?" I asked. "We didn't count," they said. "We *saw* the 111." . . .

"And why did you murmur '37,' and repeat it three times?" I asked the twins. They said in unison "37, 37, 37, 111." . . .

"How did you work that out?" I said, rather hotly. They indicated, as best they could, in poor, insufficient terms – but perhaps there are no words to correspond to such things – that they did not "work it out," but just "saw" it, in a flash. John made a gesture with two outstretched fingers and his thumb, which seemed to suggest that they had spontaneously *trisected* the number, or that it "came apart" of its own accord, by a sort of spontaneous, numerical "fission." They seemed surprised at my surprise – as if *I* were somehow blind; and John's gesture conveyed an extraordinary sense of immediate, *felt* reality.[1]

On another occasion, Sacks found the twins firing six-digit numbers at each other. He wrote the numbers down and later found them to be all prime numbers, whereupon he obtained a list of prime numbers and the next day joined the twins in their game:

1 Oliver Sacks, *The Man Who Mistook His Wife for a Hat and Other Clinical Tales* (New York: Harper & Row, 1987), ch. 23, pp. 199–200.

I decided to join in, and ventured a number, an eight figure prime. They both turned towards me, and then suddenly became still, with a look of intense concentration, and perhaps wonder on their faces. There was a long pause – the longest I had ever known them to make, it must have lasted a half-minute or more – and then suddenly, simultaneously, they both broke into smiles. . . . Then John, who always took the lead, thought for a very long time – it must have been five minutes, though I dared not move, and scarcely breathed – and brought out a nine figure number; and after a similar time his twin Michael responded with a similar one.[2]

The game continued, and in less than an hour the twins were up to twenty-digit numbers, which Sacks was unable to check because his book stopped at ten-digit primes.

Again, we need an explanation of what distinguishes beliefs that constitute foundations, an explanation that will do justice to the diversity of human capacities brought out, for instance, by Sacks's twins. Despite interesting progress towards this desideratum, especially in recent decades, to this day it remains elusive.

In spite of its failures, says W. V. Quine,

epistemology still goes on, though in a new setting and a clarified status. Epistemology, or something like it, simply falls into place as a chapter of psychology and hence of natural science. It studies a natural phenomenon, viz., a physical human subject. This human subject is accorded a certain experimentally controlled input – certain patterns of irradiation in assorted frequencies, for instance – and in the fullness of time the subject delivers as output a description of the three-dimensional external world and its history. The relation between the meager input and the torrential output is a relation that we are prompted to study for somewhat the same reasons that always prompted epistemology; namely, in order to see how evidence relates to theory, and in what ways one's theory of nature transcends any available evidence.[3]

Here are two central planks of Quine's epistemology:

(P1) Epistemology is now a branch of psychology that studies the causal relations between sensory input and theoretical output.

(P2) Engaging in such a study now leads to the conclusion that the sensory input that causes man's theoretical output does not determine it, and that man's theoretical output is hence nearly all arbitrary free creation.

The first thesis, P1, is already in the passage cited earlier. As for P2, we

2 *Ibid.*, p. 203. My thanks to Steven Hales for showing me the relevance of Sacks's writings.
3 "Epistemology Naturalized," in *Ontological Relativity and Other Essays* (New York: Columbia University Press, 1969), pp. 82–3.

are told in *The Roots of Reference* that science is in large measure a "free creation." Theoretical science is hence free-floating, but it is not alone. Even logic is in the same boat: "The steps by which the child was seen to progress from observational language to relative clauses and categoricals and quantification had the arbitrary character of historical accident and cultural heritage; there was no hint of inevitability."[4]

But in what sense is theory "arbitrary" relative to the available evidence? Completely arbitrary it cannot be, surely, lest it be as arbitrary as any superstition or mere conjecture. Quine seems to agree when he writes: "The channels by which, having learned observation sentences, we acquire theoretical language, are the very channels by which observation lends evidence to scientific theory. . . . We see, then, a strategy for investigating the relation of evidential support, between evidence and scientific theory. We can adopt a genetic approach, studying how theoretical language is learned. For the evidential connection is virtually enacted, it would seem, in the learning."[5]

If our theory of the world results from our free and arbitrary play of thought, and if nevertheless it is so related causally to observation as to be *by definition* "evident," that only prompts the question of how such "evidence" could possibly relate to knowledge. For Quine, "[the] answer is naturalism: the recognition that it is within science itself, and not in some prior philosophy, that reality is properly to be identified and described."[6]

But this is no answer unless science provides not only the measure but also the very content of reality. By definition, epistemology recapitulates the genesis of scientific theory, which in turn determines all of ontology and metaphysics, since, by definition, what exists is what science postulates. Science hence arranges a forced wedding of epistemology with metaphysics. Correct epistemology, linked by definition with science, cannot possibly fool us on the content and nature of reality, since, by definition, it is science's say-so that determines what is so. Thus we obtain a guarantee that scientific theory enjoys epistemic justification and fits reality correctly – for such justification and reality are both defined by reference to such theory.

Doubt begins with the question of how we are to distinguish any science worthy of the title. If both reality and epistemology are defined by reference to science, it would be viciously circular now to define science by reference to reality or epistemology. How, then, are we to

---

4 "The Nature of Natural Knowledge," in Samuel Guttenplan, ed., *Mind and Language* (Oxford: Clarendon Press, 1975), p. 80.
5 *Ibid.*, p. 76.
6 "Reply to Stroud," in *Midwest Studies in Philosophy* 6 (1981): 474.

distinguish science from pseudoscience? How are we to draw and understand this distinction?

Quine's positivist answer offers first the following criteria for a scientific "system of the world": (a) it must predict a certain number of observations, (b) it must be finitely axiomatized, and (c) it must contain nothing unnecessary for the prediction of observations or the derivation of observation conditionals – of the form "if such-and-such were observed, then so-and-so would be observed." Such a system of the world is a "tight fit" over the relevant observations or observation conditionals. (I have simplified somewhat, but, I believe, without serious distortion.)

Observation is hence crucial for Quine. Beyond observation is a symbolic network valued according to whether it fits observation tightly, according to its success in entailing correct observation conditionals.

Problems remain. For example, if truth and reality are determined by science, and the content of science is determined by appeal to correct observation conditionals, how is the correctness of such conditionals determined? What is the basis of such correctness? Is there some observational reality that is fundamental and not derivative from any science?[7]

And there is, in addition, a notorious problem always faced by positivism. Quine says approximately the following:

> (Q) Two things are determined by the genesis and content of science: first, what counts as "evidence"; second, the nature and content of reality; and correct science is itself determined by its "tight fit" over observation.

Nevertheless, we have seen that the third criterion for such a tight fit requires that any system that fits this tightly must contain nothing unnecessary for the derivation of correct observation conditionals. Consider now the very doctrine Q itself. Since Q is not needed for the derivation of any observation conditional, we must conclude that Q is *not* itself true. Apparently, if we combine Q with the account of a "tight fit," we obtain a self-refuting whole. This sort of self-refutation has always posed a serious problem for positivism, and Quine's positivism is no exception – as has been noted by Hilary Putnam.[8]

Putnam rejects positivism in favor of a doctrine that makes respectable room for itself, for philosophy in general, and even for values and norms. He proposes, therefore, an explication of truth and reality not in terms of science and observation but in terms of reason, of what would be rationally acceptable in ideal epistemic conditions. Now, the content of

7 Quine's naturalization is discussed further in Chapter 6.
8 "Why Reason Can't Be Naturalized," in *Realism and Reason*, Vol. 3 of his *Philosophical Papers* (Cambridge: Cambridge University Press, 1983).

what could thus turn out acceptable is not limited to the observable, nor even to what science may offer us, but includes also moral and other evaluations, as well as political views, philosophy, and the humanities generally. Putnam's doctrine is thus more sensibly inclusive than failed positivism – and has, of course, its attractions. Nevertheless, it is not entirely free of problems and must face, for example, the following:

Consider this proposition, which seems in fact true, but which in any case *might* be true (where the brackets function as a nominalizing device):

(P1) [No one is in ideal epistemic conditions.]

Proposition P1 is equivalent to

(P2) [P1 is true.]

which in turn amounts to

(P3) [Anyone who were to consider P1 in ideal epistemic conditions would accept it.]

But P3 is absurd; yet it is said to amount to P1, which is surely not absurd. Putnam's doctrine suffers therefore from a sort of self-refutation.[9]

Having taken a wrong turn, let us return to our start. The doctrine of foundations was said to suffer essentially the same problem in each of its three parts. The given, what is present to consciousness, can be grasped either by intuitive reason (when it is a rational axiom) or by introspection (e.g., when it is a matter of one's present sensory experience). But in neither case can we see with clarity the general limits of the epistemic mechanism involved. What do we intuit rationally? Everything necessary and *simple*, as are, for example, the simplest logical truths? That seems promising until we recall that what is simple and obvious for Ramanujan may not be so for others.

As for introspection, does one know *foundationally* everything one believes through introspection of one's own experience? Perhaps one *is* able to know foundationally that one has sensory experience of a white triangle against a black background. What if the figure is not a triangle, but a dodecagon, however, and one lacks the capacity to distinguish dodecagons by sight? If so, then even if (a) one in fact has a visual experience as if before one there were a dodecagon against a black background and (b) one believes that one is having such an experience – that is, an experience as if one had before one a dodecagon against a black background – still it does *not* follow that (c) one knows foundationally

9 This argument is developed in detail by Alvin Plantinga in his "How to Be an Anti-Realist," *Proceedings and Addresses of the American Philosophical Association* 56 (1982): 47–70, where he kindly acknowledges its provenance.

what one thus believes, with no need of supporting reasons or inferences.

And the like is true of observation, as we saw earlier. Mere observation of a dodecagonic surface against a black background, giving rise to a belief that one sees such a surface, is not sufficient to make that belief a case of knowledge.

Note the realist posture of all such foundationalism. Criteria for knowledge are proposed on the basis of necessary truths, sensory experiences, or objective surfaces – all of which enjoy their own character independently of what anyone may believe. When such foundationalism fails, many turn away from the presupposed realism toward a conception of language or worldview or conceptual scheme as something that constitutes reality. This we saw in Quine, for whom science determines reality. And we saw it also in Putnam, for whom reality is again constituted by language and thought, the ideal if not necessarily the actual. But we also saw the problems of incoherence faced by these doctrines.

Yet others do not adopt antirealism but do turn coherentist. Davidson, for example, argues that an allegedly foundationalist idea, that of "confrontation between what we believe and reality," is "absurd," thus opening the way for coherentism, subsequently offered as a better alternative: "What distinguishes a coherence theory is simply the claim that nothing can count as a reason for holding a belief except another belief. Its partisan rejects as unintelligible the request for a ground or source of justification of another ilk."[10] In explanation and support we are referred to Rorty, who claims that "nothing counts as justification unless by reference to what we already accept, and there is no way to get outside our beliefs and our language so as to find some test other than coherence."[11]

Suppose

   (a) that for a belief to be justified is for the subject to justify it or to have justified it;
   (b) that for one to justify a belief (really, successfully) is for one correctly and seriously to use considerations, reasons in its favor; and
   (c) that seriously and correctly to use considerations or reasons in favor of a belief is to use (i) other things one believes with justification and (ii) their (justifiedly believed) appropriate connection with the belief targeted for justification.

10 Donald Davidson, "A Coherence Theory of Truth and Knowledge," in Dieter Henrich, ed., *Kant oder Hegel?* (Stuttgart: Klett-Cotta, 1983), pp. 423–38, 426.
11 Richard Rorty, *Philosophy and the Mirror of Nature* (Princeton, N.J.: Princeton University Press, 1979), p. 178.

These are apparently involved in Davidson's and Rorty's view of epistemic justification as inevitably *argumentative*. So much seems defensible. What seems disastrous is the view of knowledge as a matter of just true belief that is thus (argumentatively) justified (even leaving aside the Gettier problem). If one is going to think of justification as thus essentially argumentative, then one must leave room for some other way in which a belief can amount to knowledge besides its being thus justified. But Davidson and Rorty oppose the very idea of a belief's amounting to knowledge through some causal process, through some sheer "confrontation" with reality.[12]

Fortunately, there is another way to overcome the problems of foundationalism. This alternative approach starts by recognizing those problems as follows: (a) Something is missing in a believer who accepts a necessary truth that is too complex for that believer to know it *just* on the basis of believing it; (b) something is also missing in the introspective belief that one has visual experience of a dodecagon when this figure is too complex for one to discriminate it and identify it *just* by introspection; and (c) finally, something is similarly missing in the observational belief that one has a dodecagonic surface before one when such surfaces are too complex for one to discriminate and identify them *just* by sight. What is missing in each of these cases is not just a matter of greater simplicity in the object of belief, however, because another subject might perfectly well have direct knowledge of similarly complex truths, by rational intuition, by introspection, or by observation. It is not just the intrinsic complexity of the truth involved that matters, therefore, but at most its excessive complexity *for that subject*. What the subject needs is a certain capacity, a certain faculty or intellectual virtue: that of distinguishing necessary truths up to a certain degree of complexity, or perhaps that of distinguishing dodecagons and other such figures by simple inspection.

According to this alternative approach, direct, foundational knowledge must be right not just by accident but by means of a noninferential faculty that enables the formation of beliefs on the matter in question with a high success ratio.

Other problems also yield to this approach. Recall our knowledge

12 This will be discussed later in some detail: with respect to Rorty, in Chapter 6, "Nature Unmirrored, Epistemology Naturalized," and with regard to Davidson, in Chapter 7, "Theories of Justification: Old Doctrines Newly Defended." If we view justification thus as essentially argumentative, then we probably need also a further idea of the *aptness* of a belief, an idea that is most likely to involve a causal relationship between that belief and reality, mediated though it might be by the intellectual virtue or faculty that gives rise to the belief. This conditional is defended most explicitly in Chapter 14, "Methodology and Apt Belief."

through memory of names, of places, of how things work, of history and geography, and so forth. When one recalls the name of one's own child, for example, one's belief derives neither from rational intuition nor from inference based on present or recalled observation or sensory experience. Accordingly, such belief is not based on the traditional foundations of reason, introspection, or observation, present or recalled. Despite its lack of such traditional foundations, such a belief surely does amount to knowledge. Surely the name of one's own child can remain knowledge through brute memory.

Our alternative approach in terms of faculties and intellectual virtues can, of course, make room for memory. Memory, like inference, is a faculty whose inputs are beliefs. Such faculties are virtuous in proportion to their capacity to emit true outputs from true inputs. In the case of inference, the outputs are different from the inputs. Memory, by contrast, retains its inputs and delivers the same later as outputs when appropriate. Such, anyhow, is the way of *good* memory. And someone blessed with good memory can know a name just by recall. According to our alternative approach, then, to know is to believe through a faculty or intellectual virtue.[13]

This approach also has its problems to face. It needs to be developed and defended. That is the main overall objective of the essays in this collection, which defend an account of knowledge with two main ideas: that of intellectual virtue and that of epistemic perspective.

Part I of the collection is on the nature of knowledge. The first chapter contains the following three things, among others:

(a) A distinction between "subjective," *internal* justification, on one hand, and "objective," *external* justification, on the other – both required for knowledge.

(b) A discussion of evidence one does not possess, and of the social aspect of knowledge, and of how these go beyond the subjective or internal rationality of belief.[14]

(c) A defeasibility framework of justification, according to which

13 My approach is in some respects akin to the reliabilist externalism of Ramsey, Armstrong, Dretske, Goldman, Nozick, Swain, and others. The most recent and extensively developed reliabilism is discussed in Chapter 8 and is compared with the present approach. My account is different in important respects from reliabilism, especially as concerns the need for doxastic ascent and epistemic perspective, as may be seen especially in Parts III and IV.

14 A further social aspect of knowledge is recognized through the place allowed to testimony (e.g., in condition oj_5), whose status as a source of knowledge is defended later, in Chapter 12. Also relevant here is a relativization of knowledge to epistemic community, which comes to the fore in Chapter 2. But note well: The commitment here is to a kind of benign relativism uninfected by any sort of subjectivism or conventionalism.

positive evidence for a belief can be defeated or overridden by additional facts.

A belief can amount to knowledge only if it is (i) internally justified, by being a rational belief that accords with the evidence given, and *also* (ii) externally justified, by meeting requirements like those imposed by (b) and (c) above. The second chapter widens the externalism thus present already in the first.

(d) It is required not only that the subject's *evidence* not be false – that there be no falsehood in any internal structure of assumptions, presumptions, premises, reasons, and so forth, that underlies any belief amounting to knowledge – but *also* that the subject who knows must be "in a position to know."

Whether or not one is thus in a position to know is, moreover, determined by factors beyond internal subjectivity, factors that go beyond rational justification and pertain, for example, to the faculties and context of the subject. And with these external factors comes also a relativization of knowledge to epistemic community.[15]

The recognition of a general distinction between internal and external factors relevant to whether a subject knows is supplemented (in Chapter 14) by a contrast between aptness and justification of belief and applied (in Chapter 15) to questions about the viability of reflexive equilibrium and of analytic epistemology itself, as well as to questions of relativism. However:

(e) The contrast between the aptness and the justification of a belief does not remove the need for two varieties of justification, the subjective and the objective, as in (a).

A subject may have an internally justified belief B that derives from fine faculties of perception, memory, introspection, and abduction, in an environment E generally favorable to such faculties, while yet in this particular instance the abductive and other rational support is essentially flawed by falsehood. Such a flaw must be precluded through a requirement of *objective* justification, something a belief needs – in addition to aptness and subjective justification – in order to constitute knowledge. Chapter 2 – "How Do You Know?" – adds a further commitment:

(f) Normative epistemic properties must *supervene* or *derive* from properties that are *not* normatively epistemic, where normatively

15 This distinction between internal and external aspects involved in knowledge then plays an increasing role, especially in Chapters 8, 14, and 15.

epistemic properties are those involved in knowledge, such as those that specify how rational or how apt is someone's belief within certain circumstances.[16]

A modest *epistemic perspectivism* enters with the remaining chapters in Part I,[17] which present the following thesis:

(g) One needs an epistemic perspective for full reflexive knowledge – knowledge that surpasses mere "thermometer" or "servo-mechanic" or even "animal" proto-knowledge.

This thesis is developed later,[18] where the epistemic perspective is crucial to proposed solutions for the generality problem and the new evil-demon problem. It is this large role played by the epistemic perspective that prompts the label "virtue perspectivism" for the view under development.

Two main alternatives in epistemology today are reliabilism and coherentism:

(h) Reliabilism and coherentism each contain important insights, but any deep enough defense of either must make room for important elements of the other.

These competing alternatives are often discussed in what follows,[19] where virtue perspectivism emerges gradually as an irenic alternative, one variously defended in Parts II and III, and developed more positively and explicitly in Part IV.[20]

16 See the account of what it is for a set to *fully validate* an epistemic proposition, account I in the appendix to that chapter. This commitment remains throughout, but see especially Chapters 9 and 10. The appendix to Chapter 9 shows how a framework of prima facie justification is compatible with the supervenience of justification.
17 Chapters 3 and 4.
18 Chapters 8, 11, 12, and 16.
19 For reliabilism, see Chapter 7 and especially Chapter 8, which explains how virtue perspectivism differs from reliabilism. For coherentism, see especially Chapters 7, 11, and 12.
20 Much remains to be done, however; for example, virtue epistemology needs to be compared with virtue ethics, as each will likely support the other. Cf. John Greco, "Virtue Epistemology," in *The Blackwell Companion to Epistemology*, J. Dancy and E. Sosa, eds. (Oxford: Basil Blackwell, in press).

PART I

What is knowledge, and how is it possible?

1

The analysis of "knowledge that p"

On Edmund Gettier's interpretation,[1] the Ayer and Chisholm analyses of the concept of knowledge are sufficiently similar to analysis A, below, to be called the same.

Analysis A:

A person S has knowledge that p iff

    (i) p is true;
    (ii) S believes that p;
    (iii) S is justified in believing that p.

Gettier presents us with two counter-examples to this view. I will now briefly set forth the principle of the second, which is both simpler than the first and not essentially different from it *qua* counter-example to A.

Suppose S has good evidence for his belief that p, from which in turn he deduces that p ∨ q. But, unknown to S, (~p) & q. So, all three conditions for knowledge specified in the view under examination are fulfilled; but we still do not want to say that S *knows* that p ∨ q.

Here is a proposed analysis of the concept of knowledge, proposed as a solution to the Gettier problem:

> If p is "basic," belief that p requires no justification, subjective or objective. If p is "non-basic," a person S has *subjective* justification for belief that p iff:

sj_1: There is a set of statements, $e_1, e_2, \ldots, e_n$, each of which S believes to be true.

sj_2: S's belief that e_i is true is itself subjectively justified whenever e_i is not a basic statement requiring no justification.

sj_3: S believes that the truth of the e_is provides strong-enough evidence for p, and either is subjectively justified in having this belief or the belief is a (basic) "canon" or "axiom."

sj_4: There is no set of statements, $f_1, f_2, \ldots, f_n$, which S believes to furnish strong-enough evidence for ~p and to be true.

sj_5: S is justified in not believing that there is any set of f_is with true members, which casts sufficient doubt on p to make it false that the union of the set of e_is and the set of f_is supplies strong-enough

1 Edmund Gettier, "Is Justified True Belief Knowledge?" *Analysis* 23 (1963): 121–3.

evidence for p; or else his not believing this requires no justification given the situation.

sj_6:   S is subjectively justified in believing each of the e_is in the context of the others to have positive evidential force for p, unless his belief requires no justification.

sj_7:   S would regard as not strong enough, in the context of the disconfirming evidence he might reasonably be expected to have, any set evidentially weaker *vis-à-vis* p than the set of e_is.

(The last two requirements allow us to include the first and second provisos in the analysis of objective justification.)

Making use of the concept of subjective justification one can also formulate a definition of objective justification.[2]

If p is non-basic, S has *objective* justification for belief that p iff:

oj_1:   There is a set of e_is which subjectively justifies S in believing that p *and* such that each of the e_is is *as a matter of fact true*.

oj_2:   This set of e_is does support belief that p with sufficient strength and there is no superfluous e_i, i.e., none in the context of the others lacking all evidential connection with p; nor is there any which, in the context of the others, supports ~p. Further, S is objectively justified in believing each of the e_is to have positive evidential force for p, in the context of the others, unless his belief requires no justification.

oj_3:   There is no set of f_is which discredits p even in the context of the e_is, and the members of which are true and such that S could reasonably be expected to have found out or otherwise know their truth.

oj_4:   If there is some evidence for ~p which S believes, the contrary evidence of the e_is overcomes it, i.e., is still strong enough even in this context to justify belief that p.

oj_5:   If S's belief that p is true is based substantially on a report that p or that one or more of the e_is is true, then the reporter *has objective justification* for the belief that p is true or that the e_is in question are true, respectively.

The reason for including provisos sj_5 and oj_3 is counter-examples such as the following:

Suppose that A and B are outside room R and seven persons P_1–P_7 come out of the room. A takes four of these, P_1–P_4, into his office and B

---

2   A word of warning: In the discussion of the two types of justification I do not strictly adhere to ordinary usage. In particular, "objective justification" is a somewhat "technical" expression.

takes the remaining three, P_5–P_7, into his office. Each of the seven subjects is asked the same question: "Is there a chair in room R?" P_1–P_4 answer: "Yes." P_5–P_7 answer: "No." When P_1–P_4 emerge from A's office they are interviewed by B. A, however, does not think it necessary to interview P_5–P_7.

Now if we don't include the provisos in question, the following absurdity is countenanced by our analysis: A could know that there is a chair in room R on the basis of the testimony he heard, whereas B couldn't on the basis of the testimony *he* heard. But B has just as much evidence for the proposition that there is a chair in the room as A does, i.e., four affirmative answers. And, furthermore, he has a wider range of data bearing on the issue. It would thus be preposterous to deny him entitlement to knowledge while granting it to A. And this is just what our condition is meant to preclude.

A striking fact is brought to light by this part of the analysis: besides justification for "believing that . . ." or for "believing that not . . ." justification for "not believing that . . ." is also involved in the concept of knowledge. In our example we pass the judgment that A is not justified in *not believing* that there is any counter-evidence to his belief, inasmuch as the testimony of P_5–P_7 is readily available (where we presume, of course, that P_5–P_7 are honest, reliable, and so forth, and that A knows them to be so. One could make the counter-example more convincing by adding such conditions as: room R is known by A to be very large and to have thick columns which cast dark shadows, etc.).

An example will perhaps make it clear why I regard sj_5 and oj_3 as quite strong enough. An historian who is justified in believing that Caesar crossed the Rubicon does not necessarily *believe that* there never will be a set of f_is such as that in sj_5 or oj_3. A methodology-conscious historian might well have such a belief but he *need not* to justifiedly make the judgment concerning Caesar. On the other hand, it is certainly required that he should *not believe that* there ever will be any such set of f_is and that either he be justified in not so believing or that his not so believing require no justification.

It is worth observing that a definition of "knowledge" in terms of objective justification would be a recursive definition. Before trying to show this, let me explicate some terminology: In what follows, "Se_i" stands for "the set of e_is", and "Sf_i" for "the set of f_is". Also, a proposition is "basic" iff it does not stand in any need of justification. S knows it simply because it is true and he believes it. "I have two hands and am now writing with my right hand" is such a one, in an ordinary context. Philosophical doubt is surely possible with respect to it, but "knowledge" being at least partly a normative term, our question ultimately calls for a decision. I won't here go into the matter of how one would identify a "basic" proposition. It may even be that a proposition which is basic in one context would not be so in another (e.g., when it conflicts with a whole body of established truth). Notice, also, that "basic" too is partly a normative term: "worthy of credence without any need for grounds." One thing at any rate is clear (at least within contexts): we do recognize "basic" propositions. Questions come to an end; and rightly so.

In conclusion, I advance as the correct (recursive) definition of "knowledge that p":

S knows that p iff

    (i) p is true;
    (ii) S believes that p;

(If p is "basic" (i) and (ii) are both necessary and sufficient for S's knowing that p. If p is "non-basic," (iii) too is needed:)

    (iii) S is objectively justified in believing that p; that is,
        (1) there is an Se_i, such that: S knows that the members of Se_i are true, and that $Se_i \rightarrow p$;[3] where none of the e_is is superfluous or supports $\sim p$ in the context of the others, and S does not believe otherwise, being in fact justified in believing each e_i to have positive evidential force for p, in the context of the others, unless his belief requires no justification; and S would regard any weaker Se_i as not strong enough in the context of the disconfirming evidence he might reasonably be expected to have;
        (2) there is no Sf_i
            (a) which is true and discredits p to such an extent that "$Se_i \rightarrow p$", while true in a neutral context, is not true in the context of Sf_i; and
            (b) the truth of the members of which S could reasonably have been expected to have found out, or otherwise know, together with the truth of (a);
        (3) S does not believe there is any Sf_i which fulfills 2(a) and is justified in not so believing unless his not so believing requires no justification; and
        (4) if S's belief that p is based substantially on the report that p, or that e_i, then the reporter knows that p or that e_i.

---

3 "$\rightarrow$" means "provides strong enough evidence for."

2

How do you know?

Despair of knowing what knowledge is dates back to Plato's *Theaetetus*. Most recently, the trinitarian view of knowledge as justified true belief has been refuted, and a multitude of problems has appeared. Progress on this question is perhaps fated to be asymptotic. But such progress as can now be made depends, in my opinion, on a careful study of the conditions within which a correctly believed proposition is a bit of knowledge. In what follows I hope to enhance our knowledge of knowledge by contributing to such a study.

I

An accepted truth is knowledge only if evident. What then is it for something to be evident? One short answer is this: a proposition is evident to someone provided he is (theoretically) justified in believing it.[1] But under what further circumstances is the truth of a proposition evident to someone? This is our first main question.

To begin with, there are two general situations where it is evident to someone *S* that *p*. *First*, there is the situation where it is self-evident to *S* that *p*, i.e., where from the fact that *S* correctly believes that *p* we may infer that it is evident to *S* that *p*. Our inference here cannot be logically valid as it stands, however, since logic alone will not enable us to infer that anything is evident just from the fact that it is correctly believed. Some extralogical principles must be invoked to validate such an inference.

Such principles are clearly needed, in any case, provided we want to account for (and not deny) our empirical knowledge. Accordingly, they have long been recognized and accepted. The Greek Sceptics perceived the problems involved clearly and made some definite suggestions.[2]

---

1 The parenthetical qualification is meant to rule out as irrelevant whatever practical reasons there might be for having a belief, such as those of a sick man whose belief that he will recover is essential to his recovery.
2 Thus the theory of Carneades of Cyrene is presented by Sextus Empiricus in his *Outline of Pyrrhonism* and in his *Against the Logicians*. This theory is discussed by Roderick M. Chisholm in his *Theory of Knowledge* (Englewood Cliffs, N.J.: Prentice-Hall, 1966), pp. 41–4.

19

Descartes and Hume were in fundamental agreement about epistemic principles: There is first the self-evident, which includes some obvious general truths and some particular claims, mainly about one's subjective states; anything else that is evident must be made so by being deduced from the self-evident. This much, it seems to me, they both accepted, even if it led them in very different directions: Descartes to his baroque system, and Hume to his desert landscape. Coming to more recent philosophy, the principles underlying the "criteria" of Wittgenstein and others seem best understood as epistemic principles.[3] Discussion of epistemic principles and epistemic scales is to be found in Chisholm's writings.[4] Finally, the third of Sellars' Matchette Lectures, delivered at the University of Texas, is a discussion of "Epistemic Principles."[5] (Among the correlates of such principles in Sellars' philosophy are his principles of "trans-level inference.")[6]

What would such epistemic principles look like? What would be some examples? Let us introduce the schematic letter "p" to be replaced by declarative clauses. The following might then be a correct epistemic principle schema: "If S correctly believes that it occurs to him that p, then it is evident to S that it occurs to him that p."

Other examples of correct principle schemata yielding self-evident propositions are those corresponding to basic a priori truths, such as "If S believes that either p or it is false that p, then it is evident to S that either p or it is false that p." Here again from S's mere correct belief of a proposition that p (e.g., that either it is snowing or it is false that it is snowing) we may infer that it is evident to S that p, and hence such propositions count as self-evident for S. Moreover, as distinguished from the group about propositional attitudes the present group of propositions are self-evident-if-evident for every person. That either it is snowing or it is not snowing is self-evident-if-evident for everyone, but it is self-evident-if-evident only to Tom that it occurs to *him* that snow is white since it is true only of Tom that if he correctly believes that concrete proposition, we can infer that it is evident to him.

We have seen how the first general situation where it is evident to S that p is one where it is self-evident to S that p. But obviously there are known

3 Cf. Norman Malcolm, *Knowledge and Certainty* (Englewood Cliffs, N.J.: Prentice-Hall, 1963), pp. 113–17.
4 See *Perceiving: A Philosophical Study* (Ithaca, N.Y.: Cornell University Press, 1957), and *Theory of Knowledge*.
5 The lectures were delivered in 1970 but are as yet unpublished.
6 See *Science, Perception, and Reality* (London: Routledge & Kegan Paul, 1963), p. 88. Trans-level inference is also discussed in "Empiricism and the Philosophy of Mind," in *Minnesota Studies in the Philosophy of Science*, Vol. 1, ed. Herbert Feigl and Michael Scriven (Minneapolis: University of Minnesota Press, 1956). This essay is also Chapter 5 of *Science, Perception, and Reality*.

facts that are not self-evident. Hence if a fact can't be known without being evident, there must be facts that are evident but not self-evident. And, more generally, there are propositions that are evident but not self-evident. This is of course the *second* general situation where it is evident to someone S that p. Now when it is evident to S that p but not self-evident to S that p, then that S correctly believes that p is not sufficient to establish it as evident to S that p, even with the help of the epistemic principles. What then *is* thus sufficient?

The answer I wish to propose is, in first approximation, that in such circumstances what makes it evident to S that p is a non-empty set of propositions α such that α validates the proposition that it is evident to S that p. Vaguely put, the idea is simply that if you know that p, but it is not self-evident to you that p, then you must have grounds for believing that p, and these grounds must make it evident to you that p. But to give your grounds for believing that p is not necessarily to give a complete epistemic explanation of how it comes to be evident to you that p. For often grounds that you have for believing that p cannot be groundless but require grounds of their own, and these may require grounds in turn, and so on. A complete epistemic explanation will not stop until it has adduced the grounds for every ground that has grounds.

It therefore appears that we need more than just the idea of a set of grounds that grounds the proposition that p for S. We need the idea of a set of grounds that *fully* grounds the proposition that p for S, the idea of a set that gives a complete epistemic explanation of how it comes to be evident to S that p.

But how are we to define this idea of a set's fully grounding a proposition for a subject at a time? Shall we say that α fully grounds x (for S at t) when for every ground y in α there is a subset α' of α such that α' grounds y? But what if $\alpha = \{$that the triangular card is approximately equilateral, that the triangular card is approximately equiangular$\}$ and $x =$ that each of the card's angles has approximately 60°? This appears to fulfill the conditions specified, and yet α can hardly be said to provide a complete epistemic explanation for how it comes to be evident that each of the card's angles has approximately 60°. For instance, how do we know that there is a triangular card at all, or that it is approximately equilateral in the first place?

Adapting an idea of Frege's, shall we say that α fully grounds x iff α is the class of ancestral grounds of x? (Here y is an ancestral ground of x iff $(\forall \alpha)\{[x \in \alpha \ \& \ (\forall z)(\forall w)[(w \in \alpha) \ \& \ (z \text{ is a ground of } w) \supset (z \in \alpha)]] \supset y \in \alpha\}$; i.e., y is an ancestral ground of x iff y is a member of every class containing x and all grounds of members.)

The main problem with this definition derives from cases of epistemic

21

over-determination. In such cases the class of ancestral grounds of x will contain superfluous grounds. This will turn out to be unfavorable to our purposes, mainly because a defective ground – say a false ground – surely need not flaw every fully grounding class, not if it's a superfluous ground. And yet, according to the Fregean idea, there is only *one* fully grounding class, and it *will* contain *every* ancestral ground, superfluous or not.

My suggestion is therefore this: α fully grounds x for S at t if and only if there is a set of subsets of α which form a sequence $C_1, \ldots, C_n$, such that (i) C_1 grounds x, (ii) for each member y of any subset C_i, such that y requires grounds, the successor of C_i C_{i+1}, grounds y and (iii) the last subset, C_n, contains no ground that requires grounds.

We are finally in a position to answer our first main question. A proposition x is evident to someone S in either of two general situations: *either* x is self-evident to S *or* there is a set of propositions that fully grounds x for S. But we may consider the first of these a special case of the second, if we allow that the null set fully grounds self-evident propositions. Thus we may conclude that *a proposition x is evident to S if and only if there is a set of propositions that fully grounds x for S.*

If I am right thus far, the well-known triadic account of knowledge as correct, evident belief is then equivalent to an account (1) according to which S knows that p provided that both (a) S correctly believes that p, and (b) there is a set of propositions that fully grounds that p for S.

Supposing this account correct, every bit of knowledge would be supported by a pyramid such as that shown in Figure 2.1. Each node of such a pyramid is a proposition. Thus the *apex* node is the-proposition-that-p_1, and the first *terminal* node from the left is the-proposition-that-p_{111}.

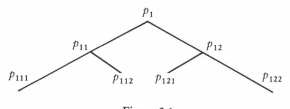

Figure 2.1

Such "epistemic pyramids" must satisfy certain requirements:

1. (Let us call node x a "successor" (i.e., a *direct* successor) of node y relative to pyramid P provided there are A and B such that (i) A stands for x on P and B stands for y on P; (ii) A and B are connected

by a straight line on P; (iii) B is closer to the apex node than A; and (iv) there is no C such that C stands for a proposition on P, and A, B, and C are connected by a straight line and B is closer to the apex node than C, and C is closer to the apex node than A.) The set of all nodes that (directly) succeed a given node must ground that node.

2. Each node must be a proposition that is evident to S.
3. If a node n is not a proposition that is self-evident to S then it must have successors, it must be succeeded by further nodes that ground the proposition n.
4. Each branch of an epistemic pyramid must terminate.

It follows that to each set that fully renders x evident to S there corresponds at least one epistemic pyramid for S and x. And we thus have a second account of knowledge that is also a close equivalent of the traditional account:

(2) S knows that p iff
   (a) it is true that p;
   (b) S believes that p; and
   (c) there is an epistemic pyramid for S and the proposition that p.

However, it is a well-known fact that the traditional account of propositional knowledge is inadequate. Therefore, if the above account is really equivalent to the traditional account, it should be similarly inadequate. And so it is.

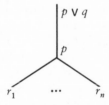

Figure 2.2

Consider Figure 2.2, the pyramid (schema) for S and the proposition that $p \vee q$. Supposing that S correctly believes that $p \vee q$, the three clauses in our account are satisfied. And yet S may not know that $p \vee q$, nevertheless. For it may be false that p, and the preceding diagram may be the *only* kind of epistemic pyramid available for S and the proposition that $p \vee q$, any other such pyramid being simply an "expansion" of the above, i.e., a pyramid obtainable by correctly adding further nodes.

23

(Obviously, if there were another kind of pyramid, where instead of p we found q, then S might still know that $p \vee q$, in spite of the falsity of p.)[7]

A further restriction on pyramids immediately suggests itself: *to support knowledge epistemic pyramids must be non-defective, i.e., must contain only true nodes.*

According to Keith Lehrer the new requirement still leaves our account open to an interesting objection. Consider the following statements:

P_1: Mr. Nogot, who is in my office, owns a Ford;
P_2: Mr. Havit, who is in my office, owns a Ford; and
H: Someone in my office owns a Ford.

And imagine ". . . that I have seen Mr. Nogot drive a Ford on many occasions and that I now see him drive away in it. Moreover, imagine that he leaves his wallet at my house and that I, being curious, examine its contents. Therein I discover a certificate asserting that Mr. Nogot owns the Ford I have just seen him drive away. This would supply me with evidence E consisting of true statements, which would completely justify my believing P_1, and, therefore, H. But now imagine that P_1 is false (due to some legal technicality), and P_2 is true, though I have no evidence for P_2. In this case, I do not know H, but all of Mr. Sosa's requirements for knowledge might well be met."[8]

However, it is in general false that if one is justified in believing p and p entails q, then one is justified in believing q. I can surely believe the axioms of a theory and yet lack sufficient justification for believing many of the theorems. For many of the theorems may as yet be unproved.

Consequently, we must reject the general principle that if e provides good (inductive or deductive) grounds for p, and p entails q, then e provides good grounds for q. The point can also be put like this: even if your justifiably believing e and your believing p on the basis of your belief of e would together imply that your believing p is justified, and even if p entails q, it still would *not* follow that your justifiably believing e and your believing q on the basis of your belief of e would together imply

---

7 I have here translated the objection raised originally by Edmund L. Gettier against the traditional account of propositional knowledge. See his "Is Justified True Belief Knowledge?" *Analysis* 23 (1963): 121–3 (reprinted in the Bobbs-Merrill reprint series).
8 Keith Lehrer, "Knowledge, Truth and Evidence," reprinted in *Knowing*, ed. M. D. Roth and L. Galis (Washington, D.C.: University Press of America, 1984). The requirements to which Lehrer refers were made in my "Analysis of 'Knowledge that p'," *Analysis* 25 (1961): 1–8 (reprinted in the Bobbs-Merrill reprint series) (see Chapter 1 in this volume). These requirements featured, in different terminology, the one now under review, viz., the requirement that for S to know that p there must be a non-defective pyramid of knowledge for S and the proposition that p. Indeed, the account of knowledge as correct belief buttressed by a non-defective pyramid is virtually my earlier account pruned of inessential elements.

that your believing q is justified. (Moreover, this would not follow even on the assumption that you do believe q and believe it on the basis of your belief of e.)

Thus I am puzzled by Lehrer's statement that E ". . . would completely justify my believing P_1, and, *therefore*, H." (My emphasis.) I see no reason for accepting this inference. Would my believing E and my believing H on the basis of E imply that my believing H is justified? Not necessarily, for whether I am justified surely depends on whether I see a connection between E and H. If I believe axioms of a theory and believe a theorem on their basis I still may not be justified in believing that theorem. For I may believe the theorem on the basis of the axioms mistakenly and without having seen a real connection.

Normally, we would establish a connection between E and H by way of the likes of P_1 or P_2. Suppose that from among such statements only P_1 is evident to you in some normal case. In that case you could make no connection between E and H except by way of a falsehood. Put another way, in that case there would be no non-defective pyramid for you and H. Therefore, our requirement would not be met by Lehrer's example after all. To be sure, there may be ways of connecting E and H without involving P_1. Perhaps there is some such way that does not violate the requirement, but I confess that I can't think of one.[9]

II

Despite the merits of the present account, however, I believe it can be shown to be too narrow. For it allows as determinants of what one knows only what one correctly believes with rational justification. But reflection will reveal much else that is equally relevant.

In the first place, what one is rationally justified in believing obviously depends on the data in one's possession. But what data one has can depend on how much and how well one investigates. Consider, therefore, the following possibility. What if A is rationally justified in believing x given his body of data D_1 whereas B is not rationally justified in believing x given his body of data D_2, where D_2 includes D_1 but is much more extensive as a result of A's irresponsible negligence and B's commendable thoroughness? The present account might unfortunately grant A knowledge while denying it to B, for A's neglect so far has no bearing on any epistemic pyramid.

9 In favor of this reply to Lehrer's example, I would also urge that the proviso that one must not "reason" via a falsehood gives us the simplest, most natural solution to the Gettier problem, and that we should therefore let it fall only under the impact of a forceful counter-example. For a further defense of the proviso, see Chapters 3 and 4.

We have considered a situation where someone lacks knowledge owing to his misuse of his cognitive equipment, either by letting it idle when it should be functioning or by busily employing it dysfunctionally. Another situation where someone lacks knowledge despite having rationally justified correct belief might be called the Magoo situation – where S lacks adequate equipment to begin with (relative to the question in hand: whether p).[10] It is because of this type of lack that despite his extensive experience with cable cars, Mr. Magoo does not know that his cable car will arrive safely when, unknown to him, bombs are raining all around it. Of course, even if you have less than 20–20 vision you can still know that there is an elephant in front of you when you see one there. So not just any defect will make your equipment inadequate for a judgment on the question whether p. I would venture that it must be a defect that prevents you from acquiring information that (i) a normal inquirer in the epistemic community would acquire in that situation *and* (ii) makes a difference to what you can reasonably conclude on the question whether p (or at least to how reasonably you can draw the conclusion).

The possibility of inadequate cognitive equipment requires a further and more striking departure from the traditional conception of knowledge. Earlier we considered a situation where, despite having warranted correct belief, someone lacks knowledge owing to his neglectful data-collection. There lack of knowledge could be traced back to epistemic irresponsibility, to substandard performance blamed on the investigator. In the present example, blame is out of place. By hypothesis, Magoo conducts impeccable "inquiry" both in arriving at his data and on the basis of his data. But he still falls short of knowledge, despite his warranted, correct belief. His shortcoming is substandard equipment, for which we may suppose him to be blameless. Hence something other than epistemic justification or correct belief can help determine what one knows or does not know. Even if one correctly believes that p with full rational justification and free of irrational or neglectful unbelief, one may still be in no position to know, because of faulty cognitive equipment.

In all of the foregoing cases, someone misses or is liable to miss available information which may be highly relevant and important and may make a difference to what he can conclude on the question in hand. In each case, moreover, he seems culpable or discredited in some sense: he would seem less reliable than otherwise for his role in any such case. But there appear to be situations where again someone misses available information with no culpability *or* discredit. Harman gives an example

---

10 The Magoo situation is the situation of that unfortunate nearsighted and hearing-impaired cartoon character who fortunately escapes disaster at every turn.

where S reads in a newspaper that some famous person has been assassinated, but does not read the next edition, where all reports of the assassination are denied by highly authoritative and trustworthy people. If practically the whole country reads the next edition and people don't know what to believe, does S alone know of the assassination, provided the next edition is in fact a pack of lies?[11] I suppose we would be inclined to say that he does not know (especially if had he read the next edition, *he* would not have known what to believe). But what if only two or three people get a chance to read the next edition before it is recalled by the newspaper? Should we now say that out of millions who read the first story and mourn the loved leader not one knows of his death? I suppose we would be inclined to say that the fake edition and the few deceived by it make no difference concerning what everybody else knows. It seems plausible to conclude that knowledge has a further "social aspect," that it cannot depend on one's missing or blinking what is generally known.

Our departures from the traditional conception of knowledge put in relief the relativity of knowledge to an epistemic community. This is brought out most prominently by the requirement that inquirers have at least *normal* cognitive equipment (e.g., normal perceptual apparatus, where that is relevant). But our new requirement – that inquirers not lack or blink generally known relevant information – also brings out the relativity. A vacationer in the woods may know that p well enough for an average vacationer, but he won't have the kind of knowledge his guide has. A guide would scornfully deny that the tenderfoot really knows that p. Relative to the epistemic community of guides (for that area) the tenderfoot lacks relevant generally known information, and misses relevant data that the average guide would grasp in the circumstances.

These departures from the traditional account may make better sense if we reflect that the honorific term "knowledgeable" is to be applied only to those who are reliable sources of information, surely an important category for a language-using, social species.

We have now taken note of two types of situation where correct, fully warranted belief falls short of knowledge owing to no neglect or faulty reasoning or false belief. Despite commendable thoroughness and impeccable reasoning unspoiled by falsehood, one may still fail to be "in a position to know," owing either to faulty cognitive equipment or to missed generally known information. I am not suggesting that these are the only ways to be out of position to know. I have no complete list of epistemic principles describing ways of arriving at a position to know or

11 Gilbert Harman, "Induction," in Marshall Swain, ed., *Induction, Acceptance and Rational Belief* (Dordrecht: Reidel, 1970), esp. Sect. IV, pp. 95–7. Cf. Chapter 1 in this volume.

of being blocked from such a position. My suggestion is only that there are such principles, and that in any case we must go beyond the traditional emphasis by epistemologists on warrant and reasoning as determinants of knowledge. Despite the importance of warranted correct belief in determining what we know, the Gettier examples show that it is not alone enough to guarantee knowledge. What is more, warranted correct belief supported by reasoning *unspoiled by falsehood* seems immune to Gettier examples, but it still falls short of knowledge, as we have seen.

My conclusion is that to understand knowledge we must enrich our traditional repertoire of epistemic concepts with the notion of *being in a position to know (from the point of view of a K, e.g., a human being)*. Thus a proposition is evident (from the point of view of a K) to a subject only if *both* he is rationally justified in believing it *and* he is in a position to know (from the K point of view) whether it is true. It may *be* (and not just appear) evident to Magoo from *his* point of view that he will reach the other side safely, but it seems wrong to say of Magoo as he steps into the cable car with bombs raining all around that it *is* quite evident to him that he will arrive safely. It seems wrong *for whom* to say this? For one of us, naturally; that is, for a normal human from *his* point of view. And since a normal human could not help seeing and hearing the bombs, from the human point of view Magoo is not in a position to know that he will arrive safely, inasmuch as he is missing relevant information that a normal human would gather in the circumstances. Hence Magoo does not have *human* knowledge that he will arrive safely, for it is not evident to him from the human point of view that he will so arrive.

Our latest account was this:

(3) S knows that p iff
    (a) it is true that p;
    (b) S believes that p; and
    (c) there is a non-defective epistemic pyramid for S and the proposition that p.

It will be recalled that every node of such a pyramid must be true *and* evident. And for every node n that has successors, the successors must serve as grounds that give the subject S rational warrant for believing n. What now seems too narrow about this account emerges with the explanation of what a pyramid of knowledge is, and of what the evident is. For in this explanation what is evident to S is identified with what S is rationally justified in believing. But it now seems plain that for x to be evident to S, *two* conditions must be satisfied: (i) that S be rationally justified in believing x, and (ii) that S be in a position to know whether x is

28

true. And we must also take note of the relativity of knowledge to an epistemic community. Let us therefore replace (3) with the following:

(4) *S* knows (from the *K* point of view) that *p* iff
   (a) it is true that *p*;
   (b) *S* believes that *p*; and
   (c) there is a non-defective epistemic pyramid (from the *K* point of view) for *S* and the proposition that *p*.

Every node of such a pyramid must now be true and evident from the *K* point of view.

Normally when epistemologists discuss knowledge (of the colors and shapes of surrounding objects, of one's own or one's neighbor's mental states, and so on), they plainly do so from the *human* point of view. But other points of view are possible even in ordinary conversation. The expert/layman distinction is replicable in many different contexts, and with each replication we have a new epistemically relevant distinction in points of view, with expert knowledge on one side and layman knowledge on the other.

Neither Magoo nor the newspaper reader who alone has not seen the new edition is in a position to know (from the human point of view) about the relevant subject matter. Thus we can understand their ignorance and, by parity of reasoning, the ignorance of all those who are out of position to know that *p* because they lack either adequate cognitive equipment or relevant information that is generally known to those who have taken an epistemic stand on the question whether *p* (where to suspend judgment *is* to take an epistemic stand, whereas to be totally oblivious to the matter is not).

Doubtless we cannot hope here for such precision as is attainable in explaining, e.g., what it is to be a chess bishop. But chess is defined by a set of artificial conventions, whereas it is doubtful that epistemic principles are either artificial or conventional. At present, in any case, our understanding of what it is to be rationally justified or of what it is to be in a position to know is about as vague as our understanding of what it is to be moral, or well-mannered, or to speak grammatically. It would be very difficult to remove such vagueness, and it might turn out to be impossible.[12] In that case, Russell's view that knowledge is an inherently vague notion would have been vindicated. Meanwhile it is surely wise to elicit as much precise content as possible from our epistemic practice, for content unelicited is missed understanding.

12 Cf. Malcolm, *op. cit.*, pp. 114–15.

APPENDIX

What it is for S's belief that p to be fully grounded has been explained earlier by means of our epistemic pyramids. That answer points in the right direction, but it can be made more precise: e.g., by clarifying the grounding relation. Moreover, we have found that a fully grounded correct belief is not necessarily knowledge, and this for at least two reasons: (i) it may rest directly or indirectly on some false ground, and (ii) the believer may not be in a position to know.

We have tried to allow for these possibilities by broadening epistemic pyramids, by making room for our new epistemic notion of being-in-a-position-to-know, and by noting that to support knowledge epistemic pyramids must be non-defective, i.e., must contain no false nodes. But pyramids are objectionable for other reasons as well: (i) they may mislead by suggesting that terminal nodes provide a "foundation" in one or another undesirable sense, or by suggesting that terminal nodes must come first in time, so that one may later build on them; (ii) more seriously, there is an unacceptable vagueness in the very idea of such a pyramid, which derives mainly from the vagueness of the "grounding" relation in terms of which pyramids were defined. What follows is an attempt to solve these problems by switching pyramids upside down into trees, and by providing a more precise definition of such trees. To achieve greater precision, however, we must first enrich our conceptual resources. Each of the three main concepts to be defined – (I), (II), and (III) – seems to me a source of light, and by this light we shall then trim our trees to a more precise outline.

(I) α *fully validates* S-epistemic proposition e if and only if there is a set of subsets of α that form a sequence, $C_1, \ldots, C_n$, such that (i) C_1 validates e, (ii) each S-epistemic member of any subset C_t is validated by the immediate successor of C_t, C_{t+1}, and (iii) no member of the last subset, C_n, is S-epistemic.

This account of full validation makes use of a battery of technical concepts. Among them are *validation* and *S-epistemic proposition*, each of which requires explanation.

(II) *S-epistemic propositions*: of these (i) some are to the effect that some other proposition x has some epistemic status relative to S (i.e., to the effect that S believes x and how reasonably); and (ii) others are to the effect that S is in a position to know whether a certain proposition is true. (i) and (ii) are the varieties of "positive S-epistemic propositions." Logical compounds of such propositions are also S-epistemic, but no other propositions are S-epistemic.

(III) *Epistemic validation.* Let *A*, *B*, and *C* be sets of propositions.

1. *A epistemically implies* that *p* if and only if *A* and the epistemic principles together logically imply that *p*, but neither does so alone.

2. *A absolutely validates* S-epistemic proposition *e* if and only if *A* has only true members and epistemically implies *e*.

3. *A confirms* S-epistemic proposition *e* if and only if (a) *A* is a set with only true members, and (b) supposing the true, positive S-epistemic propositions are at most those entailed or absolutely validated by *A*, *e* follows epistemically from this together with *A*.

4. *A validates* S-epistemic proposition *e* if and only if *A* confirms *e*, *A* has only true members, and for every *B* with none but true members, such that *A* ∪ *B* does not confirm *e*, there is a *C* with none but true members such that *A* ∪ *B* ∪ *C* does confirm *e*.

(Note that 3 is included only for convenience, since *A confirms p* if and only if *A* ∪ {that the true, positive S-epistemic propositions are at most those entailed or absolutely validated by *A*} *absolutely validates p.*)

That completes the explanation of full validation (defined above). Note that what is fully validated by a set is always an S-epistemic proposition; and that the propositions in the validating set need not all be S-epistemic and that indeed perhaps none is S-epistemic. For example, some may be "self-certifying" or "self-discrediting" by specifying, with respect to a proposition *x*, that *S* correctly believes *x*, where this is sufficient for *x* to have a certain (positive or negative) epistemic status for *S*, given the epistemic principles; other *non*-epistemic members of a validating set may specify *S*'s perceptual or cognitive basis for a belief he has; others may certify the adequacy of *S*'s cognitive equipment relative to the epistemic community; and others yet may guarantee that *S* is not missing relevant generally known information.

(For convenience, in what follows let us terminologically stipulate that α (fully) validates that a proposition is evident, certain, reasonable, etc., for a subject when and only when the set α "(fully) renders certain, reasonable, etc.," that proposition for that subject; and that α (fully) validates that *S* is in a position to know that *p* when and only when α "(fully) puts *S* in a position to know that *p*.")

There is some simple reasoning behind the definition of full validation and behind the idea that if *S* knows that *p* then there must be a set that fully validates that it is evident to A that p. The reasoning boils down to this: Supposing that both circular justification and infinite regress are ruled out, it would seem that a chain of justification must eventually reach a last link that either is self-validating or helps validate further links without itself requiring validation.

Let us emphasize, however, that this will not commit one to a picture of knowledge according to which there is a bedrock of self-evident propositions. It is perfectly consistent with the present theory that part of what makes *any* proposition evident be its coherence with a network of mutually supporting propositions. Since there is bound to be a multitude of such coherent networks, however, a non-arbitrary narrowing of the field must be supported by something other than coherence. And this is where the last subset in the sequence of subsets of a fully validating set may be invoked. However, it is not required that the last subset include any self-evident belief; for example, it may contain some merely self-certifying correct belief, i.e., a proposition specifying that some other proposition x is correctly believed, where this suffices for x to have *some* positive epistemic status, however lowly: acceptability, for instance (i.e., being such that not believing it is *not* preferable to believing it).

The concepts recently defined enable us to construct an account (5) according to which S knows that p provided that both (a) S correctly believes that p,[13] and (b) there is a set of propositions that fully and non-defectively renders it evident to S that p (where a set "non-defectively renders it evident to S that p" if and only if it does so without attributing to S any false belief).[14]

Supposing this account correct, every bit of knowledge has a tree like that shown in Figure 2.3, the "ranks" of which (RI, RII, and RIII) correspond to our epistemic subsets discussed above (in the definition of full validation).

Note that each node of such a tree is a proposition. Thus the "root" node is the-proposition-that-p_1, and the first terminal node (from the left) the-proposition-that-p_{111}.[15]

There is an important difference between these trees and our earlier

---

13 Whether knowledge entails belief at all is of course a vexed question of long standing, but there is no room for it here. A helpful and interesting discussion is found in Keith Lehrer's "Belief and Knowledge," *Philosophical Review* 77 (1968): 491–9.

14 Here, in the account of concepts (I)–(III) above, and in what follows, the relativity of knowledge to an epistemic community is left implicit, as it normally is in ordinary thought and speech.

15 Strictly speaking, what we have here is obviously a *partial tree schema*. For convenience, however, I speak of trees even when I mean partial tree schemata. Also, it should not be thought that every tree must have exactly three ranks (RI, RII, and RIII). On the contrary, a tree may have any number of ranks, so long as it has more than one.

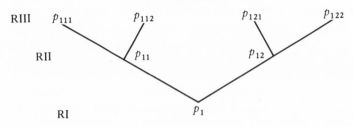

Figure 2.3

pyramids. Except for terminal nodes, every node of a tree is an S-epistemic proposition, whereas not a single node of a pyramid need be epistemic at all. Pyramids display propositions that are evident to A (*not* propositions that such and such other propositions are evident to S), and they also show which propositions ground (for S) any proposition for which S has grounds. Trees display true epistemic propositions concerning S and they also show what "makes these propositions true" *via* epistemic principles (i.e., what successors "validate" these propositions). A tree must do this for *every* epistemic proposition that constitutes one of its nodes. That is to say, trees contain no epistemic terminal nodes. It is in this sense that trees provide *complete* epistemic explanations of the truth of their root nodes.

The following requirements flow from the fact that trees are intended to correspond to the fully validating sets defined by (I) above, and from the fact that the ranks of trees are to correspond to the subsets $C_1, \ldots, C_n$ of (I).

1. (Let us call node x a "successor" (i.e., a *direct* successor) of node y relative to tree T provided there are A and B such that (i) A stands for x on T and B stands for y on T; (ii) A and B are connected by a straight branch on T; (iii) B is closer to the root node than A; and (iv) there is no C such that C stands for a proposition on T, and A, B, and C are connected by a straight branch and B is closer to the root node than C, and C is closer to the root node than A.) The set of all nodes that (directly) succeed a given node must validate that node.

2. If a node n is an S-epistemic proposition, then n must have successors, it must branch out into a set of further nodes that validate n. (Trees are supposed to correspond to sets that fully validate S-epistemic propositions, and any such set is to provide, in a sense, a "complete" explanation of how the S-epistemic proposition comes to be true.)

3. The proposition that-p_1 must be S-epistemic.

4. Each branch of a complete tree of evidence must terminate. (And in some cases the terminal node specifies that S correctly believes x, and is

the sole successor of its immediate predecessor, which is to the effect that *x* has a certain epistemic status for *S*.)

5. A non-defective tree of evidence for *S* must attribute no false belief to *S*. This applies not only to terminal nodes but also to non-terminal nodes. We know that a non-terminal node must be an *S*-epistemic proposition, given the nature of the consequents of epistemic principles and the fact that it is *S*'s knowledge that is in question.[16] That is to say, each non-terminal node must be a proposition concerning a certain other proposition (or certain other propositions) and either (i) to the effect that it is (they are) believed by *S* and how reasonably, or (ii) to the effect that *S* is in a position to know whether it is (they are) true, or (iii) some logical compound of propositions of types (i) or (ii). Propositions of types (i) or (iii) may attribute belief to *S*. If the tree is to be non-defective, no such belief can be false.

Finally, if the root node of a non-defective tree of evidence is the proposition that it is evident to *S* that *p*, let us call such a tree not just a tree of evidence, but a *tree of knowledge* for *S* and the proposition that *p*.

In conclusion, we may now be sure that to each set that fully renders it evident to *S* that *p* there corresponds at least one tree of knowledge for *S* and the proposition that *p*. And we thus have an equivalent for our account of knowledge (5) as correct belief in what has been fully and non-defectively rendered evident:

S knows that *p* iff
  (a) *S* correctly believes that *p*; and
  (b) there is a tree of knowledge for *S* and the proposition that *p*.

---

16 But it should be noted that terminal nodes are not restricted to the last (or top) rank of a tree. On the contrary, any number of them may appear in any rank.

3

On our knowledge of matters of fact

The traditional conception of knowledge as justified true belief has collapsed under weighty objections. Some of these are well known; but others, though equally weighty and puzzling, have attracted comparatively little attention.

I

It is sometimes objected that if we require that knowers always be able to ground what they know, provided it is not self-evident, then what ordinarily passes for knowledge would be little of the sort. I happen to know, for example, that Alamogordo is north of El Paso, but I doubt that I could establish it from memory: I cannot cite any authoritative map or encyclopaedia where I saw or read it, etc. In spite of this, however, it seems to me that even the traditional account can be defended here. For even though I may not remember what specific evidence I had in coming to know the relative position of the two towns, I can still remember *that I once had such evidence*, and perhaps what type of evidence it was, and that I have not since then found any contrary evidence. And this, I think, is enough to justify my continuing to believe. Indeed, even just the fact that one seems to remember may be enough for those of us with a good memory.

Much of our mathematical knowledge has a similar basis. Few of us can produce mathematical proofs at will. Even if we cannot now produce a proof, nevertheless, we may still remember well that we once did, or at least that we once saw it done, and this sometimes suffices to justify present belief.

Other doubts about the traditional account cannot be removed so easily. Suppose, for example, that I hallucinate a bear in the shadows of my cabin, when there happens indeed to be one there. Can this not be a case of justified true belief (that there is a bear) with no knowledge? Cases of this sort plausibly elicit a further requirement for knowledge: a causal connection of some sort involving the object of belief.[1] Thus, for knowledge

---

1 See, for example, the instructive papers in Volume 64 (1967) of the *Journal of Philosophy* by Alvin Goldman ("A Causal Theory of Knowing") and Brian Skyrms ("The Explication of '*S* knows that *p*' "). Goldman requires a causal connection between the belief and its object, whereas Skyrms requires one between the grounds of the belief and its object.

of the bear in the shadows, perhaps I need a (more or less costly) causal interaction with it.

Other examples lead to the same view:

A volcano and its lava. Someone sees lava and infers a past volcano, which indeed there was, but *its* lava is gone, the present lava having been placed there later.[2]

Smoke and fire. Someone sees smoke and infers fire but the smoke he sees comes from a source other than the fire which by coincidence is indeed there.[3]

The traditional account of knowledge as justified true belief is called into question by "causal" examples such as these and that of our hallucinatory bear.

An alternative account of knowledge designed to deal with such anomalies is due to Fred Dretske:

(D) S knows P if and only if S has a conclusive reason R for believing P.

(D′) S has a conclusive reason R for believing P if and only if
    (a) R is a conclusive reason for P (i.e., R would not be the case unless P were the case);
    (b) S believes without doubt, reservation, or question that P is the case, and he believes this on the basis of R; and
    (c) (i) S knows that R is the case, or
        (ii) R is some experiential state of S.[4]

Many other accounts of empirical knowledge cluster around such a conception of conclusive reasons. Compare, for instance, the proposals of Skyrms and of Rozeboom.[5] Indeed, Armstrong's explication of inferential knowledge is so similar to (D) that we may speak of an Armstrong-Dretske explication of inferential knowledge.[6] Our discussion will focus

---

2 This derives from Goldman, p. 361.

3 This derives from Skyrms, p. 385.

4 Fred Dretske, "Conclusive Reasons," *Australasian Journal of Philosophy* 49 (1971): 1–22; see particularly pp. 12–13. Dretske calls attention on p. 13 to the necessity for "minor embellishments," and closes by reminding us that the account must be "... properly qualified along the lines suggested. . . ." But I can't imagine how qualification along the lines suggested could help to solve the difficulties to be canvassed here.

5 Both reprinted in *Knowing*, ed. M. D. Roth and L. Galis (Washington, D.C.: University Press of America, 1984).

6 See Armstrong's *Materialist Theory of the Mind* (London: Routledge & Kegan Paul, 1969), especially pp. 200–4. Moreover, the conception of conclusive reasons under review is used by Dretske himself to explain knowledge by sight in his important *Seeing and Knowing* (Chicago: University of Chicago Press, 1969).

on (D), therefore, as representative of a conception of empirical knowledge with wide acceptance among students of the subject.

In the first place, it should be noted that (D'a) presupposes conditions C such that C & R together guarantee P. That is to say, R alone need not guarantee P by law of nature. Thus a barometer reading may be a conclusive reason for rain in one set of conditions (working barometer, etc.) but not in another (defective barometer, etc.). However, it seems essential to impose an independence requirement (I) to the effect that

... C must be logically and causally independent of the state of affairs expressed by P.[7]

Otherwise there would be disastrous counter-examples to the explication of conclusive reasons. Thus if C is P itself or anything Q that either alone or in conjunction with a law of nature entails P, then *every* state of affairs would be a conclusive reason R for P. For, so long as Q is held constant R would not be the case unless P were the case, no matter what R is, inasmuch as the constant presence of Q would of itself suffice to ensure that P, too, would be present. Independence requirement I is imposed to preclude this unacceptable result. What remains to be seen is whether I is itself acceptable.

It will now be argued that I is *not* acceptable, inasmuch as out of the cases where R is a conclusive reasons for P, (i) some are cases where one of the essential conditions C is caused by P, and (ii) some are cases where one of the essential conditions C causes P. (In what follows "$\boxed{P}$(. . .)" will represent "It is physically necessary (it follows from laws of nature but not from laws of logic) that . . .'; and "$\boxed{L}$(. . .)" will represent "It is logically necessary that . . .".)

(i) Suppose that a certain meter would not read m had there not been an explosion of force f. The meter reading might then surely serve as a "conclusive reason" for an estimate of the force. And yet one of the conditions C essential in ensuring that $\boxed{P}$((C & the meter reads m) ⊃ the explosion had force f) may well be the meter's being "in working condition." But there are easily imaginable circumstances where the meter's being in working condition is itself causally dependent on the explosion's having had force f.

(ii) Consider an instrument which when put in contact with a man's skull will indicate whether the man is sleeping or awake (S or A). One of the conditions C ensuring that $\boxed{P}$((C & the instrument indicates A) ⊃ A) may well be that the instrument be in contact with the man's skull. But this can surely be causally responsible for the man's being awake.

7 Dretske, "Conclusive Reasons," pp. 7–8.

It follows that we cannot require the complete causal independence of conditions C from state of affairs P. For (i) shows that P may be a cause of one of the conditions C, and (ii) shows that one of the conditions C may be a cause of P.

Let us therefore supplement (D') not with the discredited I but with the following alternative conception of what it is for R to be a conclusive reason for P:

> R is a conclusive reason for P if and only if there is a condition C such that
> (i) $\boxed{P}$((R & C) is actual $\supset$ P is actual);
> (ii) C is actual;
> (iii) Not-$\boxed{P}$(C is actual $\supset$ P is actual); and
> (iv) Not-$\boxed{L}$((R & C) is actual $\supset$ P is actual).

This seems to me a considerable improvement, but still not good enough. For it can be trivialized as follows. Suppose there is a Q such that (i) $\boxed{P}$(Q $\supset$ P), and (ii) Q is actual. Then *any* state R will qualify as a conclusive reason for P, inasmuch as (R $\supset$ Q) will always meet the foregoing conditions on C.

The problem of finding an adequate conception of "conclusive reasons" is sure to overlap largely with the problem of finding an adequate conception of "standard conditions," or so it seems to me.[8] Here we must be satisfied with some such understanding of "R is a conclusive reason for P" as "In the circumstances, R ensures or causally suffices for P." With this understanding, let us now return to the account of empirical knowledge under review.

It is a virtue of (D) that it deals adequately with the problematic cases described earlier. Thus consider the case where someone sees lava and infers a past volcano, which indeed there was. Its lava has been removed, however, and replaced by other lava later. The subject, S, believes in the past volcano (P) on the basis of the present lava (R). But since R is not a conclusive reason for believing P in the circumstances – the site for dumping the new lava was chosen at random – and since nothing else is a conclusive reason that S has for believing P, account (D) entails that S does not know about the past volcano. Similar reasoning applies in many other such cases. Thus, similar reasoning will show that if someone S sees smoke and infers fire, where the smoke he sees comes from a source other than the fire which by coincidence is indeed there, then ordinarily S does not

---

8 Actually "conclusive reason" seems unfortunate terminology for the notion intended, but let us not quibble over that.

know about the fire if his belief about the fire is based on the smoke he sees.

Despite its wide-ranging success, however, (D) has unacceptable flaws. Two different types of cases will help to show some of them.

Suppose first that I am driving along paying close attention to my speed when my car is hit by something that, unknown to me, simultaneously puts out of order the normal speedometer mechanism and pierces through to the speedometer with the effect that the needle reading remains a function – the normal function – of the speed (e.g., because of the pressure exerted on the needle by the air entering through the hole). Here speedometer readings remain conclusive reasons for my judgments about the speed. According to (D), if I believe that my speed is 60 m.p.h. because the speedometer reads 60 m.p.h., then I know what my speed is despite the fact that the speedometer mechanism is out of order and it is only by accident and luck that I am right.

There is a second type of case that to my mind also shows a serious inadequacy in (D). It has been reported in the newspapers that researchers are investigating the possibility that palm patterns are causally correlated with certain genetic conditions that are in turn so correlated with certain illnesses. Suppose now (i) that a pattern P is indeed so correlated with the onset of illness I in middle age, (ii) that a young palmreader Y as part of her indoctrination was taught that P indicates the onset of I in middle age, (iii) that this particular bit of palmreader lore was adopted not as a result of any noticed correlation, but at the urging of an unscrupulous leader with his own dark motives, and (iv) that Y believes client X will contract I in middle age, on the basis of his palm pattern P. According to (D) we must now grant Y knowledge that X will contract I in middle age, despite the fact that the most advanced medical technology of the time would be powerless to make such a prediction. (Hypochondria yields similar examples.)

I conclude that the conception of empirical knowledge represented by (D) is seriously flawed. Both flaws recently considered derive, in my opinion, from the same unfortunate omission. (D) omits requiring any cognizance by S of the connection between R and P. But it is surely because they have the wrong conception, if any, of that connection that both the speedometer-reader and the palm-reader (and the hypochondriac) fall short of knowledge, despite their correct belief on the basis of "conclusive reasons."

If the conception of empirical knowledge represented by (D) is flawed, what is the alternative? How *should* we conceive of propositional knowledge?

II

In earlier chapters I have suggested that knowledge is correct belief in what is evident, each bit of knowledge requiring a pyramid such as that shown in Figure 2.1 (on p. 22). Speaking somewhat loosely, we may say that such pyramids provide complete epistemic explanations of how S comes to know something, and we may describe them generally as follows: Each node of such a pyramid is a proposition. If the proposition is not self-evident to S then it must have successors on the pyramid. The successors of a node must together make that node evident. Each branch of a (complete) pyramid must terminate. Finally (and to solve the Gettier problem), we must require that each node be true.

Epistemic principles determine the conditions under which a proposition is evident to someone. Perhaps very few such principles are needed. (One corresponding to deduction, one or two corresponding to induction (enumerative and hypothetical) and nothing more?) In any case, however many there may be, I assume there are some. If a proposition is evident but not self-evident, then presumably something makes it evident, something entails that it is evident, *via* the epistemic principles. More strictly speaking, that p is evident is then entailed by a set of propositions together with some epistemic principles, but not by the set alone, nor by the principles alone.

I will not pretend to have given here a precise or complete account of pyramids of knowledge. That task was already carried out earlier, or so I hope. Fortunately, what we have here is sufficient for understanding and assessing what follows. The leading ideas required are simply these: (a) that you know only when you believe correctly what is evident to you; (b) that if something is evident to you, you must believe it not only correctly but with good reason, i.e., your belief must be reasonable; and (c) that the reasoning (implicit or explicit), if any, which supports your reasonable belief must not be flawed by a falsehood, i.e., must not include as an essential component any false assumption, presumption, claim, judgment, belief, or the like.

Before us, then, is an account of knowledge (S) according to which S knows that p if and only if

(1) it is true that p;
(2) S believes that p; and
(3) there is a pyramid of knowledge for S and the proposition that p.

This has been developed earlier as a general account of knowledge.[9] In this chapter I wish to consider more specific questions concerning empirical knowledge, or knowledge of matters of fact.

Let us begin with our "causal examples." It will now be argued that the present understanding of knowledge (S) draws support from such examples.

Consider first a case in which I release a pencil held above my desk, whereupon it falls to its impact with the desk and the consequent noise. Supposing I knew of this causal sequence before it occurred, how do we account for my knowledge? Take the first two links in the chain: the release, and the fall. Given my knowledge of the release, how do we account for my knowledge (in advance) of the fall?

Certainly I have no sufficient warrant to believe that all pencils drop when released. The exceptions that crowd in are so varied and numerous that there is no need to single one out. Worse yet, I could not realistically attempt to pick out with any precision present conditions within which pencils always drop when released. And surely not many of us could do so. What is more, I do not see how an appeal beyond universality ("All pencils . . .") to probability ("Most pencils . . .") is of any use at all. How then can I know that the fall will follow the release?

My own suggestion is this. I am justified in believing that in present conditions the pencil *would* fall if released, i.e., that there is a conjunction of conditions C present such that (a) the release and C together necessitate the fall (in philosophical jargon: "nomologically imply" the fall) but (b) neither C nor the release does so alone. (That-p nomologically implies that-q if and only if that-p and laws of nature together logically imply that-q, but that-p does not alone logically imply that-q.)

Actually, what we would think in the circumstances is of course that a release "guarantees" or "ensures" a fall. But when I ask myself what this means, the foregoing suggestion strikes me as a good possibility. For a further test, let us now apply it to some examples in the light of our theory.

Imagine a tribe that knows the correlation between a certain pattern of barometer readings and rain, but not the underlying theory. On a new occasion they take note of an occurrence of the pattern and correctly predict rain. But the pattern is caused, not by the atmospheric conditions, but by a defective spring.[10]

Presumably, the tribe is justified in predicting rain on the basis of

9 In Chapter 2.
10 This derives from Skyrms, *op. cit.*, p. 382.

barometric pattern P only because they think it very likely that in the circumstances the pattern "guarantees" or "ensures" rain. But what warrants this belief of theirs? Isn't it the numerous relevantly similar occasions when rain has been observed to follow an occurrence of pattern P? I say "relevantly similar" for if the tribesmen believed that, say, the position of the barometer made a difference, then surely they could not be sure that the new instance of P would be followed by rain unless the present position of the barometer was one of those already checked out. I suggest therefore that the (mostly implicit) reasoning that underlies the prediction is this: "There are circumstances C present whose conjunction with P has on many occasions guaranteed rain, and such that C and an occurrence of P together now guarantee (nomologically imply) that rain will follow, but C does not do so alone."[11]

If the tribe had reason to suspect that some circumstance made the new situation importantly different from those in the past, they would need to approach a prediction with at least much greater caution. For instance, suppose that all previous observations had been made at the top of one of their mountains, whereas in the new situation the barometer is in a valley. Anyone aware of this (given his ignorance of the underlying theory) would be in a worse rational position for prediction than otherwise. I explain this by noting that he has less reason to think that there are circumstances C present now and in the previous cases, such that C and the occurrence of P together guarantee rain (i.e., nomologically imply it).

Experimental and applied scientists must have a keener, better developed sense for what is likely to prove relevant. The rest of us rely on our duller common-sense judgment. But we all must often make assumptions of relevant similarity if we are to gather serviceable experience.

How then does all of this bear on our refusal to attribute knowledge to the tribe with the newly defective barometer? If I am right, their prediction of rain depends for its justification on their having sufficient grounds to think that there are conditions C present such that C and the occurrence of pattern P together necessitate rain. And their grounds for this surely rest on the claim that the present situation is relevantly similar to a sufficient number of those in the past where occurrences of P have always preceded rain. What this in turn comes to is a claim that, given the observed past cases where rain has followed P, we may now infer that it cannot all be just a coincidence, that on the contrary the cases must share

---

11 Of course I am not suggesting that the tribe must make such an inference consciously and in detail, any more than I must consciously infer the presence of people in a crowd from their voices, their appearance, their movements, etc., even though my knowledge of their presence is nevertheless dependent on my sensing such factors.

a set of conditions C such that (i) C and P together nomologically imply rain, (ii) C does not do so alone, and (iii) C is now present.

If they must have at least this much by way of justification, then we can see in the light of our theory why the tribe with the defective barometer fails to know of the coming rain. For the defective spring presumably ensures that there is no such conjunction of conditions C, inasmuch as it makes the *pattern P/rain* sequence a mere coincidence in the present case. But then the tribe's reasoning to the conclusion that rain will follow depends essentially on a false assumption, which means that their conclusion is supported only by pseudo-pyramids.

What I have been attempting is in effect an explication or at least a partial explication of the idea of standard conditions. The tribe can predict rain on the basis of a new occurrence of pattern P *only on the assumption that the conditions are standard* (for that sort of inference). But what is it for the conditions to be "standard" (for the sort of thing, i.e., for a prediction of rain on the basis of an occurrence of P)? My foregoing suggestions can be viewed as a first step to an answer. Those suggestions can also be applied *mutatis mutandis* to our other examples, such as the case of smoke and fire.

If I see smoke in the distance and infer that there is a fire there, normally I do so on the assumption that the conditions are standard (for that sort of inference). This is what accounts for my failure to know when the smoke comes from a source other than the fire which by coincidence is indeed there. In standard conditions – the conditions where the smoke-fire correlation has been established – the smoke comes from the fire. When the smoke originates elsewhere, part of my essential grounds is false (and the conditions are nonstandard); hence my belief rests only on pseudo-pyramids.

Notice that my being right only by coincidence is unimportant. In another case the smoke might come from a smoke bomb which in the circumstances could only have been set off by the fire which does set it off and whose smoke is out of sight. Here the smoke *would* not have been there had the fire not been there. So *in one sense* it is not merely a coincidence that I am right. Still, since I am unaware of the connection between the smoke and the fire, I fail to know of the fire even in this case. I fail to know because my inference from the smoke to the fire assumes the falsehood that the conditions are standard, i.e., relevantly similar to those present in the many past cases where the smoke-fire correlation has been established. Since my inference assumes that falsehood, my conclusion is supported only by pseudo-pyramids. Hence the present account explains why it is no knowledge.

43

Since analogous reasoning applies to the case of the planted lava, and to other such examples, I infer a virtue of the present account: that it will yield the correct results with respect to such "causal examples".

III

Our recent line of reasoning has limitations, however, some of which are brought out by the following types of examples: (i) classification of entities within kinds, (ii) identification of persons and other entities, and (iii) defective cognitive equipment.

(i) Classification of entities within kinds

Fruit carts are fruitful sources of knowledge: here is an apple, there a peach, yonder a mango, and so on. Any adequate theory of knowledge must be able to explain such knowledge. How then is it to be explained by the present theory?

It might be thought that the line of reasoning used for the causal examples will now serve equally well. Thus it might be argued that when S knows that this is an apple by seeing that it is one, the apple presents him with a look L that given the circumstances it would not present to him were it not an apple.[12] This might be said to serve as implicit reasoning that underlies S's knowledge that it is an apple: "Thus if the real apple before him has a wax covering, then S may not know, despite his justified true belief, that it is an apple; if he does not know, it is because a falsehood flaws his reasoning. The circumstances (the wax cover, etc.) make it false that the object would not present him with look L were it not an apple".

The slack in this line of reasoning derives from the fact that a thing's appearance does not determine its kind. The possibility of plastic surgery, imitations, mutations, etc., should make this clear. Hence unless the circumstances take up the slack it would *always* be false (even in cases of true knowledge by sight) that the object would not look thus were it not an apple. However, I see no way for the circumstances to take up the slack, i.e., to rule out all such possibilities as imitation, mutation, etc., short of including some such condition as: if it looks like an apple, then it is an apple (material conditional). But if this is allowed as part of the circumstances then even in the circumstances of the wax-covered apple it

---

12 This is one of Dretske's requirements for seeing that the thing is an apple (advanced on p. 82 of *Seeing and Knowing*). Our discussion will show that this exposes that account to fatal objections, and discloses further difficulties in account (D), presented earlier.

will be true that it would not look the way it does were it not an apple. For the circumstances will include the fact that if it looks like an apple, it is an apple (material conditional), in virtue of the truth of the consequent.

It may be replied that the conditional "If it looks like an apple, then it is an apple" must be interpreted as strong rather than material. It must be interpreted as tantamount to "It cannot look like an apple without being an apple". But here we are back with the original problem. If to be able to tell an apple by its look when it looks like an apple, the apple must be in circumstances encompassing that it absolutely cannot look like an apple without being an apple, then we can never tell an apple by its look when it looks like an apple; for the look of a thing never absolutely determines its kind, and in particular it is never true that the piece of fruit before you absolutely cannot look like an apple without being an apple.

If we cannot account in the way suggested for our knowledge of a thing's kind, how then are we to do so? Here it seems to me that what Peirce called "abduction" offers our best hope.[13] Confronted by the fruit cart in the right environment, with the expected odors, and so on, we implicitly jump to our conclusions – here is an apple, there a peach, yonder a mango, etc. – as the best explanations of our experience. It is important to note that the direction of the conditional is now reversed. Our reasoning now requires that if it is an apple then it looks like an apple (rather than the reverse). Indeed our reasoning requires the thesis that it looks like an apple *because* it *is* an apple (i.e., this best explains its look).

We are finally approaching a position to explain why S does not know that it is an apple when the apple is covered with wax and made to look like an apple. It is not because his reasoning requires *that the object before him would not look thus were it not an apple* (which is admittedly false since a plum could equally well have been covered with wax and made to look like an apple). For this would still be false even when it is a naked apple in plain view, and if required as an essential part of the reasoning it would infect not only pseudo-knowledge but also true knowledge.

It may be replied here that if the wax-covered apple is really an apple then surely *it* absolutely could not look like an apple without being an apple, for no non-apple could possibly be identical with it, which is an apple. Once an apple, necessarily an apple. This reasoning is a consequence of the most natural reading of "the object before him would not

13 Recent methodology of science gives this type of inference prime importance. See W. V. Quine's "Two Dogmas of Empiricism," *Philosophical Review* (1951): 20–43, and "Posits and Reality," in *Basis of Contemporary Philosophy*, ed. S. Uyeda (Tokyo: Waseda University Press, 1960); K. Popper's "Three Views Concerning Human Knowledge," in his *Conjectures and Refutations* (New York: Basic Books, 1963): and G. Harman's "Inference to the Best Explanation," *Philosophical Review* 74 (1965): 88–95.

look thus were it not an apple". Unfortunately, it in turn has the consequence that the look of the thing (along with everything else about it) becomes in a sense irrelevant: if the object before him is really an apple then, regardless of what F may be, if it is F then "the object before him would not be F were it not an apple". F may be *looking green, being upside down*, anything whatever that just happens to be true of the apple.

Therefore, we must read "the object before him would not look thus were it not an apple" in a different and perhaps unnatural way, as "it could not be true that the object before him looked thus and was not an apple". *And this reinstates our earlier critique.* Suppose an apple is covered with wax and made to look like an apple, with the result in the circumstances that S does not know from its look that it is an apple, despite his true justified belief to that effect. It is reasonable to try to account for S's lack of knowledge here by attributing to him some essential reasoning that though justified is still false. But the required reasoning must not include the claim that it *could not* be true that the object before him looked thus (the way it looks to him) and was not an apple. It must be granted that this would be false, since if the object before him were a non-apple made to look like an apple, then it *would* be true that the object before him looked thus (apple-like) and was not an apple. Nevertheless, the falsehood would carry over unwanted to cases of true knowledge. Thus if the reasoning that underlies our classification of a thing into a natural kind by its look requires the claim that it could not be true that the object had that look without falling into that natural kind, we could never know a thing's natural kind from its look, could never tell an apple by its look. For, regardless of the look or the kind, surely it *could* always be true that an object (before us or not) had that look without being of that kind.

I have argued that invoking Peircian "abduction" offers our best hope of explaining knowledge of a thing's kind by its appearance. When we know an apple by its appearance, it is because we can abduct that it is an apple, i.e., because we can reason that the idea that it is an apple (a naked apple) best explains our data or experience, that the character of our experience has its source in the presence of an apple (a naked apple). But now we can see why S does not know that the thing before him is an apple when it is an apple covered with wax and made to look like an apple. S's reasoning is flawed by a falsehood. What explains the apple-look of the thing is *not* – as S reasons – its being an apple (a naked apple), but its having been covered with wax and made to look like an apple.

No peculiarity of the fruit cart example has played an essential role in our reasoning. The same arguments go through if we shift to animals, plants, artifacts, etc. Therefore I conclude that abduction is quite generally the key to understanding our knowledge of a thing's kind by its appearance.

(ii) Identification of persons and other entities

The same key will open understanding of this new type of knowledge. When I identify someone as Sara, it is not because in the circumstances she could not look thus to me without being Sara. After all, even if she has no twin sister, it is quite conceivable that she have had one. So it seems always false that someone could not look the way he does without being whoever he is. More strictly speaking, it seems always false that if someone has a certain look then he must be a certain person.

This suggests that when I identify Sara I accept its being Sara before me as the best explanation of my relevant experience and data. It is because it *is* Sara before me that it looks like Sara before me.

Not that its being Sara by itself determines its looking like Sara before me. When I identify Sara by her look I remember her look. Speaking more accurately, therefore, what I accept is that likeness (through time) is best explained by identity (through time), or at least that what best explains sufficient likeness is identity with allowance for cosmetics, aging, and so on. We thus implicitly rely for identification on assumptions about people's gradual change in appearance in the normal course of events, making due allowance for cosmetics, etc. This seems quite obvious. What I wish to highlight here is the direction of our assumption, which is not that likeness implies identity but the reverse. How then can we infer identity from likeness without affirming the consequent or the like? By inferring first that it is identity that best explains the likeness, the likeness between what is now seen and what is remembered as having looked thus.

We are approaching a position to explain why I do not know that it is my friend Tom before me just by seeing that it is he, when unknown to me Tom has been totally disfigured by an accident and is now just made up to look like he did before the accident. It is not because my reasoning requires the falsehood that the person before me could not look thus were it not Tom. It must of course be granted that this *is* a falsehood: after all, Tom might have had an identical twin. But its correlate would also be false when I correctly and with full knowledge identify Sara, who has not been disfigured. The falsehood would therefore indiscriminately infect not only pseudo-identification but also true and knowledgeable identification.

The reasoning that allowed us to understand knowledge of a thing's kind by its appearance can now be reproduced here *mutatis mutandis*, leading to the conclusion that abduction once again offers our best hope. When I know that it is Sara before me by her look it is because I can abduct that it is she, i.e., because I can reason that the idea that it is Sara best explains the appearance of the person before me. But now we can see why I do not know by his appearance that it is Tom before me when it is Tom disfigured and made to look like Tom. My reasoning is flawed by a falsehood. What explains the man's looking just like Tom is *not* – as I reason – his being Tom, etc. (although he is indeed Tom), but his having been made up to look like Tom.

There is an important difference between the reasoning that gives us predictive knowledge from instruments or other causal indicators of the future (e.g., barometers) and the reasoning that yields knowledgeable identification of an entity or its kind. Advanced knowledge that p is obtained by noting that the data (the instrument reading or other indication) would not be what it is, in the circumstances, were it not the case that p, i.e., in the circumstances the body of data necessitates that p. Identification of an entity or its kind when embodied in knowledge that p is obtained rather by noting that if it is true that p, then (in the circumstances) that necessitates and best explains the data. The direction of the reasoning is reversed in an important respect: in one case the data are believed to necessitate that p, whereas in the other that p is believed to necessitate the data.

There is also an important similarity in our treatment of the two types of knowledge: in both cases we have explained pseudo-knowledge by attributing false reasoning to the protagonist. But not all pseudo-knowledge can be explained thus.

(iii) Defective cognitive equipment

Cases of this sort might be called Magoo situations – where someone lacks adequate cognitive equipment. It is because of this lack that, despite his extensive experience with cable cars, Mr. Magoo does not know that his cable car will arrive safely when, unknown to him, bombs are raining all around it. Some may be tempted to assimilate Magoo situations to the cases solved earlier by attributing false reasoning to the protagonist. It might be argued that Magoo falls short of knowledge despite legitimate and fully justifiable reasoning because he must be making a false assumption somewhere in his reasoning. Thus perhaps he is assuming that there are no dangers ahead, an assumption that might easily be exploded. Although this account of Magoo situations may seem initially attractive, I will now try to show a serious flaw in it.

What distinguishes the Magoo situation from our own situation as we predict the pen's fall on the basis of its release? In each case there is extensive knowledge which establishes a correlation that seems currently applicable. In each case extensive experience justifies the presumption that there must be some condition C whose presence explains an E-P correlation by virtue of the fact that E and C nomologically implies P. Furthermore, the current situation in each case sufficiently resembles the past situations (from the point of view of the protagonist) to justify the further presumption that C is currently present. Both we and Magoo may thus be sure that P is forthcoming.

For Magoo E includes his grasp, such as it is (kinesthetic, tactual, visual, etc.), of his entry into the cable car, P is his arriving safely, and C is a complicated condition involving a path free of perturbations to the other side.

For us E includes our experience of releasing the pen, P is the pen's fall, and C is a complicated condition involving the absence of magnets, high-pressure air streams, etc.

It is because of the *apparent sameness* of the new situation and the past situations where the release-fall correlation was established that we are able to predict the fall in the new situation. But then is not Magoo's situation *to his mind* apparently quite the same as the past situations where the cable-car-ride/safe-arrival correlation was established by him?

It is for this reason that, in Chapter 2, I elicited from Magoo situations a distinctive aspect of the concept of knowledge: those who aspire to knowledge must have adequate cognitive equipment to begin with – relative to the question in hand. Of course, even if you have less than 20-20 vision you can still know that there is a barn in front of you when you see one there. Not just any defect will make your equipment inadequate for a judgment on the question whether p. I venture that it must be a defect that precludes your acquiring information that (i) a normal inquirer in the epistemic community would acquire in that situation, and (ii) makes a difference to what you can reasonably conclude on the question whether p (or at least to how reasonably you can draw the conclusion).

In this essay I have tried to enhance our understanding of empirical knowledge: first, by considering an attractive and prominent account of such knowledge, which reflection exposed as seriously flawed on several counts; and, secondly, by showing how an alternative account draws support from each of several varieties of empirical knowledge: (a) advance knowledge based on causal indicators, (b) knowledge based on familiar, common-sensical correlations, such as smoke-fire, (c) classification of things into kinds, and (d) identification of persons and other entities.

According to the alternative account here supported, knowledge is correct belief in what is evident to you. In conclusion, the pseudo-knowledge of those with impaired or missing cognitive equipment was shown to resist the explanation that had served for the pseudo-knowledge correlated with (a)–(d). This calls for elaboration of our account of knowledge, and elsewhere I try to answer the call.[14]

14 In Chapters 1, 2, and 4 of this book.

4

Presuppositions of empirical knowledge

In the following pages five cases of abnormality are examined. It is argued that each reveals presuppositions that apparently underlie much of our commonplace empirical knowledge. And it is also argued that together they support a certain account of such knowledge, one that yields the following ideas: (a) that you know only when you believe correctly what is evident to you; (b) that for something to be evident to you, you must believe it reasonably, your belief must be reasonable; and (c) that the framework of beliefs, assumptions, experiences, or what not, if any, that supports your reasonable belief must not be flawed by a falsehood, i.e., must not involve as an essential component any false presupposition, assumption, presumption, claim, judgment, belief, or the like.

A. RECOGNITION AND CLASSIFICATION

1. The strange case of the masked burglar

It may well be thought that the framework (explicit or implicit) that underlies the recognitional judgment that here again is N before me is approximately this: (a) on past occasions when it has looked N-like, it has been due to the fact that it was N himself before me with what, in the circumstances, was his natural look; (b) here again something looks N-like in circumstances like those in the past when N has presented to me his natural N-like look; (c) if so, then here again it looks N-like because once again it is N himself before me, with his natural look in the circumstances.

Note, however, the heavy burden placed on the notion of "one's natural look in the circumstances." Someone who habitually uses heavy makeup may look different on arising than he does post-toilette. Could he in each case be said to have his natural look in the circumstances? Those who have never seen him without makeup, and could not recognize him if they did, may still recognize him easily from his post-toilette appearance.

Even a disguise may mediate recognition. Thus a clown with a certain distinctive look may be recognized by his fans, though they would not know him without his disguise. Does he have his "natural look in the circumstances" when he gives a performance?

If the notion of one's natural look is not helpful, is that of one's *normal* look more so? It does seem right to say that the clown has his normal look during his performance. Here, perhaps, are some of the relevant presumptions: (a) on past occasions when it has looked N-like, it has been due to the fact that it was N himself before me with what, in the circumstances, was his normal look; (b) here again something looks N-like in circumstances like those in the past when N has presented to me the N-like look that he normally presents in such circumstances; (c) if so, then here again it looks N-like because once again it is N himself before me, with his normal look in the circumstances.

Suppose that a certain Mr. B is burglarizing the theater in which he works as an actor. When he hears the watchman, who knows him by sight, Mr. B slips on one of the many excellent masks lying there in the dark, so as to avoid recognition as he makes his escape. Completely unknown to Mr. B, however, that mask has been made using *him* as a model, for a forthcoming production involving twins. The watchman gets a good look at Mr. B and does "place" him, of course, but does he *know* who it is?

To be recognized knowledgeably on the basis of one's normal look in the circumstances surely it cannot be just an accident or a coincidence that one presents that look. It is presumed that there is some stable condition (bone structure, for example) that remains nonaccidentally and is responsible for the look. That the stable condition need not be just plain bone structure is shown by such examples as that of the heavy makeup and that of the clown. In these cases the stable condition is rather a well-entrenched intention to look a certain way. It is such an intention that repeatedly leads to the characteristic look which permits recognition. If the clown is tied down and if a certain look is picked at random out of millions and he is given that look, and if his fans are then invited in, they do of course "spot" him right away if the chosen look is by amazing coincidence his characteristic look, but surely they do not know that it is he. They fall short of knowledge because their reasoning is flawed by a falsehood. They presume that there is some stable condition which has in the past consistently led to the clown's characteristic look and thus remains nonaccidentally – being so consistently present, it is not credible that it should remain just by accident – and again leads to that look. (And this is further presumed to explain the presence of the look now.) But this is a false presumption, for the stable condition that has repeatedly led to the look involves such well-entrenched intentions of the clown's as that of making a living, and so on, and more immediately the simple intention to have the characteristic appearance, at least during working hours. And it is not this condition that presently leads to his having the look, but only the intentions of his captors, and the results of their random choice procedure.

Returning to the masked burglar, the actor Mr. B, what accounts for the watchman's failure to know that it is the actor before him, though it is indeed the actor and he does look the way he normally has looked to the watchman in the past? The watchman notes the look of the actor and plumps for the obvious explanation that here again is the actor himself. If he fails to know, as he does, what falsehood flaws his reasoning (or the presumptions that underlie his "recognition" of the actor)? According to my suggestion, he presumes that there is some stable condition which has in the past consistently led to the actor's characteristic look and thus has remained nonaccidentally – being so consistently present, it is not credible that it should have remained just by accident – and again leads to that look. (And this is presumed to explain the look now.) But this is a false presumption, for the stable condition that has repeatedly led to the look is the actor's facial bone structure, etc., and it is not that condition which presently leads to his having the characteristic look but only his fortuitous wearing of a certain mask.

If we have thus spotted a false presumption on which the watchman relies essentially for his justified thought that it is the actor Mr. B before him, we have an explanation for his failure to know. For among the ideas yielded by the account of knowledge presupposed here is the requirement that if a thought of yours is to be knowledge, then its support must not involve any falsehood as an essential component (e.g., as a presumption or presupposition).

Our first "presupposition" that apparently underlies much commonplace empirical knowledge has appeared:

(P1) For an entity to be recognized knowledgeably on the basis of its normal look in the circumstances it cannot be just an accident or a coincidence that it presents that look. On the contrary, it is presupposed that there is some stable condition (bone structure, for example) that remains non-accidentally and non-coincidentally and is responsible for the look.

2. The strange case of Dr. No and Mr. Oui

Our principals are S and identical twins, Dr. No and Mr. Oui. S has known Oui all his life, meets him and (apparently) recognizes him daily, and (apparently) knows him as well as he knows anyone. Unknown to S, however, Dr. No has followed an orbit closely parallel to that of his twin brother Mr. Oui, and it is only an incredible accident that S has never seen or heard of Dr. No. On a new occasion S thinks it is Oui before him, since it looks just like Oui before him. S's belief that he does sight Oui is indeed right. Unfortunately, as usual Oui's exact look-alike, No, is nearby. Although quite right, it now appears, S has no right, no right to be sure.

If S has no right in that case, however, what right have we when we recognize our twinless closest friends? Surely there need be no relevant difference between S and us on the perceptual input or on the memory or reasoning resulting in the judgment that it is the friend in question (Mr. Oui in one case, twinless Mr. Friend in the other) before one. No matter how complete and varied we make our incoming information through time about Mr. Friend, or how subtle we make the reasoning processes to which that input is subjected, or how strong we make the resulting conviction that it is Friend before us, all of this can be duplicated *mutatis mutandis* in the case of S and the inseparable twins. We could just make S's orbit adjoin Oui's orbit more frequently, to the effect of much greater and more varied relevant input; we could make S's senses more acute, S more alert, gifted with a photographic long-range memory, and so on without apparent limit, so that S's belief that he sees Mr. Oui would appear only more reasonable than our belief that we see our Mr. Friend. If S does sight Oui with no right to be sure, it now appears that we have no greater right when we sight even our best friends.

Here again we must try to explain a distinction where there appears to be no difference. Why urge our claim to knowledgeably identify our closest friend, Mr. Friend, while rejecting S's claim to knowledgeably identify Mr. Oui? Once again, I believe, the distinction is derivable from the fact that in one case the supporting grounds are flawed by a falsehood whereas in the other they are not. In both cases, I suggest, the grounds (explicit or implicit) supporting the judgment that it is person P before one includes assumptions like the following: (a) that there are relatively very few look-alikes (few twins, triplets, accidental look-alikes, and so on); (b) that people generally have insufficient reason to go through what (with present technology) it would take to change their appearance so as to look like someone else; (c) that person P, in particular, has no natural or artificial look-alike, or if he does it would not be around here now, given his usual orbit (or given some other equally plausible grounds).

Where we recognize Mr. Friend by sight, these assumptions are all applicable, since by hypothesis Mr. Friend has no look-alike. Where S is said to recognize Mr. Oui by sight, however, assumption (c) seems inapplicable. Given Dr. No's presence nearby and given the circumstances, it is only by chance that S sights Oui rather than No. But some such assumption as (c) seems essential for S's warrant to believe that if it looks like Oui before him, in the circumstances it is because Oui is before him. I say "some such" assumption because although normally we do not exclude look-alikes from any more precisely defined volume than "around here now" or "the present general vicinity" – nevertheless, in special circumstances we do work with more precisely given volumes such as: *right in front of us and in the room*, or the like. For instance, where what is right in front of us and in the room is a police line-up, and we know that look-alikes of the suspect have been ruled out by fingerprints, there we may know by sight that the suspect himself is before us, despite the fact that his double is in the next room. The fact remains, nevertheless, that in general we are not privy to any such special information, and must rely on vaguer assumptions such as (c), whose falsehood would invalidate our claim to recognize or identify person P, as it invalidates S's claim to identify Oui.

My conclusion: although S's judgment that he sees Oui is both reasonable and correct, and although S does have as much right to it as we do to believe that it is Mr. Friend before us, inasmuch as there is exactly parallel input, processing, and output – nevertheless, we do recognize Mr. Friend and know by sight that it is he before us, whereas S does not know by sight (or otherwise) that it is Oui before him. The important difference is that our supporting grounds are *not* flawed by a falsehood, whereas S's grounds *are* flawed by some such falsehood as (c') that either Oui has no natural or artificial look-alike, or, if he does, it would not be around here now, given its usual orbit (or given some equally plausible grounds). For it is only in virtue of some such justified presumption that S could justifiably presume further that if his object of sight looks like Oui, in the circumstances, that's because it *is* Oui. This further presumption is essential for the identification of Oui by S, and an analogous presumption would seem essential in general for one's identification by sight of any spatio-temporal enduring individual. Thus we have our second general assumption that underlies some of our commonplace empirical knowledge:

(P2) For an entity to be recognized knowledgeably on the basis of its normal look in the circumstances, it must normally be presupposed to be no mere accident or coincidence that if in the circumstances the object of sight has a certain characteristic look then it is the entity in question.

Our first two general presuppositions of (much) empirical knowledge can be derived from a more general principle of knowledgeable recognition:

(R) For an entity to be recognized knowledgeably on the basis of its normal appearance in the circumstances, it must normally be presupposed that if in the circumstances something presents that appearance, it does so because it is the entity in question presenting its normal appearance in normal circumstances (i.e., in circumstances relevantly similar to those in which it has in our experience presented that appearance).

Analogous examples and arguments support a principle of knowledgeable classification analogous to the principle of knowledgeable recognition:

(C) For an entity to be classified knowledgeably as a K on the basis of its look in the circumstances, it must normally be presupposed that if in the circumstances anything presents that look, it does so because it is a K presenting its normal look in normal circumstances (i.e., in circumstances relevantly similar to those in which Ks have in our experience presented that appearance).

B. INDUCTIVE PREDICTION AND RETRODICTION

3. The strange case of the nail and the magnets

Someone, S, is about to release a nail and predicts its fall. Unknown to him, however, there are powerful magnets overhead and underfoot such that the nail will fall as usual but under the influence of the magnets, next to which gravity is negligible. Surely S's prediction that the nail will fall does not amount to knowledge, but why not? What goes wrong?

These questions can be answered by reference to a certain form of enumerative induction (EI). When we encounter a remarkable correlation between A and B, we are often entitled to conclude that the correlation can't have been just a big accident, that there must have been some connection. If B has thus followed A with remarkable consistency, we may conclude that there must have been some connection, that "something must have attached B to A." If on a new occasion we find that to our best observation there is no significant difference in the circumstances and that A is present, we presume that the circumstances are propitious for the inference from A to B, that is to say, that there is something present that has in the many past cases attached B to A. Thus an EI schema would appear thus:

(1) B has accompanied A with remarkable consistency.
(2) The consistency is so remarkable that it can't have been just an accident or a mere coincidence.
(3) Some persistent circumstance must have attached B to A.
(4) Here again is A and there is no apparent difference between the

present circumstance and the past circumstances in which B has been observed consistently to accompany A.

(5) So, here again that persistent circumstance is present.

We may rephrase (5) by saying that "the circumstances are propitious for the inference from A to B."

Our EI schema makes use of something that requires explanation – the notion of a circumstance C "attaching" a state of affairs B to a state of affairs A. This obtains if and only if, relative to C, A would not hold if B did not hold. Thus, in first approximation,

> C is a circumstance that attaches B to A on occasion O if and only if (i) A, B, and C all hold on occasion O, and (ii) A and C would not both hold if B did not hold.

Returning to S's prediction that the nail will fall, perhaps we can now see why his justified true belief does not amount to knowledge. If in the EI schema, (1)–(5) above, we let A = Release and B = Fall, we have a good summary of the framework that supports S's prediction that the nail will fall. But his bit of EI seems flawed by a falsehood. For it is *not* the persistent circumstance K1 (involving gravity and so on), which has regularly attached a fall to a release, that does so again in the new situation. In the new situation it is rather a complicated circumstance K2 (involving the magnets) that does so.

We have thus arrived at a further general assumption underlying much of our knowledge:

> (P3) Knowledge based on causal indicators (smoke-fire, barometer-rain, speedometer-speed, pencil release-pencil fall, etc.) requires a reasonable presupposition that propitious circumstances prevail.

The notion of propitious circumstances having helped us to solve the case of the nail and the magnets, let us now test it against a harder case.

4. The strange case of the buoyant coconuts

A tribe has found through long experience that the variety of coconut found on their island floats on their streams and rivers. One evening two unrelated changes take place. First, lead is injected into all of their coconuts, which raises their average specific gravity (or weight/volume quotient) to such an extent that were the density of the island water to remain constant the coconuts would sink rapidly in it. But the second change is of course a temporary and compensating rise in the density of water, which takes place as a result of a unique complex of circumstances (including perhaps torrential rains and mud slides high up in the mountains and undetected by the islanders). Having noticed, observed, or sensed nothing different in their environment, the islanders naturally continue to believe that their coconuts float. It seems clear, however, that with the environmental changes they lose the knowledge that their coconuts float, if only temporarily. And yet there *is* a circumstance C that was present in all the earlier cases where the buoyancy of coconuts was established and such that in that circumstance nothing could be a coconut in water without floating. The circumstance C is simply that their coconuts have a lower specific gravity than their water, a circumstance that remains unaltered through the changes in specific gravity and density. If the islanders knew that such a circumstance held constant then of course their knowledge of the buoyancy of coconuts in water would be unaffected by the changes. But by hypothesis the islanders do not know that any such circumstance holds constant (through the changes).

Nevertheless, are not the islanders entitled to use a bit of EI as follows?

(1) Floating has followed plunging with remarkable consistency.
(2) The consistency is so remarkable that it can't have been just a big accident or a mere coincidence.
(3) Some persistent circumstance must have attached the floating to the plunging.
(4) Here again is a plunging and there is no discernible difference between the present circumstances and the past circumstances in which floating has been observed consistently to follow plunging.
(5) So here again that persistent circumstance is present, and the circumstances are propitious for the plunging/floating inference.

My answer is that I see no way to deny the islanders about as much right to such a framework as many of us have to the similar frameworks that support for us our ordinary predictions and retrodictions. In the case where despite such right S did not know that the nail would fall – because of the magnets – an explanation of why S's justified true prediction did not amount to knowledge had some plausibility. The explanation was that statement (5) in his bit of EI was essential but false. Is there a similar explanation for why the islanders' justified true prediction that a certain coconut will float does not amount to knowledge? Is their statement (5) essential but false? Unfortunately the answer seems to be that it is not false but true. For there is indeed a persistent condition that has in the past attached floatings to plungings and that is again present on the new occasion, namely the circumstance that the island coconuts always have a lower specific gravity than the water.

I draw two tentative conclusions: (i) that our EI schema does not go deep enough, and that there are elements of commonplace enumerative induction that it leaves out; and (ii) that once we have filled in the missing elements we should be able to spot the falsehood that stops the islanders' justified true prediction short of knowledge.

On reflection it seems plausible that our earlier EI schema should be supplemented as follows:

(1) B has accompanied A with remarkable consistency.
(2) The consistency is so remarkable that it can't have been just an accident or a mere coincidence.
(3) Some persistent circumstance C must have attached B to A.
(4) C's persistence is so remarkable that it can't have been just an accident or a coincidence.
(5) Here again is A and there is no apparent (non-trivial) difference between the present circumstances and the past circumstances in which B has been observed to accompany A (where a discerned purely temporal difference would be a trivial difference).
(6) Given (4), C can now be assumed to remain – it would not be a mere accident or coincidence – unless there are apparent (non-trivial) differences.
(7) Hence, the circumstances are propitious for the inference from A to B.

The islanders do have a right to this fuller EI schema, of course, about as much right as many of us do if we use it to support a prediction of a pencil's fall on the basis of its release. But it now appears that a falsehood flaws the islanders' supporting framework. In particular, their version of (6) is false. The islanders turn out to be wrong in their presumption that their coconuts and water remain stable by nature, since there are significant changes in specific gravity and density whose coincidence is a mere accident or coincidence. Their temporary failure to know that coconuts float (at the time of the changes) is hence due to this falsehood that infects their grounding.

Our fourth strange case therefore suggests a fuller likely presupposition of empirical knowledge, one that subsumes the earlier (P3) but goes beyond it. I mean the following principle (P) of prediction, retrodiction, and other knowledgeable claims based on causal indicators.

(P) Commonplace empirical knowledge based on causal indicators rests on a presupposition that circumstances are "propitious" for an inference from the (supposed) "indicator" A to what it indicates, B, i.e., on a presupposition that the non-accidental persistence of a circumstance C accounts for the remarkable A-B

59

correlation in our experience, and that here again C can be assumed to remain (non-accidentally) and attaches (will attach) B to A unless there are apparent non-trivial differences. (This summarizes our fuller EI schema.)

Consider finally a fifth and last strange case:

5. The strange case of the smoke bombs

An observer sees a fire being built and predicts smoke, which is indeed forthcoming, but only via a smoke bomb to be placed on the fire, since the fire itself is smokeless, as are all fires in that general area. Does the observer, Mr. O, know about the forthcoming smoke? That depends, it seems to me, on further, so far unspecified circumstances. If there is a taboo of long standing on fires devoid of smoke bombs, so that Mr. O's fire/smoke regularity has been mediated by smoke bombs all along, then it seems clear that in the new case he does know of the coming smoke on the strength of the present fire. But what if it is only a fantastic accident that in Mr. O's experience fires have always been accompanied by smoke bombs, and that if Mr. O had seen a fire at a different time or place, that fire might not have brought forth any smoke? Then it seems not so clear that Mr. O does know of the coming smoke thanks to the fire. His supposed knowledge seems impugned by the fact that it is inapplicable outside the spatio-temporal volume checked.

And yet surely the desert nomad's common sense is not impugned by the fact that it is inapplicable in the mountains. The nomad's knowledge that it takes no less than so long to make water boil (in the desert) is not impugned by the fact that unknown to him it takes less, with lower atmospheric pressure, in the mountains. Shall we say, similarly, that Mr. O's knowledge that where there's fire there's smoke is not impugned by the fact that outside the discontinuous spatio-temporal volume checked, conditions are importantly different, so that either fire or smoke might be there without the other? Surely not: but why not? The important condition C inside the spatio-temporal volume checked is the relevant presence of a smoke bomb in every fire. Outside the spatio-temporal volume checked there seems to be no standing condition that assures a smoke bomb for every fire. But actually this is an illusion, since we can rule by hypothesis (H) that it is equally true inside and outside the volume checked that for every fire there is a related smoke bomb, though this is true only contingently. Shall we say that what impugns Mr. O's supposed knowledge is the fact that H is true only contingently? But the atmospheric pressure required for the truth of the desert nomad's belief about boiling water seems to be just as contingent a part of his environment.

To be sure, given the accidental or coincidental character of the smoke-bomb/fire correlation, our feeling is that in such circumstances a fire is not a reliable sign of coming smoke, and thus gives no knowledge of it. And yet given that for every fire there is a related smoke bomb, a fire is not only a reliable sign of the coming smoke, but in conjunction with that circumstance necessitates the smoke by law of nature. In what respect then is Mr. O in an inferior position to the nomad? After all, the nomad's prediction that some water will boil in no less than so long, on the basis of its being tepid water in a container just placed on a fire, is equally dependent on contingent circumstances, such as the atmospheric pressure.

The difference seems to be that whereas the nomad can presume that there are stable conditions C that remain constant for the purpose of the new prediction, our observer, Mr. O, lacks any similar assurance in his situation. The nomad can rely on the natural stability of the makeup, powers, properties, and relations of substances in his environment and from this flows the stable atmospheric pressure that unknown to him underlies the reliability of his predictions concerning the boiling of water. By contrast, the natural stability of the environment does not yield the smoke-bomb/fire correlation; nor is there any similar grounding for this correlation, which is by hypothesis entirely accidental or coincidental.

Perhaps we can now see how the nomad may ground his wisdom on our preceding seven-fold form of enumerative induction (EI) roughly as follows: water has always taken approximately so long to boil; that can't have been just a big accident or coincidence; so, there must have been circumstances *whose continued presence was no mere accident or coincidence*, such that given those circumstances water must always boil in approximately that length of time; and to all appearances the circumstances now are the same in all relevant respects, so it is no mere accident or coincidence that the continued presence of the effective circumstances does extend to the present, inasmuch as it can be assumed stable by nature unless there are noticeable (non-trivial) differences.

Can the observer, Mr. O, reason similarly that smoke has always accompanied fire, that this can't have been just a big accident or coincidence, that hence there must have been conditions whose continued presence was no mere accident or coincidence, such that given those conditions smoke must always accompany fire; and so on? The answer is, I suggest, that while he *can* properly reason thus, his reasoning is flawed by a falsehood, for the continued presence of conditions sustaining the fire/smoke regularity *is* a mere accident or coincidence. It is only because smoke bombs continue fortuitously to accompany the smokeless fires of the region that the fire/smoke regularity survives. I conclude that although Mr. O does fall short of knowledge (despite his justified true belief) when on a new occasion he predicts the coming smoke on the strength of the observed fire, he also fails to meet the conditions of our account. For the grounding of his prediction is flawed by a falsehood.

C. CONCLUSION

In this chapter I have tried to dispose of several anomalies for an account of knowledge explained and defended in earlier chapters. The relevant ideas drawn from that account are: (a) that you know only when you believe correctly what is evident to you; (b) that for something to be evident to you, you must believe it reasonably, your belief must be reasonable; and (c) that the framework of beliefs, assumptions, experiences, or whatnot, if any, that supports your reasonable belief must not be flawed by a falsehood, i.e., must not involve as an essential component any false assumption, presumption, claim, judgment, belief, or the like.

Accounting for the anomalies in terms of these ideas has helped to highlight some "presuppositions of empirical knowledge":

(R) A principle of knowledgeable recognition: For an entity to be recognized knowledgeably on the basis of its normal appearance in the circumstances, it must normally be presupposed that if in the circumstances something presents that appearance, it does so because it is the entity in question presenting its normal appearance in normal circumstances (i.e., in circumstances relevantly similar to those in which it has in our experience presented that appearance).

(C) A principle of knowledgeable classification: For an entity to be classified knowledgeably as a K on the basis of its appearance in the circumstances, it must normally be presupposed that if in the circumstances anything presents that appearance, it does so because it is a K presenting its normal look in normal circumstances (i.e., in circumstances relevantly similar to those in which Ks have in our experience presented that appearance).

(P) A principle of prediction, retrodiction, and other knowledgeable claims based on causal indicators: Commonplace empirical knowledge based on causal indicators rests on a presupposition that circumstances are "propitious" for an inference from the (supposed) "indicator" A to what it indicates B, i.e., on a presupposition that the non-accidental persistence of a circumstance C accounts for the remarkable A-B correlation in our experience, and that here again C remains non-accidentally and attaches (will attach) B to A unless there are apparent non-trivial differences.

PART II
Theories of justification

5

Epistemology today:
a perspective in retrospect

I. PHENOMENALISM

According to the main tradition, knowledge is either direct or indirect: direct when it intuits some perfectly obvious fact of introspection or a priori necessity; indirect when based on deductive proof stemming ultimately from intuited premises. Simple and compelling though it is, this Cartesian conception of knowledge must be surmounted to avoid skepticism. Seeing that the straight and narrow of deductive proof leads nowhere, C. I. Lewis wisely opts for a highroad of probabilistic inference. But how can one arrive at a realm inaccessible through direct knowledge having set out from one thus accessible? How could probabilistic inference offer any help? There are two different answers to these questions in Lewis's writings, and he moves from one to the other under pressure of well-known objections from perceptual relativity. Our action divides into three acts, which we now review in turn.

Act One: According to Lewis a statement about one's surroundings, such as P (that there is a sheet of paper before one), has analytic implications for one's experience, these being statements estimating the probability of outcomes for one's experience yielded by various action-cum-experience combinations. Thus our statement P is said by Lewis to have as one of its analytic consequences that if $s1$ (a visual sheet of paper presentation is given to one) and $a1$ (one seems to oneself to move one's eyes), then in all probability $e1$ (a seen displacement of the presentation follows for one).[1] It is by verifying a great number of such analytic consequences for experience in the form of probability estimates that one comes to know one's physical surroundings.[2]

Act Two: An objection to Lewis brought by R. M. Chisholm is essentially similar to the following: (a) If P & Q does not analytically

---

1 Here and in what follows lower-case p, q, r, etc., will stand for declarative sentences, and the corresponding capital letters will represent the corresponding nominalizations: thus P will represent the nominalization of the sentence represented by p, i.e., that p, etc. Occasionally capital P, Q, R, etc., will be used as statement variables, however, but the context should always remove any ambiguity.
2 Cf. C. I. Lewis, *An Analysis of Knowledge and Valuation* (La Salle, Ill.: Open Court, 1946), Book II, Chapter VIII.

imply a given statement then P alone cannot possibly do so, and this holds good quite generally and irrespective of the character of the given statement: in particular it holds independently of whether or not the given statement is a statement of probability. (b) According to Lewis, P above analytically implies that if ($s1$ & $a1$) then in all probability $e1$. But the conjunction of P and the following statement will analytically imply no such thing: (q) I am unable to move my eyes but am subject to delusions such that I think I'm moving them: I often seem to myself to be moving them, but, when I do, no seen displacement of any presentation ever follows for me. Since P & Q does not analytically imply that if ($s1$ & $a1$) then in all probability $e1$, it follows that P cannot possibly do so. What is more, the relativity of perception to nonexperiential circumstances makes it clear that there will always be such defeaters as Q of any supposed analytical implications for experience of the likes of P. But then, in the absence of such analytical implications, we are back where we started. How can we begin with knowledge of our experience and end up with knowledge of our surroundings if there are no analytical implications linking pure exemplars from one realm with those from the other?[3]

Act Three: In response Lewis abandons analytical implications in favor of a doctrine whose embryo may well have been lodged already between the lines of his earlier theory. According to this new doctrine we should look to probability where earlier we set our hopes on analytical implication. It is true that P does not analytically imply that if ($s1$ & $a1$) then in all probability $e1$. But it may still be true that if p then in all probability if ($s1$ & $a1$) then $e1$. Put another way, the new doctrine affirms that (($S1$ & $A1$) $\to$ $E1$) is highly probable relative to P.[4] It is true, of course, that (($S1$ & $A1$) $\to$ $E1$) is *not* probable relative to P & Q. But this is now harmless, since something can be probable relative to P without being probable relative to P & Q. Accordingly, Lewis rests content with the view that one's perceptual knowledge lies on a basis of probability statements relating one's experience and one's physical surroundings. For appropriate objective P and experiential E, such statements might affirm that E is very probable relative to P, or that not-E is very probable relative to not-P. Such statements might link a great number of experiential outcomes $E1, \ldots, En$ with a given P. By verifying such experiential outcomes, one could then raise the credibility of an objective P.[5]

Critical notes: How do we obtain the statements that according to

---

3 Cf. R. M. Chisholm, "The Problem of Empiricism," *Journal of Philosophy* 45 (1948): 512–17.
4 The symbol "$\to$" here helps to represent merely material conditionals.
5 Cf. C. I. Lewis, "Professor Chisholm and Empiricism," *Journal of Philosophy* 45 (1948): 517–24.

Lewis link our experience with our surroundings enabling us to cross that gap in knowledge? As Lewis well knows, if we are to make the inference from experience to surroundings that he would have us make, we must somehow have access to the required premises, and among these premises are clearly to be found the statements that link our experience with our surroundings. How then do we acquire the linking knowledge thus required? In Act One Lewis could and did answer that such knowledge is a priori, as befits knowledge of analytic implications. In Act Three this answer remains, in default of any other, buttressed by the claim that the relevant probability statements linking experience and surroundings are true in virtue simply of their meaning. But it now reduces briskly to absurdity. For the relevant correlations between experience and surroundings are surely contingent matters dependent in each case on a great number of other contingencies, including the presence or absence of a Cartesian demon, who would as soon and about as easily make our experience *mostly* illusory as only *sometimes* illusory.[6]

If the premises linking our experience with our surroundings are not necessary a priori truths, then how could we possibly come to know them without falling into a vicious circle or an infinite regress? Two ways out of this dilemma have been explored in recent years.

Foundationalists have held that the nature of the experience-surroundings link that is preeminently relevant has been misconceived by those who argue as does Lewis. The relevant link is not a statement, probabilistic or not, that can serve as a premise for an inference, probabilistic or deductive, leading to knowledge of our surroundings. The relevant link is provided instead by epistemological principles declaring perceptual beliefs prima facie justified if held in the right experiential circumstances, as perhaps when one believes oneself to be in the presence of something white when prompted by the relevant visual experience caused by a snowball seen in good light. Our foundationalists hence deny that knowledge must be intuitively obvious and direct or else inferential and indirect.[7] For the foundationalist of today perceptual knowledge is

---

6 Roderick Firth, in "Radical Empiricism and Perceptual Relativity," *Philosophical Review* 59 (1950): 164–83, 319–31, and Richard Fumerton, in his "Defence of Phenomenalism" (unpublished), show how surprisingly defensible phenomenalism can be made, even to an unbeliever. Nevertheless, even if phenomenalism were in fact true metaphysics, I fear this would help little or not at all to cross our gap in epistemology. Section (II)(E) considers some recent versions of verificationism.

7 Recent years have seen the development of a rich diversity of foundationalisms, so that here I can cite only some of the important contributions: R. M. Chisholm, "Theory of Knowledge," in R. M. Chisholm et al., eds., *Philosophy* (Englewood Cliffs, N.J.: Prentice-Hall, 1964), pp. 243–344; R. Firth, "Coherence, Certainty, and Epistemic Priority," *Journal of Philosophy* 61 (1964): 545–57; R. M. Chisholm, *Theory of Knowledge* (Englewood Cliffs, N.J.: Prentice-Hall, 1966); A. Quinton, "The Foundations of

not intuitively obvious knowledge, but neither is it inferential knowledge, either deductive or probabilistic. He therefore abandons the rigorously sparse main tradition in favor of a richer epistemology with other sources of epistemic justification beside intuitive obviousness and deductive proof. Among these other sources might be found, for instance, the source of justification for a perceptual judgment provided by the fact that it is prompted by the right sensory experience or the like. It is then a task for epistemology to make us conscious of the full complement of such principles, or at least to approach that objective as an ideal. Thus far the foundationalist way out. What is the alternative?

According to coherentism, the misconception of the tradition is located not in its view of the experience-surroundings links – which are indeed correlational statements, universal or probabilistic, nomological or accidental, but in any case statements of a statistical correlation between the character of one's experience and the nature of one's surroundings. Rather is the misconception of the tradition located in the use it would have us make of such statements as premises for inferences leading to indirect knowledge of our surroundings. For the coherentist we do not arrive at our knowledge of the world through a linear chain of inferences from premises to conclusions. What would possibly serve as the ultimate premises of such a chain leading by deductive or probabilistic inference to all other links? Justification is not transmitted thus discretely and linearly, but dawns rather on a whole body of beliefs along with sufficiently comprehensive coherence, coherence that is logical, probabilistic, and explanatory.[8]

Knowledge," in B. Williams and A. Montefiore, eds., *British Analytical Philosophy* (London: Routledge & Kegan Paul, 1966), pp. 55–86; A. Quinton, *The Nature of Things* (London: Routledge & Kegan Paul, 1973). The most fully developed version of foundationalism is that worked out by J. Pollock in his book *Knowledge and Justification* (Princeton University Press, 1974). For defenses of foundationalism, including discussion of specific objections, see also: M. Pastin, "Modest Foundationalism and Self-warrant," *American Philosophical Quarterly*, monograph series no. 9 (1975); W. P. Alston, "Has Foundationalism Been Refuted?" *Philosophical Studies* 29 (1976): 287–305, and "Two Types of Foundationalism," *Journal of Philosophy* 73 (1976): 165–85; R. Audi, "Psychological Foundationalism," *The Monist* 61 (1978): 592–610; and J. Van Cleve, "Foundationalism, Epistemic Principles, and the Cartesian Circle," *Philosophical Review* 88 (1979): 55–91.
8 Cf. W. V. O. Quine, "Two Dogmas of Empiricism," in his collection *From a Logical Point of View* (Cambridge, Mass.: Harvard University Press, 1953); W. S. Sellars, "Empiricism and the Philosophy of Mind," in H. Feigl and G. Maxwell, eds., *Minnesota Volumes in the Philosophy of Science*, Vol. 1 (Minneapolis: University of Minnesota Press, 1956), and "Givenness and Explanatory Coherence," *Journal of Philosophy* 70 (1973): 612–24; B. Aune, *Knowledge, Mind, and Nature* (New York: Random House, 1967); N. Rescher, *The Coherence Theory of Truth* (Oxford University Press, 1973); G. Harman, *Thought* (Princeton University Press, 1973); K. Lehrer, *Knowledge* (Oxford University Press, 1974); and L. Bonjour, "The Coherence Theory of Empirical Knowledge," *Philosophical Studies* 30 (1976): 281–312.

According to Lewis, in our epistemology of perception we have no choice but either the nebulous coherentism of a Bosanquet or his own foundationalism of obvious ultimate premises and linear chains of inference. In thus restricting our choice he ironically overlooks or rejects the further alternative actually adopted by most of his foundationalist successors. This is made doubly ironical because it is this third alternative that Lewis himself adopts in his epistemology of memory.

We now turn our attention away from Lewis towards the alternative that he so mysteriously neglects, that of contemporary foundationalism. Let us consider such foundationalism not primarily against the familiar background of ordinary perceptual judgments of shape or color, but rather against the less familiar background of our perceptual judgments of reidentification.

II. REIDENTIFICATION

A. *The problem set*

"The third one from the left is the culprit," says the witness facing the lineup. How does he know? Generalized, this turns into the epistemological problem of reidentification. We can think of it as the problem of how we know that a single thing has two properties of certain sorts, one a retrospective individuator and the other a contemporaneous individuator. These may be explained as follows:

(D1) A property is an *individuator* iff it can possibly be exemplified, but it cannot possibly be exemplified by more than one thing at a time.

(D2) A property is *retrospective (prospective)* iff its exemplification at any given time t involves particular or general reference to the past (future) with respect to that time t.

(D3) A property is *contemporaneous* iff it is neither retrospective nor prospective.

Having had breakfast, being an alumnus, and being a culprit are retrospective properties; being awake, being tall, and being at home are contemporaneous properties; and being about to wake up, being a future President, and being destined to die are prospective properties.

Being the third one from the left in a certain police lineup is thus a contemporaneous individuator, and being the culprit (the one who robbed the bank) is a retrospective individuator. The most familiar cases of problematic reidentification are cases where the problem is whether or not a retrospective individuator and a contemporaneous individuator are coinstantiated or coexemplified. Our police lineup example is a case in point.

Note, however, that such cases constitute nothing more than a special subdivision of the more general problem of how we know that two individuators, of whatever temporal sorts, are coinstantiated or coexemplified. And this, in turn, is only a special subdivision of a still more general problem, that of how we know that two properties, whether individuators or not, are coexemplified.

Naturally, if one knows oneself to have a given property F and knows oneself to have a further property G, then by putting these two bits of knowledge together one can easily arrive at knowledge that F and G are coexemplified. This is knowledge of coexemplification through knowledge of co-self-exemplification. The more difficult cases are those which do not involve self-attribution. Suppose I know that something has property F without knowing whether or not I have F, and suppose I know further that something has property G without knowing whether or not I have G. What would it take to put me in a position to know still further that the two properties are not only exemplified but are exemplified by one and the same thing? The following discussion is restricted to knowledge of physical bodies, so that our main question may be formulated thus: How do we ever know with respect to properties F and G of physical bodies, not only that each is exemplified but also that the two are coexemplified?

B. *Illative vs collative coinstantiative knowledge*[9]

Our question has an easy answer in certain special cases. Thus if a given property F with rich content is known to be exemplified, this can easily yield much knowledge of coexemplification. Take, for example, the property of being cubical. Knowledge that this property is exemplified yields knowledge that the following properties are all combined in some one thing: being six-sided, being eight-cornered, being twelve-edged, and many more. Such coinstantiative knowledge may be labelled "deductively illative" (relative to given prior knowledge) since it derives from simple deductive inference drawn from the knowledge (that a given property is instantiated). Coinstantiative knowledge may also be "inductively illative" (relative to some given knowledge) as when a glance at a ball midway down an inclined plane yields not only the knowledge of where it is but also the knowledge of where it was just prior to this and knowledge of where it will soon be. With respect to the properties of

---

9 According to my dictionary, the primary meaning of "collate" is "to compare critically".

having been at the top, being midway down, and being destined for the bottom, we thus determine not only that each is exemplified but also that the three are coexemplified by a single thing. We do not arrive at such coinstantiative knowledge simply by unaided deduction from the given knowledge, however, since we must implicitly depend on further assumptions about regularities, and about initial and boundary conditions.

How do we collate a bit of memory-retrospective knowledge and a bit of perceptual-contemporaneous knowledge to obtain some recognitional-coinstantiative knowledge? Through memory we know that a given retrospective individuator $I1$ is exemplified and through perception we know that a given contemporaneous individuator $I2$ is exemplified.[10] What enables us to put them together for the conclusion that a single thing exemplifies both $I1$ and $I2$? One simple and familiar answer is: "*Resemblance (of content).*" And what could be more plausible than the notion that perceptual recognition takes place through noticed resemblance?[11]

C. Problems for resemblance

It seems to some a necessary truth known a priori that a snowball must be composed of a quantity of snow diverse from it (diverse since there are changes in the quantity of snow that destroy the snowball). Yet the snowball is as similar in all perceptual respects to the quantity of snow (at any time when they both exist) as it is possible for any physical body to be with respect to anything (including itself). The snowball and the quantity of snow hence resemble each other maximally at any time when they both exist, and also across many times that they both survive. The resemblance criterion thus leads us to the apparent absurdity that the snowball and the lump of snow are one, or to the equally absurd conclusion that one can become the other. What has gone wrong?

It seems inevitable, in any case, that a set of justified beliefs can possibly lead to absurdity.[12] Even so logically straightforward a matter as believing the conjunction of some severally justified premises, on the basis of the premises collectively, yields at best the prima facie justifica-

10 Actually the yet more general case is one where one knows with respect to one of two individuators that it *was* exemplified either at some time or other or at some more specific time in the past, and with respect to the other that it is now exemplified, and somehow by collating those two bits of knowledge one comes to know that a single thing did exemplify the one and does exemplify the other. Generalizing thus would require the introduction of a battery of tensed modes of exemplification, however, which would complicate our discussion without a compensating gain.
11 Cf. Pollock, *op. cit.*, Chapter Six, for a thorough defense of this view.
12 For an illuminating treatment of this, see Richard Foley's "Justified Inconsistent Beliefs," *American Philosophical Quarterly* 16 (1979): 247–59.

tion of that conjunctive conclusion. For the conjunctive conclusion may display an absurdity so patent as to override easily the prima facie justification issuing from its logical sources. Thus, many of us are humble enough to grant that at least one of our beliefs is false. Someone with a powerful enough intellect could consider the conjunction of all his beliefs. Could he not combine enough humility and self-knowledge to deny that conjunction quite reasonably? Consider then his new set of beliefs including that denial. Conjoining its severally justified members would yield a conclusion whose intrinsic absurdity might override the prima facie justification deriving from its premises. An extension of this argument makes it reasonable to suppose that even basic sources of justification could not be exempt from leading to outright absurdities by valid forms of inference. Perhaps the simplest way for the foundationalist to deal with such cases is to say that the prima facie justification that would be lent to such a conclusion for someone misguided enough to draw it could always be overridden by its intrinsic absurdity. And this reinstates resemblance of content as a possible basic source of prima facie justification, even despite the perfect similarity between a snowball and the quite distinct lump of snow that constitutes it, and despite the fact that a piece of gold might emerge through indiscriminable neighboring stages from a mere lump of mud. This demotion of deduction from *absolute* to *prima facie* (and defeasible) justifier may thus serve to solve such epistemic paradoxes as that of the preface and that of the lottery.

D. Limits of resemblance

Not all collative judgments of identification or coinstantiation can be grounded in such resemblance, nor even all such *perceptual* judgments, as shown by those that span sensory modalities. Take the judgment that what now feels cold and round to my touch is identically the same as what now looks white and round to my eyes. Surely we are often in possession of such knowledge. How do we get it? What justifies us in believing even so much as simply that we touch what we see? Resemblance seems clearly of little use here, since the arrays of properties corresponding to our several sensory modalities have at best only minimal similarity of content. A more promising answer would develop the notions of visual and tactual-kinesthetic spatial fields, and would point to the pervasive correlations between the two isomorphic fields, so that when something looks round at a place in visual space, something would feel round at the tactual-kinesthetic image of that place, and so on. This might then be offered as a basic source of prima facie justification for identifying what looks round there with what feels round there. For convenience let us refer to this as the "correlation-cum-isomorphism" justification for such coinstantiative judgments.

Unfortunately, that does not explain how we know that what looks white is the same as what looks round (and the same as, let's say, what looks to be some distance away from something black). But here we might perhaps supplement our basic sources of justification for coinstantiative judgments by appeal to a notion of visual properties being "co-located" in visual space. For it could then be said that if looking round to one and looking white to one are co-located in one's visual space, that prima facie justifies a judgment that the two properties are not only co-located but also coinstantiated.

E. On foundationalist strategy

The strategy of some contemporary foundationalism now seems clear: multiply epistemic principles in order to provide for the sources of justification required for our rich knowledge in its various dimensions. But the danger in a free use of such a strategy also seems clear, for a wide scattering of diverse principles does not make for a satisfactory epistemology.

There have been attempts to provide a unity of sorts for a scattered epistemology by appeal to a notion of meaning.[13] Thus we are told that the various epistemic principles are all true by virtue of their very meaning. That there is something white before one could not possibly mean what it does without visual experience of white serving as a source of prima facie justification for believing it. It is by virtue of its very meaning that the following principle, or the like, is true: that believing oneself to be in the presence of something white would be prima facie justified through being prompted by a visual experience of white in good light, etc. This is a somewhat unusual notion of meaning, however, for insofar as a principle or proposition may be said to be true simply by virtue of its meaning this must amount to saying that it is true by virtue simply of its content or its identity. And since a proposition's content or identity or in any case its meaning is surely essential to it, the claim that a proposition or principle is true simply in virtue of its meaning reduces to the claim that it is necessarily true. Two things are worth noting in this connection: first, that at least for those who accept the notion of necessity at all it has not been a matter of controversy that basic epistemic principles would be necessary truths; second, that it does not seem anyhow to show deeper unity in a scattered set of diverse principles that

13 Cf. Pollock, op. cit., esp. Chapter One, and Quinton, The Nature of Things, op. cit., Part II.

they all turn out to be necessary truths. We wish our epistemology to be systematic to the extent possible, and a set of necessary truths does not necessarily constitute a system.

It is possible that we have not been quite fair. Possibly those who speak of meaning in the present connection have in mind something like the following:

> A proposition P is true in virtue simply of its meaning iff the concepts or properties constitutive of P, and P itself, cannot possibly be grasped or understood by anyone who does not accept P.

In that case propositions other than epistemic principles would be true-by-meaning: e.g., that nothing cubical is spherical. Further, the notion that epistemic principles are true-by-meaning might be rejected on the grounds that only what is obvious can be true-by-meaning. But this assumption is itself not obvious. For the acceptance-implied-by-understanding required for truth-by-meaning may be not so much the acceptance-in-occurrent-consciousness involved in obviousness as rather a kind of acceptance-shown-in-conduct, where the conduct involved may be either physical or intellectual.

This most recent idea promises an epistemology with more satisfactory unity. Consider, for instance, the epistemic principles for intellectual passage from experience to the objective external world. These would now have the status of principles that anyone must accept (in his intellectual procedure) if he is to have so much as a grasp of the concepts (geometric, temporal, chromatic, etc.) that for us define the external world.

Unfortunately, the idea seems questionable, since someone congenitally blind but with sensitive skin and someone sighted but with congenitally insensitive skin could apparently argue about the geometry of their common surroundings. If the blind man were given visual experience, moreover, he might acquire the concepts required for grasping the conditions of visual experience that lead his neighbor to a justified belief that there is something round before him. And it seems further that someone blind might acquire such concepts without yet embodying in his cognitive practice the epistemic principles linking visual experience and physical roundness that he is thus enabled to understand.

Our example, like Molyneux's, serves to suggest the following possibility. Consider first, once again, the supposed requirement that anyone with a grasp of our objective geometric and chromatic concepts must accept in his cognitive (perceptual) practice the epistemic principles that in fact guide our intellectual passage from experience to the objective world, if unintentionally and even unconsciously so. Our Molyneux-like example now suggests that this requirement is weaker than it might seem, that it applies at most only to beings with our perceptual mechanisms. There may be routes of epistemic access to objective geometric and even chromatic facts that we, because of our perceptual limitations, cannot dream of. Why could not a better endowed being to whom many such routes were open take note of ours (thus grasping them) without accepting them either consciously or in his practice?

Such a being could perhaps question whether a belief that one neighbors something round prompted in normal conditions by visual experience of roundness would thereby be prima facie justified. Could he not determine, through his other routes of access to objective properties, that in fact a visual-experience-of-roundness in the conditions that normally prevail is usually due not to something round but rather to something oval? And should that not give us pause about the necessary truth of the epistemic principle linking visual experience of roundness with neighboring physical roundness? It seems to me that the foregoing discussion does at least raise a reasonable doubt that such a specific epistemic principle would be *either* one that cannot be understood without being accepted, *or even* a necessary truth. A more subordinate status for such specific principles is also suggested by our discussion, something like that of the contingent maxim that stabbing people with pins just for enjoyment is bad or wrong, which for the utilitarian would rest if true on the principle of utility via assumptions about the effects of stabbing, and for a deontologist would rest if true on some categorical principle via the assumption that to engage in such conduct would be to treat someone merely as a means, or the like.

Systematic epistemology requires principles more basic than one linking visual experience of roundness with neighboring physical roundness. We need principles that will play a role in epistemology analogous to the role played in utilitarian ethics by a principle of utility and in formalist ethics by a categorical imperative. Perhaps true principles of that sort are simply inaccessible in epistemology (or even in ethics, for that matter), but surely it is worth our while to look for them, since our philosophy would be more satisfactory for being thus systematic.

In contrast with the foundationalism already examined, coherentism appears attractively unified and simple. But let us have a closer look.

III. COHERENTISM

The seductive simplicity of coherentism is only cosmetic. A little probing exposes its true complexity.

First of all, there appear to be independent varieties of coherence: e.g., deductive, probabilistic, and explanatory.

What is more, and no matter how variegated coherence may be, the warrant of a belief cannot derive simply from its coherence within a homogeneous and unstructured body of beliefs. Two cases will be described in support of this claim.

A. Self-abstraction

Take first a particular subject S, and his body of beliefs. Many of his beliefs will be first-person beliefs about himself. The *self-abstract* of a body of propositions believed by S is obtained by replacing the object of every such first-person belief by a propositional function with a gap for an individual concept replacing every first-person reference by S (to himself). Thus if S takes himself to be seated, then the self-abstract of the body of propositions that he believes will include *not* whatever proposition he would express by "I am seated" but rather the propositional function expressed by the open sentence "x is seated."

Such a self-abstract of the body of propositions believed by S can then be *uniformly instantiated* by filling in the individual-concept gaps in its propositional functions with a single individual concept. Thus if the self-abstract contains the propositional function x *is seated* and the propositional function x *is awake*, then a uniform instantiation of that self-abstract would contain two propositions involving one and the same individual concept C: one proposition predicating being seated with respect to C, and another predicating being awake with respect to C.

Allow me now to mention the self-abstract of the body of propositions that I now believe. And let us consider the uniform instantiation of that self-abstract obtained by filling in its individual-concept gaps with the single individual concept: *the holder of the median Social Security number for Rhode Island (or of the lower of the two middle ones, if there isn't a median one).*[14] The resulting body of propositions B has about the same degree of comprehensiveness and coherence – deductive, probabilistic,

---

14 Let us assume here that in fact I believe neither that I am nor that I am not the holder of that number. And let us assume also that I have *no* belief about the holder of that number that I do not have about myself, *except* possibly for propositions that follow necessarily from the very existence of someone holding that number: e.g., the proposition that the holder of that number *is* the holder of that number. (Alternatively, if I do have some such belief, e.g., the belief that it is improbable that I am the holder of such a number, then the *self-abstract* of my body of beliefs can be required to *drop* its propositional functions that correspond to such beliefs. This would surely make a negligible difference to overall coherence or comprehensiveness, given that my body of beliefs is not abnormally small.) On present usage, finally, an "individual concept" does not necessarily involve essential properties of whatever individual corresponds to the individual concept; others may prefer to replace my "individual concept" with "identifying concept" or "identifying description" or the like.

and explanatory – as my present body of beliefs. And yet it is clear that no one would be at all justified in holding B as his entire body of beliefs, nor would anyone be justified in holding any member of B simply in virtue of its being held as part of comprehensive and coherent B.

B. Present-abstraction

The *present-abstract* of a body of propositions believed by S is obtained by replacing the object of every present-tense belief on the part of S by a propositional function with a gap for an individual-time-concept replacing every reference to the present on the part of S. Thus if S believes that it is now raining, then the present-abstract of the body of propositions that he believes will include *not* whatever proposition he would express by "It now rains" but rather the propositional function expressed by the open sentence "It rains at t".

Such a present-abstract of the body of propositions believed by S at some time can then be *uniformly instantiated* by filling in the individual-time-concept gaps in its propositional functions with a single individual-time-concept. Thus if the present-abstract contains the propositional functions *It rains at t* and *It is dark at t*, then a uniform instantiation of that present-abstract would contain two propositions involving one and the same individual-time-concept T: one proposition predicating being a time when it rains with respect to T, and another predicating being a time when it is dark with respect to T.

Take now the present-abstract of the body of propositions that some one of us now believes. And let us consider the uniform instantiation of that present-abstract obtained by filling in its individual-time-concept gaps with the single individual-time-concept: *two thousand years from now*.[15] The resulting body of propositions has about the same degree of comprehensiveness and coherence – deductive, probabilistic, and explanatory – as the original body of beliefs. And yet it is clear that no one would be at all justified in holding B as his entire body of beliefs, nor would anyone be justified in holding any member of B simply in virtue of its being held as part of comprehensive and coherent B.

C. Conclusions about coherentism

Self-abstraction and present-abstraction show that cognitive warrant cannot derive from undifferentiated coherence. It seems clear that our ordinary bodies of belief as we know them depend essentially for their

15 Qualifications analogous to those in the preceding note are in order here.

warrant on the special character of some of their contents. First-person beliefs and present-tense beliefs have a special role. A body of beliefs lacking these altogether may be as comprehensive and coherent as could be desired without the slightest degree of cognitive warrant.

IV. EPISTEMOLOGY

We have now touched on four epistemologies: the rigorous Cartesianism of obvious intuition and deductive proof; Lewis's supplement, with probabilistic inference as a further source of indirect knowledge; unsystematic foundationalism, i.e., any form of contemporary foundationalism committed to a wide diversity of basic principles; and, finally, probabilistic, explanatory, or logical coherentism. It is worth noting that despite their many and sometimes vigorous disagreements, advocates of these four doctrines share a deeper commitment that binds them together as a community of inquirers. Knowledge for them all falls within a dimension of assessment or evaluation for which we have no better label than (cognitive) justification. Would-be knowledge always has a location within that dimension founded on its non-evaluative properties. Thus the justification of a belief may perhaps supervene on its basis in perception, memory, or inference. Just what the justification of belief is founded on or supervenes upon is exactly what the four epistemologies disagree about. But they agree that it is indeed founded on something, and take their task to be developing a theory of such foundations.[16] It is for this reason that in their view epistemology can be fully naturalized only by returning it to nature, six feet under.

In an area so long and intensively explored it is not unlikely that each of the main competing alternatives has grasped some aspect of a many-sided truth not wholly accessible through any one-sided approach. The counsel to open minds and broaden sympathies seems particularly apt with regard to basic issues so long subject to wide disagreements. Let us therefore consider the most widely divergent basic doctrines with a view to reconciling their positive insights, to the fullest extent possible.

The divide between Cartesian rationalism and Humean empiricism is subsidiary to the more profound divide discerned by the genius of Peirce: that between Descartes' deductivist foundationalism and Peirce's own abductivist coherentism. In any case, whether Peirce's own or merely

---

16 They are thus all varieties of a kind of foundationalism that we may dub "formal" to distinguish it from the more substantive foundationalism that is only one of its instances, coherentism being another. Compare in this connection "The Foundations of Foundationalism," Chapter 9 of this volume.

suggested by his writings, abductivist coherentism is worth considering; but first it demands explication.

By "abduction" we shall mean a form of epistemic support of the same general sort as hypothetical induction, the hypothetico-deductive method, inverse induction, the inference to the best explanation, and explanatory induction. But just what, in more specific terms, is this form of support?

Here, in first approximation, is an abductivist principle of epistemic support: Belief of P is prima facie justified if based on justified belief of Q and justified belief that P would explain Q.

It is worth noting, first of all, that I am here using "abduction" and its cognates more broadly than Peirce. Unlike Peirce we do not restrict abduction to a form of conscious reasoning whereby one arrives at reasonable explanatory conjectures. Our abductivist principle departs from Peirce's conception in two respects: first, it deals with belief and not with mere conjecture; and, second, it is not restricted to the conscious fixation of belief (or the conscious conjecturing of hypotheses) under the control of explicit volition. It is meant to apply to all beliefs that satisfy its conditions, whether consciously fixed or not. Our abduction is therefore not quite Peirce's abduction but rather something closer to his method of "hypothesis," which he explains as follows:

Induction is where we generalize from a number of cases of which something is true, and infer that the same thing is true of a whole class. . . . Hypothesis is where we find some very curious circumstance, which would be explained by the supposition that it was a case of a certain general rule, and thereupon adopt that supposition. . . . Hypotheses are sometimes regarded as provisional resorts, which in the progress of science are to be replaced by inductions. But this is a false view of the subject. Hypothetic reasoning infers very frequently a fact not capable of direct observation. . . . The essence of an induction is that it infers from one set of facts another set of similar facts whereas hypothesis infers from facts of one kind to facts of another.[17]

Is our abductivist principle acceptable? Not quite as it stands, it seems to me, but there is perhaps no better way to improve and deepen it than by considering objections to it found in the recent literature. There are two rather different sorts of objections that we ought to consider. First, there is the thoroughgoing objection according to which no principle of this sort could be right since it would always lead to unacceptable absurdity. And, second, there is the more restricted objection not to the principle but only to an application, and more specifically to its application in elucidating perceptual knowledge.

17 From: *The Collected Papers of Charles Sanders Peirce* (Cambridge, Mass.: Harvard University Press, 1932), Vol. 2, 2.619–24, 641–4.

The thoroughgoing objection distills to something essentially like this: That the abductivist principle cannot possibly be right, since it would lead to the possibility of a single epistemic source of prima facie support for an outright absurdity. For a single phenomenon Q may have incompatible possible explanations P and P'. Abduction and deduction in tandem would therefore lead to prima facie support for the absurdity $P \& P'$.[18]

Two ways to meet the thoroughgoing objection come to mind. The first would modify the principle so as to require that one justifiably believe not only Q and that P would explain Q but also that one can then think of no equally good explanation. This would guarantee that the abductivist principle would never lead us to a pair of incompatible beliefs both prima facie justified. But we also have a less strenuous response to the thoroughgoing objection, and that is to argue that the consequence drawn is no *reductio*. For it seemed clear in our discussion of resemblance as a prima facie justifier of reidentificatory judgments that there is no way to preclude the possibility that a single basic source S of prima facie justification may lead to prima facie justification for an outright absurdity. Our best recourse at that time seemed clearly to involve appeal to the absurd character of the absurdity as a defeater of its prima facie justification derived from source S in tandem with deduction. That being so, we might now argue similarly as follows. Each of two incompatible explanations, P and P', might be prima facie justified through abduction, deduction then leading further to prima facie justification for the absurd conjunction $P \& P'$, but the very absurdity of this conjunction would surely override the prima facie justification that it derived from its premises. If that is a convincing argument, and it does seem so to me, we have thereby met the thoroughgoing objection to our abductivist principle.

Let us turn next to objections not to the principle itself but to its application in elucidating perceptual knowledge. Here there are two main objections: first, the objection from vicious circularity; and, second, the objection from inadequacy of premises. We consider these in turn.

Objection 1: "According to the abductivist principle, I believe the proposition P (that there is a sheet of paper before me) with prima facie justification if I believe it in part on the basis of my justified belief of V (that a visual sheet of paper presentation is given to me) and my justified belief that P would explain V. And for one to be justified in believing that P would explain V, one must be justified in believing at least that P would imply V. In order to know an objective proposition such as P on the basis of an experiential proposition such as V, by means of the abductivist principle, one must presuppose a linking proposition like the proposition

18 Cf. Pollock, *op. cit.*, Chapter Eight, esp. Sections 1, 2, and 7.

that if P is true that brings with it the truth of Q (in present circumstances). And just how does one acquire justification for believing any such proposition linking one's experience and one's surroundings? Appeal to a noticed correlation between situations in which a proposition like P is true and those in which a proposition like V is true is unavailing. For it presupposes some means of arriving at knowledge of P or the like, and that is precisely our lack, which we mean to fill with the abductivist principle when we apply it to perceptual knowledge of objective propositions like P. In sum, abduction cannot be a basic source of knowledge of our objective surroundings, since abduction always requires a prior justified belief whose justification cannot in turn have been abductive on pain of a vicious regress or circularity." Is there any recourse for the abductivist?[19]

Reply 1: The abductivist should appeal to a broader conception of the explanans than that required for the objection. More strictly it is not just the presence of something white and rectangular before one that explains one's visual presentation of something white and rectangular. The fuller explanans that more strictly explains the presentation includes as a further conjunct that one's circumstances are such that, in them, the presence of something white and rectangular before one would cause one to have a visual presentation of something white and rectangular.

The key point is that the explanans belief of which is prima facie justified by abduction is not the narrow proposition that there is something white and rectangular before one. What abduction most directly justifies is rather the broader explanans with two conjuncts: first, that there is such a thing before one; and, second, that its presence there would in the circumstances cause a visual presentation of something white and rectangular. It is then a simple matter to detach by deduction the narrower proposition that there is something white and rectangular before one.

It may be objected further that if the subject is aware of a better explanation for Q than that provided by P, then he can hardly be justified in accepting P on the basis of his joint beliefs of Q and of the proposition that P would explain Q. This is not conclusive, however, since we might simply speak of defeat or overriding in such a case, but it does seem most reasonable to modify the abductivist principle in response to the objection so that it reads as follows:

> One is prima facie justified in accepting P by basing it on justified belief of Q and on justified belief that P is the best of all accounts that one recognizes as possible explanations of Q.

19 Cf. Chisholm, *Theory of Knowledge*, 2nd ed., Chapter Four, Section 2.

Objection 2: The second of our two objections to the application of abduction in elucidating perceptual knowledge is the objection from inadequacy of premises.[20] This objection may be summarized as follows when addressed to our modified abductivist principle:

(1) The abductivist principle is correctly applicable only when the explanandum Q involved is a general regularity or correlation.

(2) None of us has a grasp of any general regularities or correlations connecting phenomena pertaining only to his experience, or at least not nearly of enough such regularities to serve as an adequate basis via abduction for any significant portion of our rich knowledge of the objective world.

(3) Therefore, one cannot begin with knowledge pertaining simply to his experience and move correctly via abduction to any significant portion of our rich knowledge of the objective world.

Reply 2: The argument seems valid, though not formalized in full detail. And the second premise seems quite true. But the first premise does not carry much conviction. If the fact that it would serve to explain something known is a source of the credibility of a hypothesis, I cannot see why the source should be thought to dry up entirely when the thing known is not a regularity but just, let us say, a particular fact. Maybe the credibility provided to a hypothesis by its power of explaining a particular fact should be thought to be less than that provided by its power of explaining a regularity, but I cannot think it plausible that it would be nil. Nor does it seem plausible that the power of explaining regularities should always yield more credibility than the power of explaining particular facts. Could that not depend on the number and variety of the regularities when compared with the number and variety of the particular facts (to mention only two other factors that seem relevant)?

Our vast frameworks of common sense and scientific would-be-knowledge seem to me structures held together epistemically mainly by abduction. This holds good not only of such theoretical knowledge as we have attained in the sciences but even of perceptual knowledge, memory knowledge, and much introspective knowledge.[21] Could it hold good of all knowledge whatever? Could it be the abductivist principle that explains how it is that a justified belief is justified, no matter what the justified belief might be?

20 Cf. W. S. Sellars, "Phenomenalism," in his *Science, Perception, and Reality* (London: Routledge & Kegan Paul, 1963), Chapter 3.
21 For the general lines of how abduction may combine with resemblance to play an important role in perceptual reidentification, see Chapter 3 of this volume, esp. Section (III)(ii).

It seems clear that our abductivist principle could not possibly do so much, for that would be incompatible with the supervenience of epistemic justification on factors all free of any epistemically evaluative or normative content. If our abductivist principle in its present form were indeed adequate and required to explain how it is that a justified belief is justified, no matter what the justified belief, then such justification could not possibly be supervenient in the sense indicated. For note that according to the abductivist principle as it now stands, the justification of any belief justified on its basis would always flow from factors some of which would include epistemically evaluative or normative content. This should be clear on inspection.

It may be replied that what we need in order to surmount our difficulty is a bold leap away from a conception of the transfer of justification as a linear stepwise procedure, to a more global conception of justification as something that dawns on a system of beliefs with sufficiently comprehensive abductivist or explanatory coherence. But this is open to decisive objections from the fact that it detaches the justification of a body of beliefs from its surroundings and its history.[22]

If abduction serves to justify belief only on a basis of already justified belief, then if justification must ultimately supervene on the nonepistemic, there must be some sources of justification that unlike abduction does not simply justify on the basis of the already justified. In a sense, there must be some basic sources of justification, justification that can then be transferred by means of abduction, induction, deduction, or any other means of transferring justification. What could possibly play the role of such a basic source of justification?

Experience, some will say, only experience could provide the basic data to which we can then apply our inferential machinery for the transference of justification. For us experience is at best a way station, however, since we have seen that experience in its various modalities is linked with objective chromatic and geometric beliefs by nothing more than derivative principles. And these, for systematic epistemology, must rest on more fundamental principles required to give them unity. Our response may reasonably be rejected, nevertheless, on the grounds that the beliefs for which experience is to serve as a basic source are not our objective chromatic and geometric beliefs or the like but rather only certain of our beliefs about experience itself. Since our experience is so variegated, however, both in respect of broad modalities, and even within modalities, and since not just any belief about experience can be justified simply in

22 See Section III in this chapter. And compare Chapter 10 of this volume, esp. Sections 4, 8, and 9.

virtue of the character of the experience (cf. being shaped like a regular chiliagon, attributed to a visual image), it seems clear that even restricting ourselves to introspective beliefs about experience, there will be a great number of scattered individual principles with no systematic unity. What might these principles have in common? What more basic epistemic principles could they derive from?

Infallibility, some might propose, is the basic source of foundational justification, and it is only because such beliefs as the beliefs that I think, that I exist, that I am thinking of sphericity, and the like, are infallible that they all count as foundationally justified. Moreover, when a headache cannot be ignored, the belief that it exists is justified, and now that we have appeal to infallibility we need not rest with the special, highly specific principle that introspective beliefs in headaches are justified. Such a specific principle is now nothing more than a secondary principle whose validity derives from the more fundamental principle about the justifying power of infallibility, along with the assumption that introspective beliefs about headaches are indeed infallible.[23]

There are some difficulties of detail with infallibility as a source of justification. Let us pass over these, however, in order to focus on what appears the most serious and persuasive substantive problem: namely, that it is hard to be sure that the full variety of introspective beliefs whose basic justification we need as a foundation for the rest of our knowledge will turn out all of them to be infallible beliefs. Why make so strong a requirement? Why not require only that the belief in question have its source in an intellectual virtue, in a way of forming beliefs that leads to the truth, given the subject's normal state and surroundings (normal relative to that sort of belief). Intellectual virtues are hence ingrained modes of intellectual procedure that tend to give us truth, just as practical virtues are ingrained modes of practical conduct that tend to yield what is good.

Having followed a route quite unlike ours, Peirce arrives at a very similar conclusion. But he restricts its scope to thought under conscious control (or at least he does so in the passage from which I will quote), leaving out spontaneous perceptual, introspective, and memory judgments. According to Peirce, in judging our ideals of conduct,

we consider what the general effect would be of thoroughly carrying out our ideals. Just so certain ways of reasoning recommend themselves because if

---

23 According to Brentano, one ". . . can be said to have direct, affirmative, and therefore factual evidence concerning the existence of a thing only if it would be contradictory to say that, although he is thinking of the thing, the thing does not exist." See p. 132 of the English edition, edited by R. M. Chisholm, of Brentano's *The True and the Evident* (New York: Humanities Press, 1966).

84

consistently carried out they must lead to the truth. The parallelism, you perceive, is almost exact.[24]

Introspection may now be regarded as a secondary source of justification that derives its justificatory power from its status as an intellectual virtue for beings like us. There is moreover a welcome bonus in our acceptance of intellectual virtue as a basic source of justification. For now the commitments to the use of deduction, of induction, and of abduction, commitments that we embody, may themselves surely count as intellectual virtues and hence need not be accepted as basic sources of justification. Instead, we may now think of them all as secondary sources derivative from a principle of intellectual virtue.

24 *The Collected Papers of Charles Sanders Peirce*, Vol. 1, 1.608.

6

Nature unmirrored, epistemology naturalized

A. KNOWLEDGE AND JUSTIFICATION

To know, you must at least be right; but you can be right without knowing. If you say that the dice will come up 7, you may be right without knowing. If you know you are most likely cheating, one die perhaps showing 4 on all six of its faces while the other shows 3. But if you are right on a roll of fair dice you must simply have guessed right.

What distinguishes the cheater who knows from someone who is right only by luck? For one thing, the cheater predicts with a good basis. He is justified in his belief.[1] But not just any sort of justification is thus relevant to knowledge, as shown by the bearing of confidence on success. The athlete, for example, tries to be confident. The fact that it will help gives him practical justification for confidence. But even if bound to win and thus to be right in the object of his confidence, such practical justification moves him no closer to knowledge than is the honest player who simply guesses right. What *would* bring him thus closer to knowledge is not the instrumental value of his confidence, but information about the skills and abilities of the competitors. It is such information that would give him *epistemic* justification for confidence that he will best the competition. Positive thinking is often justified in practice by its power. Despite the advantages it confers, which recommend it to prudence, optimism need not be justified in a way that makes for knowledge. Confidence becomes knowledge not through bribes but by credentials.

There may also be moral reasons for trusting people unless they disappoint our trust, religious reasons for faith in a divinity, and prudential reasons for someone ill to feel assured of his recovery. But trust, faith, and assurance are not made knowledge by such backing of moral, religious, or prudential reasons. Only epistemic justification will serve for that. In predicting right the cheater at dice knows through epistemic justification. The honest player predicts right without knowing because he lacks such justification.

Epistemic justification is a normative or evaluative property that shares with such properties generally three important features. It is *superve-*

---

1 Gender-unspecific reference is occasionally made here with "he" and its cognates, which may then be read as "she or he" or "her or him" or the like.

nient. Its attribution is *universalizable*. And it is *governed by principles*. It is supervenient because whenever it applies to a belief (or the like), there must be more basic properties of that belief such that any belief with such properties would be equally epistemically justified. Its attribution is universalizable because if a belief is epistemically justified, then any belief similar to that belief in all relevant respects would be equally epistemically justified. And it is governed by principles because the epistemic justification of a belief must always derive from certain intrinsic or relational properties of it, so that any belief just like it in respect of all such properties must be equally well justified. A principle is thus implied, one that governs epistemic justification by making it consequent on antecedent properties of belief.

The three important features of epistemic justification are indeed so closely related in logical space as to seem three faces of a single feature. The three may easily be seen to go together by necessity. And they all amount to the notion that justification always has conditions in virtue of which it applies. In terms of this we may now distinguish two projects of epistemology.

B. UNDERSTANDING AND VALIDATION

Epistemology has two main projects sometimes confused: a project of Understanding, and one of Validation. The first is that of understanding how it is that one would know whatever it is that one might know, of what conditions one would need to satisfy with respect to a proposition in order to know its truth. As we have seen, this is bound to involve an account of the conditions that make for epistemic justification. The other main project is that of ensuring that to the greatest extent possible our supposed knowledge really meets such conditions, which in some or even in many cases might involve actually *changing* our situation so as to meet conditions that we had not theretofore met.

The Project of Understanding is that of finding as simple, general, and convincing an account as we are able to find of the conditions within which our belief of a proposition has the kind of epistemic authority (justification, evidence, warrant) required for one to know its truth. Having completed the Project of Understanding to his full satisfaction, a philosopher of knowledge may find his work only just begun. For he may find that very little of what we all take ourselves to know can possibly be real knowledge given his account of what this requires in the way of epistemic authority. He may thus be brought to face a Project of Validation, of so changing his situation with regard to more and more of the propositions that we commonly take ourselves to know that he may come

87

to satisfy the conditions necessary for knowledge by his own (earlier) account.

C. EPISTEMIC RATIONALISM

Descartes is one such philosopher of knowledge. He concludes that we know only what we intuit or deduce: that our acceptance of a true proposition can have the epistemic justification (authority, warrant, status, call it what one will) required for knowledge only if it is either itself a rational intuition or the outcome of logical deduction from nothing but rational intuitions as ultimate premises. Thus he concludes his Project of Understanding with an account of utmost simplicity explaining how one would know whatever it is that one might know; with an utterly simple theory of the conditions required for the epistemic authority of true knowledge: "Intuition and deduction are the most sure routes to knowledge and the mind should admit no others." It is then hard to miss the looming fact that almost nothing of what we ordinarily take for knowledge satisfies the conditions laid down. Descartes attacks this windmill with a few rusty relics – as they now seem to us – in a vain attempt to carry out the consequent Project of Validation.

More recent tilts at neighboring windmills include logicism's attempt to found mathematics on obvious logic, and phenomenalism's attempt to found physics on phenomena, or so it is generally supposed. These attempts abetted the rationalist project of showing our supposed knowledge provable from the obvious. Their apparent failure leaves the rationalist in an awkward position. For he is now caught in the incoherence of supposing himself in possession of a vast body of knowledge none of which he can apparently have by his own account of knowledge as proof from the obvious. Skepticism would extricate him and offers its arms. Embracing it may be best if one holds knowledge unattainable except by conclusive proof. But doing so would neglect all knowledge that is not perfect, conclusive superknowledge.

Litte of what we take ourselves to know in science and ordinary life is thus superknown. One response is to insist that superknowledge is the only true knowledge and to accept the skeptical outcome that there is little we really know in science and common sense. But that response is simplistic. And it helps little to be told that ordinary talk of knowledge is interpretable and largely acceptable as talk of *approximations* to superknowledge. That is just empty unless the *dimensions* of approach are specified and explained.

If one is not just stipulating that "knowledge" (superknowledge) is to be attained only by déductive proof, however, then it is far from obvious that there is no other means. What is really at issue, of course, is how to attain justification, epistemic or cognitive justification, the kind of justification pertinent to knowledge.

D. RELIABILISM

An alternative to failed rationalism is a broader reliabilism, of which rationalism may be thought a special case. Reliabilism requires for the epistemic justification of belief that it be formed by a process reliable in an environment normal for the formation of such belief. Rationalism requires such a process to be perfectly reliable, whatever the context, to induce justification in its product beliefs. But we may of course give up such rationalism while yet retaining reliabilism. Suppose we require less of justification-inducing processes. Reliabilism then remains a kind of foundationalism. Every bit of knowledge still lies atop a pyramid of knowledge. But the building requirements for pyramids are now less stringent. A belief may now join the base not only through perfectly reliable rational intuition but also through introspection, perception, or memory. And one may now erect a superstructure on such a basis not only by deduction but also by induction, both enumerative and hypothetical or explanatory.

E. FOUNDATIONALISM ASSAILED

For several decades now foundationalism has been repeatedly attacked. Dewey and Wittgenstein are only two of the best-known critics. A warm admirer, Richard Rorty, now renews the offensive with his widely read *Philosophy and the Mirror of Nature*. Philosophy since Descartes and Locke is funded mainly by epistemology, according to Rorty, and since epistemology is now bankrupt, philosophy finds itself fundless. What breaks epistemology is moreover its dependence on a foundationalism requiring direct mirroring of reality through sensory experience. But this "confuses justification with causation." Realizing that justification is a matter of relations among propositions turns justification holistic. Since the standards of justification are legislated by society, finally, " . . . justification is not a matter of a special relation between ideas (or words) and objects, but of conversation, of social practice."

Justification for Rorty works not like a mirror but like a salon, and this social character makes justification holistic rather than foundational. *Philosophy and the Mirror of Nature* is largely variations on that main theme and its consequences. Parts of the theme are sounded repeatedly in the central chapters.[2]

Rorty's attack on foundationalism depends crucially on his charge against the tradition of a disastrous confusion between causation and justification. How now can such a charge be made to stick? One might so define justification that for a belief (assertion, assumption, claim, thought, or what have you) to have the status of being justified: (a) it must have *been justified*, a process of (its) justification must have taken place; and (b) this process must have involved the giving of reasons or arguments, must have involved conversation, at least *in foro interno*. But glue so thin won't make it stick for long.

Not that it is outrageous, or even unacceptable, to define justification thus as necessarily the outcome of a justificatory process of providing reasons or arguments. But argument will often have premises that are "ultimate," not having been supported by argument or buttressed by reasons. Ultimate premises are one and all *unjustified*, therefore, and yet some way must be found to distinguish those that in a given context can be used by a given thinker to help justify other things from those that are there then useless for that purpose.[3] I can argue for quite some time in favor of the proposition that there are at least one thousand sheep in this room: for I can claim that there are at least 1001, in favor of which in turn I can allege the presence of at least 1002; and so on. But eventually I must reach ultimate premises, if only because I fall asleep. Such ultimate premises will of course be unjustified since unbuttressed by reasons or arguments. Still that is not what precludes them from adequately justifying anything, since *all* ultimate premises must be equally unjustified and ultimate premises there must surely be for *any* complete argument that is not regressive or circular.

(An argument is *complete* relative to a thinker or community and a time if and only if there is no premise of that argument that has been argued for without circularity by that thinker or in that community up to that time. If an argument does have premises argued for by that thinker or in that community, then there is a more inclusive "argument" of which the immediate premises serve as lemmas. If within a stretch of time one relies essentially on P as a premise in arguing for Q, and within that same

---

2 For examples, see pages 152, 157, 159, 170, and 174 of Richard Rorty, *Philosophy and the Mirror of Nature*. (Copyright © 1979 by Princeton University Press. Excerpts reprinted by permission.)

3 Compare Chisholm's distinction, concerning ultimate premises, between considering them facts that constitute their own evidence and considering them facts that are evidence without being evident. "In the one case we are reminded of the prime mover that moves itself, and in the other, of the prime mover unmoved." *Theory of Knowledge*, 2nd ed. (Englewood Cliffs. N.J.: Prentice-Hall, 1977), p. 25.

stretch relies essentially on Q in arguing for P, then one incurs circularity relative to that stretch of time.)

What then distinguishes ultimate premises that do from those that do not justify conclusions drawn by equally valid inferences?

First we need some terminology, and if "epistemic justification" is already preempted by definition, we may perhaps use "epistemic author-ity" as a broader term for the positive epistemic status required for knowledge. There would then be two ways for a belief (assumption, presupposition, thought, etc.) to have such epistemic authority: (a) as the outcome of a process of justification, of the giving of reasons or arguments in its favor; or (b) in some other way, as it surely must on any occasion when it functions as an ultimate premise.

F. NATURE UNMIRRORED

The main outlines of Rorty's view of human knowledge and its so-called "theory" may be discerned in the following passages from *Philosophy and the Mirror of Nature*:

[The] notion of a [foundational] "theory of knowledge" will not make sense unless we have confused causation and justification in the manner of Locke.[4]

If . . . we think of "rational certainty" as a matter of victory in argument rather than of relation to an object known, we shall look toward our interlocutors rather than to our faculties for the explanation of the phenomenon.[5]

[We] can think of knowledge as a relation to propositions, and thus of justifica-tion as a relation between the propositions in question and other propositions from which the former may be inferred. Or we may think of both knowledge and justification as privileged relations to the objects those propositions are about. If we think in the first way, we will see no need to end the potentially infinite regress of propositions-brought-forward-in-defense-of-other-propositions. It would be foolish to keep conversation going on the subject once everyone, or the majority, or the wise, are satisfied, but of course we *can*. If we think of knowledge in the second way, we will want to get behind reasons to causes, beyond argument to compulsion from the object known, to a situation in which argument would be not just silly but impossible. . . . To reach that point is to reach the foundations of knowledge.[6]

In order to defend Sellars and Quine, I shall be arguing that their holism is a product of their commitment to the thesis that justification is not a matter of a special relation between ideas (or words) and objects, but of conversation, of

4 *Op. cit.*, p. 152.
5 *Ibid.*, p. 157.
6 *Ibid.*, p. 159.

social practice. Conversational justification, so to speak, is naturally holistic, whereas the notion of justification embedded in the epistemological tradition is reductive and atomistic. I shall try to show that Sellars and Quine invoke the same argument, one which bears equally against the given-versus-nongiven and the necessary-versus-contingent distinctions. The crucial premise of this argument is that we understand knowledge when we understand the social justification of belief, and thus have no need to view it as accuracy of representation.[7]

For Sellars, the certainty of "I have a pain" is a reflection of the fact that nobody cares to question it, not conversely. Just so, for Quine, the certainty of "All men are animals" and of "There have been black dogs". . . . More broadly, if assertions are justified by society rather than by the character of the inner representations they express, then there is no point in attempting to isolate privileged representations.

Explaining rationality and epistemic authority by reference to what society lets us say, rather than the latter by the former, is the essence of what I shall call "epistemological behaviorism," an attitude common to Dewey and Wittgenstein.[8]

Irrespective of what Quine, Sellars, Dewey, or Wittgenstein may have accepted, it is evident in the book that Rorty himself embraces the "epistemological behaviorism" that he attributes to them all. His doctrine apparently boils down to the following five main tenets. (See, for instance, the passages quoted above.)

(R1) *The inferential conception of justification*: A proposition – or its acceptance – is justified by inferring it from premises from which it may be inferred, and only thus.

(R2) *The normative conception of inference*: Some inferences are permissible, and some impermissible.

(R3) *The social foundation of inferential norms*: Inferential norms are legislated by society and have no deeper foundation.

(R4) *The confusion of causes with reasons*: No belief – not even an observational belief – is justified in virtue of a special causal relation to its object(s), or because it "mirrors Nature." That is to confuse causation with justification in the manner of Locke.

(R5) *The two sources of epistemic authority*: The epistemic authority of an assertion may derive from inference and argument (and thus indirectly from social approval through legislation that permits such inference or argument), but it may also derive from social approval of such assertions directly, without need of argument, as in the case of "I am in pain," which society clears epistemically for issue in almost any context. Whether

7 *Ibid.*, p. 170.
8 *Ibid.*, p. 174.

92

argument is socially required will no doubt depend on the context.

Surprisingly enough it follows from R1–R5 that in a straightforward sense Rorty is as clearly a foundationalist as is anyone in the tradition of modern epistemology. This may be seen in the following consequences:

(C1) Every assertion with epistemic authority has either direct authority or indirect authority.

(C2) Any assertion with indirect authority has such authority in virtue of having been justified through argument or inference ultimately from assertions all of which have direct authority.

(C3) An assertion made in a certain context has direct authority only if it is of a sort approved by society for issue without prior argument in such a context: e.g., "I am in pain" for nearly any context.

(C4) What makes argument or inference permissible is its relation to norms legislated by society.

The foundation is thus always provided by assertions with direct authority. The superstructure is built by argument or inference on that foundation. This is outright foundationalism, even if what provides authority at the foundation is not the taking of the given but the approval of society, and even if what permits the erection of the superstructure is social legislation.

Accordingly, if traditional foundationalism were refuted by a charge of confusing causation (mirroring Nature) with justification, conventionalist foundationalism would seem equally well refuted by a charge of confusing convention (direct social approval) with justification.

What now are the grounds for conventionalist foundationalism? How is it itself by its own account founded? Is its authority direct or indirect? Surely not all of C1 through C4 are directly cleared by society for issue in the context of a philosophy book or discussion, without need of argument. True enough, it may be answered, but now they have the support of philosophical argument, so the relevant claim is that they now have indirect authority.

When we look for the purported sources of such conventionalist foundationalism, however, we find quasi-stipulative definitions, like R1, and reasonably plausible assumptions, like R2. But we also find that most of the work is done by assertions that have no direct social approval, like R3 and R5. And these lack any kind of evident authority, either direct or indirect. No valid argument for them issues from premises all cleared by society for issue and acceptance without argument in the context of a philosophy book or discussion. I for one have been unable to discern or state any such argument.

The salon account of knowledge – conventionalist foundationalism – was fashioned as an alternative to a more traditional mirror account: reliabilist foundationalism. Our doubts on the salon turn us back to the mirror, to the view of knowledge as accurate reflection in a mirror so constituted as to be generally accurate in its reflections, as accurate reflection in a reliable mirror.

G. RELIABILIST FOUNDATIONALISM

Two problems arise for reliabilist foundationalism, and they both point in the same direction. In the first place, there is the possibility of reliable mechanisms for noninferential acquisition of belief other than introspection, memory, and (ordinary) perception. Clairvoyance, for instance, would be one such mechanism. If magic or surgery suddenly gives one such a gift, however, one finds oneself predicting things "out of the blue," with too little discernible connection to the rest of one's beliefs. Such a prediction might turn out to be right, of course: and not just by luck, either, since by hypothesis it derives from the operation of a reliable faculty. But I could not easily think it epistemically justified simply on that account. For anyone similarly minded this raises a doubt as to the adequacy of mere reliability to induce justification.[9]

It might be objected that we are in fact no better off with our present faculty of memory than we would be with clairvoyance. In a room with more than one door, one yet remembers which one used to come in. And often it is just brute, direct memory that enables one to know what one remembers. That is of course to set apart the coherence of what one remembers with the rest of one's beliefs, but then such coherence does not in our example distinguish one's having entered through one door from one's having entered through any of the others. Unless one rejects such memory as a source of knowledge, then, how can one consistently reject clairvoyance? The problem for clairvoyance relative to a normal human today is, I think, its failure to meet the challenge of doxastic ascent. If a normal human today were suddenly to receive the gift of clairvoyance he would be helpless to explain the source of beliefs delivered by his new gift and how that source operates. These is much that we know at least implicitly about memory and its mode and conditions of

9 The example of clairvoyance is used persuasively by Laurence Bonjour to similar effect in "Externalist Theories of Empirical Knowledge," *Midwest Studies in Philosophy*, Vol. 5, ed. Peter A. French, Theodore E. Uehling, Jr., and Howard K. Wettstein (Minneapolis: University of Minnesota Press, 1980).

reliable operation. And it is largely this that enables discrimination in favor of memory and against suddenly endowed clairvoyance. But that is not to say that clairvoyance could never reach or surpass the status of memory as a source of knowledge. Of course it could, if we learned as much about it as we know about our memory. And there is no evident reason to rule out a priori that one might conceivably be gifted with such clairvoyance and learn even more about it than one presently knows about one's memory.

The challenge of doxastic ascent might well be thought a pseudo-challenge, however, since it would deny knowledge to infants and animals. Admittedly, there is a sense in which even a supermarket door "knows" when someone approaches, and in which a heating system "knows" when the temperature in a room rises above a certain setting. Such is "servo-mechanic" knowledge. And there is also an immense variety of animal knowledge, instinctive or learned, which facilitates survival and flourishing in an astonishingly rich diversity of modes and environments. Human knowledge is on a higher plane of sophistication, however, precisely because of its enhanced coherence and comprehensiveness and its capacity to satisfy self-reflective curiosity. Pure reliabilism is questionable as an adequate epistemology for such knowledge. The challenge of doxastic ascent does seem pertinent at least here, and it signals the promise of comprehensive coherence as a source of epistemic authority.

A second problem for reliabilist foundationalism forms an obstacle to its developing a theory of knowledge. An important component of a reliabilist theory of knowledge would surely be a list of reliable faculties: perception, memory, introspection, inference, and perhaps others. But how could one justify the addition of a faculty to the list except by use – direct or indirect – of that very faculty? And is that not as viciously circular as declaring a source reliable by accepting its reports at face value and inferring that it issues truth? Such reasoning is unreliable and in any case unacceptable. We may perhaps avoid vicious circularity by allowing a faculty to gain support from the use of other faculties. But these would need support of their own and how could they gain it except by each leaning on the others? Reliabilism is thus driven to seek refuge in a wide enough circle, which it must regard as benign, perhaps in virtue of its wide diameter. And this in effect appeals to comprehensive coherence.

H. COHERENCE

Coherentism can be a more radical response to the failure of rationalism. Radical coherentism rejects the generic view of which rationalism is a species. In this it departs more widely from rationalism than does the reliabilism just briefly considered. But reliabilism deeply enough developed leads to a kind of coherentism anyhow, or so our brief discussion does suggest.

The coherence invoked by coherentism cannot amount to mere logical consistency, since for any body of beliefs with n independent beliefs, the number of alternative equally consistent and comprehensive bodies of belief is 2 to the nth power or more, which for any ordinary body of beliefs will surely be a very large number. But it is absurd to suppose that any of us would have been equally well justified in believing any of such equally consistent alternatives to his actual body of beliefs.

If consistency is too weak as an account of coherence, pairwise logical equivalence is both too strong and too weak: too strong since no body of beliefs realistically numerous enough to be actual would have only pairwise equivalent members; too weak since any such body of beliefs would then cast an equally coherent image comprised of all its negations.

If it is clear what comprehensive coherence cannot be, it is not so clear what it is. There is certainly no compelling and simple analysis of it, nor is there even any widely accepted complete account, no matter how complex. Features of it there are which have been widely discerned, and with these we must rest content, at least for now if not longer. Among these features of a comprehensively coherent body of beliefs are to be found, besides its comprehensiveness – both in plurality and in scope – also its high degree of interconnection: logical, probabilistic, confirmational, and explanatory.

In addition to such features, a high degree of consistency is also a plausible requirement. But the notion of such degree may seem repugnant to the all-or-nothing intuitive character of logical consistency. Despite the absolute character of a notion of logical consistency pertaining to propositions singly or even to sets of propositions, there does yet appear a further useful notion of degree of consistency for bodies of belief. Even if two bodies of belief are equally inconsistent in the "inconsistency, period" sense, one may be more (extensively) inconsistent than the other in another useful sense. For one may contain a highly localized inconsistency of no great moment, while the other is riddled with absurdities of global or at least general importance. A body of beliefs tends to be more coherent the less generally inconsistent it is.

I. PERSPECTIVAL COHERENCE

Even though a belief may be a part of a body of beliefs highly coherent and comprehensive, and that belief may seem *thereby* justified, it cannot be just the coherence and comprehensiveness of the containing body that make it justified. For we can find an equally coherent and comprehensive body whose members are clearly *not* justified. Since the argument is detailed elsewhere,[10] I will not give it here, but will stop only briefly to consider how coherentism might respond.

To block this refutation coherentism must require that for comprehensive enough coherence a body of beliefs need include an epistemic perspective, an account at least in broad outline of the ways in which member beliefs in various categories acquire epistemic justification: an account of how one gets to know various sorts of things covered by beliefs in that body.

That amounts to a form of coherentism aptly labelled "perspectival" for requiring an epistemic perspective in any world view adequate to induce knowledge-making justification in member beliefs. Such perspectivism may with equal justice be thought a form of foundationalism, however, since (a) it does not countenance mere coherence, no matter how comprehensive, as a sufficient source of justification, and (b) foundationalism for its part does not reject coherence as *one* factor relevant to epistemic justification.

Perspectivism may also agree extensively with forms of foundationalism on how we know. Both will cite perception on how we know the external world, memory on the past, introspection of the contents of our consciousness, induction on the future, and so on. But such agreement is bounded when the perspectivist assigns to perception, memory, introspection, induction, and the like, not the status of fundamental sources of justification, but rather that of reliable sources of truth, of true belief. For it is this that puts them in his epistemic perspective.

J. EPISTEMOLOGY OF EPISTEMOLOGY

Even if it is true that comprehensive coherence requires the various conditions already noted, how do we know that it does require such conditions? Different answers seem apt for different conditions. Regarding consistency, comprehensive coherence obviously requires at least a high degree, and one grasps such an obvious truth by one's faculty of reason. Thus one may be said to grasp that coherence requires consistency through the same faculty that enables one to grasp the principles constitutive of such consistency: that nothing is diverse from itself, that nothing both has and lacks a property, and the like.

The Greek analogy between reason and vision also comes under

10 See Chapter 11, Section H, in this book.

vigorous attack in Rorty's book. But is it really so absurd to draw such an analogy? What after all is the so-called human faculty of sight? May it not be regarded as something intrinsic to human beings: as a set of intrinsic properties that grounds their ability to grasp truths of a certain sort in the right circumstances? More specifically, may it not be regarded as the set of intrinsic properties in a human that grounds his ability to grasp without conscious inference certain simple truths about the colors, shapes, etc., of neighboring middle-sized unscreened objects in good light, etc.? One may of course discover much more about such properties. We know that in normal humans they include the possession of eyes, a nervous system including a brain, and much more in greater and greater scientific detail. But the basic idea seems clear enough to common sense without need of such detail.

If human beings eye a snowball in good light and ask themselves whether something white and round is before them, with few exceptions they will answer yes. Nearly all of us would thus grasp such a truth without need of conscious inference. And there is no apparent absurdity in proposing at least the beginning of an explanation for such agreement by attributing to those in agreement a certain faculty about which we may learn more and more thus improving our explanation without obvious limit. It's because of their common possession of a faculty of sight that humans agree so generally in grasping truths about the color and shape of unscreened middle-sized objects in their well-lit environment.

Given what our faculty of sight amounts to, is it really so absurd to attribute to ourselves a faculty of reason? There is after all considerable agreement when we ask ourselves whether it is or is not possible for something to be diverse from itself, or to both have and lack one and the same property. If we are right in attributing to ourselves a faculty of sight to explain our remarkable agreement about colors and shapes, what is so wrong in laying claim to a faculty of reason for explaining equally general agreement about identity and contradiction? Of course the postulation of such a faculty does not go very far toward explaining our grasp of basic truths of logic and our consequent agreement on them, no further than does the postulation of sight with regard to colors and shapes.

If our defense of the analogy between sight and reason is adequate, it sustains invoking a faculty of reason to meet the challenge of how we know principles of logic constitutive of consistency – like the impossibility of self-diversity – or principles of epistemology constitutive of coherence, like the need of high consistency for coherence. The answer in each case would be that such truths are manifest to reason. Developing that answer would of course involve saying more about the set of properties whose possession by humans constitutes their having the faculty of reason. That is enabled by scientific progress, and further relevant progress is hoped for in cognitive science and neurophysiology. But even without such progress it seems to me we are no less justified in attributing to ourselves a faculty of reason than we were in laying claim to a faculty of sight before the dawn of a physiology and psychology of sight; and, for that matter, no less justified than we were in attributing to objects a property of heat before developing a science of thermodynamics.

Such a defense is not available for all features we have claimed for coherence. And there may indeed be an element of stipulation in focusing on a kind of coherence that includes not only logical consistency but also a high degree of explanatory, probabilistic, and confirmational interconnection. A more important question is this: What justifies us in thinking that coherence so defined or characterized gives the key to epistemic justification, that it is the comprehensive coherence of a body of beliefs that induces epistemic justification in its members? The answer of any advocate of such a view is already determined by his view. He must surely answer that his view is itself justified fundamentally because of its own degree of coherence with the rest of his beliefs, and in particular with the relevant data. But has he a right to that answer without explaining more fully just what is involved in comprehensive coherence? Don't we need either an outright definition of the notion or a more precise specification of the principles that delineate its scope of application? That seems a weak objection, however, especially when compared with the fact that we can legitimately attribute causes to an event, knowledge to a subject, and explanatory power to an account even in the absence of any precise and general philosophical definition or account of causation, knowledge, or explanation. It seems quite conceivable accordingly that we reach a position to propose comprehensive coherence as a fundamental source of epistemic justification; that the epistemic justification of our proposal flow from its coherence with a sufficiently comprehensive set of data and related beliefs; and that all this be so despite our lack of a precise definition of comprehensive coherence or even a complete theory with all the principles that delineate its scope of application.

How indeed would one discover such principles for the comprehensive coherence that induces justification except through the relevant coherence of proposed principles with a sufficiently comprehensive set of relevant data and other beliefs? Testing for such coherence is after all little else than the familiar philosophical method of counter-examples. What does one do in assessing a proposed counter-example if not to consider how well a proposed principle or definition coheres with something that seems intuitively right? When one proposes a counter-example to a philosophical theory (e.g., to a principle or a definition) one claims concerning a described situation that it is possible, that such-and-such would be true in it, and that these facts are jointly incompatible with the philosophical theory. One thereby charges that the philosophical theory fails to cohere well with intuitive data already part of our body of beliefs.

K. HOW TO NATURALIZE EPISTEMOLOGY

If to naturalize epistemology is to surpass the traditional concern with conclusive proofs that refute the skeptic, opening it to interdisciplinary influence from the scientific studies of cognition, then reliabilism at least encourages if it does not require that epistemology be thus naturalized. For reliabilism would serve as an overarching doctrine of epistemology, as a very general account of the conditions required for epistemic justification. And it would then fall to the studies of cognition to specify just which processes reliably engender true belief and how, thus giving substance and strength to our overall theory of knowledge. A common-sense correlate of such a theory of knowledge is our view of ourselves as possessed of faculties like sight, taste, touch, etc., by the use of which we gain knowledge of our physical surroundings. But we have seen how defending that view of ourselves on a reliabilist basis involves us in coherentism: in allowing each faculty included to rest on the use of others for support of its inclusion. And the same would seem to hold for any more scientific development of such a view of ourselves. Reliabilism more closely examined seems therefore to require a kind of coherentism as a source of epistemic justification.

There is in any case a more radical way to naturalize epistemology, one provided already by its locus classicus, Quine's "Epistemology Naturalized."[11]

Two dogmas of empiricism according to Quine remain "unassailable" despite the failure of phenomenalism.

One is that whatever evidence there is for science is sensory evidence. The other . . . is that all inculcation of meanings of words must rest ultimately on sensory evidence.[12]

Phenomenalism's is not the only failure relevant to epistemology: so is the failure of any logicism which dared to hope for a reduction of mathematics to obvious logic. In spite of these failed hopes, for Quine,

epistemology still goes on, though in a new setting and a clarified status.

---

11 *Ontological Relativity and Other Essays* (New York: Columbia University Press, 1969).
12 *Op. cit.*, p. 75.

Epistemology, or something like it, simply falls into place as a chapter of psychology and hence of natural science. It studies a natural phenomenon, viz., a physical human subject. This human subject is accorded a certain experimentally controlled input – certain patterns of irradiation in assorted frequencies, for instance – and in the fullness of time the subject delivers as output a description of the three-dimensional external world and its history. The relation between the meager input and the torrential output is a relation that we are prompted to study for somewhat the same reasons that always prompted epistemology: namely, in order to see how evidence relates to theory, and in what ways one's theory of nature transcends any available evidence.[13]

That in brief is Quine's naturalization of epistemology. Already *Word and Object* had told us that

we can investigate the world, and man as a part of it, and thus find out what cues he could have of what goes on around him. Subtracting his cues from his world view, we get man's net contribution as the difference. This difference marks the extent of man's conceptual sovereignty – the domain within which he can revise theory while saving the data.[14]

And in others of his writings one may even better appreciate the full extent that Quine allows to man's conceptual sovereignty: an extent great enough that science is described as in large measure a "free creation."[15]

But it is not only theoretical science that floats free of any firm mooring. Even crucial logical features of the most basic common sense are in the same boat.

The steps by which the child was seen to progress from observational language to relative clauses and categoricals and quantification had the arbitrary character of historical accident and cultural heritage; there was no hint of inevitability.[16]

Two central planks of Quine's epistemology are hence these:

(P1) Epistemology is now a branch of psychology that studies the causal relation between sensory input and theoretical output.

(P2) Engaging in such a study now leads to the conclusion that the sensory input which causes man's theoretical output does not determine it, and that man's theoretical output is hence nearly all arbitrary free creation.

But if science is in large measure a "free creation," and if even our basic logical framework is "arbitrary," what reason can we then have for

13 *Ontological Relativity and Other Essays*, pp. 82–3.
14 *Word and Object* (Cambridge, Mass.: MIT Press, 1960).
15 *The Roots of Reference* (La Salle, Ill.: Open Court, 1974).
16 "The Nature of Natural Knowledge," in *Mind and Language*, ed. Samuel Guttenplan (Oxford: Clarendon Press, 1975), p. 80.

thinking that our view of the world around us is not just a massive illusion? And if in fact it gets things largely right, must that not be just a lucky accident that gives no knowledge, seeing its character as free and arbitrary creation?

One gathers that Quine would rule such questions illegitimate whole-sale doubt.[17] Epistemology cannot legitimately indulge in such universal questioning of science, for the very problem of knowledge of the world presupposes science. It is only the posit of physical objects with their respective regularities that raises the problem of illusion. Without that posit there is no contrast between physical appearance and reality.

Such reasoning does not quiet philosophical doubt, unfortunately, for the problem of knowledge presupposes not *acceptance* of science as believed truth but at most *supposition* of science as relevant possibility. Thus Quine's own plank P2 (above) gives renewed relevance and vigor to a famous Russellian reductio:

(R1) If the scientific account of the (supposed) world around us – including our bodies, their environment, and the relations between the two – is false even in its broad outlines, then we lack scientific knowledge even in broad outline of the world around us.

(R2) If the scientific account of the (supposed) world around us is true at least in its broad outlines, that rules out any possibility that we really know such a world even in broad outline.

(R3) Therefore, we lack scientific knowledge even in broad outline of the world around us.

It seems trivial and uncontroversial both that the conclusion follows validly and that the first premise is true. Everything turns on the second premise. But according to hypotheses concerning language acquisition and theory formation endorsed by Quine, our theory of the world is very largely an arbitrary free creation relative to the evidence that prompts it, our sensory stimulations. And if such hypotheses are borne out, that would seem to establish premise R2 about as conclusively as could be feared.

Yet Quine certainly rejects the conclusion that we have no scientific knowledge, and with it of course the premise (R2) that if science is true we can have no such knowledge. Still, given the arbitrary character attributed to science we are owed some explanation of how it can

Thus we are told on p. 68 of "The Nature of Natural Knowledge," *op. cit.*, that the " . . . positing of bodies is already rudimentary physical science; and it is only after that stage that the sceptic's invidious distinctions can make sense."

nevertheless amount to knowledge. Insofar as we are provided such explanation, here is its key:

The channels by which, having learned observation sentences, we acquire theoretical language, are the very channels by which observation lends evidence to scientific theory. . . .
We see, then, a strategy for investigating the relation of evidential support, between observation and scientific theory. We can adopt a genetic approach, studying how theoretical language is learned. For the evidential relation is virtually enacted, it would seem, in the learning.[18]

Quine's response to the Russellian reductio would thus apparently be that our theory of the world is not only true but also epistemically justified (evident) to the extent that it is reached through channels by which we acquire theoretical language. Premise R2 would thus be rejected and the skeptical conclusion avoided.

The response fails to satisfy because it seems incoherent. Humanity soon goes beyond observation to theory – very soon for Quine since it does so even for elementary common sense. Once having taken such a step, we enter the ambit of conceptual sovereignty, where thought has free play. Not even the elementary logical framework of common sense escapes such sovereignty. Even it has "the arbitrary character of historical accident and cultural heritage." If found among early results of a science of language and theory, this threatens to substantiate Russell's second premise. And surely the threat is not met simply with the thought that the channels by which theoretical language is learned themselves automatically determine the relation of evidential support. A ditch dug at random in primordial ooze will not likely lead to the fountain of truth. If our theory of the world is significantly the outcome of free and arbitrary play of thought, then if it is still so related causally to observation as to be by definition "evident," that only raises the question of what such "evidence" could possibly have to do with knowledge.

Quine has very recently returned to this question with the following remarks by way of answer.[19]

What then does our overall scientific theory really claim regarding the world? Only that it is somehow so structured as to assure the sequences of stimulation that our theory gives us to expect. . . .
In what way then do I see the Humean predicament as persisting? Only in the

18 "The Nature of Natural Knowledge," op cit., p. 74.
19 "Reply to Stroud," in Midwest Studies in Philosophy, Vol. 6, ed. Peter A. French, Theodore E. Uehling, Jr., and Howard Wettstein (Minneapolis: University of Minnesota Press, 1981), p. 474. Cf. Barry Stroud's "The Significance of Naturalized Epistemology," ibid., pp. 455–73.

fallibility of prediction: the fallibility of induction and the hypothetico-deductive method in anticipating experience.

I have depicted a barren scene. The furniture of our world, the people and sticks and stones along with the electrons and molecules, have dwindled to manners of speaking. Any other purported objects would serve as well, and may as well be said already to be doing so.

So it would seem. Yet people, sticks, stones, electrons, and molecules are real indeed, on my view, and it is these and no dim proxies that science is all about. Now how is such robust realism to be reconciled with what we have just been through? The answer is naturalism: the recognition that it is within science itself, and not in some prior philosophy, that reality is properly to be identified and described.

One might as well say:

> The people, sticks, stones, and places of fiction are real indeed, on my view, and it is these and no dim proxies that fiction is all about. Now how is such robust realism to be sustained? The answer is fictional realism: the recognition that it is within fiction itself, and not in some prior philosophy, that reality is properly to be identified and described.

Fictional realism is no answer, however, for the characters of pure fiction do not really exist, and it is not within fiction that reality is properly to be identified and described. No indeed, but why not? Presumably because if pure fiction happens somehow to be true (as well it might if purely general, which it quite well might be), that would be nothing more than a mere accidental coincidence that no one could have reasonably expected working only from within the fiction. And it is of course coherent with this to hold fiction free and arbitrary creation.

Not to be countenanced as equally coherent is acceptance of science as reality-claims court coupled with denial that it is anything but free and arbitrary creation.

The incoherence is not removed, moreover, if one now adds:

(Q1) "What then does our overall scientific theory really claim regarding the world? Only that it is somehow so structured as to assure the sequences of stimulation that our theory gives us to expect."

(Q2) "Yet people, sticks, stones, electrons, and molecules are real indeed."

(Q3) "[It] is within science itself, and not in some prior philosophy, that reality is properly to be identified and described."

If it is within science that we settle, to the extent possible for us, the

104

contours of reality; and if science really claims regarding the world only that it is so structured as to assure certain sequences of stimulation; then how can we possibly think reality to assume the contours of people, sticks, stones, and so on?

We cannot have it all three ways: (Q1), (Q2), and (Q3) form an incoherent triad. If we trust science as the measure of reality, and if we think there really are sticks and stones, then we can't have science accept only a world "somehow so structured as to assure" certain sequences of stimulations or the like. Our science must also claim that there really are sticks and stones.

What is more, if science is really the measure of reality, it cannot undercut itself by saying that it really isn't, that it is only convenient "manners of speaking" to guide us reliably from stimulation to stimulation.

We have now considered two ways to naturalize epistemology. A moderate way is promised by reliabilism, which offers itself as a leading principle under which common sense and cognitive science could fill in a more and more elaborate account of reliable cognitive processes or methods. But reliabilism appeared to require coherentism at a crucial juncture in such building of a theory of knowledge.

A more radical way is apparently advanced by Quine, who seems at times to propose outright replacement of epistemology with psychology. That proposal is undermined, however, by his own talk of evidential relations, manners of speaking, and "properly" identifying and describing reality. What is more, Quine's reflections do not clearly add up to a coherent epistemology.

Moderate reliabilism threatens comprehensive coherentism, while radical naturalism threatens comprehensive incoherence. Is there a more promising way to naturalize epistemology?

L. EPISTEMOLOGY NATURALIZED

In the absence of any compelling reason to restrict the naturalization of epistemology to a psychological study of the relation between stimulations and language or theory, it would be arbitrary not to include the evolutionary epistemology of Campbell, Popper, Shimony and others; the genetic epistemology of Piaget; the cognitive innatism of Chomsky; and even the history of science and the sociology of knowledge. These then are studies of cognition that promise new vigor and substance for theory of knowledge. But just how would this promise be realized?

Epistemologists who move to such areas risk suspicion of having simply abandoned their field. For it is not perfectly obvious how scientific study of the causal conditions of knowledge can bear on philosophical study of the nature of knowledge and the conditions on which it (epistemic justification) supervenes.

One radical way to naturalize epistemology is of course to forsake it in favor of science, to let it wither and return it to Nature. But in the absence of argument that it deserves such a fate, that is trivial and unilluminating.

Under reliabilism epistemology is naturalized because one turns to the studies of cognition for detailed accounts of the modes of belief acquisition that induce justification through reliability. But pure reliabilism remains under shadow of doubt for its eventual need of coherentism.

Recall however that epistemology traditionally adopts two main projects. It adopts the Project of Understanding, of understanding as simply and generally as possible the conditions upon which epistemic justification supervenes. But on occasion it adopts also the Project of Validation, of actively bringing about the satisfaction of such required conditions by those of our beliefs which do not already satisfy them, and perhaps by new beliefs as well. (Thus nearly all of Descartes' *Meditations*.)

Accordingly, if comprehensive coherence is a fundamental source of epistemic justification, why not co-opt the studies of cognition as important elements of our Project of Validation. That is, after all, exactly what they could be, since if philosophical and successful enough they would enhance the comprehensive coherence of our world view.[20] But if so what then sets them apart as especially apt for inclusion in epistemology? Would not all of inquiry be equally apt, since it all would enhance comprehensive coherence?

Yes and no. Yes, under comprehensive coherentism all of inquiry does form part of the Project of Validation. No, it is not all equally apt for inclusion in epistemology: for there are two important features that set apart the studies of cognition.

In the first place, epistemology is especially concerned with coherence and comprehensiveness in our view of our cognitive faculties and accomplishments. That is one reason why studies of cognition have special pertinence to epistemology.

We have seen moreover how comprehensive coherentism must turn perspectival by requiring the presence of an epistemic perspective in any body of beliefs comprehensive enough to induce the epistemic justifica-

---

20 Compare the place in philosophy recognized for some such studies of cognition by Roderick Firth, under the title of "epistemological rule utilitarianism," in his 1980 Presidential Address to the APA's Eastern Division, "Epistemic Merit, Intrinsic and Instrumental," *Proceedings and Addresses of the American Philosophical Association* 55 (1981): 5–23.

tion of members.[21] It is here especially that the studies of cognition have the spotlight. For they promise epistemology the elaboration in finer and finer detail of precisely that epistemic perspective crucial for comprehensive enough coherence in our world view.

M. SUMMARY

This chapter has been structured as follows:

A. *Knowledge and justification*: the nature of epistemic justification and its supervenience
B. *Understanding and validation*: two projects of epistemology, one to understand justification, the other to promote it
C. *Epistemic rationalism*: a simple foundationalism of intuition and deduction
D. *Reliabilism*: a broader foundationalism
E. *Foundationalism assailed*
F. *Nature unmirrored*: Rorty reviewed
G. *Reliabilist foundationalism*: two problems
H. *Coherence*: a more radical response to the failure of rationalism
I. *Perspectival coherence*: the requirement of an epistemic perspective and its relation to foundationalism
J. *Epistemology of epistemology*
K. *How to naturalize epistemology*: Quine reviewed
L. *Epistemology naturalized*: through the project of validation

21 See Section I in this chapter.

7

Theories of justification:
old doctrines newly defended

A. THE "ABSURDITY" OF FOUNDATIONS

Foundationalism has drawn fire repeatedly of late and stands multiply accused of itself resting on no better foundation than a "myth of the given," and of requiring the evident absurdity of a "test" that compares our beliefs with reality itself in the absence of any intermediary concepts or beliefs. A recent salvo was fired by Donald Davidson in an important essay. Let us now examine the damage.

Davidson's "Coherence Theory of Truth and Knowledge"[1] argues both against foundations and in favor of coherence. It attacks foundationalism for requiring a confrontation intrinsically absurd, and it objects to specific foundational "sources of justification" outside the scope of our beliefs. That is on the negative. On the affirmative, it presents and defends a coherentist alternative.

An allegedly foundationalist idea, that of "confrontation between what we believe and reality" is first argued to be "absurd," thus opening the way for coherentism, subsequently offered as the alternative.

What distinguishes a coherence theory is simply the claim that nothing can count as a reason for holding a belief except another belief. Its partisan rejects as unintelligible the request for a ground or source of justification of another ilk. (426)

In explanation and support we are referred to Rorty, who claims that "nothing counts as justification unless by reference to what we already accept, and there is no way to get outside our beliefs and our language so as to find some test other than coherence."[2]

Confrontational foundationalism, according to Davidson,

must be wrong. We have been trying to see it this way: a person has all his beliefs about the world – that is, all his beliefs. How can he tell if they are true, or apt to

1 Donald Davidson, "Coherence Theory of Truth and Knowledge," in Dieter Henrich, ed., *Kant oder Hegel?* (Stuttgart: Klett-Cotta, 1983), pp. 423–38. Parenthetical page references in this text will be to that essay. Compare also "Empirical Content," *Grazer Philosophische Studien*, 17/17 (1982): 471–89, where Davidson traces in detail some historical background of his theory of knowledge.
2 Richard Rorty, *Philosophy and the Mirror of Nature* (Princeton, N.J.: Princeton University Press, 1979), p. 178.

be true? Only, we have been assuming, by connecting his beliefs to the world, confronting certain of his beliefs with the deliverances of the senses one by one, or perhaps confronting the totality of his beliefs with the tribunal of experience. No such confrontation makes sense, for of course we can't get outside our skins to find out what is causing the internal happening of which we are aware. (429)

What we have shown is that it is absurd to look for a justifying ground for the totality of beliefs, something outside this totality which we can use to test or compare with our beliefs. (431)

Suppose:

(a) that for a belief to be justified is for the subject to justify it or to have justified it;

(b) that for one to justify a belief (really, successfully) is for one correctly and seriously to use considerations, reasons in its favor; and

(c) that seriously and correctly to use considerations or reasons in favor of a belief is to use (i) other things one believes with justification and (ii) their (justifiedly believed) appropriate connection with the belief targeted for justification.

These are apparently involved in Davidson's view of epistemic justification as inevitably *argumentative*. They are at least one way to make sense of his remarks, and no better way comes to mind, nor even any as good. Compare now the organon conception of justification (O), according to which a belief is justified if and only if it is obtained through appropriate application of an adequate organon. Clearly all organon justification must be argumentative justification. Perhaps the view that all epistemic justification is argumentative justification derives its currency, or some of it, from the attraction of the organon conception. In any case, it is worth noting the connection between the two, and two things bear emphasis in that connection: first, that the organon conception of justification will be indicted of vicious circularity or regress in Part I of Chapter 14; and second, that theoretical epistemology *need not* be tied to practical epistemology in the way required by the organon conception. For these facts may lead us to question the view of epistemic justification as inevitably argumentative.

Suppose, again, that to justify a belief is to reason or argue in favor of its object from premises believed with justification; and that the only way a belief can come to be justified is by the justifying of it through such argumentation or reasoning. Then it is beyond doubt that no full source of such justification for a belief can fail to include other beliefs. And if confrontation is the attempt to give such argumentative justification to a belief while leaning on no other beliefs, then confrontation is necessarily futile and indeed absurd. Certainly such argumentative justification must always be acquired coherentially if this means only that its acquisition requires appeal to other beliefs used as premises or reasons.

A crucial question yet remains open to doubt, however, and is not settled by *that* argument: the question, namely, whether *such* justification is always required for knowledge, whether it is argumentative justification that figures among the "primary conditions for knowledge" (423). For if some sort of epistemic authority can come to a belief independently of any *justifying* of it by argument from premises, and if such epistemic authority can help to make a belief knowledge even in the absence of any justifying of that belief by any argument from premises, then we might after all have a source of epistemic authority that is *neither* "confrontational" nor "coherential" (as these terms are here defined). Again: if there is a sort of epistemic justification that may accrue to a belief independently of any *justifying* of it by any reasoning on given grounds, and if such epistemic justification can help to make a belief knowledge even absent any justifying of that belief by any reasoning on given grounds, then we might after all have a foundational source of epistemic justification.

Note the caution. It would not follow that in fact there *is* such a non-confrontational but foundational source. It *would* follow, however, that such a source of justification or authority has not yet been *ruled out* by the argument advanced.

But in what *sense* could there possibly be an epistemic "source" of justification which was not somehow a process of arguing or reasoning on the basis of already justified beliefs? My answer is based on the supervenience of the epistemically evaluative. Suppose S and Twin-S live lives indistinguishable physically or psychologically, indistinguishable both intrinsically and contextually, on Earth and Twin-Earth respectively. Surely there can then be no belief of S epistemically justified without a matching belief held by Twin-S with equal epistemic justification. Epistemic justification must accordingly supervene upon or derive from physical or psychological properties of the subject of belief, properties either intrinsic or contextual.

All epistemic justification, authority, warrant, or any other epistemic status of belief hence derive from what is not epistemically evaluative. Any epistemically justified belief must have non-epistemic properties which make it thus justified, so that any other belief sharing all such properties would be equally epistemically justified. Would it not be proper and natural to speak of such properties as "sources" of justification? Not just causal sources, either, not just causes of the belief, but providers or sustainers of its epistemic status as justified. The important point now is that *argument or reasoning from something already believed*

110

with justification could not possibly serve as *such* a source of epistemic justification. For the property of a belief of its *having been supported by argument from something already believed with justification* is not a non-epistemic property, since it talks of *justification*, epistemic justification, already attained.

It may still be argued that the epistemic justification of any belief must anyhow derive from its coherence-inducing relations (of logic, say, and probability and explanation) to *other beliefs* already in place. Nothing said here so far rules this out. But now the argument in its favor cannot be the simple and apparently conclusive platitude that the argumentative justification of a belief requires appeal to other beliefs already in place. For such justification by the already justified cannot serve as a source of justification in our present sense. Since it is a justification-including source, it cannot serve as a non-epistemic source of justification. And if freed of such epistemic content, if conceived simply as argument from premises (justified or not) or reasoning from grounds (justified or not) then, far from being the *only* source of justification, it is not even clearly a sufficient source of justification at all.

The first of Davidson's arguments against foundationalism is hence inconclusive. Yes, confrontation is of course absurd if it means arguing seriously and correctly in favor of something so as to justify belief in it, *without appeal to anything already accepted or believed with justification.* What is not so obvious, however, and may in fact be false, and has yet to be given adequate support, is the assumption crucial to the attack on foundationalism: the assumption, namely, that besides justification by argument or reasoning from other beliefs, there is no alternative source of epistemic justification (or authority, warrant, etc.); that besides such *argumentative justification* there is only the absurd confrontational source of testing our target belief by comparing it with reality *neat*, unfiltered by any belief; of arguing for it without appeal to any believed premises; of reasoning to it with no reliance on any believed grounds. No argument we have yet seen rules out the possibility of a source of justification or authority *not* constituted by any reasoning or arguing *at all*, or by any testing properly so-called.

There is a second prong to Davidson's anti-foundations argument, the attack on specific foundationalist proposals. This attack is inconclusive, nor do we find here any claim to the contrary, since it is said only "to review very hastily some of the reasons for abandoning the search for a basis for knowledge outside the scope of our beliefs" (427). Even if it conclusively refutes its specific foundationalist targets, moreover, that still falls short of refuting foundationalism itself.

Coherentists aim to replace foundationalism with a positive doctrine of

111

their own. Even if what they say against foundationalism is inconclusive, moreover, we need to consider what there is to be said in favor of their alternative view.

B. THREE DEFENSES OF COHERENTISM

Foundationalism is sometimes defended by appeal to an elimination argument, as follows. What sort of (complete) account could there be of how a particular belief gets to be justified? There seem to be just three options: (a) The belief is justified by inference from other beliefs, and these in turn are severally justified by their respective inferences, whose premises are thus justified in turn, and so on *ad infinitum*. (b) The belief is justified by other beliefs, and these by others in turn, including perhaps some of the original beliefs, etc., with justification circling back, sooner or later: B might be justified by C1, . . . , Cn, where each of the C's is justified by other beliefs in turn, and so on, until at some stage we reach B itself once again. (c) The belief is justified by other beliefs, and these respectively by other beliefs yet, and so on, until we reach beliefs that are not justified by appeal to other beliefs: these then would be ultimate premises, premises that do not require further, believed premises for an inference that would provide them in turn with justification of their own. Their justification does not derive from inferential relations to other beliefs. Instead, they are self-justified, or require no justification at all, or are justified in virtue of some property or relation that involves no inference from other beliefs, nor any relation of psychological grounding or support by other beliefs, but requires only perhaps that the belief be a perceptual belief, and derive directly from the subject's pertinent sensory experience at the time.

Sometimes the circle and the infinite regress are ruled out of account by appeal to our *first* beliefs. The justification of these, we are told, cannot be due to inference from earlier beliefs, for by hypothesis there are no earlier beliefs.[3] In response, there is first Wittgenstein's observation that " . . . light dawns gradually over the whole." Our first beliefs may hence arrive as a large package with many parts intricately interrelated. Despite being first beliefs, therefore, each may arrive already tied by psychological relations to many other beliefs. And if so, why may not the justification of each derive from being thus intricately backed by inferential or grounding relations?

3 See, e.g., Anthony Quinton, "The Foundations of Knowledge," in B. Williams and
   A. Montefiore, eds., *British Analytical Philosophy* (London: Routledge & Kegan Paul,
   1966), pp. 55–86; reprinted in R.M. Chisholm and R.J. Swartz, eds., *Empirical Knowledge* (Englewood Cliffs, N.J.: Prentice Hall, 1973).

Perhaps it will be argued in response that such relations cannot be just cotemporaneous, but must hold across time: e.g., inferring is a process that takes time. But this is far from being evident. For one thing, many of the things that I believe at the moment are based on reasons that I have right now. Thus I believe right now that 456,982 is divisible by 2 without remainder, but that is only because I believe that any number whose usual expression (as a numeral in our system) ends in 2, is divisible by 2. Here I have two beliefs at the very same present moment, and yet one is based on the other, which provides my reason for believing the first. If someone insists that reasoning and inference require time, so that true inferential relations among beliefs must hold across time, we should probably just relinquish the term "inference", and use instead "rational support" or some such term as our label for a broader relation that can hold between a "supported" belief and one or more "supporting" beliefs, all at the same time.

Besides, if inference cannot be instantaneous, then it is not clear that there is any deductive inference at all. Thus if I have certain premises P1, . . . , Pn each of which I am justified in believing, and I come to see that conclusion C follows from them deductively, it does not follow that I am thereby justified in believing C. For C may be quite absurd on the face of it, or it may conflict directly with other beliefs already in place, and very well supported. The deduction of C from P1, . . . , Pn may hence fail to justify C, even if P1, . . . , Pn were severally very highly justified; instead, the deduction may succeed only in reducing P1, . . . , Pn collectively to absurdity. Only the justified acceptance of P1, . . . , Pn at the later time t – after the subject has seen the entailment of C by these premises jointly – rationally supports that subject's justified acceptance of C, at that very same time t.

Having answered the foregoing objections against the circle, we still face the demand for an explication of the concept of coherence and for some positive reasons in favor of coherentism as our account of epistemic justification.

According to radical coherentism, the basic source of epistemic justification is the internal coherence of a comprehensive body of beliefs.[4] What is coherence? In his recent book *The Structure of Empirical Knowledge*, Laurence Bonjour gives the following account of the coherence of a system of beliefs SB.

---

4 Major contributions to coherentist epistemology precede our period: e.g., the works of Sellars, Rescher, and Harman, where "our period" spans the middle to late eighties, the years covered in my "state of the art" paper (from which this discussion is drawn), "Beyond Scepticism, to the Best of our Knowledge," *Mind* 97 (1988): 153–88.

1. SB must be logically consistent.
2. SB is coherent in proportion to its degree of probabilistic consistency.
3. SB's coherence is increased in proportion to the number and strength of inferential connections among its components.
4. SB's coherence is diminished to the extent to which it is divided into inferentially isolated sub-systems.
5. SB's coherence is decreased in proportion to the presence of unexplained anomalies.

That is certainly a start on a characterization of coherence – surely an object of desire, obscure though it may be, to every epistemology, and especially so to coherentism. There is, however, a problem with this particular characterization, one that it will share with any account that makes room for deductive, inferential connections as sources of coherence; and the problem seems especially nasty for those accounts similar to the present one in placing a premium on such strong connections as sources of justification. The problem is that any two beliefs in anyone's head would seem to be deductively connected, or at least too easily connectable. Take B(p) and B(q). From B(p) the subject may easily arrive at B($q \supset p$), and from B(q) similarly he may arrive at B($p \supset q$). But then he has a direct two-way connection between his original arbitrarily selected beliefs B(p) and B(q), and it is a connection than which there is none more obvious or deductively cogent. In each case he may appeal to modus ponens, and to the premises it requires. The coherentist, of all people, is in no position to cry vicious circle! But then how are we to rule out our always available tight little circle, one which might easily be broadened at will *ad infinitum*?

A further problem concerns requirement 1: surely an isolated logical inconsistency will not spoil a body of beliefs and render it useless as a justifier of its member beliefs. This becomes particularly pressing with increasing awareness of how easy it is to uncover paradoxes just below the surface of common sense.

Coherentism is not refuted just because its central concept is less than crystal clear, however. We can appeal to coherence in giving an account of justification even if it would be desirable eventually to have a better account of coherence. In this respect the concept of coherence joins a distinguished battery of central philosophical concepts, such as explanation, causation, entailment, inference, and others.

Shelving the question of how to explicate coherence, however, we still face the demand for positive reasons in favor of coherentism, a demand that the coherentist might attempt to meet along the following lines. First

114

of all, suppose we accept the coherence of a belief B within a body of beliefs as sufficient for the epistemic justification of that belief B. Would this not enable us to bypass vexing skeptical arguments which depend on drawing a distinction between a realm to be known and a screen providing all the epistemically prior knowledge on which alone we must base any real knowledge of the realm, except only for whatever we might know a priori through armchair reflection. The coherentist rejects any such cleavage of our knowledge. For him our knowledge is constituted by a unified system of beliefs each dependent causally and epistemically on others. There is no separable foundation that underlies an entire super-structure, no screen providing our exclusive access to the realm that lies beyond. No matter where we turn in our system of beliefs, the source of our justification is to be found in adjacent, supporting beliefs, themselves dependent in turn on yet others for their own justification, until eventually we circle back to beliefs already noted and used earlier. That, then, is one reason in favor of coherentism: by enabling us to reject foundation-alist doctrines of epistemic priority, it makes possible a principled rejection of the notorious skeptical reasoning employed for instance by Descartes.

There is moreover a second notable reason in favor of coherentism, one that involves once again a prominent argument from elimination. If we rule out the infinite regress option as something beyond the capacities of limited humans, we are left with only two options: coherentism and foundationalism. So, if we are able to cast sufficient rational doubt on foundationalism, and we can defend coherentism against the objections made to it, as above, that would constitute a sufficient positive case in its favor. And this is indeed the strategy used by Laurence Bonjour in developing his version of coherentism in a recent book and in several articles.

1. Laurence Bonjour

Bonjour argues that foundationalism is unacceptable at its very core, where it explains its foundations and urges that they must be noninferentially justified. This is unacceptable, we are told, since there must be something that *makes* a foundational belief FB foundationally justified, something noninferential of course. Suppose what makes FB foundationally justified is simply that it is the taking of the given. Then, argues Bonjour, how can that fact make a believer justified in believing FB unless the believer has some idea that beliefs which are takings of the given tend to be true? Moreover, the believer must not only have a pretty good idea

115

that this is so, but must use this idea in arriving at the belief FB. Otherwise he would be accepting FB just by luck or happy accident, and such beliefs cannot count as justified. This is why Bonjour turns to coherentism. And just what is it that according to pure coherentism makes one's beliefs epistemically justified? According to such coherentism, a belief B on the part of a subject S is justified if and only if B is a member of subject S's comprehensively coherent body of beliefs. But don't we now have an objection to such coherentism just like the objection pressed by Bonjour against foundationalism? Can belief B be justified merely by its happening to be a member of such a coherent belief system, even if the subject has no knowledge of this, and does not even so much as believe it? Recall the objection to the form of foundationalism we selected as an example: a belief B cannot be foundationally justified simply in virtue of being the taking of the given, if the subject is ignorant of that fact and ignorant also of the fact that takings of the given tend to be correct and true (which we suppose to be a fact, since if it is not a fact then that itself will undercut the claim of B to be foundationally justified through being the taking of the given). Ironically, that objection to foundationalism itself fails to cohere nicely with the view which is then proposed in place of foundationalism, the view namely that a belief B can be justified simply in virtue of belonging to a sufficiently coherent system of the subject's beliefs at the time. For the subject may be ignorant of the fact that his belief is indeed a member of such a system, and may also be ignorant of the fact that such coherent systems tend to be true and correct.

Bonjour's own response to this problem is to adduce the "Doxastic Presumption," according to which one is right about the contents of one's own belief system. This is said to be a presumption required for epistemic reflection to begin, and it is nothing more than a background presumption beyond justification. Not that skepticism with regard to this presumption is unintelligible. It is quite intelligible and it cannot be ruled out by coherentist reasoning. But it is just put aside when we make the Doxastic Presumption, a presumption that needs to be made for epistemic reflection to "begin" at all. When we ask for the justification of such and such beliefs of our own, we are presupposing already that we do have such and such beliefs! If epistemic reflection ensues, it can then continue to presuppose the presumption which underlies the very question raised.[5]

There are a number of problems with this approach:

(a) Epistemic reflection does not necessarily presuppose the Doxastic Presumption. Only some epistemic reflection does so, surely. First of all

5 Laurence Bonjour, *The Structure of Empirical Knowledge* (Cambridge, Mass.: Harvard University Press, 1985), Chapter 5.

the Doxastic Presumption is not even presupposed by all epistemic reflection that begins by picking out a certain belief B – or certain beliefs B1, . . . , Bn – and then wonders what justifies the selected beliefs; it is not even presupposed by such reflection unless the selected beliefs B1, . . . , Bn are *all* of the beliefs of the subject at the time. Besides, epistemic reflection may just take the form of asking general questions such as: What is human knowledge? What is the epistemic justification involved in human knowledge? What are the conditions required for possessing such justification? It is ever possible for anyone to have knowledge? How is it possible for anyone ever to have knowledge? And so on, for quite a number of questions that can arise in epistemic reflection without requiring for their formulation that the subject presuppose anything so powerful as the Doxastic Presumption – namely, the assumption, with regard to each of that subject's beliefs, that she both has that belief and is not unjustified in thinking herself to have it.

(b) Besides, even if one presupposes that one does have a belief B in raising the question of what justifies one in accepting that belief, this does not exempt one from having to face the question of what accounts for one's justification for believing that one does have belief B, at the time. If it were that easy to exempt oneself from having to face such questions of justification, then one could deal with epistemology very comfortably. For it would be possible to exempt oneself easily from providing an account for how one becomes justified in believing that-p, for any proposition, that-p, which one might care to select. It would be easy enough to arrange that with just a bit of strategic presuming, for just the fact that one presumes something apparently suffices to exempt one from having to provide an account of how one becomes justified in believing or in presuming whatever it is that one thereby believes or presumes.

(c) But the most serious problem for the present use and defense of the Doxastic Presumption is that the reasoning employed seems quite irrelevant to the challenge before us. In order to see this more clearly it may be useful to review the dialectical situation. Bonjour argues against foundationalism that what it provides as its explanation of our justification for our allegedly basic beliefs is unacceptable. For example, we cannot accept the claim of a foundationalist, concerning our basic beliefs that allegedly amount simply to taking the given, that such beliefs are justified simply in virtue of the fact that they *are* just takings of the given. Surely, Bonjour exclaims, the subject must be aware at a minimum that such a belief is indeed a taking of the given, and must be aware further that takings of the given tend to be right. If the subject does not have even that much by way of metaperspective, then it cannot be right to call her justified in accepting the belief in question. So much for the foundationalist. And just what

117

would Bonjour's coherentist propose that we put in place of the foundationalist explanation of justification and how it arises? "Coherence, of course; it is the internal systematic coherence of a body of beliefs that makes its member beliefs justified." But Bonjour must now face his own question: Can the subject with that body of beliefs enjoy justification for her member beliefs simply because in fact they do cohere nicely? Must the subject not have some awareness of that fact and also of the fact that coherent beliefs tend to be right? But how then might she be justified in such further metabeliefs? Can it be just their own coherence within the wider body of beliefs including both her object beliefs and her metabeliefs? Bonjour rejects this sort of self-referring coherentism as vicious. But what recourse is he then left? How might he then explain how such metabeliefs can acquire justification? His response is to say that they do *not* acquire justification. What happens is that we presume ourselves to have a certain body of beliefs, and to be at least approximately right in thus presuming. On the basis of such implicit presumption, then, presumably along with a presumption that such coherence tends to go with truth, one can then provide justification to the member beliefs in one's system. But is it enough just to presume that we do have such a body of beliefs and to be approximately correct? I do not mean to suggest that we should require absolute and perfect correctness. I mean to suggest, rather, that even if it follows from what we thus presume that the member beliefs of our present body of beliefs tend to be right – and hence, for each member belief, that it is likely to be right (relative to its being in one's system) – yet that is not sufficient to render our member beliefs justified. For even on the assumption that the Presumption is true, what we base logically on it, at least implicitly, does not become *justified* simply because it is thus based logically on such a proposition assumed to be true. After all, it is not merely the *truth* of our premises that is required for our conclusion to be justified. We need to assume also that our acceptance of such premises is *justified*. Now Bonjour does emphasize that the Doxastic Presumption is not supposed to function as a premise in the account of how through coherence our object beliefs gain justification. Instead, it is supposed to function merely as an implicit presumption. But whatever distinction there may be between the way in which a premise supports or underlies a conclusion and the way in which a presumption does so, it seems equally necessary, if the supported belief is to be justified, that what supports it must be not only true but also itself justified, in whatever way may be appropriate at the level involved (whether it is the level of premises or the level of presumptions). Surely a wild and arbitrary presumption assumed to be true may enable one to reach certain conclusions which would be unattainable logically in the absence of such a presumption; and reaching our conclusions on *that* basis might ensure that they would be true conclusions, but would it be sufficient to ensure that one would be *justified* in accepting them? Surely not.

In any case Bonjour has a separate way of defending the Doxastic Presumption. The defense is not now that epistemic reflection by its very nature involves assuming that one has a certain body of beliefs, and assuming that one is right at least approximately in attributing to oneself such a body of beliefs, so that one may continue to make such a presumption as one continues to reflect epistemically, etc. That is the sort of defense that we have just considered. The new defense argues rather that even if all we obtain from our epistemic project is a conditional result, that is not devoid of value. Even if we must yield to skepticism on the question of how we could ever know that we were correct in making the Doxastic Presumption, we might still go ahead and make the Presumption, and then argue that on that condition, on the condition that we are right in making that presumption, we can see how we are justified in so much else. And this may still be an illuminating epistemic result. Of course it has already been argued that even assuming oneself correct in making the Presumption, that is not enough to enable an explanation of how one becomes justified in much else, for it seems required for such explanation that we presume not only our correctness in making the Presumption but also our justification – and it is this precisely that has been granted to be out of reach. Let that pass now, however, for even if we assume that we are justified in making the Presumption, and explain thereby how on that basis we can then be justified in so much else, it is far from clear why *such* coherentism stands out as preferable to a corresponding foundationalism. After all, the givenist foundationalist can similarly conditionalize, arguing as follows. Perhaps the fact that a belief B of ours is the taking of the given is not by itself enough to yield justification for that belief. Perhaps we need to have some awareness of the fact that B has that feature of being the taking of the given, and perhaps we must realize as well that beliefs with that feature tend to be correct. However, we might just make a Givenist Presumption – that we are correct and justified in such beliefs that are takings of the given. And we might then be able to explain on that basis how we are then also justified in much else that we believe. And this might still be an illuminating epistemic result, even if we must yield to the skeptic on the question whether we are indeed justified in our beliefs which are takings of the given. I fail to see how Bonjour's approach would enable one to discriminate in such a comparison between a sort of conditionalized coherentism and a corresponding conditionalized foundationalism. Even if one could discriminate somehow, moreover, such conditionalization would yield at best a deeply unsatisfying and thoroughly skeptical outcome of the following sort. We *would* be justified in some of our contingent beliefs about the external world, other minds, the past, and the future, *if and only if* we were justified in our Doxastic Presumption. *But we can never be justified in any such presumption*, according to Bonjour, since he grants this to follow from the stance that he adopts and makes crucial for his critique of foundationalism. The obvious conclusion of such coherentism, then, is that we can never be justified in any of our contingent beliefs about the external world, other minds, the past, and the future. Few skeptics have gone so far!

2. Donald Davidson

In discussing Davidson earlier, we found both a trivial version of coherentism and the suggestion of a more interesting version. The trivial version requires for the truth of coherentism only that confrontation be absurd, only that the justifying of a belief by arguing or reasoning inevitably involve the use of believed propositions as premises or reasons. Coherentism is then trivially undeniable. But in that case the interesting question becomes whether it is *such* justification that figures as one of the primary conditions for knowledge. Put another way, the question to face is then what can possibly serve as a non-epistemic source of epistemic justification. What can no longer serve as *such* a source is the feature of a belief of its having been epistemically justified by appeal to justified premises or reasons. For that is obviously epistemic.

We now have reason to believe that there must be some "source" of epistemic justification other than the property of a belief of its having been justified by epistemically good reasoning or argument. What now might possibly count as such a source? No longer will it do to urge that there is no answer but the internal coherence of our body of beliefs since "confrontation" is absurd. That is now insufficient, since the absurdity of "confrontation" does not rule out any source of epistemic justification that is foundational without being absurdly "confrontational." Suppose a proposed source of justification for a belief which is not just the property of its having been supported on the basis of already justified beliefs nor just the property of its cohering with a comprehensive and coherent enough body of one's own beliefs; perhaps some such source as its deriving from perception, introspection, or memory, or deriving from a reliable faculty of one's own. No reason has yet been provided to show that there can be *no* such foundational source of epistemic justification. But let us anyhow put aside the possibility of such foundationalism, and let us turn instead to coherence among one's beliefs as basic "source" of justification. Why opt for such coherence?

"What distinguishes a coherence theory," according to Davidson, recall, is "simply the claim that nothing can count as a reason for holding a belief except another belief. Its partisan rejects as unintelligible the request for a ground or source of justification of another ilk" (426).[6] Davidson joins Rorty's attack on foundationalism as involving a disastrous confusion between causation and justification. How, now, is such a charge to be supported? One might simply conceive of justification as by definition always argumentative. But such support is too insubstantial, and insufficient to the task.

Not that it's outrageous, or even unacceptable, to conceive of justification thus as necessarily the outcome of a justificatory process of providing reasons or arguments. But argument will often have premises that are "ultimate", not having been supported by argument or buttressed by reasons. No ultimate premise is *argumentatively justified*, therefore, and yet some way must be found to distinguish those that in a given context can be used by a given thinker to help justify other things from those that are there then useless for that purpose. I can argue for quite some time in favor of the proposition that at least n Fs occupy location L (for any n, F, and L you please) by simply alleging the presence there of at least $n + 1$, in support of which in turn I allege the presence of at least $n + 2$, and so on. But any such argument by any of us must eventually end, if we are all finite, and anyhow must eventually reach ultimate premises. Such ultimate premises will of course fail to be argumentatively justified. Can it be their being unbuttressed by argument that makes ineffectual any argument that hangs from them? Not obviously, since *all* ultimate premises must be equally unbuttressed and ultimate premises there must likely be for *any* complete argument that avoids vicious circularity and regress.

An argument seems viciously regressive if it requires a sequence of premises, and premises for these premises, and premises for these in turn, and so on *ad infinitum*. No human mind seems spacious enough to hold such an argument. (And even could such an argument be grasped and endorsed, that would not make one justified in holding the conclusion, as is shown by the case of the n Fs at location L.)

One incurs circularity relative to a stretch of time if within it one both relies essentially on P as a premise in arguing for Q and relies essentially on Q in arguing for P. Is such circularity vicious?

There is really no evident vice in accepting P on the basis of support that includes *in part* one's acceptance of Q while yet one accepts Q on the

6 See footnote 1.

basis of support that includes *in part* one's acceptance of P. The appearance of vice derives more from the metaphor of "support," which may just be inapt at this point, than from any intrinsic absurdity in such mutual epistemic support. Indeed, there had better be no vice or absurdity in such mutuality of support: sooner or later we find it unavoidable anyhow.

If there is no evident vice in mutuality of support, neither is it evident that such mutuality or coherence is an epistemic source of justification (much less a basic source, and least of all *the* basic source). We have seen moreover that *such* coherence does *not* have absurd "confrontation" as its only rival for being an epistemic source of justification. No longer does an argument by elimination of alternatives seem obvious, therefore, and we need some other reason to find virtue in coherence as source of justification.

According to Davidson, what we need in favor of coherence is some reason to think that any belief coherent with a total body of beliefs is likely to be true. And he has the credit of facing that need squarely and arguing ingeniously and imaginatively to fill it. His argument has two main threads, though exactly how they intertwine is not really obvious.

One thread has the leading idea that the content of a belief is determined by its causal role in such a way that given the identities and contents of our beliefs, they could not possibly be globally false, for if they were generally caused in some way other than the way they are in fact generally caused, then they would have different contents and identities, they would not be the beliefs they are, they would be about something else.

The other main thread has as its leading idea a principle of charity which requires that, to know the mind of another, one interpret him as importantly and widely in agreement with oneself. For suppose our world changed only just enough to accommodate the presence of a superinterpreter who knows all there is to know about one's physical being including one's behavioral dispositions, linguistic or not, and who is omniscient about logic, mathematics, physical science, history, geography, cosmology, etc. If one's mind would be knowable to such an interpreter but only through his charitable attribution of wide and important agreement to the two of us, then it is hard to see how one's present body of beliefs could possibly fail to be widely and importantly right.

Many questions arise about these intriguing ideas. Here I will mention only some that seem either especially salient or especially pertinent to their proposed use in epistemology.

First, even if both threads prove sound, how do they uphold the importance of coherence in epistemology? Coherence seems epistemi-

122

cally superfluous. A set of totally independent beliefs would seem to enjoy an equal presumption of truth. It is not enough to answer that there could not be any total set of largely independent beliefs. Surely that beliefs must cohere and that a total set of beliefs must be widely and importantly true does not show it to be the coherence of the beliefs that makes them justified. For there are many other properties that a total set of beliefs must also have: it must be plural, the members must be caused, the members must have effects, etc. – all this in accordance with the assumptions used by Davidson for the very argument under study. And then nothing would permit a choice between coherence and these other properties equally essential to beliefs, so as to distinguish coherence as especially pertinent to epistemology.

Second, the very double-threaded argument used to uphold the epistemic importance of coherence serves equally to uphold foundational reliability. For it shows equally that beliefs by their very nature must be reliably caused so as to be mostly true. Hence, if what it shows about coherence displays the importance of coherence to epistemology, then what it shows about reliability would seem to display the equal importance of reliability to epistemology.

Third, and finally, the form of Davidson's argument seems in fact to give a certain priority to reliability, since the way it tries to sustain coherence is by showing it to be an intellectual virtue, a reliable source of truth. By its very form the argument therefore at least suggests reliability as epistemologically most basic, inasmuch as even coherence is to be validated by reference to it.[7, 8]

3. Keith Lehrer

It has always been a main objection to coherence theories that people have the ability to spin out coherent tales bearing no relation to their surroundings and that their coherence is surely insufficient to render

---

7 This even if by arguing thus one secures the *coherence* within one's world view of the claim that coherence is reliable.
8 I do not deny the truth of Davidson's main positive conclusions nor the suggestiveness and value of his main arguments. I agree on the importance of coherence for epistemology, and I agree especially on the necessity to argue that coherence is bound to be reliable and an intellectual virtue. Indeed I have myself argued elsewhere for these same conclusions: cf. "The Coherence of Virtue and the Virtue of Coherence," in the proceedings of the naturalized epistemology conference held by the History and Philosophy of Science Department of the University of Pittsburgh in the spring of 1981, edited by Peter Machamer, in *Synthese* 64 (1985): 3–28; see Chapter 11 in this volume.

My thanks to Gerald Barnes for his commentary at the Davidson Conference, and to the Rutgers philosophical community for helpful discussion at my preconference seminar on Davidson's epistemology, based on an earlier version of this essay.

them suitable objects of belief. Keith Lehrer's radical coherentism seemed in its early stages[9] open to some such problem of detachment from reality. More recently,[10] however, Lehrer has made some important improvements. For one thing, *two* forms of justification are now recognized. *Personal* justification remains very subjective and detached from the world: one is personally justified in accepting a proposition P iff P coheres with one's *corrected* system obtained by dropping everything accepted towards epistemically unworthy goals: for example, with greed, or pride. Besides such personal justification, now we also have *verific* justification, and this requires that what one accepts cohere with what remains of the corrected acceptance system when it is purged of all *falsehood*. The world is therefore very much in "contact" with one's verific system, since determinative of its contents.

According to Lehrer's new theory:[11]

(C) P coheres with the system A of S iff $(\forall Q)[(Q$ competes with P for S on the basis of A$)|\supset.(Q$ is either beaten or neutralized for S, on the basis of A, as a competitor of P$)]$.

The important novelties lie in the notion of a proposition being beaten; that of its being neutralized, and that of two propositions competing. All of these notions are now defined in terms of the following primitive locution:[12]

(R) It is *more reasonable* for S to accept that p on the assumption that c than to accept that q on the assumption that d, on the basis of system A.

So it is clear that the sort of coherence defined by C cannot serve as a basic source of *all* normative epistemic status. Whether something is "more reasonable" than something else is itself a normatively epistemic matter. Hence the coherence defined by C cannot provide a basic explanation of the positive epistemic status enjoyed by P relative to S with system A.

However, there is still a sense in which a kind of probabilistic coherence underlies justification even under the new theory, since according to it: other things being equal, the more probable a statement is, the more reasonable one is to accept it, where probability here is conditional on one's pertinent acceptance system.

---

9 E.g., in his book *Knowledge, op. cit.*
10 E.g., in his paper "The Coherence Theory of Knowledge," *Philosophical Topics* 14 (1986): 5–27.
11 *Ibid.*, p. 11.
12 *Ibid.*, p. 9.

Four main questions about Lehrer's theory seem in order. First, it is not quite clear what the term "acceptance" amounts to. It is said to be akin to a performative term and it is said to be quite distinct from "belief" in its intension and extension. Acceptance is supposed to be more subject to our voluntary control and more explicitly conscious than belief. But does one accept at a time only that which one consciously, occurrently, and voluntarily "accepts" at that time? And what *constitutes* the accepting? Does it require an utterance of "I accept" or the conscious and deliberate issuing of some other appropriate sign? Or does it require some explicit mental act at that time? The more voluntary and conscious acceptance is required to be, the thinner our acceptance system. But the acceptance system determines what we know and with too thin an acceptance system we would know too little.

My second question concerns the sort of conditional probability that is supposed to yield knowledge. It is said to be probability conditional on the purified acceptance system. But suppose the purified acceptance system retains acceptances $A(p)$ and A(It is highly probable that one is right in $A(p)$). Suppose it is only by luck that these acceptances are retained, and suppose the acceptance system has been purged of lots and lots of falsehood including most of our higher level claims about our own reliability. Would not the proposition that p still be highly probable conditional on the acceptance system? But how plausible is it to suppose that one might thereby know or be justified? (Here we need to hear more about the fourth condition of knowledge.)

My third question concerns the lack of any requirement of mutual coherence among co-ordinate members of one's acceptance system. Can a mere helter-skelter collection of acceptances yield knowledge or even justification so long as there is "up and down" coherence? Do we not also need "sideways" coherence among the members of the system at the same doxastic level?

The fourth and final question returns to the problem of detachment. Suppose one's acceptance system can answer the three earlier questions: that is highly coherent, etc. Might it not still clash in some important sense with all one's experience at that time? And can it still yield knowledge and justification in that case?

Lehrer's views and my own have converged increasingly. We have increasingly agreed on the importance of coherence and on the need for a requirement of "objective justification." (See Chapter 1 above, and compare Lehrer's recent requirement of *verific* along with *personal* justification.) We have both also independently stressed the explanatory value of doxastic ascent, as well as the need for a distinction between reflective knowledge and animal knowledge. It is true that Chapter 10 below argues

125

extensively against a requirement of doxastic ascent, but it is a very strong requirement of doxastic ascent for justification, such that one could never be justified or at least could never be foundationally justified in a certain belief in the absence of doxastic ascent to further beliefs about that belief. Rejection of this strong requirement, because it is vicious, is compatible with appreciation of the epistemic value of doxastic ascent. The value of doxastic ascent may be appreciated, for example, in connection with an assessment of the place of coherence in epistemology. Consider the "referential origin" provided by the I/now cluster, around which so much of our referential system is organized. Replace your I and now concepts in your belief system systematically with some arbitrary S and t concepts (say, *the bearer of such and such a Social Security number* and *1 January 1990*). Such "referential origin transfer" leads to the following argument against coherentism. If your original belief system was largely coherent, then the new one will be about equally so: *unless* we require for the right sort of coherence (comprehensive enough coherence) that there be doxastic ascent, enough to provide one with an epistemic perspective on one's own body of knowledge. This requirement will suffice to meet the "referential origin transfer argument" against coherence. But of course any such requirement of doxastic ascent to an epistemic perspective will likely block infants and lower animals from the sort of knowledge made possible by such ascent. We must therefore distinguish such "reflective" knowledge from mere "animal" knowledge (and one might even acknowledge the sort of servomechanic "knowledge" we allow to thermostats and supermarket doors). Reliabilism is perhaps best understood as an account of such animal knowledge, though the generality and evil demon problems would yet need to be faced.

Still there remain the four questions for the specific way in which Lehrer develops his coherentism. The first three of these may turn out to be answerable by appeal to some overlooked features of Lehrer's theory or by technical adjustments to it. The fourth question seems more weighty, and it has long weighed on coherentism (especially as it developed in the analytic traditions, starting with Neurath, though Bradley is quite another matter on this point, and can hardly be accused of overlooking experience). So we come to the sort of view whose opposition to coherentism has long turned on its vivid awareness of experience as a crucial factor in our empirical knowledge.[13]

13 Suppose somehow experience could be brought *within* the framework whose coherence justifies its member beliefs. That would surely mitigate and might even solve coherentism's problem of detachment from experience. If it is to be more than verbal magic with "coherence," however, the proposal must come with a conception of experience suitable for allowing it a place in coherent frameworks. And that would seem to mean a

C. INTERNALIST FOUNDATIONALISM

Here there are two main forms: (a) evidentialism, and (b) criteriology.[14]

(a) Evidentialism

This is the view that there is a relation among propositions – "fitting" or "being supported" or the like – such that a proposition is justified for one iff it "fits" or "is supported by" the relevant evidence that one "has." This sort of view has long been implicit in the writings of Roderick Chisholm, and recently it has received an explicit defence by Richard Feldman and Earl Conee.[15]

So far as I can see there is nothing positively incoherent with evidentialism. One can define notions of epistemic justification in that way; and one can later add a well-groundedness requirement for knowledge: namely, that in order to know that p one must believe that p on the basis of the evidence for it that one has and which it fits. Still, an important question for this approach is that of our prospects for success in defining an appropriate relation of *fitting* among propositions without doing so by reference to what thinkers might reliably believe in various circumstances. Let me mention three possible obstacles.

First, an abstract theory of confirmation would encounter the problem of projectibility. Confirmational relations would seem to pertain not only to the forms of the relata but also to their conceptual content: blue and green would be allowed, but grue and bleen would not. Here perhaps one could try restricting allowable concepts to those apt in certain ways for reliable human use, but that of course would go beyond the abstract theory.

Second and perhaps more seriously, the theory of fitting would have to deal with the relations between experience and introspective or perceptual beliefs. Consider just the simpler problem of the relation between experi-

conception according to which experience is to a significant extent *propositional.* (Recent work toward such a conception includes Michael Pendlebury's "Perceptual Representation," *Proceedings of the Aristotelian Society* 87 (1986–7): 91–106; and my own "Experience and Intentionality," *Philosophical Topics* 14 (1986): 67–85.) But even so there will likely remain relations like that of (non-propositional) pain to the belief that one is in pain, which induce justification without being in any recognized sense relations of coherence, and simply require an outright concession to traditional foundationalism.

14 The two varieties of foundationalism to be considered are both "internalist," again, because each places the basic sources of epistemic justification *within* the mind of the believer (except of course for necessary and a priori principles, which are supposed to be internalistically accessible through thought or reflection).

15 R. Feldman and E. Conee, "Evidentialism," *Philosophical Studies* 48 (1985): 15–44.

ence and introspective beliefs. Some experiences in a certain sense "directly fit" some introspective beliefs. But not all experiences directly fit the introspective beliefs that describe them correctly. Thus my belief that at the center of my visual field there lies a white triangle against a black background would so fit the corresponding experience. But my belief that my visual field contains a 23-sided white figure against a black background would *not* directly fit that experience. If I had this last belief simply on the basis of that experience my belief might still be ill-grounded and not a candidate for knowledge.

Possibly the notion of a reliable faculty or virtue is more basic than that of *fitting*. It seems conceivable that if we ever develop a theory of fitting, it will be not a purely a priori and abstract theory prior to epistemology but rather an a posteriori theory dependent on what we are able to discover about our own epistemic competence. (This is not to say that either deductive logic or the probability calculus is thus derivative. *These* theories might yet be *invoked* in explaining reliable mechanisms or faculties.)

A third problem with evidentialism is related to the second. John Stuart Mill would often object to "intuitionist" moral theories by deploring their lists of retail intuitions with no apparent unity, thus charging them with a problem of "scatter." Suppose evidentialism stops with a scattered set of principles. For example, suppose it includes principles admitting green and blue but ruling out bleen and grue, and suppose it includes principles that allow direct introspection of triangularity but not direct introspection of octagonality or of 23-sidedness. Obviously there would then be a problem of scatter – and that does not yet consider the appropriate experience-introspection ties suitable for extraterrestrials. The problem is that if we hold the abstract level of *fitting* to be *fundamental* we may then lack the resources for greater theoretical unity.[16]

(b) Criteriology

John Pollock is an internalist foundationalist who has recognized the problem of theoretical unity. He now calls it the most serious problem a theory could face other than plain falsity. His solution is not to turn externalist or coherentist, however, but rather to deepen the criteriology

---

16 The third edition of Chisholm's *Theory of Knowledge* (Englewood Cliffs, N.J.: Prentice-Hall, 1989) recognizes such difficulties and offers solutions. Note that the problem here is a special case of the quite general problem for foundational empiricism presented in the first few pages of the Introduction to this volume. Cf. Richard Feldman, "Evidence," in *The Blackwell Companion to Epistemology*, J. Dancy and E. Sosa, eds. (Oxford: Basil Blackwell, in press).

that he has always favored. His search for deeper unity includes the following elements: (i) the notion that concepts are defined by their justification conditions; (ii) the claim that epistemic rules are rules of prima facie justification or the overriding of such justification; (iii) the view that epistemic rules are rules *by which we reason*; and (iv) the thesis that our acceptance of such rules is essentially implicit and procedural, and that it reaches consciousness only through the persistent reflection of epistemology.[17]

Pollock now uses an analogy with bicycle riding to explain the sort of unity he sees in criteriology. A bicycle rider also embodies procedural rules that he can occasionally override, and these rules are also mostly implicit and subconscious, and they have normative content as well. What unifies such rules, moreover, is simply that they specify how one rides a bike (correctly and, for the most part, actually).

I have some hesitation about the analogy between reasoning and bike riding, and it amounts roughly to this. Good bike riding has a content and meaning external to the pertinent rules. For good bike riding can be described in some such rule-external way as this: traversing space astride a bicycle propelled by one's pedalling while avoiding falls, etc. And rules like that of turning the handlebars in the direction of one's otherwise impending fall, etc., are given real and illuminating unity through their subservience to the external end of smooth riding.

But it seems otherwise with reasoning as viewed by criteriology. What is the outcome of a bit of reasoning? Usually it is some cognitive attitude with respect to one or more concepts. The problem now is that for criteriology there is an internal and necessary connection involved in *such* reasoning and *that* attitude to *those* concepts. For the concepts in question are *defined* as the concepts to which one justifiably takes *such* an attitude by *such* reasoning in *such* circumstances.[18] The unity of criteriology is not the unity of bike riding, therefore, but at most the unity of chess. The rules of chess are constitutive of that game just as for criteriology the rules of reasoning are constitutive of reasoning with *our* concepts. For criteriology there is no such thing as good reasoning with our concepts understandable apart from its rules, rules which can then be unified by their subservience to such good reasoning. For criteriology good reasoning with our concepts is defined by its rules just as chess is defined by its rules. What then *is* the unity of chess? For that is the unity

17 J. Pollock, *Contemporary Theories of Knowledge* (Totowa, N.J.: Rowman & Littlefield, 1987).
18 Digression: Can't some people systematically reason better than others in reaching the same beliefs? Surely different people may have different ways to *acquire* the same beliefs (though not *all* such ways may qualify as "reasoning")? Yet recall in this connection items (iii) and (iv) in the beginning paragraph of this section.

criteriology might hope to find in its epistemic rules. So far as I can see the unity of chess is that of an invented practice, invented and adopted because it coheres nicely and defines a challenging and amusing activity. There seems no other *point* to chess than its constituting a rule-bound activity which is an amusing challenge to beings with roughly our intelligence. But it is hard to believe that there is no better way to think of reason. It is hard to see reason as conventionally invented, nor can I see it as constituted by a set of rules held together by nothing more than their mutual adjustment for the sake of an amusing challenge to humans.[19]

D. SUMMARY

This chapter has been structured as follows:

A. *The "absurdity" of foundations*: a defense of foundationalism against an attack due to Donald Davidson.

B. *Three defenses of coherentism*: general discussion of coherentism, followed by consideration of positive proposals by three coherentists: (1) Laurence Bonjour, (2) Donald Davidson, and (3) Keith Lehrer.

C. *Internalist foundationalism*: where we return to foundationalism, and more particularly to the forms recently advanced by (1) Richard Feldman and Earl Conee and (2) John Pollock.

19 The externalism/internalism issue has appeared in the last two sections, but only partially and indirectly. For a fuller, better-focused view of it and of related questions, such as the nature of epistemic justification, see Alston's "Concepts of Epistemic Justification" and "Internalism and Externalism in Epistemology," both of which are reprinted in his *Epistemic Justification: Essays in the Theory of Knowledge* (Ithaca, N.Y.: Cornell University Press, 1989) and my "Methodology and Apt Belief," Chapter 14 in this volume. Further defense of foundationalist internalism may be found in Paul Moser's *Empirical Justification* (Dordrecht: Reidel, 1985).

8

Reliabilism and intellectual virtue

Externalism and reliabilism go back at least to the writings of Frank Ramsey early in this century.[1] The generic view has been developed in diverse ways by David Armstrong, Fred Dretske, Alvin Goldman, Robert Nozick, and Marshall Swain.[2]

A. GENERIC RELIABILISM

Generic reliabilism might be put simply as follows:

> S's belief that p at t is justified iff it is the outcome of a process of belief acquisition or retention which is reliable, or leads to a sufficiently high preponderance of true beliefs over false beliefs.

That simple statement of the view is subject to three main problems: the generality problem, the new evil-demon problem, and the meta-incoherence problem (to give it a label). Let us consider these in turn.

The generality problem for such reliabilism is that of how to avoid processes which are too specific or too generic. Thus we must avoid a process with only one output ever, or one artificially selected so that if a belief were the output of such a process it would indeed be true; for every true belief is presumably the outcome of some such too-specific processes, so that if such processes are allowed, then every true belief would result from a reliable process and would be justified. But we must also avoid processes which are too generic, such as perception (period), which surely can produce not only justified beliefs but also unjustified ones, even if perception is on the whole a reliable process of belief acquisition for normally circumstanced humans.[3]

1 Frank Ramsey, *The Foundations of Mathematics and Other Logical Essays* (London: Routledge & Kegan Paul, 1931).
2 David Armstrong, *Belief, Truth and Knowledge* (Cambridge University Press, 1973); Fred Dretske, "Conclusive Reasons," *Australasian Journal of Philosophy* 49 (1971): 1–22; Alvin Goldman, "What Is Justified Belief?" in George Pappas, ed., *Justification and Knowledge* (Dordrecht: D. Reidel, 1979); Robert Nozick, *Philosophical Explanations* (Cambridge, Mass.: Harvard University Press, 1981), chapter 3; Marshall Swain, *Reasons and Knowledge* (Ithaca, N.Y.: Cornell University Press, 1981).
3 This problem is pointed out by Goldman himself (*op. cit.*, p. 12), and is developed by

The evil-demon problem for reliabilism is not Descartes's problem, of course, but it is a relative. What if twins of ours in another possible world were given mental lives just like ours down to the most minute detail of experience or thought, etc., though they were also totally in error about the nature of their surroundings, and their perceptual and inferential processes of belief acquisition accomplished very little except to sink them more and more deeply and systematically into error? Shall we say that we are justified in our beliefs while our twins are not? They are quite wrong in their beliefs, of course, but it seems somehow very implausible to suppose that they are unjustified.[4]

The meta-incoherence problem is in a sense a mirror image of the new evil-demon problem, for it postulates not a situation where one is internally justified though externally unreliable, but a situation where one is internally unjustified though externally reliable. More specifically, it supposes that a belief (that the President is in New York) which derives from one's (reliable) clairvoyance is yet *not* justified if either (a) one has a lot of ordinary evidence against it, and none in its favor; or (b) one has a lot of evidence against one's possessing such a power of clairvoyance; or (c) one has good reason to believe that such a power could not be possessed (e.g., it might require the transmission of some influence at a speed greater than that of light); or (d) one has no evidence for or against the general possibility of the power, or of one's having it oneself, nor does one even have any evidence either for or against the proposition that one believes as a result of one's power (that the President is in New York).[5]

B. GOLDMAN'S RELIABILISMS

How might reliabilism propose to meet the problems specified? We turn first to important work by Goldman, who calls his theory "Historical Reliabilism," and has the following to say about it:

The theory of justified belief proposed here, then, is an *Historical* or *Genetic* theory. It contrasts with the dominant approach to justified belief, an approach that generates what we may call (borrowing a phrase from Robert Nozick) *Current Time-Slice* theories. A Current Time-Slice theory makes the justificational status of a belief wholly a function of what is true of the cognizer *at the*

Richard Feldman in "Reliability and Justification," *The Monist* 68 (1985): 159–74.
4 This problem is presented by Keith Lehrer and Stewart Cohen in "Justification, Truth, and Coherence," *Synthese* 55 (1983): 191–207.
5 This sort of problem is developed by Laurence Bonjour in "Externalist Theories of Empirical Knowledge," in *Midwest Studies in Philosophy, Vol. 5: Studies in Epistemology*, ed. P. French et al. (Minneapolis: University of Minnesota Press, 1980).

time of the belief. An Historical theory makes the justificational status of a belief depend on its prior history. Since my Historical theory emphasizes the reliability of the belief-generating processes, it may be called *Historical Reliabilism.*[6]

The insights of externalism are important, and Goldman has been perceptive and persistent in his attempts to formulate an appropriate and detailed theory that does them justice. His proposals have stimulated criticism, however, among them the three problems already indicated.

Having appreciated those problems, Goldman in his book[7] moves beyond Historical Reliabilism to a view we might call rule reliabilism, and, in the light of further problems,[8] has made further revisions in the more recent "Strong and Weak Justification." The earlier theory, however, had certain features designed to solve the new evil-demon problem, features absent in the revised theory. Therefore, some other solution is now required, and we do now find a new proposal.

Under the revised approach, we now distinguish between two sorts of justification:

A belief is *strongly justified* if and only if it is well formed, in the sense of being formed by means of a process that is truth-conducive in the possible world in which it is produced, or the like.

A belief is *weakly justified* if and only if it is blameless though ill-formed, in the sense of being produced by an unreliable cognitive process which the believer does not believe to be unreliable, and whose unreliability the believer has no available way of determining.[9]

Notice, however, that it is at best in a *very* weak sense that a subject with a "weakly justified" belief is thereby "blameless." For it is not even precluded that the subject take that belief to be very ill-formed, so long as he is in error about the cognitive process that produces it. That is to say, S might hold B, and believe B to be an output of P, and hold P to be an epistemically unreliable process, while in fact it is not P but the equally unreliable P' that produces B. In this case S's belief B would be weakly justified, so long as S did not believe P' to be unreliable, and had no available means of determining its unreliability. But it seems at best extremely strained to hold S epistemically "blameless" with regard to

6 See Goldman, "What Is Justified Belief?" pp. 13–14.
7 Alvin Goldman, *Epistemology and Cognition* (Cambridge, Mass.: Harvard University Press, 1986); *idem.*, "Strong and Weak Justification," in *Philosophical Perspectives, Vol. 2: Epistemology (1988)*: 51–71.
8 Some of these are pointed out in my "Beyond Scepticism, to the Best of our Knowledge," *Mind* 97 (1988): 153–88.
9 Goldman, "Strong and Weak Justification," p. 56.

holding B in such circumstances, where S takes B to derive from a process P so unreliable, let us suppose, as to be epistemically vicious.

The following definition may perhaps give us a closer approach to epistemic blamelessness.

> A belief is *weakly justified (in the modified sense)* if and only if it is blameless though ill-formed, in the sense of being produced by an unreliable cognitive process while the believer neither takes it to be thus ill-formed nor has any available way of determining it to be ill-formed.

With these concepts, the Historical Reliabilist now has at least the beginnings of an answer both for the evil-demon problem and for the meta-incoherence problem. About the evil demon's victims, those hapless twins of ours, we can now say that though their beliefs are very ill-formed – and are no knowledge even if by luck they, some of them, happen to be true – still there is a sense in which they are justified, as justified as our corresponding beliefs, which are indistinguishable from theirs so far as concerns only the "insides" of our respective subjectivities. For we may now see their beliefs to be weakly justified, in the modified sense defined above.[10]

About the meta-incoherence cases, moreover, we can similarly argue that, in some of them at least, the unjustified protagonist with the wrong (or lacking) perspective on his own well-formed (clairvoyant) belief can be seen to be indeed unjustified, for he can be seen as subjectively unjustified through lack of an appropriate perspective on his belief: either because he positively takes the belief to be ill-formed, or because he "ought" to take it to be ill-formed given his total picture of things, and given the cognitive processes available to him.

Consider now the following definition:

> A belief is *meta-justified* if and only if the believer does place it in appropriate perspective, at least in the minimal sense that the believer neither takes it to be ill-formed nor has any available way of determining it to be ill-formed.

Then any belief that is weakly justified (again, sticking to the unmodified sense) will be meta-justified, but there can be meta-justified beliefs which are not weakly justified. Moreover, no strongly justified belief will be weakly justified, but a strongly justified belief can be meta-justified. Indeed one would wish one's beliefs to be not only strongly justified

---

10 I will use the modified sense in what follows because it seems clearly better as an approach to blamelessness; but the substance of the critique to follow would apply also to the unmodified sense of weakly justified belief.

but also meta-justified. And what one shares with the victim of the evil demon is of course not weak justification. For if, as we suppose, our own beliefs are strongly justified, then our own beliefs are not weakly justified. What one shares with the evil demon's victim is rather meta-justification. The victim's beliefs and our beliefs are equally meta-justified.

Does such meta-justification – embedded thus in weak justification – enable answers both for the new evil-demon problem and for the problem of meta-incoherence? Does the victim of the evil demon share with us meta-justification, unlike the meta-incoherent? The notion of weak justification does seem useful as far as it goes, as is the allied notion of meta-justification, but we need to go a bit deeper,[11] which may be seen as follows.

C. GOING DEEPER

Beliefs are states of a subject, which need not be occurrent or conscious, but may be retained even by someone asleep or unconscious, and may also be acquired unconsciously and undeliberately, as are acquired our initial beliefs, presumably, whether innate or not, especially if deliberation takes time. Consider now a normal human with an ordinary set of beliefs normally acquired through sensory experience from ordinary interaction with a surrounding physical world. And suppose a victim in whom evil demons (perhaps infinitely many) inplant beliefs in the following way. The demons cast dice, or use some other more complex randomizer, and choose which beliefs to inplant at random and in ignorance of what the other demons are doing. Yet, by amazing coincidence, the victim's total set of beliefs is identical to that of our normal human. Now let's suppose that the victim has a beautifully coherent and comprehensive set of beliefs, complete with an epistemic perspective on his object-level beliefs. We may suppose that the victim has meta-justification for his object-level beliefs (e.g., for his belief that there is a fire before him at the moment), at least in the minimal sense defined above: he does not believe such beliefs to derive from unreliable processes, nor has he any available means of determining that they do. Indeed, we may suppose that he has an even stronger form of meta-justification, as follows:

S has meta-justification, in the stronger sense, for believing that p iff (a) S has weaker meta-justification for so believing, and (b) S has

11 Though, actually, it is not really clear how these notions will deal with part (d) of the problem of meta-incoherence: cf. Goldman, *Epistemology and Cognition*, pp. 111–12.

meta-beliefs which positively attribute his object beliefs in every case to some faculty or virtue for arriving at such beliefs in such circumstances, and further meta-beliefs which explain how such a faculty or virtue was acquired, and how such a faculty or virtue, thus acquired, is bound to be reliable in the circumstances as he views them at the time.

And the victim might even be supposed to have a similar meta-meta-perspective, and a similar meta-meta-meta-perspective, and so on, for many more levels of ascent than any human would normally climb. So everything would be brilliantly in order as far as such meta-reasoning is concerned, meta-reasoning supposed flawlessly coherent and comprehensive. Would it follow that the victim was internally and subjectively justified in every reasonable sense or respect? Not necessarily, or so I will now try to show.

Suppose the victim has much sensory experience, but that all of this experience is wildly at odds with his beliefs. Thus he believes he has a splitting headache, but he has no headache at all; he believes he has a cubical piece of black coal before him, while his visual experience is as if he had a white and round snowball before him. And so on. Surely there is then something internally and subjectively wrong with this victim, something "epistemically blameworthy." This despite his beliefs being weakly justified, in the sense defined by Goldman, and despite his beliefs being meta-justified in the weaker and stronger senses indicated above.

Cartesians and internalists (broadly speaking) should find our victim to be quite conceivable. More naturalistic philosophers may well have their doubts, however, about the possibility of a subject whose "experience" and "beliefs" would be so radically divergent. For these there is a different parable. Take our victim to be a human, and suppose that the demon damages the victim's nervous system in such a way that the physical inputs to the system have to pass randomizing gates before the energy transmitted is transformed into any belief. Is there not something internally wrong with this victim as well, even though his beliefs may be supposed weakly and meta-justified, as above?

It may be replied that the "internal" here is not internal in the right sense. What is internal in the right sense must remain restricted to the subjectivity of the subject, to that which pertains to the subject's psychology; it must not go outside of that, even to the physiological conditions holding in the subject's body; or at least it must not do so under the aspect of the physiological, even if in the end it is the physiological (or something physical anyhow) that "realizes" everything mental and psychological.

Even if we accept that objection, however, a very similar difficulty yet remains for the conception of the blameless as the weakly justified or meta-justified (in either the weaker or the stronger sense). For it may be that the connections among the experiences and beliefs of the victim are purely random, as in the example above. True, in that example the randomness derives from the randomizing behavior of the demons involved. But there is no reason why the randomizing may not be brought inside. Thus, given a set of experiences or beliefs, there may be many alternative further beliefs that might be added by the subject, and there may be no rational mechanism that selects only one to be added. It may be rather that one of the many alternatives pops in at random: thus it is a radically random matter which alternative further belief is added in any specific case. Our evil demon's victim, though damaged internally in that way, so that his inner mental processes are largely random, may still by amazing coincidence acquire a coherent and comprehensive system of beliefs that makes him weakly justified and even meta-justified, in both the weaker and stronger senses indicated above. Yet is there not something still defective in such a victim, something that would preclude our holding him to be indiscernible from us in all internal respects of epistemic relevance?

Consider again the project of defining a notion of weak justification, however, a notion applicable to evil-demon victims in accordance with our intuitions; or that of defining a notion of meta-justification as above, one applicable equally to the victims and to ourselves in our normal beliefs. These projects may well be thought safe from the fact that a victim might be internally defective in ways that go beyond any matter of weak or meta-justification. Fair enough. But then of course we might have introduced a notion of superweak justification, and provided sufficient conditions for it as follows:

> S is superweakly justified in a certain belief if (1) the cognitive process that produces the belief is unreliable, but (2) S has not acquired that belief as a result of a deliberate policy of acquiring false beliefs (a policy adopted perhaps at the behest of a cruel master, or out of a deep need for epistemic self-abasement).

Someone may propose that a similarity between the victim of the evil demon on one side and ourselves on the other is that we all are superweakly justified in our object-level beliefs in fires and the like. And this is fair and true enough. But it just does not go very far, not far enough. There is much else that is epistemically significant to the comparison between the victim and ourselves, much else that is left out of account by the mere notion of superweak justification. Perhaps part of what is left out is what the notion of weak justification would enable us to capture,

137

and perhaps the notion of meta-justification, especially its stronger variant, would enable us to do even better. Even these stronger notions fall short of what is needed for fuller illumination, however, as I have tried to show above through the victims of randomization, whether demon-derived or internally derived. In order to deal with the new evil-demon problem and with the problem of meta-incoherence we need a stronger notion than either that of the weakly justified or that of the meta-justified, a stronger notion of the internally or subjectively justified.

D. A STRONGER NOTION OF THE "INTERNALLY JUSTIFIED": INTELLECTUAL VIRTUE

Let us define an intellectual virtue or faculty as a competence in virtue of which one would mostly attain the truth and avoid error in a certain field of propositions F, when in certain conditions C. Subject S believes proposition P at time t out of intellectual virtue only if there is a field of propositions F, and there are conditions C, such that: (a) P is in F; (b) S is in C with respect to P; and (c) S would most likely be right if S believed a proposition X in field F when in conditions C with respect to X. Unlike Historical Reliabilism, this view does not require that there be a cognitive process leading to a belief in order for that belief to enjoy the strong justification required for constituting knowledge. Which is all to the good, since requiring such a process makes it hard to explain the justification for that paradigm of knowledge, the Cartesian cogito. There is a truth-conducive "faculty" through which everyone grasps their own existence at the moment of grasping. Indeed, what Descartes noticed about this faculty is its infallible reliability. But this requires that the existence which is grasped at a time t be existence at that very moment t. Grasp of earlier existence, no matter how near to the present, requires not the infallible cogito faculty, but a fallible faculty of memory. If we are to grant the cogito its due measure of justification, and to explain its exceptional epistemic status, we must allow faculties which operate instantaneously in the sense that the outcome belief is about the very moment of believing, and the conditions C are conditions about what obtains at that very moment – where we need place no necessary and general requirements about what went before.

By contrast with Historical Reliabilism, let us now work with intellectual virtues or faculties, defining their presence in a subject S by requiring

> that, concerning propositions X in field F, once S were in conditions C with respect to X, S would most likely attain the truth and avoid error.

138

In fact a faculty or virtue would normally be a fairly stable disposition on the part of a subject *relative to an environment*. Being in conditions C with respect to proposition X would range from just being conscious and entertaining X – as in the case of "I think" or "I am" – to seeing an object O in good light at a favorable angle and distance, and without obstruction, etc. – as in "This before me is white and round." There is no restriction here to processes or to the internal. The conditions C and the field F may have much to do with the environment external to the subject: thus a moment ago we spoke of a C that involved seeing an external object in good light at a certain distance, etc. – all of which involves factors external to the subject.

Normally, we could hope to attain a conception of C and F which at best and at its most explicit will still have to rely heavily on the assumed nature of the subject and the assumed character of the environment. Thus it may appear to you that there is a round and white object before you and you may have reason to think that in conditions C (i.e., for middle-sized objects in daylight, at arm's length) you would likely be right concerning propositions in field F (about their shapes and colors). But of course there are underlying reasons why you would most likely be right about such questions concerning such objects so placed. And these underlying reasons have to do with yourself and your intrinsic properties, largely your eyes and brain and nervous system; and they have to do also with the medium and the environment more generally, and its contents and properties at the time. A fuller, more explicit account of what is involved in having an intellectual virtue or faculty is therefore this:

> Because subject S has a certain inner nature (I) and is placed in a certain environment (E), S would most likely be right on any proposition X in field F relative to which S stood in conditions C. S might be a human; I might involve possession of good eyes and a good nervous system including a brain in good order; E might include the surface of the earth with its relevant properties, within the parameters of variation experienced by humans over the centuries, or anyhow by subject S within his or her lifetime or within a certain more recent stretch of it; F might be a field of propositions specifying the colors or shapes of an object before S up to a certain level of determination and complexity (say greenness and squareness, but not chartreuseness or chiliagonicity); and C might be the conditions of S's seeing such an object in good light at arm's length and without obstructions.

If S believes a proposition X in field F, about the shape of a facing surface before him, and X is false, things might have gone wrong at interestingly different points. Thus the medium might have gone wrong unknown to the subject, and perhaps even unknowably to the subject; or something within the subject might have changed significantly: thus the lenses in the eyes of the subject might have become distorted, or the optic nerve might have become defective in ways important to shape recognition. If what goes wrong lies in the environment, that might prevent the subject from knowing what he believes, even if his belief were true, but there is a sense in which the subject would remain subjectively justified or anyhow virtuous in so believing. It is this sense of internal virtue that seems most significant for dealing with the new evil-demon argument and with the meta-incoherence objection. Weak justification and meta-justification are just two factors that bear on internal value, but there are others surely, as the earlier examples were designed to show – examples in which the experience/belief relation goes awry, or in which a randomizer gate intervenes. Can something more positive be said in explication of such internal intellectual virtue?

Intellectual virtue is something that resides in a subject, something relative to an environment – though in the limiting case, the environment may be null, as perhaps when one engages in armchair reflection and thus comes to justified belief.

> A subject S's intellectual virtue V relative to an "environment" E may be defined as S's disposition to believe correctly propositions in a field F relative to which S stands in conditions C, in "environment" E.

It bears emphasis first of all that to be in a certain "environment" is *not* just a matter of having a certain spatio-temporal location, but is more a matter of having a complex set of properties, only some of which will be spatial or temporal. Secondly, we are interested of course in non-vacuous virtues, virtues which are not possessed simply because the subject would never be in conditions C relative to the propositions in F, or the like, though there may be no harm in allowing vacuous virtues to stand as trivial, uninteresting special cases.

Notice now that, so defined, for S to have a virtue V relative to an environment E at a time t, S does not have to be *in* E at t (i.e., S does not need to have the properties required). Further, suppose that, while outside environment E and while not in conditions C with respect to a proposition X in F, S still retains the virtue involved, *relative to E*, because the following ECF conditional remains true of S:

> (ECF) that if in E and in C relative to X in F, then S would most likely be right in his belief or disbelief of X.

If S does so retain that virtue in that way, it can only be due to some components or aspects of S's intrinsic nature I, for it is S's possessing I together with being in E and in C with respect to X in F that fully explains and gives rise to the relevant disposition on the part of S, namely the disposition to believe correctly and avoid error regarding X in F, when so characterized and circumstanced.

We may now distinguish between (a) possession of the virtue (relative to E) in the sense of possession of the disposition, i.e., in the sense that the appropriate complex and general conditional (ECF) indicated above is true of the subject with the virtue, and (b) possession of a certain ground or basis of the virtue, in the sense of possessing an inner nature I from which the truth of the ECF conditional derives in turn. Of course one and the same virtue might have several different alternative possible grounds or bases. Thus the disposition to roll down an incline if free at its top with a certain orientation, in a certain environment (gravity, etc.), may be grounded in the sphericity and rigidity of an object, or alternatively it may be grounded in its cylindricality and rigidity. Either way, the conditional will obtain and the object will have the relevant disposition to roll. Similarly, Earthians and Martians may both be endowed with sight, in the sense of having the ability to tell colors and shapes, etc., though the principles of the operation of Earthian sight may differ widely from the principles that apply to Martians, which would or might presumably derive from a difference in the inner structure of the two species of being.

What now makes a disposition (and the underlying inner structure or nature that grounds it) an intellectual virtue? If we view such a disposition as defined by a C-F pair, then a being might have the disposition to be right with respect to propositions in field F when in conditions C with respect to them, relative to one environment E but not relative to another environment E'. Such virtues, then, i.e., such C-F dispositions, might be virtuous only relative to an environment E and not relative to a different environment E'. And what makes such a disposition a virtue relative to an environment E seems now as obvious as it is that having the truth is an epistemic desideratum, and that being so constituted that one would most likely attain the truth in a certain field in a certain environment, when in certain conditions *vis-à-vis* propositions in that field, is so far as it goes an epistemic desideratum, an intellectual virtue.

What makes a subject intellectually virtuous? What makes her inner nature meritorious? Surely we can't require that a being have all merit and virtue before it can have any. Consider then a subject who has a minimal virtue of responding, thermometer-like, to environing food, and suppose him to have the minimal complexity and sophistication required for having beliefs at all – so that he is not literally just a thermometer or the like. Yet we suppose him further to have no way of relating what he senses, and his sensing of it, to a wider view of things that will explain it all, that will enable him perhaps to make related predictions and exercise related control. No, this ability is a relatively isolated phenomenon to which the subject yields with infant-like, unselfconscious simplicity. Suppose indeed the subject is just an infant or a higher animal. Can we allow that he knows of the presence of food when he has a correct belief to that effect? Well, the subject may of course have reliable belief that there is something edible there, without having a belief as reliable as that of a normal, well-informed adult, with some knowledge of food composition, basic nutrition, basic perception, etc., and who can at least implicitly interrelate these matters for a relatively much more coherent and complete view of the matter and related matters. Edibility can be a fairly complex matter, and how we have perceptual access to that property can also be rather involved, and the more one knows about the various factors whose interrelation yields the perceptible edibility of something before one, presumably the more reliable one's access to that all-important property.

Here then is one proposal on what makes one's belief that-p a result of enough virtue to make one internally justified in that belief. First of all we need to relativize to an assumed environment, which need not be the environment that the believer actually is in. What is required for a subject S to believe that-p out of sufficient virtue relative to environment E is that the proposition that-p be in a field F and that S be in conditions C with respect to that proposition, such that S would not be in C with respect to a proposition in F while in environment E, without S being most likely to believe correctly with regard to that proposition; and further that by comparison with epistemic group G, S is not grossly defective in ability to detect thus the truth in field F; i.e., it cannot be that S would have, by comparison with G:

(a) only a relatively very low probability of success,
(b) in a relatively very restricted class F,
(c) in a very restricted environment E,
(d) in conditions C that are relatively infrequent,

where all this relativity holds with respect to fellow members of G and to their normal environment and circumstances. (There is of course some variation from context to context as to what the relevant group might be when one engages in discussion of whether or not some subject knows something or is at least justified in believing it. But normally a certain group will stand out, with humanity being the default value.)

142

E. INTELLECTUAL VIRTUE APPLIED

Consider now again the new evil-demon problem and the problem of meta-incoherence. The crucial question in each case seems to be that of the internal justification of the subject, and this in turn seems not a matter of his superweak or weak or meta justification, so much as a matter of the virtue and total internal justification of that subject relative to an assumed group G and environment E, which absent any sign to the contrary one would take to be the group of humans in a normal human environment for the sort of question under consideration. Given these assumptions, the victim of the evil demon is virtuous and internally justified in every relevant respect, and not just in the respects of enjoying superweak, weak, and meta justification; for the victim is supposed to be just like an arbitrarily selected normal human in all cognitively relevant internal respects. Therefore, the internal structure and goings on in the victim must be at least up to par, in respect of how virtuous all of that internal nature makes the victim, relative to a normal one of us in our usual environment for considering whether we have a fire before us or the like. For those inclined towards mentalism or towards some broadly Cartesian view of the self and her mental life, this means at a minimum that the experience-belief mechanisms must not be random, but must rather be systematically truth-conducive, and that the subject must attain some minimum of coherent perspective on her own situation in the relevant environment, and on her modes of reliable access to information about that environment. Consider next those inclined towards naturalism, who hold the person to be either just a physical organism, or some physical part of an organism, or to be anyhow constituted essentially by some such physical entity; for these it would be required that the relevant physical being identical with or constitutive of the subject, in the situation in question, must not be defective in cognitively relevant internal respects; which would mean, among other things, that the subject would acquire beliefs about the colors or shapes of facing surfaces only under appropriate prompting at the relevant surfaces of the relevant visual organs (and not, e.g., through direct manipulation of the brain by some internal randomizing device).[12]

We have appealed to an intuitive distinction between what is intrinsic or internal to a subject or being, and what is extrinsic or external. Now when a subject receives certain inputs and emits as output a certain belief or a certain choice, that belief or choice can be defective either in virtue of

12 As for the generality problem, my own proposed solution appears in Chapter 16 of this volume.

an internal factor or in virtue of an external factor (or, of course, both). That is to say, it may be that everything inner, intrinsic, or internal to the subject operates flawlessly and indeed brilliantly, but that something goes awry – with the belief, which turns out to be false, or with the choice, which turns out to be disastrous – because of some factor that, with respect to that subject, is outer, extrinsic, or external.[13]

In terms of that distinction, the victim of the demon may be seen to be internally justified, just as internally justified as we are, whereas the meta-incoherent are internally unjustified, unlike us.

My proposal is that justification is relative to environment. Relative to our actual environment A, our automatic experience-belief mechanisms count as virtues that yield much truth and justification. Of course relative to the demonic environment D such mechanisms are not virtuous and yield neither truth nor justification. It follows that relative to D the demon's victims are not justified, and yet *relative to A their beliefs are justified*. Thus may we fit our surface intuitions about such victims: that they lack knowledge but not justification.

In fact, a fuller account should distinguish between "justification" and "aptness"[14] as follows:

(a) The "justification" of a belief B requires that B have a basis in its inference or coherence relations to other beliefs in the believer's mind – as in the "justification" of a belief derived from deeper principles, and thus "justified," or the "justification" of a belief adopted through cognizance of its according with the subject's principles, including principles as to what beliefs are permissible in the circumstances as viewed by that subject.

(b) The "aptness" of a belief B relative to an environment E requires that B derive from what relative to E is an intellectual virtue, i.e., a way of arriving at belief that yields an appropriate preponderance of truth over error (in the field of propositions in question, in the sort of context involved).

As far as I can see, however, the basic points would remain within the more complex picture as well. And note that "justification" itself would

---

13 This sort of distinction between the internal virtue of a subject and his or her (favorable or unfavorable) circumstances is drawn in "How Do You Know?" – Chapter 2 in this volume. There knowledge is relativized to epistemic community, though not in a way that imports any subjectivism or conventionalism, and consequences are drawn for the circumstances within which praise or blame is appropriate (see especially the first part of Section II).

14 For this sort of distinction, see, e.g., "Methodology and Apt Belief," Chapter 14 in this volume. The more generic distinction between external and internal justification may be found in "The Analysis of 'Knowledge That *P*'," Chapter 1 in this volume.

then amount to a sort of inner coherence, something that the demon's victims can obviously have despite their cognitively hostile environment, but also something that will earn them praise relative to that environment only if it is not just an inner drive for greater and greater explanatory comprehensiveness, a drive which leads nowhere but to a more and more complex tissue of falsehoods. If we believe our world not to be such a world, then we can say that, relative to our actual environment A, "justification" as inner coherence earns its honorific status, and is an intellectual virtue, dear to the scientist, the philosopher, and the detective. Relative to the demon's D, therefore, the victim's belief may be inapt and even unjustified – if "justification" is essentially honorific – or if "justified" simply because coherent then, relative to D, that justification may yet have little or no cognitive worth. Even so, relative to our environment A, the beliefs of the demon's victim may still be both apt and valuably justified through their inner coherence.

The epistemology defended in this volume – virtue perspectivism – is distinguished from generic reliabilism in three main respects:

(a) Virtue perspectivism requires not just any reliable mechanism of belief acquisition for belief that can qualify as knowledge; it requires the belief to derive from an intellectual virtue or faculty (a notion defined more fully in Chapter 16).

(b) Virtue perspectivism distinguishes between aptness and justification of belief, where a belief is apt if it derives from a faculty or virtue, but is justified only if it fits coherently within the epistemic perspective of the believer – perhaps by being connected to adequate reasons in the mind of the believer in such a way that the believer follows adequate or even impeccable intellectual procedure (see Chapter 14). This distinction is used as one way to deal with the new evil-demon problem. (See Chapter 16, Section D.)

(c) Virtue perspectivism distinguishes between animal and reflective knowledge. For animal knowledge one needs only belief that is apt and derives from an intellectual virtue or faculty. By contrast, reflective knowledge always requires belief that not only is apt but also has a kind of justification, since it must be belief that fits coherently within the epistemic perspective of the believer (see Chapter 13, Section IX). This distinction is used earlier in this chapter to deal with the metaincoherence problem, and it also opens the way to a solution for the generality problem. (See Chapter 16, Section D.)

PART III

Intellectual virtue and epistemic perspective: a view presented

9

The foundations of foundationalism

There is a controversy in contemporary philosophy over the question whether or not knowledge must have a foundation.[1] On one side are the foundationalists, who do accept the metaphor and find the foundation in sensory experience or the like. The coherentists, on the other side, reject the foundations metaphor and consider our body of knowledge a coherent whole floating free of any foundations. This controversy grew rapidly with the rise of idealism many years ago, and it is prominent today not only in epistemology proper but also in philosophy of science and even in ethics.

The discussion of this issue has been lamentably hampered by confusion and misunderstanding, and in this neither side is wholly innocent. The reflections that follow are not meant to settle the controversy, but only to help us understand it more clearly.

I

Foundationalism is often defended as the only acceptable alternative to an infinite regress of justification. It is now in fashion to reply that an infinite regress is not objectionable so long as we do *not* require that all members of the regress be actually held, actually justified beliefs, but only that each member be justifiable by reference to its successor. Actual justification will proceed only so far as the occasion demands, but it could always proceed further, if further doubts were pressed (as we are told by Wittgenstein, e.g., early in the *Blue Book*). Although a helpful observation, that surely will not render the regress palatable to those who would not swallow it in the first place. For they will still be puzzled as to how there could be an infinite regress of the justifiable. Their puzzlement needs to be spelled out, however, for though it has some initial plausibility, neither its content nor its justification is immediately obvious.

Any satisfactory treatment of the problem must focus on the linking relation of justification chains. Let us consider some possibilities. Suppose the linking relation is defined as follows:

1 The ideas in this paper were first presented in a seminar at the University of Texas, and the paper was delivered at a Rice University Conference on Foundationalism and Non-foundationalism.

149

(J1) P justifies (would justify) Q iff that P is justified is sufficient for Q to be justified (iff if P were justified that would be sufficient for Q to be justified, where for simplicity we abstract from subject and time).

On this first conception of the linking justification relation an infinite regress seems quite possible. Consider the following infinite sequence σ:

(P1) That there is at least one real number in the interval (0–1)
(P2) That there are at least two real numbers in the interval (0–1)

.
.
.
.

It seems plausible that, on conception (J1), P2 justifies P1, P3 justifies P2, and so on *ad infinitum*. The whole infinite chain of beliefs might even be held by some believers, perhaps by all of us, given that the beliefs involved can be dispositional. What is more, this infinite regress may even consist wholly of *justified* beliefs.

Those who reject an infinite regress of justification perhaps have in mind not a sufficiency relation of justification such as (J1) but rather a dependence relation such as the following: (J2) P depends on Q (for its justification) iff P would not be justified if Q were not justified.

But here again it is not at all obvious that an infinite chain is unacceptable. In fact, the very chain about the real numbers between 0 and 1 is a real possibility. May not the justification of P_i depend on the justification of P_{i+1}, for all i, in the sense of (J2)? Presumably someone S may be such that for each link of the chain in question he is justified in believing it because he is justified in believing the proposition I: that there is a non-denumerable infinity of real numbers in the (0–1) interval. Thus the whole chain may well be an all-or-nothing matter for S, in the sense that S is justified in believing either all the members or none. If so, then of course in the sense of J2 his justification for believing any of the members depends on his justification for believing any of the others, and so there is the regress.

In response to these objections the opponent of the infinite regress of justification might attempt to introduce some further, more complex linking relation, so as to isolate the kind of justification chain which according to his intuition could not possibly be infinite. That seems to me unnecessary, however, for the roots of the anti-regress intuition may be brought to light without need of any more elaborate justification relation than the simple (J1).

150

II

The foundationalism controversy at this time can be clarified by a distinction between "formal foundationalism" and "substantive foundationalism." Substantive foundationalism is opposed to coherentism but formal foundationalism is opposed not to coherentism but to what I shall label (epistemic) "pessimism."

Formal foundationalism may be held with respect to the study of normative or evaluative principles of any sort. For instance, it may be held in ethics as well as in epistemology. Formal foundationalism in ethics tries to fix the goodness of events or states, or the rightness of actions, perhaps recursively. Thus a simple utilitarian theory might say that

    (i) every event of someone undergoing pleasure is good,
    (ii) every event that causes a good event is good, and
    (iii) every event that is good is so in virtue of (i) or (ii).

(This is of course absurdly simple-minded but it will serve as an example of a foundationalist ethical theory.)

Analogously, formal foundationalism in epistemology would say that

    (i) every belief with a certain non-epistemic property F is justified,
    (ii) if a belief bears relation R to a set of justified beliefs then it is itself justified, and
    (iii) every belief that is justified is so in virtue of (i) or (ii).

There are various familiar candidates for the role of property F or of relation R. Thus property F may be indubitability or infallibility of belief, and relation R may hold between a belief B and a set α of further beliefs when B is deductively based on α. But these are only some examples.

Formal foundationalism is reminiscent of the recursive definition of the natural numbers (N):

    (i) 1 is an N.
    (ii) *If* x is an N, *then* if y is the successor of x, y is an N.
    (iii) Whatever is an N is so simply in virtue of (i) and (ii) above.

What a recursive definition tries to do may be thought of as the specification of a class. Thus:

The class of natural numbers is the smallest class α such that:

    (i) $1 \in \alpha$, and
    (ii) if $x \in \alpha$, then if y is the successor of x then $y \in \alpha$.

More generally, a recursive definition picks out as a basis a class of elements, and it may do so by specifying a property that they alone have in common. Thus a recursive definition of the class of entities that have property F may take the following form:

(D) The class of entities that have F is the smallest class α such that:
(i) (x) $(x$ has G only if $x \in \alpha)$; and
(ii) *if* $(x_1 \in \alpha)$ & . . . & $(x_n \in \alpha)$, and R $(x_1, \ldots, x_n, y)$, *then* $y \in \alpha$.

Call G the *basis* (the basis property), and R the *generator* (or generating relation). The formal foundationalist now has a twofold task. For F = the property of being a justified belief, he must identify an appropriate basis (or basis property) G and an appropriate generator (or generating relation) R. If such an account is to be illuminating, however, there must be restrictions on the basis G. Thus it cannot be allowed that G = F. And there must be similar restrictions on the generator R.

Formal foundationalism in epistemology holds that the notion of epistemic justification or warrant is recursively definable in terms of a necessary truth with the form of D above, using a non-epistemic basis and a non-epistemic generator.

Is there an alternative to foundationalism thus understood? If there is a class of justified beliefs at all, must it be specifiable in some illuminating way, at least recursively, or can it just be the class of justified beliefs and that's that? There is no obvious reason to think that the class of blue things must be recursively specifiable in terms of a basis and a generator that are color-neutral. Why should we think that the class of justified beliefs must be recursively specifiable in terms of a basis and a generator that are epistemically neutral?

So far as I can see the main reason in favor of formal foundationalism – antecedent to an actual, compelling foundationalist theory – is the apparently supervenient or consequential character of the evaluative generally and of epistemic justification in particular. For example, an apple may be a good apple in virtue of certain of its non-evaluative properties: in virtue, let us say, of being sweet, juicy, large, etc. If so, then its evaluative property of being a good apple "supervenes" upon its complex of non-evaluative properties that includes being sweet, juicy, large, etc. And this means that any sweet, juicy, large, etc., apple would also be a good apple. This example introduces the concept of the "supervenient" to be defined in what follows. According to the doctrine of supervenience, evaluative and normative properties always supervene on non-evaluative, non-normative properties.

An acceptable formal foundationalist theory would specify a particular non-epistemic basis and generator, which would give more precise content to the doctrine of supervenience or consequentialism, and would fulfill its promise. For such a formal foundationalism would assure us that for every case of a justified belief, its being justified is supervenient on a set of non-epistemic facts involving only the basis property of the recursion and its generating relation. (And note that the very same defense can be given for foundationalism in ethics, where, of course, utilitarianism is only one example of such foundationalism.)

It should be noted that formal foundationalism does not entail a doctrine of objectively unique foundations for empirical knowledge. For there might be several alternative recursive specifications of the class of justified beliefs, making use of different bases and generators, without any evident criterion for selecting one as objectively correct. If so, there might be different bases determining different foundations, none objectively prior or superior to the others.

That being so, if (just for the sake of an example) we presuppose a definition of the justified using indubitability as the basis and deduction as the generator, we may then think of the set of indubitable beliefs as the foundation of empirical knowledge. If so, we will be right only relative to our definition. For if the foundation is what is picked out by the basis property, then the indubitable is the foundation only relative to the definition that uses indubitability as the basis property. And so long as other definitions, using other bases, are equally possible and on a par with ours, the relativity is ineliminable.

Pessimism is to be distinguished from the more radical position that simply rejects supervenience. The *doctrine of supervenience* for an evaluative property ϕ is simply that, for every x, if x has ϕ then there is a non-evaluative property (perhaps a relational property) ψ such that

(i) x has ψ, and
(ii) necessarily, whatever has ψ has ϕ.

The denial of this for an evaluative property ϕ is a doctrine of the *autonomy* of ϕ. It holds that ϕ can be exemplified even though it does not supervene on any non-evaluative properties of what exemplifies it.

Formal foundationalism entails the doctrine of supervenience for epistemic justification, but is also considerably stronger. It requires in addition a certain faith in our intellectual powers, or a certain confidence in the manageable simplicity of the sphere of the relevant values (i.e., epistemic if the foundationalism is epistemic, ethical if it is ethical, aesthetic if it is aesthetic, and so on).

Accordingly, since pessimism is the denial of formal foundationalism and *not* of the weaker doctrine of supervenience, pessimism is a weaker

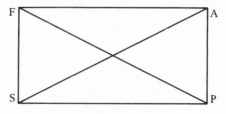

Figure 9.1

claim than the doctrine of autonomy. For pessimism is compatible with supervenience and requires only a certain skepticism about our ability to comprehend the principles that underlie such supervenience, perhaps because they are infinite in number or degree of complexity.

The four doctrines mentioned determine a square of opposition as in Figure 9.1. (But first let us agree on some convenient abbreviations:

S for the doctrine of supervenience.
A for autonomy, the negation of S.
F for formal foundationalism.
P for pessimism, the negation of F.

All of the above are to be taken implicitly as relative to a given property or a given set of properties.) Here F and A are contraries, S and P subcontraries, F and P contradictories, and S and A contradictories. Finally F entails S and A entails P.

Far from being pessimist, the coherence theory in epistemology is a kind of formal foundationalism. For it does try to provide principles that specify the conditions within which beliefs are justified. Thus a coherentist might choose coherence within a set of a certain sort as his basis and deduction as his generator. For example, a coherentist may hold that a belief is justified if 'and only if *either* it coheres within a large and diverse set of beliefs held by the subject *or* it is deduced by the subject from a set of such beliefs. In fact the coherentist usually has an all-encompassing basis that absorbs all generators, but this is quite compatible with formal foundationalism, though it is a limiting case.

Coherentism is opposed not to formal foundationalism but at most to substantive foundationalism. The conflict here is over what basis to choose in the recursive definition of justification. Obviously, there are grades of coherentism and of foundationalism. Radical coherentism holds that *only* coherence can serve as a basis. Radical foundationalism holds that coherence *never* serves as a basis, that the basis property which gives a belief B access to the foundation never makes reference to *other* beliefs

154

of the subject, except of course such beliefs as B itself may refer to. And various intermediate positions are clearly possible.

An infinite regress of justification is incompatible neither with formal foundationalism nor even with radical foundationalism. Thus recall our infinite sequence σ:

(P1) That there is at least one real number in the interval (0–1);

(P2) That there are at least two real numbers in the interval (0–1).

.

.

.

I can think of no compelling reason why there could not be a sequence of justified dispositional beliefs in P1, P2, . . . such that each member of the sequence is justified in our sense (J1) by its successor. This is not ruled out by formal foundationalism. What formal foundationalism would require of such a sequence, however, is that for each of its members there be a possible finite epistemic account or explanation of how its justification supervenes on the non-epistemic (such an explanation to be carried out perhaps by means of a non-epistemic basis G and a non-epistemic generator R).

It seems to me, therefore, that the foundationalist misplaces his objection when he focuses on the infinite regress of justification. What he really opposes is pessimism. His fundamental thesis is formal foundationalism, which we have found to be a form of the doctrine of supervenience.

G. E. Moore was optimistic enough about the possibility of a normative ethics, i.e., of an ethical theory or system, that he wrote as follows in *Principia Ethica*:

When A asks B what school he ought to send his son to, B's answer will certainly be an ethical judgment. And similarly all distribution of praise or blame to any personage or thing that has existed, now exists, or will exist, does give some answer to the question "What is good?" . . . But this is not the sense in which a scientific Ethics asks the question. Not one, of all the many million answers of this kind, which must be true, can form a part of an ethical system; although *that science must contain reason and principles sufficient for deciding on the truth of all of them.*[2]

For Moore a scientific ethics must have a kind of completeness which, given that it is comprehensible, it can have only if pessimism is false and formal foundationalism true.

By way of contrast, compare W. D. Ross's opposing view:

2 G. E. Moore, *Principia Ethica* (Cambridge University Press, 1903), p. 3 (my italics).

For the estimation of the comparative stringency of . . . prima facie obligations no general rules can, so far as I can see, be laid down.[3]

Ross's view is pessimist, but it may well be true, not only for ethics but also for epistemology. It seems unrealistic to suppose that either subject admits of the kind of completeness required by Moore. Only an evaluative monist, perhaps Mill, could reasonably believe otherwise. Mill himself was well aware of this, and made it the basis of scorn for pluralist "intuitionism." The pluralist must abandon all hope of attaining Moorean completeness, for there is no *general* answer accessible to our limited intellects for the question of how to resolve value conflicts or moral dilemmas.

Here we must distinguish between a general *method* for resolving such conflicts or dilemmas, and its *application*. The value monist can have a method, even if it may be difficult to apply. Thus it may be difficult to tell whether a certain action would lead to more pleasure than any alternative, but at least the monist radical hedonist can tell us that it is right if and only if it does in fact do so.

Even if it turns out that one must in the end yield to pessimism, moreover, one can still reject autonomism. Suppose one resigns oneself to the fact that given epistemic pluralism (several different *basic* sources of justification) there is no possibility of a complete epistemology, such that every correct attribution of justification to a belief would follow logically from the principles of our complete epistemology and certain non-epistemic facts about the belief. Even so, one might still reasonably reject autonomism and accept supervenience by holding that for every justified belief there must be a property ψ (perhaps a very complex relational property) such that

   (i) that belief has ψ,
  (ii) ψ is not a normative epistemic property, and
 (iii) necessarily, whatever belief has ψ is a justified belief.

Here again the foundationalist and the coherentist could turn out to be allies. For each could surely carry on despite pessimism in an attempt to specify *as completely as possible* the conditions within which beliefs are justified. Each could retain formal foundationalism as an ideal which we might approach but probably could never reach.

Formal foundationalism leaves open the viability of coherentism even in its most radical forms, therefore, which means that *substantive* foundationalism requires additional support beyond that provided by *formal* foundationalism. We need not rehearse in detail the familiar arguments

3 W. D. Ross, *The Right and the Good* (Oxford: Clarendon Press, 1930), p. 41.

against radical coherentism, since we are not assessing the merits of that doctrine. But. these objections to coherentism should be detached from the alleged impossibility of an infinite regress of justification.[4]

III

In order to understand fully the contemporary debate about foundationalism we need to draw a further distinction besides that between formal foundationalism and substantive foundationalism. Our new distinction divides substantive foundationalism into two varieties: epistemic foundationalism and meta-epistemic foundationalism.

For simplicity, I shall again cast my remarks in terms of justified beliefs, while assuming that what I say could be recast *mutatis mutandis* in more general terms that would also cover warranted (or reasonable, or evident, etc.) assumptions (or presumptions, or suppositions, etc.) or in even more general terms that would cover the category of pieces of knowledge itself.

Epistemic foundationalism concerns the justification of beliefs about the non-epistemic, the justification of beliefs whose objects are propositions that are *not* themselves about the justification of belief or beliefs. *Meta-epistemic foundationalism* concerns the justification of beliefs about the epistemic.

To my mind the burden of argument on the issue of epistemic foundationalism now falls on the radical coherentist. What we need from him is, first of all, a convincing solution to the problem posed by the apparent multiplicity of equally coherent systems that one could accept in any given set of circumstances. In addition there is a problem for epistemic coherentism that we might label "the problem of detachment from reality." A subject might acquire a coherent system of beliefs from a randomizing evil demon. This system of beliefs, which might even include an intricate set of introspective beliefs, could be embedded in a world of any sort compatible with the existence of such a subject, at least so far as one can see at present. Thus for the coherentist there is no necessary constraint deriving from the character of the non-cognitive world, including his own subjective states, on the constitution of his system of justified beliefs. The system of justified beliefs is detached from the world beyond, in the sense that justification is an internal matter totally unaffected by what lies outside. Thus a subject of such a system of justified beliefs would have been equally well justified no matter how one

4 The Appendix takes up the question whether an epistemic framework of *prima facie* justification and its defeat can possibly be of any use to the formal foundationalist.

might have varied his surroundings and even all of his non-cognitive experience. Surely such a subject who happens to obtain his system of coherent and thus – for the coherentist – *justified* beliefs from a randomizing demon, and whose system of beliefs turns out wholly true by sheer and enormously improbable coincidence, at least does not thereby *know*. Hence the coherentist must apparently embrace a separate causal condition for knowledge, thus complicating his account of knowledge in a way that the foundationalist need not always follow. (Sometimes the foundationalist must follow suit, however, as when he defines his foundation by reference to some intrinsic character of certain beliefs.) In sum, the epistemic coherentist owes us solutions to the problem posed by the multiplicity of coherent systems, and to the problem of detachment from reality. It is not obvious, however, that if no such solutions are forthcoming, then the issue of meta-epistemic foundationalism is settled in favor of foundationalism along with the issue of epistemic foundationalism.

Meta-epistemic foundationalism is the view that there must be foundational epistemic beliefs: beliefs *about* epistemic justification that do not derive *all* of their justification from coherence or some other relation to other beliefs of the subject, but rather derive some of their justification from intrinsic plausibility or from factors external to the system of beliefs.

The issue of meta-epistemic foundationalism is closely related to the ancient problem of the *diallelus* or "the wheel," most recently given prominence by Roderick Chisholm as "the problem of the criterion." Which should come first: a method or set of criteria for determining when we have a bit of knowledge, or *particular* examples of knowledge, in terms of which we can determine criteria?

Those who give pre-eminence to method or criteria may be called *methodists*, and those who give pre-eminence to particular examples (e.g., my knowledge that I have two hands) may be called *particularists*. Note that whereas a methodist can be a skeptic, a particularist is anti-skeptical on principle. Moreover, whereas a skeptic might be a methodist and cannot be a particularist, he might be a *radical* skeptic, rejecting *both* methodism and particularism. Some Pyrrhonic Skeptics were radical in their skepticism; Locke and Hume were methodists; and Reid and Moore particularists.

Particularism and methodism are meta-epistemological positions, for they tell us which justifies which of two sorts of *epistemic* knowledge. They tell us whether our knowledge of certain epistemic principles is based on our knowledge that we have bits of knowledge of a certain related kind (e.g., of the external world, that I have two hands), or whether, conversely, our knowledge that we have bits of knowledge of a particular kind rests on our knowledge of certain related epistemic principles.

Particularism in meta-epistemology forecloses some options in epistemology. We have already seen that it forecloses skepticism. More exactly, particularism about knowledge of a certain sort (e.g., the external world, other minds, the past) forecloses skepticism with regard to knowledge of that sort.

In addition to foreclosing epistemic options, particularism raises epistemic questions. Thus particularism with respect to knowledge of any specified sort (e.g., of the external world) raises the Kantian epistemic question of how knowledge of that sort is possible, of how we arrive at bits of knowledge of that sort. Here epistemic foundationalism is one general sort of answer and epistemic coherentism is another.

In addition to the Kantian epistemic question, moreover, particularism raises a further *meta*-epistemic question, which deserves some attention.

The meta-epistemic question raised by particularism is simply this. Suppose particularism is true and our knowledge of epistemic principles of a certain sort is based on our knowledge that we have particular bits of knowledge of that sort (e.g., of the external world: say, that I have two hands). This surely raises the simple question of *how* we come to have our knowledge of the particular bits of knowledge in question. For instance, *how* does one know *that* one knows that one has two hands. Surely it can't be right to say that this is just immediate or basic or foundational knowledge and leave it at that. For one thing, that would give the particularist too easy a solution to the Kantian question. Thus in answer to the question of how he knows that he now has two hands, the particularist could just retort that he knows directly or self-evidently that he knows that he has two hands and that his knowledge that he has two hands obviously entails that he *does* have two hands. So this knowledge of the external world is founded by deduction on his self-evident and foundational knowledge that he has such knowledge. Surely that would be absurd, but how can the particularist avoid the absurdity?

The particularist may reply that our objection confuses methodological assumptions with substantive commitments. The status of his starting points, e.g., that he does know he has two hands, and so on, is that of *assumptions*, provisional assumptions made with the purpose in mind of discovering what epistemic principles might fit in with them. But if the particularist is only *supposing* that one does know one has two hands, then anything he arrives at on that basis will not be detachable from it, and this includes whatever epistemic principles he might derive. In sum, if his inquiry is based on mere assumptions it would seem that the most he could hope to show is that *if* the assumptions are indeed true *then* such

159

and such epistemic principles are true: *if* one does know that one has two hands, *then* such and such epistemic principles are true. And how are we to detach the principles?

The particularist may respond more soundly by restricting himself to particular examples of *justification* rather than knowledge. His idea would then be that such particular examples have epistemic priority over principles of justification: the principles are always to be established on the basis of such examples.

Can the particularist now answer the question of *how* one acquires justification for the belief that one *is* justified in believing that one has two hands? Why can he not answer that such a belief is foundational, basic, immediately justified, self-justified, or the like? At least it cannot now be argued so easily that this gives too facile a foundation for our knowledge that we have two hands. For the proposition that, according to the particularist, is self-evident for one is

(P) that one is justified in believing that one has two hands.

And from this it does *not* follow logically

(Q) that one does have two hands.

Therefore, belief of Q cannot be based deductively on belief of P thus giving it a foundation in the self-evident.

There is a second line of argument that may be used against the particularist, one that can conveniently draw on the concepts and terms introduced earlier. In those terms the objection is basically that particularism leads to epistemic autonomism, to the rejection of the supervenience of justification. For the whole point of particularism is to circumvent the fact that the self-evident epistemic principles are too few and weak to yield much knowledge. The particularist proposes using particular examples as data will justify the acceptance of epistemic principles that may not be *self*-evident but do fit together best with such data. Thus the particularist seems committed to the view that examples such as P above have some measure of intrinsic credibility. And at least on some accounts of intrinsic credibility it would follow that it is the truth of P that makes one's belief of it justified. But then there is after all an epistemic fact – namely, P – which is an ultimate source of justification.

The particularist may defend himself, however, without even questioning the view of the intrinsic credibility of a proposition as founded merely on its truth. For he may point out that an *epistemic* proposition can be credible simply in virtue of being true, even though its truth has a *non-epistemic* source. If so, then of course there may be purely non-epistemic *ultimate* sources of *every* epistemic fact even though some epistemic facts are self-evident. This particularism does not after all lead to epistemic autonomism:

What is more, on reflection the particularist seems uncommitted to any kind of intrinsic credibility for his data after all. His particularism does commit him to the view that his beliefs about (at least some) particular instances of justified belief – such as P above – do *not* derive their justification from some relation that they bear to beliefs of his concerning some general principles of justification. For instance, he must hold that his belief of P (or some such proposition) does *not* acquire its justification by inference from certain other beliefs of his among which there is some such epistemic principle as that anyone's beliefs about large features of his body are always justified. For if *all* his beliefs about particular instances of justified belief *were* dependent for their justification on inference from general principles of justification, then principles would always be meta-epistemically prior to instances and methodism would be true. However, one's beliefs about particular instances of justified belief may fail to derive their justification by inference from general principles of justification without being intrinsically justified. For they may derive their justification from some relation that they bear to beliefs *other* than those about general principles of justification, or by relation to sensory experience, or to some other factors external to one's body of beliefs altogether.

Epistemic foundationalism and meta-epistemic foundationalism are independent, but they are also compatible. Particularism is one form of meta-epistemic foundationalism. We have now considered two objections to it which may seem weighty but turn out to have little substance.

Are particularism, methodism, radical coherentism, and skepticism our only meta-epistemic alternatives? On reflection it is not really so obvious that there could be no other alternatives. Why must it be that *either* our particular knowledge is prior to our relevant epistemic principles *or* the converse, unless we must embrace skepticism or radical coherentism? It seems possible to reject the dichotomy, and to do so without embracing either skepticism or radical coherentism. For surely our meta-epistemic foundations can be broad enough to include both some particular instances and some general principles, without either having priority over the other. (This is not to say that we must take the same approach to every sort of knowledge. Thus methodism or particularism may be preferable with respect to some.) If first-level foundations may combine principles and instances, meta-epistemic foundations may do so as well. And if the justification yielded by first-level foundations is boosted by coherence, the same goes for meta-epistemic foundations.

It is true that even those detached from reality will have some derivative justification for their meta-beliefs that their first-level beliefs are justified. This derivative justification will derive from the coherence of such meta-beliefs with their first-level beliefs, just as it does for the sane. Such *prima facie* justification does not yield knowledge for the insane, however, given their detachment from reality, given the lack of relevant connection between their system of beliefs and the world outside. Since presumably the beliefs of the sane are not thus detached, the *prima facie* credibility carried by the meta-beliefs of the sane is supplemented by their attachment to reality rather than defeated by their detachment from reality.

IV

In sum, substantive foundationalism was first of all distinguished from formal foundationalism, and then divided into epistemic and meta-epistemic foundationalism. It was argued (a) that formal foundationalism is little more than the doctrine of supervenience; (b) that even radical coherentism is a type of formal foundationalism, but is unconvincing; (c) that substantive foundationalism concerning first-level, non-epistemic beliefs is made plausible by the weakness of its opposition, radical coherentism, which has no convincing solution for the problem of the multiplicity of coherent systems or for the problem of detachment from reality; (d) that particularism concerning meta-epistemic beliefs – the view that our knowledge that in certain particular cases we have knowledge is prior in the order of justification to the relevant epistemic principles – is made implausible by the fact that, if our knowledge of our own knowledge were just foundational, we would have an absurd foundation for any piece of knowledge by deducing its object from the self-evident fact that we had such knowledge; (e) that the particularist can defend himself soundly by restricting his data to examples of *justified belief* rather than knowledge; (f) that the particularist can also defend himself adequately against the charge that he is committed to epistemic autonomism, for he can appeal to the fact that an epistemic proposition can be both (i) self-*evident*, and (ii) such as to have a non-epistemic source of its truth; and (g) that the particularist need not even hold his epistemic data (particular cases of justified belief) to be *self*-evident: in fact he need only hold that epistemic data are not always made evident by inference from general principles of justification.

It seems fair to conclude that one cannot properly understand foundationalism without two distinctions: that between formal and substantive foundationalism, and that between epistemic and meta-epistemic foundationalism.[5]

---

5 The doctrine of supervenience used in this chapter was introduced earlier in Chapter 2. See the account of what it is for a set to *fully validate* an epistemic proposition, account I in the Appendix to Chapter 2.

APPENDIX

It may well be thought that epistemic principles that specify *prima facie* reasons are useless to the formal foundationalist, for in such a framework the absolute (and not just *prima facie*) justification of a belief derives from its satisfying certain conditions that provide *prima facie* justification where these are not overridden or defeated. It is of course the presence of the no-defeaters condition in the total situations yielding absolute justification that apparently makes the framework of *prima facie* principles useless to the formal foundationalist. For the universal presence of the no-defeaters condition in such justification-yielding situations would make all such situations epistemic, and thus we would be inevitably frustrated in our formal foundationalist project of showing how epistemic justification supervenes on non-epistemic situations.

A closer look will reveal, however, that this objection to the framework of *prima facie* principles is spurious. Suppose that the situation that yields absolute justification for Q contains the fact

(F) that there are no defeaters for P as a *prima facie* reason for Q.

If this is an essential part of the justification-yielding situation then it seems that we do not have here an explanation of how epistemic justification supervenes on the non-epistemic, for F seems *epistemic*.

It is important to be clear at this point on what formal foundationalism requires, which is that the evaluative supervene on the non-evaluative, in the sense that evaluative truths must follow from non-evaluative truths via necessary truths.

Consider now the set ß such that ß contains, for each proposition X that is a possible defeater of P as a *prima facie* reason for Q, the proposition that X is false. Presumably from that set ß it follows with necessity that there is no X such that X is a possible defeater of P as a *prima facie* reason for Q, and such that X is true. (And, if so, it follows further of course that F is true.) For suppose all members of ß are true. *Could* there then possibly be a Y such that Y was a possible defeater of P as a *prima facie* reason for Q and such that Y was true (at the same time that all members of ß were true)? Well, is there possibly some Y such that Y is *not* in fact a possible defeater of P as a *prima facie* reason for Q and such that Y *could* be such a possible defeater? Surely that seems not to be a real possibility. If something X is a possible defeater then surely it is necessarily a possible defeater, and if something Y fails to be a possible defeater then surely it necessarily so fails. I conclude that it does follow *with necessity* from ß that there is no Y such that Y is a possible defeater of P as a *prima facie* reason for Q and such that Y is true. And this is

163

tantamount to F. But ß may be presumed not to contain any epistemic proposition: no proposition in ß need be supposed to attribute a normative epistemic property or to be a logical compound of such a proposition. Thus we can perhaps see how F does after all have its source in a non-epistemic situation. If that much is right, it follows that despite appearances to the contrary, the presence of F in the situation that yields the absolute justification for Q does *not* rule out a non-epistemic source on which such justification supervenes. For even though F is epistemic we have just seen how it itself has a *non*-epistemic source, and thus how whatever has its source in *it* need not inevitably have any *ultimate* epistemic source. This shows that the foundationalist can use a framework of *prima facie* justification with a clear conscience.

10

The raft and the pyramid: coherence versus foundations in the theory of knowledge

Contemporary epistemology must choose between the solid security of the ancient foundationalist pyramid and the risky adventure of the new coherentist raft. Our main objective will be to understand, as deeply as we can, the nature of the controversy and the reasons for and against each of the two options. But first of all we take note of two underlying assumptions.

1. TWO ASSUMPTIONS

(A1) Not everything believed is known, but nothing can be known without being at least believed (or accepted, presumed, taken for granted, or the like) in some broad sense. What additional requirements must a belief fill in order to be knowledge? There are surely at least the following two: (a) it must be true, and (b) it must be justified (or warranted, reasonable, correct, or the like).

(A2) Let us assume, moreover, with respect to the second condition A1(b): first, that it involves a normative or evaluative property; and, second, that the relevant sort of justification is that which pertains to knowledge: epistemic (or theoretical) justification. Someone seriously ill may have two sorts of justification for believing he will recover: the practical justification that derives from the contribution such belief will make to his recovery and the theoretical justification provided by the lab results, the doctor's diagnosis and prognosis, and so on. Only the latter is relevant to the question whether he knows.

2. KNOWLEDGE AND CRITERIA (OR CANONS, METHODS, OR THE LIKE)

a. There are two key questions of the theory of knowledge:
   (i) What do we know?
   (ii) How do we know?
The answer to the first would be a list of bits of knowledge or at

165

least of types of knowledge: of the self, of the external world, of other minds, and so on. An answer to the second would give us criteria (or canons, methods, principles, or the like) that would explain how we know whatever it is that we do know.

b. In developing a theory of knowledge, we can begin either with a(i) or with a(ii). Particularism would have us begin with an answer to a(i) and only then take up a(ii) on the basis of that answer. Quite to the contrary, methodism would reverse that order. The particularist thus tends to be antiskeptical on principle. But the methodist is as such equally receptive to skepticism and to the contrary. Hume, for example, was no less a methodist than Descartes. Each accepted, in effect, that only the obvious and what is proved deductively on its basis can possibly be known.

c. What, then, is the obvious? For Descartes it is what we know by intuition, what is clear and distinct, what is indubitable and credible with no fear of error. Thus for Descartes basic knowledge is always an infallible belief in an indubitable truth. All other knowledge must stand on that basis through deductive proof. Starting from such criteria (canons, methods, etc.), Descartes concluded that knowledge extended about as far as his contemporaries believed.[1] Starting from similar criteria, however, Hume concluded that both science and common sense made claims far beyond their rightful limits.

d. Philosophical posterity has rejected Descartes's theory for one main reason: that it admits too easily as obvious what is nothing of the sort. Descartes's reasoning is beautifully simple: God exists; no omnipotent perfectly good being would descend to deceit; but if our common sense beliefs were radically false, that would represent deceit on His part. Therefore, our common sense beliefs must be true or at least cannot be radically false. But in order to buttress this line of reasoning and fill in details, Descartes appeals to various principles that appear something less than indubitable.

e. For his part, Hume rejects all but a miniscule portion of our supposed common sense knowledge. He establishes first that there is no way to prove such supposed knowledge on the basis of what is

---

1 But Descartes's methodism was at most partial. James Van Cleve has supplied the materials for a convincing argument that the way out of the Cartesian circle is through a particularism of basic knowledge. (See James Van Cleve, "Foundationalism, Epistemic Principles, and the Cartesian Circle," *Philosophical Review* 88 (1979): 55–91.) But this is, of course, compatible with methodism on inferred knowledge. Whether Descartes subscribed to such methodism is hard (perhaps impossible) to determine, since in the end he makes room for all the kinds of knowledge required by particularism. But his language when he introduces the method of hyperbolic doubt, and the order in which he proceeds, suggest that he did subscribe to such methodism.

obvious at any given moment through reason or experience. And he concludes, in keeping with this methodism, that in point of fact there really is no such knowledge.

3. TWO METAPHORS: THE RAFT AND THE PYRAMID

Both metaphors concern the body or system of knowledge in a given mind. But the mind is of course a more complex marvel than is sometimes supposed. Here I do not allude to the depths plumbed by Freud, nor even to Chomsky's. Nor need we recall the labyrinths inhabited by statesmen and diplomats, nor the rich patterns of some novels or theories. We need look no further than the most common, everyday beliefs. Take, for instance, the belief that driving tonight will be dangerous. Brief reflection should reveal that any of us with that belief will join to it several other closely related beliefs on which the given belief depends for its existence or (at least) its justification. Among such beliefs we could presumably find some or all of the following: that the road will be icy or snowy; that driving on ice or snow is dangerous; that it will rain or snow tonight; that the temperature will be below freezing; appropriate beliefs about the forecast and its reliability; and so on.

How must such beliefs be interrelated in order to help justify my belief about the danger of driving tonight? Here foundationalism and coherentism disagree, each offering its own metaphor. Let us have a closer look at this dispute, starting with foundationalism.

Both Descartes and Hume attribute to human knowledge an architectonic structure. There is a nonsymmetric relation of physical support such that any two floors of a building are tied by that relation: one of the two supports (or at least helps support) the other. And there is, moreover, a part with a special status: the foundation, which is supported by none of the floors while supporting them all.

With respect to a body of knowledge K (in someone's possession), foundationalism implies that K can be divided into parts $K_1, K_2, \ldots$, such that there is some nonsymmetric relation R (analogous to the relation of physical support) which orders those parts in such a way that there is one – call it F – that bears R to every other part while none of them bears R in turn to F.

According to foundationalism, each piece of knowledge lies on a pyramid like that in Figure 10.1. The nodes of such a pyramid (for a proposition P relative to a subject S and a time t) must obey the following requirements:

a. The set of all nodes that succeed (directly) any given node must

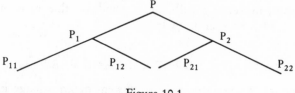

Figure 10.1

serve jointly as a base that properly supports that node (for S at t).
b. Each node must be a proposition that S is justified in believing at t.
c. If a node is not self-evident (for S at t), it must have successors (that serve jointly as a base that properly supports that node).
d. Each branch of an epistemic pyramid must terminate.

For the foundationalist Descartes, for instance, each terminating node must be an indubitable proposition that S believes at t with no possibility of error. As for the nonterminal nodes, each of them represents inferential knowledge, derived by deduction from more basic beliefs.

Such radical foundationalism suffers from a fatal weakness that is twofold:

(a) there are not so many perfectly obvious truths as Descartes thought; and
(b) once we restrict ourselves to what is truly obvious in any given context, very little of one's supposed common sense knowledge can be proved on that basis.

If we adhere to such radical foundationalism, therefore, we are just wrong in thinking we know so much.

Note that in citing such a "fatal weakness" of radical foundationalism, we favor particularism as against the methodism of Descartes and Hume. For we reject the methods or criteria of Descartes and Hume when we realize that they plunge us in a deep skepticism. If such criteria are incompatible with our enjoyment of the rich body of knowledge that we commonly take for granted, then as good particularists we hold on to the knowledge and reject the criteria.

If we reject radical foundationalism, however, what are we to put in its place? Here epistemology faces a dilemma that different epistemologists resolve differently. Some reject radical foundationalism but retain some more moderate form of foundationalism. Others react more vigorously, however, by rejecting all forms of foundationalism in favor of a radically different coherentism. Coherentism is associated with idealism – of both the German and the British variety – and has recently acquired new vigor and interest.

The coherentists reject the metaphor of the pyramid in favor of one that they owe to the positivist Neurath, according to whom our body of knowledge is a raft that floats free of any anchor or tie. Repairs must be made afloat, and though no part is untouchable, we must stand on some in order to replace or repair others. Not every part can go at once.

According to the new metaphor, what justifies a belief is not that it can be an infallible belief with an indubitable object, nor that it have been proved deductively on such a basis, but that it cohere with a comprehensive system of beliefs.

4. A COHERENTIST CRITIQUE OF FOUNDATIONALISM

What reasons do coherentists offer for their total rejection of foundationalism? The argument that follows below summarizes much of what is alleged against foundationalism. But first we must distinguish between subjective states that incorporate a propositional attitude and those that do not. A propositional attitude is a mental state of someone with a proposition for its object: beliefs, hopes, and fears provide examples. By way of contrast, a headache does not incorporate any such attitude. One can of course be conscious of a headache, but the headache itself does not constitute or incorporate any attitude with a proposition for its object. With this distinction in the background, here is the antifoundationalist argument, which has two lemmas – a(iv) and b(iii) – and a principal conclusion.

a. (i) If a mental state incorporates a propositional attitude, then it does not give us direct contact with reality, e.g., with pure experience, unfiltered by concepts or beliefs.

(ii) If a mental state does not give us direct contact with reality, then it provides no guarantee against error.

(iii) If a mental state provides no guarantee against error, then it cannot serve as a foundation for knowledge.

(iv) Therefore, if a mental state incorporates a propositional attitude, then it cannot serve as a foundation for knowledge.

b. (i) If a mental state does not incorporate a propositional attitude, then it is an enigma how such a state can provide support for any hypothesis, raising its credibility selectively by contrast with its alternatives. (If the mental state has no conceptual or propositional content, then what logical relation can it possibly bear to any hypothesis? Belief in a hypothesis would be a propositional attitude with the hypothesis itself as object. How can one depend logically for such a belief on an experience with no propositional content?)

169

(ii) If a mental state has no propositional content and cannot provide logical support for any hypothesis, then it cannot serve as a foundation for knowledge.

(iii) Therefore, if a mental state does not incorporate a propositional attitude, then it cannot serve as a foundation for knowledge.

c. Every mental state either does or does not incorporate a propositional attitude.

d. Therefore, no mental state can serve as a foundation for knowledge. (From a(iv), b(iii), and c.)

According to the coherentist critic, foundationalism is run through by this dilemma. Let us take a closer look.[2]

In the first place, what reason is there to think, in accordance with premise b(i), that only propositional attitudes can give support to their own kind? Consider practices – e.g., broad policies or customs. Could not some person or group be justified in a practice because of its consequences: that is, could not the consequences of a practice make it a good practice? But among the consequences of a practice may surely be found, for example, a more just distribution of goods and less suffering than there would be under its alternatives. And neither the more just distribution nor the lower degree of suffering is a propositional attitude. This provides an example in which propositional attitudes (the intentions that sustain the practice) are justified by consequences that are not propositional attitudes. That being so, is it not conceivable that the justification of belief that matters for knowledge be analogous to the objective justification by consequences that we find in ethics?

Is it not possible, for instance, that a belief that there is something red before one be justified in part because it has its origin in one's visual experience of red when one looks at an apple in daylight? If we accept such examples, they show us a source of justification that serves as such without incorporating a propositional attitude.

As for premise a(iii), it is already under suspicion from our earlier exploration of premise b(i). A mental state M can be nonpropositional and hence not a candidate for so much as truth, much less infallibility, while it serves, in spite of that, as a foundation of knowledge. Leaving that aside, let us suppose that the relevant mental state is indeed propositional. Must it then be infallible in order to serve as a foundation of justification and knowledge? That is so far from being obvious that it

---

2 Cf. Laurence Bonjour, "The Coherence Theory of Truth," *Philosophical Studies* 30 (1976): 281–312; and, especially, Michael Williams, *Groundless Belief* (New Haven: Yale University Press, 1977); and L. Bonjour, "Can Empirical Knowledge Have a Foundation?" *American Philosophical Quarterly* 15 (1978): 1–15.

seems more likely false when compared with an analogue in ethics. With respect to beliefs, we may distinguish between their being true and their being justified. Analogously, with respect to actions, we may distinguish between their being optimal (best of all alternatives, all things considered) and their being (subjectively) justified. In practical deliberation on alternatives for action, is it inconceivable that the most *eligible* alternative *not* be objectively the best, all things considered? Can there not be another alternative – perhaps a most repugnant one worth little if any consideration – that in point of fact would have a much better total set of consequences and would thus be better, all things considered? Take the physician attending to Frau Hitler at the birth of little Adolf. Is it not possible that if he had acted less morally, that would have proved better in the fullness of time? And if that is so in ethics, may not its likeness hold good in epistemology? Might there not be justified (reasonable, warranted) beliefs that are not even true, much less infallible? That seems to me not just a conceivable possibility, but indeed a familiar fact of everyday life, where observational beliefs too often prove illusory but no less reasonable for being false.

If the foregoing is on the right track, then the antifoundationalist is far astray. What has led him there?

As a diagnosis of the antifoundationalist argument before us, and more particularly of its second lemma, I would suggest that it rests on an Intellectualist Model of Justification.

According to such a model, the justification of belief (and psychological states generally) is parasitical on certain logical relations among propositions. For example, my belief (i) that the streets are wet is justified by my pair of beliefs (ii) that it is raining, and (iii) that if it is raining, the streets are wet. Thus we have a structure such as this:

B(Q) is justified by the fact that B(Q) is grounded on (B(P), B(P $\supset$ Q)).

And according to an Intellectualist Model, this is parasitical on the fact that

P and (P $\supset$ Q) together logically imply Q.

Concerning this attack on foundationalism I will argue (a) that it is useless to the coherentist, since if the antifoundationalist dilemma impales the foundationalist, a form of it can be turned against the coherentist to the same effect; (b) that the dilemma would be lethal not only to foundationalism and coherentism but also to the very possibility of substantive epistemology; and (c) that a form of it would have the same effect on normative ethics.

(a) According to coherentism, what justifies a belief is its membership

171

in a coherent and comprehensive set of beliefs. But whereas being grounded on B(P) and (B(P ⊃ Q) is a property of a belief B(Q) that yields immediately the logical implication of Q by [P and (P ⊃ Q)] as the logical source of that property's justificatory power, the property of being a member of a coherent set is not one that immediately yields any such implication.

It may be argued, nevertheless, (i) that the property of being a member of a coherent set would supervene in any actual instance on the property of being a member of a particular set α that is in fact coherent, and (ii) that this would enable us to preserve our Intellectualist Model, since (iii) the justification of the member belief B(Q) by its membership in α would then be parasitical on the logical relations among the beliefs in α which constitute the coherence of that set of beliefs, and (iv) the justification of B(Q) by the fact that it is part of a coherent set would then be *indirectly* parasitical on logical relations among propositions after all.

But if such an indirect form of parasitism is allowed, then the experience of pain may perhaps be said to justify belief in its existence parasitically on the fact that P logically implies P! The Intellectualist Model seems either so trivial as to be dull, or else sharp enough to cut equally against both foundationalism and coherentism.

(b) If (i) only propositional attitudes can justify such propositional attitudes as belief, and if (ii) to do so they must in turn be justified by yet other propositional attitudes, it seems clear that (iii) there is no hope of constructing a complete epistemology, one which would give us, in theory, an account of what the justification of any justified belief would supervene on. For (i) and (ii) would rule out the possibility of a finite regress of justification.

(c) If only propositional attitudes can justify propositional attitudes, and if to do so they must in turn be justified by yet other propositional attitudes, it seems clear that there is no hope of constructing a complete normative ethics, one which would give us, in theory, an account of what the justification of any possible justified action would supervene upon. For the justification of an action presumably depends on the intentions it embeds and the justification of these, and here we are already within the net of propositional attitudes from which, for the Intellectualist, there is no escape.

It seems fair to conclude that our coherentist takes his antifoundationalist zeal too far. His antifoundationalist argument helps expose some

valuable insights but falls short of its malicious intent. The foundationalist emerges showing no serious damage. Indeed, he now demands equal
time for a positive brief in defense of his position.

5. THE REGRESS ARGUMENT

a. The regress argument in epistemology concludes that we must
countenance beliefs that are justified in the absence of justification
by other beliefs. But it reaches that conclusion only by rejecting the
possibility in principle of an infinite regress of justification. It thus
opts for foundational beliefs justified in some noninferential way by
ruling out a chain or pyramid of justification that has justifiers, and
justifiers of justifiers, and so on *without end*. One may well find this
too short a route to foundationalism, however, and demand more
compelling reasons for thus rejecting an infinite regress as vicious.
We shall find indeed that it is not easy to meet this demand.
b. We have seen how even the most ordinary of everyday beliefs is the
tip of an iceberg. A closer look below the surface reveals a complex
structure that ramifies with no end in sight. Take again my belief
that driving will be dangerous tonight, at the tip of an iceberg, (I),
that looks like Figure 10.2. The immediate cause of my belief that
driving will be hazardous tonight is the sound of raindrops on the
windowpane. All but one or two members of the underlying iceberg
are as far as they can be from my thoughts at the time. In what sense,
then, do they form an iceberg whose tip breaks the calm surface of
my consciousness?

Here I will assume that the members of (I) are beliefs of the
subject, even if unconscious or subconscious, that causally buttress
and thus justify his prediction about the driving conditions.

Can the iceberg extend without end? It may appear obvious that it
cannot do so, and one may jump to the conclusion that any piece of
knowledge must be ultimately founded on beliefs that are *not*
(inferentially) justified or warranted by other beliefs. This is a
doctrine of *epistemic foundationalism*.

Let us focus not so much on the *giving* of justification as on the
having of it. Can there be a belief that is justified in part by other
beliefs, some of which are in turn justified by yet other beliefs, and
so on without end? Can there be an endless regress of justification?
c. There are several familiar objections to such a regress:
   (i) *Objection*: "It is incompatible with human limitations. No
   human subject could harbor the required infinity of beliefs."
   Reply: It is mere presumption to fathom with such assurance

173

(I)

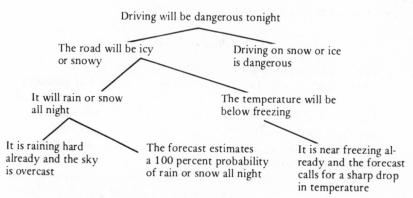

Figure 10.2

the depths of the mind, and especially its unconscious and dispositional depths. Besides, our object here is the nature of epistemic justification in itself and not only that of such justification as is accessible to humans. Our question is not whether humans could harbor an infinite iceberg of justification. Our question is rather whether *any* mind, no matter how deep, could do so. Or is it ruled out *in principle* by the very nature of justification?

(ii) *Objection*: "An infinite regress is indeed ruled out in principle, for if justification were thus infinite how could it possibly end?"

Reply: (i) If the end mentioned is *temporal*, then why must there be such an end? In the first place, the subject may be eternal. Even if he is not eternal, moreover, why must belief acquisition and justification occur seriatim? What precludes an infinite body of beliefs acquired at a single stroke? Human limitations may rule this out for humans, but we have yet to be shown that it is precluded in principle, by the very nature of justification. (ii) If the end mentioned is justificatory, on the other hand, then to ask how justification could possibly end is just to beg the question.

(iii) *Objection*: "Let us make two assumptions: first, that S's belief of q justifies his belief of p only if it works together with a justified belief on his part that q provides good evidence for p; and, second, that if S is to be justified in believing p on the basis of his belief of q and is to be justified in believing q on the basis

174

of his belief of r, then S must be justified in believing that r provides good evidence for p via q. These assumptions imply that an actual regress of justification requires belief in an infinite proposition. Since no one (or at least no human) can believe an infinite proposition, no one (no human) can be a subject of such an actual regress."[3]

Reply: Neither of the two assumptions is beyond question, but even granting them both, it may still be doubted that the conclusion follows. It is true that each finitely complex belief of the form "r provides good evidence for p via $q_1, \ldots, q_n$" will *omit* how some members of the full infinite regress are epistemically tied to belief of p. But that seems irrelevant given the fact that for each member r of the regress, such that r is tied epistemically to belief of p, there *is* a finite belief of the required sort ("r provides good evidence for p via $q_1, \ldots, q_n$") that ties the two together. Consequently, there is no apparent reason to suppose – even granted the two assumptions – that an infinite regress will require a single belief in an infinite proposition, and not just an infinity of beliefs in increasingly complex finite propositions.

(iv) *Objection*: "But if it is allowed that justification extend infinitely, then it is too easy to justify any belief at all or too many beliefs altogether. Take, for instance, the belief that there are perfect numbers greater than 100. And suppose a mind powerful enough to believe every member of the following sequence:

(σ1) There is at least one perfect number > 100
There are at least two perfect numbers > 100
               "   three   "   "

If such a believer has no other belief about perfect numbers save the belief that a perfect number is a whole number equal to the sum of its whole factors, then surely he is *not* justified in believing that there are perfect numbers greater than 100. He is quite unjustified in believing any of the members of sequence (σ1), in spite of the fact that a challenge to any can be met easily by appeal to its successor. Thus it cannot be allowed after all that justification extend infinitely, and an infinite regress is ruled out."

Reply: We must distinguish between regresses of justification

---

3 Cf. Richard Foley, "Inferential Justification and the Infinite Regress," *American Philosophical Quarterly* 15 (1978): 311–16.

that are actual and those that are merely potential. The difference is *not* simply that an actual regress is composed of actual beliefs. For even if all members of the regress are actual beliefs, the regress may still be *merely potential* in the following sense: while it is true that *if* any member *were* justified then its predecessors *would* be, still none is in fact justified. Anyone with our series of beliefs about perfect numbers in the absence of any further relevant information on such numbers would presumably be the subject of such a merely potential justificatory regress.

(v) *Objection*: "But defenders of infinite justificatory regresses cannot distinguish thus between actual regresses and those that are merely potential. There is no real distinction to be drawn between the two. For if any regress ever justifies the belief at its head, then every regress must always do so. But obviously not every regress does so (as we have seen by examples), and hence no regress can do so."[4]

Reply: One can in fact distinguish between actual justificatory regresses and merely potential ones, and one can do so both abstractly and by examples.

What an actual regress has that a merely potential regress lacks is the property of containing only justified beliefs as members. What they both share is the property of containing no member without successors that would jointly justify it.

Recall our regress about perfect numbers greater than 100: i.e., there is at least one; there are at least two; there are at least three; and so on. Each member has a successor that would justify it, but no member is justified (in the absence of further information external to the regress). That is therefore a merely potential infinite regress. As for an actual regress, I see no compelling reason why someone (if not a human, then some more powerful mind) could not hold an infinite series of actually justified beliefs as follows:

(σ2) There is at least one even number
There are at least two even numbers
"   three   "

It may be that no one could be the subject of such a series of justified beliefs unless he had a proof that there is a denumerable infinity of even numbers. But even if that should be so, it

---

4 Cf. John Post, "Infinite Regresses of Justification and of Explanation," *Philosophical Studies* 38 (1980): 31–52.

would not take away the fact of the infinite regress of potential justifiers, each of which is actually justified, and hence it would not take away the fact of the actual endless regress of justification.

The objection under discussion is confused, moreover, on the nature of the issue before us. Our question is *not* whether there can be an infinite potential regress, each member of which would be justified by its successors, such that the belief at its head is justified in virtue of its position there, at the head of such a regress. The existence and even the possibility of a single such regress with a belief at its head that was *not* justified in virtue of its position there would of course settle that question in the negative. Our question is, rather, whether there can be an actual infinite regress of justification, and the fact that a belief at the head of a potential regress might still fail to be justified despite its position does *not* settle this question. For even if there can be a merely potential regress with an unjustified belief at its head, that leaves open the possibility of an infinite regress, each member of which is justified by its immediate successors working jointly, where every member of the regress is in addition actually justified.

6. THE RELATION OF JUSTIFICATION AND FOUNDATIONALIST STRATEGY

The foregoing discussion is predicated on a simple conception of justification such that a set of beliefs ß conditionally justifies (*would* justify) a belief X iff, necessarily, if all members of ß are justified then X is also justified (if it exists). The fact that on such a conception of justification actual endless regresses – such as (σ2) – seem quite possible blocks a straightforward regress argument in favor of foundations. For it shows that an actual infinite regress cannot be dismissed out of hand.

Perhaps the foundationalist could introduce some relation of justification – presumably more complex and yet to be explicated – with respect to which it could be argued more plausibly that an actual endless regress is out of the question.

There is, however, a more straightforward strategy open to the foundationalist. For he *need not* object to the possibility of an endless regress of justification. His essential creed is the more positive belief that every justified belief must be at the head of a terminating regress. Fortunately, to affirm the universal necessity of a terminating regress is *not* to deny the bare possibility of a nonterminating regress. For a single belief can trail at once regresses of both sorts: one terminating and one not. Thus the proof of the denumerably infinite cardinality of the set of evens may provide for a powerful enough intellect a *terminating* regress for each member of the *endless* series of justified beliefs:

(σ2) There is at least one even number
   There are at least two even numbers
      "   three   "

At the same time, it is obvious that each member of (σ2) lies at the head of an actual endless regress of justification, on the assumption that each member is conditionally justified by its successor, which is in turn actually justified.

"Thank you so much," the foundationalist may sneer, "but I really do not need that kind of help. Nor do I need to be reminded of my essential creed, which I know as well as anyone. Indeed my rejection of endless regresses of justification is only a means of supporting my view that every justified belief must rest ultimately on foundations, on a terminating regress. You reject that strategy much too casually, in my view, but I will not object here. So we put that strategy aside. And now, my helpful friend, just what do we put in its place?"

Fair enough. How then could one show the need for foundations if an endless regress is not ruled out?

7. TWO LEVELS OF FOUNDATIONALISM

a. We need to distinguish, first, between two forms of foundationalism: one *formal*, the other *substantive*. A type of *formal foundationalism* with respect to a normative or evaluative property ϕ is the view that the conditions (actual and possible) within which ϕ would apply can be specified in general, perhaps recursively. *Substantive foundationalism* is only a particular way of doing so, and coherentism is another.

Simpleminded hedonism is the view that:
   (i) every instance of pleasure is good,
   (ii) everything that causes something good is itself good, and
   (iii) everything that is good is so in virtue of (i) or (ii) above.
Simpleminded hedonism is a type of formal foundationalism with respect to the good.

Classical foundationalism in epistemology is the view that:
   (i) every infallible, indubitable belief is justified,
   (ii) every belief deductively inferred from justified beliefs is itself justified, and

178

    (iii) every belief that is justified is so in virtue of (i) or (ii) above. Classical foundationalism is a type of formal foundationalism with respect to epistemic justification.

    Both of the foregoing theories – simpleminded hedonism in ethics, and classical foundationalism in epistemology – are of course flawed. But they both remain examples of formal foundationalist theories.

b. One way of arguing in favor of formal foundationalism in epistemology is to formulate a convincing formal foundationalist theory of justification. But classical foundationalism in epistemology no longer has for many the attraction that it had for Descartes, nor has any other form of epistemic foundationalism won general acceptance. Indeed epistemic foundationalism has been generally abandoned and its advocates have been put on the defensive by the writings of Wittgenstein, Quine, Sellars, Rescher, Aune, Harman, Lehrer, and others. It is lamentable that in our headlong rush away from foundationalism we have lost sight of the different types of foundationalism (formal vs. substantive) and of the different grades of each type. Too many of us now see it as a blur to be decried and avoided. Thus our present attempt to bring it all into better focus.

c. If we cannot argue from a generally accepted foundationalist theory, what reason is there to accept formal foundationalism? There is no reason to think that the conditions (actual and possible) within which an object is spherical are generally specifiable in nongeometric terms. Why should we think that the conditions (actual and possible) within which a belief is epistemically justified are generally specifiable in nonepistemic terms?

    So far as I can see, the main reason for accepting formal foundationalism in the absence of an actual, convincing formal foundationalist theory is the very plausible idea that epistemic justification is subject to the supervenience that characterizes normative and evaluative properties generally. Thus, if a car is a good car, then any physical replica of that car must be just as good. If it is a good car in virtue of such properties as being economical, little prone to break down, etc., then surely any exact replica would share all such properties and would thus be equally good. Similarly, if a belief is epistemically justified, it is presumably so in virtue of its character and its basis in perception, memory, or inference (if any). Thus any belief exactly like it in its character and its basis must be equally well justified. Epistemic justification is supervenient. The justification of a belief supervenes on such properties of it as its content and its basis (if any) in perception, memory, or inference. Such a doctrine of supervenience may itself be considered, with considerable justice, a grade of foundationalism. For it entails that every instance of justified belief is founded on a number of its nonepistemic properties, such as its having a certain basis in perception, memory, and inference, or the like.

But there are higher grades of foundationalism as well. There is, for instance, the doctrine that the conditions (actual and possible) within which a belief would be epistemically justified *can be specified* in general, perhaps recursively (and by reference to such notions as perception, memory, and inference).

A higher grade yet of formal foundationalism requires not only that the conditions for justified belief be specifiable, in general, but that they be specifiable by a simple, comprehensive theory.

d. Simpleminded hedonism is a formal foundationalist theory of the highest grade. If it is true, then in every possible world goodness supervenes on pleasure and causation in a way that is recursively specifiable by means of a very simple theory.

Classical foundationalism in epistemology is also a formal foundationalist theory of the highest grade. If it is true, then in every possible world epistemic justification supervenes on infallibility-cum-indubitability and deductive inference in a way that is recursively specifiable by means of a very simple theory.

Surprisingly enough, coherentism may also turn out to be formal foundationalism of the highest grade, provided only that the concept of coherence is itself both simple enough and free of any normative or evaluative admixture. Given these provisos, coherentism explains how epistemic justification supervenes on the nonepistemic in a theory of remarkable simplicity: a belief is justified iff it has a place within a system of beliefs that is coherent and comprehensive.

It is a goal of ethics to explain how the ethical rightness of an action supervenes on what is not ethically evaluative or normative. Similarly, it is a goal of epistemology to explain how the epistemic justification of a belief supervenes on what is not epistemically evaluative or normative. If coherentism aims at this goal, that imposes restrictions on the notion of coherence, which must now be conceived innocent of epistemically evaluative or normative admixture. Its substance must therefore consist of such concepts as explanation, probability, and logical implication – with these conceived, in turn, innocent of normative or evaluative content.

e. We have found a surprising kinship between coherentism and substantive foundationalism, both of which turn out to be varieties of a deeper foundationalism. This deeper foundationalism is applicable to any normative or evaluative property ϕ, and it comes in three grades. The *first* or lowest is simply the supervenience of ϕ; the idea that whenever something has ϕ its having it is founded on certain others of its properties which fall into certain restricted sorts. The *second* is the explicable supervenience of ϕ: the idea that there are formulable principles that explain in quite general terms the conditions (actual and possible) within which ϕ applies. The *third* and highest is the easily explicable supervenience of ϕ: the idea that there is a *simple* theory that explains the conditions within which ϕ applies. We have found the coherentist and the substantive foundationalist sharing a primary goal: the development of a formal foundationalist theory of the highest grade. For they both want a simple theory that explains precisely how epistemic justification supervenes, in general, on the nonepistemic. This insight gives us an unusual viewpoint on some recent attacks against foundationalism. Let us now consider as an example a certain simple form of argument distilled from the recent antifoundationalist literature.[5]

8. DOXASTIC ASCENT ARGUMENTS

Several attacks on foundationalism turn on a sort of "doxastic ascent" argument that calls for closer scrutiny.[6] Here are two examples:

A. A belief B is foundationally justified for S in virtue of having property F only if S is justified in believing (1) that most at least of his beliefs with property F are true, and (2) that B has property F. But this means that belief B is not foundational after all, and indeed that the very notion of (empirical) foundational belief is incoherent.

It is sometimes held, for example, that perceptual or observational beliefs are often justified through their origin in the exercise of one or more of our five senses in standard conditions of perception. The advocate of doxastic ascent would raise a vigorous protest, however, for in his view the mere fact of such sensory prompting is impotent to justify the belief prompted.

---

5 The argument of this whole section is developed in greater detail in my paper "The Foundations of Foundationalism," *Noûs* 14 (1980): 547–65; see Chapter 9 herein.

6 For some examples of the influence of doxastic ascent arguments, see Wilfrid Sellars's writing in epistemology: e.g., "Empiricism and the Philosophy of Mind," in *Science, Perception and Reality* (London: Routledge & Kegan Paul, 1963), ch. 5, especially section VIII, and particularly p. 168. Also I. T. Oakley, "An Argument for Skepticism Concerning Justified Beliefs," *American Philosophical Quarterly* 13 (1976): 221–8; and Bonjour, "Can Empirical Knowledge Have a Foundation?"

Such prompting must be coupled with the further belief that one's senses work well in the circumstances, or the like. For we are dealing here with *knowledge*, which requires not blind faith but *reasoned* trust. But now surely the further belief about the reliability of one's senses itself cannot rest on blind faith but requires its own backing of reasons, and we are off on the regress.

B. A belief B of proposition P is foundationally justified for S only if S is justified in believing that there are no factors present that would cause him to make mistakes on the matter of the proposition P. But, again, this means that belief B is not foundational after all and indeed that the notion of (empirical) foundational belief is incoherent.

From the vantage point of formal foundationalism, neither of these arguments seems conclusive. In the first place, as we have seen, what makes a belief foundational (formally) is its having a property that is nonepistemic (not evaluative in the epistemic or cognitive mode), and does not involve inference from other beliefs, but guarantees, via a necessary principle, that the belief in question is justified. A belief B is made foundational by having some such nonepistemic property that yields its justification. Take my belief that I am in pain in a context where it is caused by my being in pain. The property that my belief then has, of being a self-attribution of pain caused by one's own pain, is, let us suppose, a nonepistemic property that yields the justification of any belief that has it. So my belief that I am in pain is in that context foundationally justified. Along with my belief that I am in pain, however, there come other beliefs that are equally well justified, such as my belief that someone is in pain. Thus I am foundationally justified in believing that I am in pain only if I am justified in believing that someone is in pain. Those who object to foundationalism as in A or B above are hence mistaken in thinking that their premises would refute foundationalism. The fact is that they would not touch it. For a belief is no less foundationally justified for having its justification yoked to that of another closely related belief.

The advocate of arguments like A and B must apparently strengthen his premises. He must apparently claim that the beliefs whose justification is entailed by the foundationally justified status of belief B must in some sense function as a *necessary source* of the justification of B. And this would of course preclude giving B foundationally justified status. For if the *being justified* of those beliefs is an *essential* part of the source of the justification of B, then it is ruled out that there be a wholly *nonepistemic* source of B's justification.

That brings us to a second point about A and B, for it should now be clear that these cannot be selectively aimed at foundationalism. In particular, they seem neither more nor less valid objections to coherentism than to foundationalism, or so I will now argue about each of them in turn.

> (A') A belief X is justified for S in virtue of membership in a coherent set only if S is justified in believing (1) that most at least of his beliefs with the property of thus cohering are true, and (2) that X has that property.

Any coherentist who accepts A seems bound to accept A'. For what could he possibly appeal to as a relevant difference? But A' is a quicksand of endless depth. (How is he justified in believing A'(1)? Partly through justified belief that *it* coheres? And what would justify *this*? And so on. . . .)

> (B') A belief X is justified for S only if S is justified in believing that there are no factors present that would cause him to make mistakes on the subject matter of that belief.

Again, any coherentist who accepts B seems bound to accept B'. But this is just another road to the quicksand. (For S is justified in believing that there are no such factors only if . . . and so on.)

Why are such regresses vicious? The key is again, to my mind, the doctrine of supervenience. Such regresses are vicious because they would be logically incompatible with the supervenience of epistemic justification on such nonepistemic facts as the totality of a subject's beliefs, his cognitive and experiential history, and as many other nonepistemic facts as may seem at all relevant. The idea is that there is a set of such nonepistemic facts surrounding a justified belief such that no belief could possibly have been surrounded by those very facts without being justified. Advocates of A or B run afoul of such supervenience, since they are surely committed to the more general views derivable from either of A or B by deleting "foundationally" from its first sentence. In each case the more general view would then preclude the possibility of supervenience, since it would entail that the source of justification *always* includes an *epistemic* component.

9. COHERENTISM AND SUBSTANTIVE FOUNDATIONALISM

a. The notions of coherentism and substantive foundationalism remain unexplicated. We have relied so far on our intuitive grasp of them. In this section we shall consider reasons for the view that substantive foundationalism is superior to coherentism. To assess these reasons, we need some more explicit account of the difference between the two.

By coherentism we shall mean any view according to which the ultimate sources of justification for any belief lie in relations among that belief and other beliefs of the subject: explanatory relations, perhaps, or relations of probability or logic.

According to substantive foundationalism, as it is to be understood here, there are ultimate sources of justification other than relations among beliefs. Traditionally these additional sources have pertained to the special content of the belief or its special relations to the subjective experience of the believer.

b. The view that justification is a matter of relations among beliefs is open to an objection from alternative coherent systems or detachment from reality, depending on one's perspective. From the latter perspective the body of beliefs is held constant and the surrounding world is allowed to vary; from the former it is the surrounding world that is held constant while the body of beliefs is allowed to vary. In either case, according to the coherentist, there could be no effect on the justification for any belief.

Let us sharpen the question before us as follows. Is there reason to think that there is at least one system B', alternative to our actual system of beliefs B, such that B' contains a belief X with the following properties:

(i) in our present nonbelief circumstances we would not be justified in having belief X even if we accepted along with that belief (as our total system of beliefs) the entire belief system B' in which it is embedded (no matter how acceptance of B' were brought about); and

(ii) that is so despite the fact that belief X coheres within B' at least as fully as does some actual justified belief of ours within our actual belief system B (where the justification of that actual justified belief is alleged by the coherentist to derive solely from its coherence within our actual body of beliefs B).

The coherentist is vulnerable to counterexamples of this sort right at the surface of his body of beliefs, where we find beliefs with minimal coherence, whose detachment and replacement with contrary beliefs would have little effect on the coherence of the body. Thus take my belief that I have a headache when I do have a splitting headache, and let us suppose that this *does* cohere within my present body of beliefs. (Thus I have no reason to doubt my present introspective beliefs, and so on. And if my belief does *not* cohere, so much the worse for coherentism, since my belief is surely justified.) Here then we have a perfectly justified or warranted belief. And yet such a belief may well have relevant relations of explanation, logic, or probability with at most a small set of other beliefs of mine at the time: say, that I am not free of headache, that I am in pain, that someone is in pain, and the like. If so, then an equally coherent alternative is not far to seek. Let everything remain constant, *including* the splitting headache, except for the following: replace the belief that I have a headache with the belief that I do *not* have a headache, the belief that I am in pain with the belief that I am *not* in pain, the belief that someone is in pain with the belief that someone is *not* in pain, and so on. I contend that my resulting hypothetical system of beliefs would cohere as fully as does my actual system of beliefs, and yet my hypothetical belief that I do *not* have a headache would not therefore be justified. What makes this difference concerning justification between my actual belief that I have a headache and the hypothetical belief that I am free of headache, each as coherent as the other within its own system, if not the actual splitting headache? But the headache is *not* itself a belief nor a relation among beliefs and is thus in no way constitutive of the internal coherence of my body of beliefs.

Some might be tempted to respond by alleging that one's belief about whether or not one has a headache is always *infallible*. But since we could devise similar examples for the various sensory modalities and propositional attitudes, the response given for the case of headache would have to be generalized. In effect, it would have to cover "peripheral" beliefs generally – beliefs at the periphery of one's body of beliefs, minimally coherent with the rest. These peripheral beliefs would all be said to be infallible. That is, again, a possible response, but it leads to a capitulation by the coherentist to the radical foundationalist on a crucial issue that has traditionally divided them: the infallibility of beliefs about one's own subjective states.

What is more, not all peripheral beliefs are about one's own subjective states. The direct realist is probably right that some beliefs about our surroundings are uninferred and yet justified. Consider my present belief that the table before me is oblong. This presumably coheres with such other beliefs of mine as that the table has the same shape as the piece of paper before me, which is oblong, and a different shape than the window frame here, which is square, and so on. So far as I can see, however, there is no insurmountable obstacle to replacing that whole set of coherent beliefs with an equally coherent set as follows: that the table before me is square, that the table has the same shape as the square window frame, and a different shape than the piece of paper, which is oblong, and so on. The important points are (a) that this replacement may be made without changing the rest of one's body of beliefs or any aspect of the world beyond, including one's present visual experience of something oblong, not square, as one looks at the table before one; and (b) that is so, in part, because of the fact (c) that the subject need not have any beliefs about his present sensory experience.

Some might be tempted to respond by alleging that one's present experience is *self-intimating*, i.e., always necessarily taken note of and reflected in one's beliefs. Thus if anyone has visual experience of something oblong, then he believes that he has such experience. But this would involve a further important concession by the coherentist to the radical foundationalist, who would have been granted two of his most cherished doctrines: the infallibility of introspective belief and the self-intimation of experience.

10. THE FOUNDATIONALIST'S DILEMMA

The antifoundationalist zeal of recent years has left several forms of foundationalism standing. These all share the conviction that a belief can be justified not only by its coherence within a comprehensive system but also by an appropriate combination of observational content and origin in the use of the senses in standard conditions. What follows presents a dilemma for any foundationalism based on any such idea.

a. We may surely suppose that beings with observational mechanisms radically unlike ours might also have knowledge of their environment. (That seems possible even if the radical difference in observational mechanisms precludes overlap in substantive concepts and beliefs.)

b. Let us suppose that there is such a being, for whom experience of type ϕ (of which we have no notion) has a role with respect to his beliefs of type ϕ analogous to the role that our visual experience has with respect to our visual beliefs. Thus we might have a schema such as the following:

Human	*Extraterrestrial being*
Visual experience	ϕ experience
Experience of something red	Experience of something F
Belief that there is something red before one	Belief that there is something F before one

186

c. It is often recognized that our visual experience intervenes in two ways with respect to our visual beliefs: as cause and as justification. But these are not wholly independent. Presumably, the justification of the belief that something here is red derives at least in part from the fact that it originates in a visual experience of something red that takes place in normal circumstances.

d. Analogously, the extraterrestrial belief that something here has the property of being F might be justified partly by the fact that it originates in a φ experience of something F that takes place in normal circumstances.

e. A simple question presents the foundationalist's dilemma: regarding the epistemic principle that underlies our justification for believing that something here is red on the basis of our visual experience of something red, is it proposed as a fundamental principle or as a derived generalization? Let us compare the famous Principle of Utility of value theory, according to which it is best for that to happen which, of all the possible alternatives in the circumstances, would bring with it into the world the greatest balance of pleasure over pain, joy over sorrow, happiness over unhappiness, content over discontent, or the like. Upon this fundamental principle one may then base various generalizations, rules of thumb, and maxims of public health, nutrition, legislation, etiquette, hygiene, and so on. But these are all then derived generalizations which rest for their validity on the fundamental principle. Similarly, one may also ask, with respect to the generalizations advanced by our foundationalist, whether these are proposed as fundamental principles or as derived maxims or the like. This sets him face to face with a dilemma, each of whose alternatives is problematic. If his proposals are meant to have the status of secondary or derived maxims, for instance, then it would be quite unphilosophical to stop there. Let us turn, therefore, to the other alternative.

f. On reflection it seems rather unlikely that epistemic principles for the justification of observational beliefs by their origin in sensory experience could have a status more fundamental than that of derived generalizations. For by granting such principles fundamental status we would open the door to a multitude of equally basic principles with no unifying factor. There would be some for vision, some for hearing, etc., without even mentioning the corresponding extraterrestrial principles.

g. It may appear that there is after all an idea, however, that unifies our multitude of principles. For they all involve sensory experience and sensible characteristics. But what is a sensible characteristic? Aristotle's answer appeals to examples: colors, shapes, sounds, and so on. Such a notion might enable us to unify perceptual epistemic principles under some more fundamental principle such as the following:

> If σ is a sensible characteristic, then the belief that there is something with σ before one is (prima facie) justified if it is based on a visual experience of something with σ in conditions that are normal with respect to σ.

h. There are at least two difficulties with such a suggestion, however, and neither one can be brushed aside easily. First, it is not clear that we can have a viable notion of sensible characteristic on the basis of examples so diverse as colors, shapes, tones, odors, and so on. Second, the authority of such a principle apparently derives from contingent circumstances concerning the reliability of beliefs prompted by sensory experiences of certain sorts. According to the foundationalist, our visual beliefs are justified by their origin in our visual experience or the like. Would such beliefs be equally well justified in a world where beliefs with such an origin were nearly always false?

i. In addition, finally, even if we had a viable notion of such characteristics, it is not obvious that fundamental knowledge of reality would have to derive causally or otherwise from sensory experience of such characteristics. How could one impose reasonable limits on extraterrestrial mechanisms for noninferential acquisition of beliefs? Is it not possible that such mechanisms need not always function through sensory experience of any sort? Would such beings necessarily be denied any knowledge of their surroundings and indeed of any contingent spatio-temporal fact? Let us suppose them to possess a complex system of true beliefs concerning their surroundings, the structures below the surface of things, exact details of history and geography, all constituted by concepts none of which corresponds to any of our sensible characteristics. What then? Is it not possible that their basic beliefs should all concern fields of force, waves, mathematical structures, and numerical assignments to variables in several dimensions? This is no doubt an exotic notion, but even so it still seems conceivable. And if it is in fact possible, what then shall we say of the noninferential beliefs of such beings? Would we have to concede the existence of special epistemic principles that can validate their noninferential beliefs? Would it not be preferable to formulate more abstract principles that can cover both human and extraterrestrial foundations? If such more abstract principles are in fact accessible, then the less general principles that define the human

188

foundations and those that define the extraterrestrial foundations are both derived principles whose validity depends on that of the more abstract principles. In this the human and extraterrestrial epistemic principles would resemble rules of good nutrition for an infant and an adult. The infant's rules would of course be quite unlike those valid for the adult. But both would still be based on a more fundamental principle that postulates the ends of well-being and good health. What more fundamental principles might support both human and extraterrestrial knowledge in the way that those concerning good health and well-being support rules of nutrition for both the infant and the adult?

11. RELIABILISM: AN ETHICS OF MORAL VIRTUES AND AN EPISTEMOLOGY OF INTELLECTUAL VIRTUES

In what sense is the doctor attending Frau Hitler justified in performing an action that brings with it far less value than one of its accessible alternatives? According to one promising idea, the key is to be found in the rules that he embodies through stable dispositions. His action is the result of certain stable virtues, and there are no equally virtuous alternate *dispositions* that, given his cognitive limitations, he might have embodied with equal or better total consequences, and that would have led him to infanticide in the circumstances. The important move for our purpose is the stratification of justification. Primary justification attaches to virtues and other dispositions, to stable dispositions to act, through their greater contribution of value when compared with alternatives. Secondary justification attaches to particular acts in virtue of their source in virtues or other such justified dispositions.

The same strategy may also prove fruitful in epistemology. Here primary justification would apply to *intellectual* virtues, to stable dispositions for belief acquisition, through their greater contribution toward getting us to the truth. Secondary justification would then attach to particular beliefs in virtue of their source in intellectual virtues or other such justified dispositions.[7]

---

7 This puts in a more traditional perspective the contemporary effort to develop a "causal theory of knowing." From our viewpoint, this effort is better understood not as an attempt to *define* propositional knowledge but as an attempt to formulate fundamental principles of justification.

Cf. D. Armstrong, *Belief, Truth and Knowledge* (Cambridge, 1973); and that of F. Dretske, A. Goldman, and M. Swain, whose relevant already published work is included in *Essays on Knowledge and Justification*, ed. G. Pappas and M. Swain (Ithaca and London, 1978). But the theory is still under development by Goldman and Swain, who have reached general conclusions about it similar to those suggested here, though not necessarily – so far as I know – for the same reasons or in the same overall context.

That raises parallel questions for ethics and epistemology. We need to consider more carefully the concept of a virtue and the distinction between moral and intellectual virtues. In epistemology, there is reason to think that the most useful and illuminating notion of intellectual virtue will prove broader than our tradition would suggest and must give due weight not only to the subject and his intrinsic nature but also to his environment and to his epistemic community. This is a large topic, however, to which I hope some of us will turn with more space, and insight, than I can now command.[8,9]

12. SUMMARY

1. *Two assumptions*: (A1) that for a belief to constitute knowledge it must be (a) true and (b) justified; and (A2) that the justification relevant to whether or not one knows is a sort of epistemic or theoretical justification to be distinguished from its practical counterpart.

2. *Knowledge and criteria.* Particularism is distinguished from methodism: the first gives priority to particular examples of knowledge over general methods of criteria, whereas the second reverses that order. The methodism of Descartes leads him to an elaborate dogmatism whereas that of Hume leads him to a very simple skepticism. The particularist is, of course, antiskeptical on principle.

3. *Two metaphors: the raft and the pyramid.* For the foundationalist every piece of knowledge stands at the apex of a pyramid that rests on stable and secure foundations whose stability and security does not derive from the upper stories or sections. For the coherentist a body of knowledge is a free-floating raft every plank of which helps directly or indirectly to keep all the others in place, and no plank of which would retain its status with no help from the others.

4. *A coherentist critique of foundationalism.* No mental state can provide a foundation for empirical knowledge. For if such a state is propositional, then it is fallible and hence no secure foundation. But if it is *not* propositional, then how can it possibly serve as a foundation for belief? How can one infer or justify anything on the basis of a state that, having no propositional content, must be

8 The main ideas in this essay were first presented in a seminar of 1976–7 at the University of Texas. I am grateful to those who made that seminar a valuable stimulus, as listed in the acknowledgments at the beginning of this volume.
9 This topic is taken up in Chapters 13 and 16.

190

logically dumb? An analogy with ethics suggests a reason to reject this dilemma. Other reasons are also advanced and discussed.

5. *The regress argument.* In defending his position, the foundationalist often attempts to rule out the very possibility of an infinite regress of justification (which leads him to the necessity for a foundation). Some of his arguments to that end are examined.

6. *The relation of justification and foundationalist strategy.* An alternative foundationalist strategy is exposed, one that does not require ruling out the possibility of an infinite regress of justification.

7. *Two levels of foundationalism.* Substantive foundationalism is distinguished from formal foundationalism, three grades of which are exposed: first, the supervenience of epistemic justification; second, its explicable supervenience; and, third, its supervenience explicable by means of a simple theory. There turns out to be a surprising kinship between coherentism and substantive foundationalism, both of which aim at a formal foundationalism of the highest grade, at a theory of the greatest simplicity that explains how epistemic justification supervenes on nonepistemic factors.

8. *Doxastic ascent arguments.* The distinction between formal and substantive foundationalism provides an unusual viewpoint on some recent attacks against foundationalism. We consider doxastic ascent arguments as an example.

9. *Coherentism and substantive foundationalism.* It is argued that substantive foundationalism is superior since coherentism is unable to account adequately for the epistemic status of beliefs at the "periphery" of a body of beliefs.

10. *The foundationalist's dilemma.* All foundationalism based on sense experience is subject to a fatal dilemma.

11. *Reliabilism.* An alternative to foundationalism of sense experience is sketched.

11

The coherence of virtue and the virtue of coherence

Polyfacetic epistemology would answer the skeptic, provide how-to-think manuals, explain how we know, and more. To some it is the project of assuring oneself, of validating one's knowledge or supposed knowledge, turning it into real and assured knowledge, thus defeating the skeptic. To others it is a set of rules or instructions, a guide to the perplexed, a manual for conducting the intellect. To others yet it is a meta-discipline, but one whose purpose is not nearly so much guidance as understanding, understanding of what gives us the knowledge we do have, of what factors serve to justify so many of our beliefs well enough to make them knowledge.

What follows is epistemology as understanding, an attempt to understand the relation between epistemic coherence and intellectual virtue at the foundation of epistemology: between the comprehensive coherence prized in the thirst for understanding and the "reliability" that makes a faculty or procedure intellectually virtuous.

A. SUPERVENIENCE

The central concept of epistemology is justification: not the practical justification of action, nor even such justification of belief as may come of its being expedient or generous or charitable; but rather the cognitive justification required to distinguish belief that is knowledge from what is little more than a lucky guess. Such cognitive justification is a normative or evaluative notion involved in the guidance or assessment of the intellect. Being thus justified is hence bound to share in the supervenience of the normative and evaluative generally. If an apple is a good apple, it is so in virtue of nonevaluative properties, perhaps being juicy, sweet, and large. And any other apple just like it in respect of all such properties could not fail to be equally good. Similarly, if a belief is cognitively justified, it is so presumably in virtue of nonevaluative properties, perhaps having a certain source in perception, introspection, memory, or inference, or some combination of these. And any other belief just like it in respect of all such properties could not fail to be equally well justified.

Let us speak of nonevaluative properties of belief on which cognitive justification supervenes as "justification-making properties."

B. INTERNALISM

Internalism is the view that the justification-making properties of any justified belief must be (epistemically) internal to the mind of the subject who holds that belief, that he could always know such properties of his belief by *reflection*; that is, through mere introspection, memory, and reason (intuitive and deductive).[1]

Externalism is the complement of internalism. According to externalism there can be justification-making properties of a belief which the believer could not possibly discover merely by reflection (introspection, memory, and reason). Reliabilism, for example, today an attractive option, holds to a single, basic justification-making property of any justified belief: its having for source a reliable way of forming beliefs, one which (roughly) would normally lead such a subject to true beliefs in his normal environment. Clearly one might not always be able to tell the presence or absence of a reliable source in this sense merely by reflection, even when one's belief did in fact have such a source.

Internalism imposes a strong restriction on possible justification-making properties of belief. Since it is not a compellingly obvious restriction, simply on inspection, why might anyone be moved to accept it?

C. ANSWERING THE SKEPTIC

Answering the skeptic has widely been thought the main project of epistemology, though occasionally by such names as validating our knowledge or assuring ourselves. The skeptic to be answered, moreover, is not just he for whom religion is opium or history bunk, but he for whom there is no better alternative than solipsism or worse. Since *by one or another route* what the skeptic ends up demanding is absolute proof – deductive proof from what is perfectly obvious in the absence of any but perfectly obvious presuppositions – it is such proof from the manifest that is held up as the key to real knowledge, to what we would have if only we could validate our knowledge, if we could only assure ourselves.

Here we are interested not in the sad denouement of that familiar story, but only in the conception of knowledge and justification that goes with

---

1 Gender-unspecific reference is often made here with "he" and its cognates, which may then be read as "she or he" or "her or him," or the like.

it. For if real justification requires proof from the manifest, and only the a priori and the mental can be truly manifest, then it is plausible that whenever a belief is really justified, the subject harboring that belief could indeed discover its justification-making properties by mere *reflection*.

"Cartesianism" aptly labels the radically foundationalist view that a belief is cognitively justified if and only if its object either (a) is manifest in itself to the believer in the absence of any but manifest presuppositions (amounting thus to something *given*), or (b) is arrived at through deductive proof from ultimate premises all of which are thus manifest.

D. CARTESIANISM

Cartesianism is universally abandoned, but for different reasons and in favor of different alternatives.

Some abandoned Cartesianism for its subsequent association with an ontology of ghostly phenomena constitutive of the given. But that is an unfair charge of guilt by association.

Others abandoned Cartesianism because outside the a priori they could find only too little scope for indubitability of proposition or infallibility of belief. But these can be answered by a more modest foundationalism whose foundations require not such indubitability or infallibility, but only initial credibility or high degree of intrinsic plausibility. Even such attenuated foundationalism proves too rigorous, however, if nothing but perception, memory, and introspection is allowed to provide the initial credibility or intrinsic plausibility required at the foundation. For deduction from the perceived, introspected, or remembered still gives an unacceptably impoverished world view. Further weakening of Cartesianism has thus won general favor among the moderate, to allow not only deduction, but also induction, both enumerative and hypothetical or explanatory.

The most radical break with Cartesianism is made by those who reject the very notion of a given or foundation in any of its forms no matter how modest. And the crucial guiding principle that informs (or deforms) their dissent is close kin to internalism: that a belief cannot be justified merely because it reflects reality (even manifest reality), or because it is of a sort that while fallible still tends to reflect reality, or because it comes out of reliable process; that no such feature of belief justifies in the absence of awareness by the believer that his belief has the feature. To think otherwise is to confuse causation with justification, causes with reasons, and to accept inadequate "thermometer" or "mirror" conceptions of knowledge.

That radical rejection of manifest foundations seems to require an

194

Intellectualist Model of Justification, according to which no belief is ever justified simply by being an accurate reflection in a mirror so constituted as to be generally accurate in such reflections. A further meta-belief is always required: that there is the belief in question (and that it is of a reliable sort). Only such meta-belief makes possible sufficient justification for a particular observation or memory belief. But such introspective meta-belief must then fulfill the same requirement, surely, for if itself unjustified it could hardly justify its object belief. And introspection can no more justify in virtue of amounting merely to the taking of the given than can perception or memory, not for our radical critic of givenness. Hence there must be a meta-meta-belief, and we are off on a regress inexorably vicious to particular justified belief by any finite mind.

E. CONTEXTUALISM

A further close kin of internalism insists on inference as the key to justification: a belief is justified if and only if it represents the conclusion of valid reasoning, of a good inference. And this leads compellingly to contextualism, to the view that justification is always relative to a context defined by a set of accepted premises. Our contextualism appeals not to public debate or argument but to reasoning that need not be made public. But any finite being who engages in such reasoning must have premises to which he is not reasoning – not *then* reasoning. *All* such premises will now be on a par: those due to observation or memory as well as those imbibed with superstition. Superstition will be just as much knowledge, relative to superstition, as is knowledge based on observation or memory, relative to observation or memory.

Both views of justification most recently considered tend to agree with internalism. If an important part of what justifies a belief is always that one hold it reliable in virtue of its sort, then an important part of the justification-making property of a particular belief is always discoverable by mere reflection. But we have seen such a view lead to vicious regress. If, on the other hand, what justifies a belief is always its having been consciously inferred from certain propositions taken in the context as premises, then again what justifies one's belief is always (in principle) discoverable through mere reflection. But contextualism turns out to be a radical relativism that puts superstition on a par with knowledge.

We have now considered three views of justification in harmony with internalism: Cartesianism's view of justification as deduction from the manifest (radical foundationalism); the view of a belief's justification as including awareness of the apparent reliability of its sort (doxastic ascent); and justification as valid inference from premises provided by the context (contextual givenness). And these have all turned out at best highly problematic. Accordingly, we turn away from internalism and look to its alternative.

F. EXTERNALISM

According to externalism the factors that justify one's belief need not be open to discovery by one's own mere reflection. An attractive option compatible with externalism is reliabilism, which finds the basic source of any belief's justification in a single factor: namely, the belief's being of a reliable sort, of a sort that tends to be true. For contingent, empirical beliefs the relevant sorts have most often been thought to be causal sorts pertaining to the origin of the belief in the likes of perception or memory. And it would seem a matter for observation and science to determine whether or not a particular perceptual faculty leads reliably to truth for beings like us in an environment like ours. But we need to look more closely at just how this is to be carried out.

A simple inductive procedure would seem suspiciously circular. For it would amount to allowing ourselves the use of perceptual faculty P in arriving at a set of what we then took to be truths, which would in turn be used to reflect favorably back on faculty P for leading us to so many truths. Would it count in favor of the reliability of a newspaper that it is so often right in its reports if we accept the reports only because they appear in that newspaper? "But why restrict ourselves to the use of P in arriving at the relevant truths?" Fair enough. Suppose we had an alternative means P' of arriving at beliefs of the relevant sort, of the sort that P delivers, beliefs that can bear on the reliability of P. We would then seem to have an independent way of determining reliability of P, for we could use P' for that purpose. This is encouraging until we reflect on just how we could go about determining the reliability of P'. We could not use P' itself along with enumerative induction, again on pain of vicious circularity. But what then could we appeal to if not the likes of P itself? Introducing P' to help with P appears only to widen the circle of justification, without making it more benign.

A reliabilist justification of rationality would appeal, along lines just examined, to the reliability of rationality as shown by all the truths it delivers. All the truths it delivers by whose lights? Why, by the rationalist's lights, of course. But then the superstitious are well placed to respond with a reliabilist justification of superstition that seems, by parity of reasoning, equally effective. "Look," they might exclaim, "look at how reliable superstition is, as shown by all the truths that it delivers." All the truths that it delivers by whose lights? "Why, by the lights of the

196

superstitious, of course." Such justification seems a foot-stamping whirl to nowhere.

Admittedly the circle involved is not of the ordinary sort where we reach the conclusion only by circling back to the premises, the conclusion itself lying among the premises. Our inductive justification of the reliability of a faculty P is more like a spiral than a circle.

A particularly vicious circle of justification would have one and the same proposition P as both sole premise and conclusion.

A further vicious circle might take the form of the following argument:

> *Premise*: I believe that anything I believe is true.
> *Conclusion*: Anything I believe is true.

For here the argument is an enthymeme whose missing premise is nothing other than the conclusion.

Our spirals of justification take rather an argument form like the following (AR):

1. It is only source S that emits all and only our beliefs in $H1, \ldots, Hn$.
2. $H1, \ldots, Hn$ are all true.
3. Source S is (therefore) reliable.

Now if enumerative induction – which leads from 1 and 2 to 3 – is reliable, and if the sources of 1 and 2 are reliable, then by reliabilism proposition 3 would be emitted by a reliable source and hence credible.

Still on the assumption of reliabilism, however, an argument of the form AR above will serve to *establish* its conclusion – to demonstrate its truth and justification – only if its premises are true and justified. But note that if premise 1 is true, then given reliabilism, our acceptance of premise 2 is justified only if source S is reliable (since, given 1, the overall source of 2 will have to include S as an essential element). So there is a much more direct, deductive route to the truth of 3 from the assumptions necessarily required by reliabilism for successful use of AR as a way to establish 3. The argument to conclusion 3 from premises 1 and 2 via enumerative induction will help show 3 true and justified only if each of 1 and 2 is true and justified. But if 1 is true then to assume 2 justified is, given reliabilism, to presuppose that 3 is true. So argument form AR cannot be used to *establish* a conclusion like 3 – to demonstrate its truth and justification – without falling into a vicious spiral through the presuppositions required for such use of AR. Given the requirement for such presuppositions, the inductive argument is quite superfluous, for its conclusion is among the presuppositions required for its use.

Another way of objecting to AR as a way for the reliabilist to defend its conclusion charges that such use of it amounts to *begging the question*.

Circular question-begging particularly blatant is involved in the presence of a conclusion among its premises as in "*P*, therefore *P*."

Spiral question-begging is also vicious though it does not put the conclusion itself among the premises.

When one lists premises in support of a conclusion, presumably one advances them as both true and justified. What is vicious about the reliabilist's spiral offering of AR in justification of its conclusion is that, given reliabilism and the affirmed truth of the first premise, when he advances the second premise *as justified* he must *presuppose* the truth of the conclusion and hence beg the question (in the spiral mode).

What recourse is then left for the reliabilist who wishes to go beyond the mere affirmation of his main principle, who wishes to develop a reliabilist theory of knowledge by finding specific sources of belief that emit justified beliefs because of their reliability as sources of true belief? How could he establish his inclusion of any such source on the list of approved sources without falling into a vicious circle or spiral?

One might of course be forced to give in to a fideism of cognitive faculties by resolving to (continue to) trust our faculties in the absence of any good argument for doing so. But remember, the superstitious could match trust with trust and there would be nothing to choose between us. Our various faculties would be arrayed on our side with nothing to ground them but our trust, and his various superstitions would be arrayed on his side with no better or worse basis. And if we unify our faculties by calling them all reliable and extolling reliability, he can no less reasonably do the same for his superstitions, and what then would there be to choose between us?

G. VINDICATION

In extremis even the philosopher may perhaps be allowed appeal to the practical, to the requirements of our nature, to habits or common sense, or to our needs and desires. Some do make such appeal, even before reaching our extremity. For William James the requirements of our passionate nature have a proper bearing even on the most theoretical of questions, so long as the option is living, momentous, and forced, and so long as purely cognitive evidence does not already decide it. For James there are important issues of theology and metaphysics properly decidable by our passionate nature since the intellect is unable to decide them on its own.

Consider, for example, the following case for immortality, one I would call Kierkegaardian were it not as strikingly absent from his commentators as apparent in Kierkegaard.

The deepest, most fulfilling forms of (subjective) happiness appear to rest on various sorts of knowledge: that we love and are loved, that we have a place in a community, that we have a future in that community, that we are accomplishing something of value in our lives, and other like truths. What if it is all in fact a raft of lies, forever unbeknownst to anyone? Would that necessarily affect how (subjectively) happy we can be? Or is it not really just belief that counts, whether it amounts to knowledge or not? If believing and favoring are positive, with disbelieving and disfavoring their respective negative counterparts, then the magnitude of our happiness (positive) or unhappiness (negative) over a given matter is determined by the product of our belief/disbelief and our favoring/disfavoring with regard to that same matter. Now each of us would no doubt be pleased by the expectation of eternal bliss starting immediately. And the deeper and more vivid our conviction, the more thorough our happy appreciation. Thus the great value of *passionate* subjectivity in (such) religious conviction. Assuming one controls a faith machine applied to oneself, and ruling out undesirable future consequences, would it be irrational to opt for faith? That is very far from obvious, since nothing can be more rational than to bring about deliberately the best one can in the circumstances. And what is the best but the best *all* things considered, that is, considering all the value and disvalue that one's action and its immediate and intrinsic result bring into the world, intrinsically, inherently, and instrumentally? Given the apparent possibility of a faith machine and the rest of the situation envisaged, it does seem possible for the acceptance and harboring of a belief to be rational on a practical basis. The rationality of wishful thinking in our actual historical situation does not follow by any stretch, however, and note how careful James is to delimit its proper application to questions like those of theology or metaphysics beyond the reach of decisive cognitive evidence.

A philosopher stretching in extremis to the practical for "objective ground" may be Sellars, when he concludes that if his ". . . argument is sound, it is reasonable to accept. . . . that IPM judgments are likely to be true, simply on the ground that unless they *are* likely to be true, the concept of effective agency has no application."[2] But just what sort of ground is this? Is it practical or theoretical? Is it outright practical means/end reasoning? Or is it (at least in the first instance) a theoretical deduction of a conclusion from believed premises?[3]

2 "Givenness and Explanatory Coherence," in G. S. Pappas, ed., *Justification and Knowledge* (Dordrecht: D. Reidel, 1979), p. 180. IPM judgments are judgments of introspection, perception, or memory.

3 My colleague Felicia Ackerman remarks here that the solipsist could surely apply the concept of effective agency even if his actions would always have himself for their sole intended object.

Under the practical interpretation, the argument would be the following. We want effective agency but know we can have it only if IPM judgments are reliable, so it would please us to think IPM judgments reliable and agency thus accessible, and it would displease us to think IPM judgments unreliable and agency thus inaccessible. All of this would then give us practical grounds for accepting the reliability of introspection, perception, and memory analogous to the practical grounds on which James would repose his faith (and Kierkegaard, too, if I am not astray).

Under the theoretical interpretation, the argument would be this: We do have effective agency, but can have it only if IPM judgments are reliable, so we may conclude that they are indeed reliable. The problem here is that we cannot gauge the effectiveness of such agency without relying on IPM judgments. Of course the objective now may be not so much to reason linearly from our effectiveness to our reliability, as to heighten consciousness of some coherence-inducing features of our world view, whose coherence and comprehensiveness ultimately yield its justification. Let us reserve judgment on this proposal until the next section, however, which will contain a more general discussion of combined coherence and comprehensiveness as ultimate source of cognitive justification. As for this section, it remains only to conclude with a few general remarks about justification of theory on the basis of goals indiscriminately, of belief on the basis of desires unrestrictedly.

It is not rational belief generally that constitutes knowledge, not belief justified judging by all relevant considerations. On the contrary, knowledge requires an appropriate justification on a certain restricted basis of reasons. What we had best believe, all things considered, and what the (cognitive) evidence points to decisively *need* not coincide, as we have seen already, and could easily see anew with the aid of examples. But suppose the evident and the expedient in the way of belief do coincide so often and systematically, as things in fact stand in our actual historical situation, that it seems clearly the best policy both for individuals and for societies to give their allegiance to standards of evidence with a reasonable degree of rigor, and to avoid wishful thinking. Would that give us a foundation for cognitive values in what is best all things considered, e.g., perhaps a foundation for cognitive justification in the total welfare of the individual or the group? The question raised here is that of the autonomy of cognitive values. Do cognitive values and standards of evidence stand on their own, in isolation from other values and norms, such as those that pertain to the physical or moral welfare of the individual or his group? Our intuition that the evident and the expedient to believe need not coincide might still fail to settle this question, and this for several reasons, among which the following deserves special notice.

In scouting whether the evident and the expedient to believe can diverge, we might leash our imagination unawares with standards of evidence we actually accept for their expediency in the actual world. But such standards would seem mere derived principles issuing from deeper values. If so, then our thought experiment must free our imagination to range wider by releasing it from the standards that we actually accept. These must not be thought to display the essence of the evident but only its accidental features in our actual world.

Wider scouting might begin by postulating not just an isolated wishful thinker rewarded with satisfaction, but a society of wishful thinkers who flourish thereby. Perhaps such a society cannot be made plausible in detail; but nor does it seem obviously impossible. Even if we can imagine such a society, still we may not conclude that for them wishful thinking would yield cognitive justification – even if they would not call it "wishful thinking," of course, not with its present negative connotation anyhow. An obstacle, which looks serious, is that cognitive justification is the sort of justification relevant to knowledge, the sort of justification that distinguishes true belief that is knowledge from true belief that is little more than a lucky guess. This being so, such justification could not possibly turn out to be a property that a belief might have in complete independence from the truth of its object. But cognitive justification could turn out to be such a property of a belief *if mere wishful thinking could provide it.* So mere wishful thinking could not be a source of cognitive justification.

There might of course be possible worlds in which rational agents would and should ignore knowledge in favor of other goods, including goods constituted by beliefs of certain sorts; for example, those that provide comfort. But such beliefs would not necessarily amount to knowledge simply by their aptness for constituting such goods.

Even if cognitive values are not wholly as autonomous as, for all we have determined, they might be (perhaps because they depend for rational status on coherence with other values and with beliefs) yet reducing them to the practical now seems a forlorn hope. Vindication by practical reason is a doubtful way to objective grounds for knowledge.

H. COHERENCE

Recall our spirals of justification constituted by arguments of the form AR:

1. It is only source S that emits all and only our beliefs in $H1, \ldots, Hn$.
2. $H1, \ldots, Hn$ are all true.
3. Source S is (therefore) reliable.

We concluded from discussion of such spirals that presenting an argument like AR as a way of *establishing* its conclusion, or a way of *arguing rationally, persuasively, and conclusively* for acceptance of its conclusion, or as a *demonstration* is ineffective because it begs the question. AR does seem anyhow viciously spiral, since it could only succeed as a sound and rationally persuasive *inductive* argument through the immediately patent existence of a *deductive* argument to the *same conclusion*, one that demands nothing more as premises than the inductive argument requires as premises or presuppositions (implicit assumptions) for its successful use as a means to rational persuasion.

It is still open however that simple reasoning in accordance with AR – by contrast with presenting it as a way of justifying its conclusion – may yet be quite in order. Thus one might reach its conclusion on the causal basis of belief in its premises and acceptance of enumerative induction. According to reliabilism, then, if one receives the premises from reliable sources and if enumerative induction is a reliable form of inference, then one's conclusion comes out of a cognitive process overall reliable and hence sound.

How else indeed could one determine the reliability of one's sources of belief than by considering the accuracy of their deliverances and assessing them on that basis? In the absence of cognitive science, there appears no other way.

What is wrong in the newspaper case, even as a case of simple reasoning is, it now appears, the narrowness of one's purview in judging the newspaper reliable simply on the basis of a set of data one knows to be remediably and relevantly too narrow; namely, the reports of that very newspaper accepted at face value. (Remediably, that is, for humans generally, though not perhaps for someone in jail or in other obstructing circumstances.) So the circle can perhaps be widened to make it after all benign. Perhaps comprehensive coherence is after all a legitimate court of last appeal.

According to coherentism, for example, effective agency may indeed provide a rationale for such received sources of knowledge as introspection, perception, and memory. The way it may do so, however, is *not* by constituting a desideratum unattainable to us without such sources, thus making it a comfort to believe in them. Rather may our effectiveness as agents help by being an object of belief adding comprehensiveness and coherence to our total body of beliefs. For it may thus contribute an important measure of credibility, especially to beliefs with which it is most closely bound, such as the belief that introspection, perception, and memory are reliable sources of belief, and the belief that without these sources we could not hope for effective agency.

According to coherentism what essentially justifies any justified belief is simply its coherence with a sufficiently comprehensive and coherent body of beliefs. Coherence among beliefs is induced, moreover, by relations of deduction, explanation, and probability among the objects of belief.

Coherentism seems false. Each of us at any given time believes a set of propositions, some of them consciously or explicitly, some subconsciously or implicitly. Many of these will be about the believer as himself and many about the time of belief as the time then present. In English one would express these beliefs respectively by such sentences as those of the form " ... I ..." or " ... me ..." and by such sentences as those of the form " ... now ..." or in the present tense. The self-abstract of such a set is obtained by removing any self-concept of the believer from every one of its appearances in any proposition in the set. The present-abstract of such a set is similarly obtained by removing any concept of the temporal present (as such) from every one of its appearances in any proposition in the set. Each of these abstracts will thus have a mixed membership of propositions and propositional functions. And the propositional functions will have personal gaps (left by the self-concept(s) removed) or temporal gaps (left by the concept(s) of the present removed). The problem for coherentism is that (with minimal and negligible alteration) the self-abstract and present-abstract of one's set of believed propositions at any given time would seem uniformly instantiable with respect to a personal individual concept P and a temporal individual concept T in such a way that the result is nearly enough as coherent and comprehensive as the original without being cognitively justified in the sense relevant to knowledge.

Consider for example the following uniform instantiation of the self-abstract and present-abstract of my present set of believed propositions. Fill in every personal gap left by the removal of any self-concept of mine with the personal individual concept *the holder of the lowest mean U.S. Social Security number exactly ten years from now* and fill in every temporal gap left by the removal of any concept of the present (as such) with the temporal individual concept *exactly ten years from now*. If I had believed such a uniform instantiation of the twofold abstract of my presently believed set of propositions, I should have had an enormous number of beliefs about the holder of the relevant Social Security number of ten years from now, most of which would have been as wildly unjustified as their correlates about myself now are firmly justified in my actual and present body of beliefs. And yet the total set of propositions resulting from the transformation would bring little or no loss of coherence or comprehensiveness. For the resultant is created in the image of the original, with the concept of *the (relevant) future holder* as the image of my concept(s) of *myself*, and the concept of *the time ten years from now* as the image of my concept(s) of *the (temporal) present*. And this means that the coherence-inducing relations borne by any member (M) of the original to other members ($M1, \ldots, Mn$) must then be reflected in the resultant by corresponding relations borne by the image of that member (M') to images of the other members ($M1', \ldots, Mn'$). This is in direct opposition to the coherentist, and the burden now passes to him.

Objection: "But the resulting set would surely be incoherent, since presumably I now believe that I am not the exactly-ten-years-from-now-holder of the lowest mean Social Security number. Therefore the resulting set must contain the incoherent proposition that the ten-years-from-now holder of such a number will not then be the then holder of such a number."

Reply: Retail inconsistencies of this sort cannot have much weight, however, since for one thing we could remove them individually as part of the transformation from the original set of propositions to the resultant set. And even if we did not remove them, it is far from clear that such retail inconsistencies would detract more than negligibly from the rationality of a body of beliefs. Recall the author who in his preface takes "responsibility for the errors that remain." Surely his book is at most negligibly less rational for containing the implied incoherence than would be a similar book from an author so much less humble that he did not think to consider the very possibility of an error in his book.

Objection: "But there is a further source of incoherence in the resulting set, and it yields more than just isolated inconsistencies. For the subject will find himself believing a complicated story about someone ten years in the future – including for instance that in exactly ten years the person in question will be sitting at a keyboard – while at the same time retaining his (normal common-sense) belief that one cannot reliably predict any such thing without certain required forms of access to its subject matter. One might be able to make such a prediction reliably, of course, if one knows oneself able to ensure that the circumstances will be right; for example, that one will oneself be the holder of the relevant number, etc., and able to ensure through one's present intentions that the right actions and states will issue in those circumstances, for example, that one will indeed be sitting at a keyboard at the exact time, etc. In the example imagined, however, no such powers are attributed to the subject, nor even the belief that he has them. How then can he possibly accept the complicated predictive account while subscribing to the meta-belief that he lacks the forms of access to the predicted scenario required for its reliable prediction? "

204

Reply: In the first place, for coherentism as defined here incoherence of beliefs always derives from incoherence among propositions believed. But there is no incoherence between the following *propositions*: that exactly ten years from now the holder of a certain number will be sitting at a keyboard; and that I have no way of reliably predicting what the holder of the number will be doing exactly ten years from now. Therefore, *if* we are not to revise our conception of coherence as a matter of relations of coherence (e.g., of logic, probability, or explanation) among propositions believed; *then* we must find some further propositions in the resultant set. For we must then find propositions whose failure to cohere will account for the incoherence of the subject's beliefs when he accepts the predicted scenario while believing himself unable to make the prediction at all reliably.

Objection: "That may be so, but such propositions *can* be found. Indeed, likely candidates are not far to seek *if* we require sufficient self-awareness by the subject who accepts the resultant set. For the resultant set will then contain *not only P*, the proposition predicted, and the proposition that the subject cannot reliably make predictions of sort *X*, *but also* the propositions both that he does predict *P* and that his prediction of *P is* of sort *X*. Once these propositions are included in the resultant set we do have a kind of global incoherence among the members of the set, since there are then included in the resultant set many propositions about a time ten years in the future, while the resultant set also contains, for each of these propositions, both the proposition that the subject predicts it and the proposition that his prediction is not reliable. The resultant set would therefore be seriously incoherent after all, and not a good reflection of the coherent and comprehensive original. That being so, we may quite properly accept the original as a coherent and comprehensive source of justification while rejecting the resultant as incoherent."

Reply: The line of objection under development and consideration here is addressed to the thought experiment that we have aimed against coherentism. According to the thought experiment we can start with a total, justified body of propositions believed by any one of us and transform it into a corresponding body whose acceptance by any of us would be unjustified despite its being no less coherent or comprehensive than the original. The line of objection against this thought experiment has argued that the transformation would after all involve a terrible loss of coherence or comprehensiveness. But it has now been forced to impose certain restrictions on the subject whose body of believed propositions undergoes transformation. To avoid refutation by the thought experiment, coherentism is now requiring that the subject of the experiment must be self-aware enough to both grasp and sort his beliefs, and to catalogue his belief sorts by degree of reliability. It is only this require-ment that yields the incoherence of the set resulting from the transforma-tion in our thought experiment. But just what is the source of this requirement in coherentist epistemology? Is it supposed that no one could have a coherent and comprehensive enough set of beliefs unless he satisfied such requirements of self-awareness? We could of course inter-pret "comprehensiveness" so that the answer is trivially in the affirmative. But this would also run the risk of trivializing the controversy between coherentism and even the most radical of foundationalisms. The Carte-sian, for example, could accept such coherentism and simply argue that no body of beliefs is comprehensive enough to give justification unless it includes a substantial complement of manifest or perfectly obvious prop-ositions, and that no body of propositions is coherent enough unless every proposition in it that is not manifest is deducible from some that are. To be sure, the line of objection to our thought experiment has not gone this far, but that it may do so is a risk worth noting.

So far the coherentist has placed only the following requirements on acceptable total sets of propositions or "world views": that a world view must be coherent in all the relevant ways and comprehensive in the number and variety of its components; and also must include an account of the beliefs held by the subject, and must include an account of his reliable sorts of beliefs.

We have seen how the coherentist needs such self-awareness require-ments in order to escape refutation by our thought experiment. But each of these requirements is problematic. In the first place, it is not at all clear that no one knows anything unless he is thus aware of his own beliefs and interested in what makes for reliable belief. More importantly, to require that the subject always be aware of his own beliefs would sink us in the quicksand already skirted earlier of requiring acceptable world views to include not only P – the object of an arbitrary object-level belief – but also $B(P)$, and $B(B(P))$, and $B(B(B(P)))$, etc. One could, of course, distinguish between the coherence and comprehensiveness minimally required for knowledge and such additional coherence and comprehen-siveness as may add further increments of justification without being essential for knowledge. And it might then be argued that what is minimally required for knowledge is awareness of one's own object-level beliefs along with some notion of which sorts are reliable, and that while such awareness concerning higher and higher meta-levels of belief may add to the coherence and comprehensiveness of one's total body of beliefs, it is not minimally essential for knowledge. This seems a bitter pill of adhocness for the coherentist but it may still be just the medicine he needs.

So we have developed a form of coherentism aptly labelled "perspectival" for requiring an epistemic perspective in any world view adequate to induce knowledge-making justification in its member beliefs. Such perspectivism may with equal justice be thought a form of foundationalism, however, since (a) it does not countenance mere coherence, however comprehensive, as a sufficient source of justification, and (b) foundationalism for its part does not reject coherence as *one* factor relevant to epistemic justification.

Perspectivism may also agree extensively with forms of foundationalism on how we know. Both will cite perception on how we know the external world, memory on the past, introspection on the contents of our consciousness, induction on the future, and so on. But such agreement is bounded when the perspectivist assigns to perception, memory, introspection, induction, and the like, not the status of fundamental sources of justification, but rather that of reliable sources of truth, of true belief. For it is this that puts them in his epistemic perspective.

I. THESIS, ANTITHESIS, AND SYNTHESIS

Here in summary is the main thread of our reflection:

> *Thesis*: The essential and fundamental justification-making property of any justified belief is always its reliability in virtue of a relevant sort or kind within which it falls.

> *Antithesis*: It is not such reliability that is essential and fundamental. What essentially and fundamentally justifies a belief is, rather, its coherence with a sufficiently coherent and comprehensive body of beliefs. The fact that beliefs of a certain kind are reliable is relevant to justification only once incorporated into one's body of beliefs. And it then does have a place of honor along with beliefs representative of the cognitive self-awareness of the subject.

Admittedly, it does seem plausible today that it is reason's proper work to provide us with a maximum of explanatory coherence and comprehensiveness.

Prospects for a synthesis open, nevertheless, when we consider a world coherent enough to allow the survival of at least one knower but random or vacuous otherwise. Presumably for there to be any knowledge of the world at all there must be some lawlike mind/world regularity. Let us suppose, however, that beyond the causal regularity required at the mind/world interface there is no systematic and orderly depth either in the mind or in the world. Beyond a certain elementary level, in such a world coherent unity adds nothing to the likelihood of having the truth, and random scatter in our body of beliefs seems no less likely to get it right. How plausible is it to insist even for such a world that knowledge even of the mind/world interface is aided by the most elaborate possible webs both worldward and mindward? Surely it is very little plausible to suppose that such artificial and wholly false webs add anything at all to one's knowledge of what is there knowable. This suggests that coherence has derivative and not fundamental status as a source of cognitive justification. It justifies in our world, or so we believe, in virtue of its reliability as a source of truth. This is quite apart from its crucial role as a source of understanding: a world with no systematic depth, one that is random or vacuous except for the mind/world regularities that permit superficial knowledge is largely absurd. Such a world hence provides little scope for understanding, but it is far from obvious that it makes no allowance for knowledge at all.

J. APTNESS AND VALIDATION

By definition, a belief is *apt* for someone at a given time iff it is cognitively justified for him at that time: this in a sense requiring *not* that he have done any justifying of it through reasoning, *but only* that the belief have that evaluative epistemic status which helps distinguish a true belief that is knowledge from one little better than a lucky guess. Such status *can* be acquired for a belief by means of reasoning on the part of the believer. But it need not always be acquired thus, since there are things we know which we did not *figure out*.

By definition, a belief is *ostensibly validated* for someone at a given time iff in holding that belief at that time he ostensibly reasons correctly, with no apparent fallacies of any kind, so as to make that belief ostensibly apt.

Since there are things we know without ostensibly concluding them from any reasoning, therefore some beliefs are apt without being ostensibly validated by the believer (or for that matter by anyone).

It was once supposed that to validate a belief one had to reach it as conclusion of proof from the manifest, or else to exhibit a proof from the manifest that displayed its aptness. Even in the heyday of rationalism it was never supposed, however, that in order for any belief to be apt its proof by deductive reason is always required. Even for rationalism a belief can be apt without having for its object the conclusion of an argument used by the believer (or anyone else) to make it apt or to display its aptness. For even the rationalist grants that a belief can be apt by merely taking the given or recognizing the manifest. Despite lack of necessary overlap between the apt and the validated, one might deliberately restrict one's scope to the validated, which would narrow one's inquiry to how reasoning can provide the aptness of belief.

K. COHERENCE AS FUNDAMENTAL FOR VALIDATION

Leaving aside intuitive reason – the taking of the given, the recognition of the manifest – for the rationalist reason's proper work or function is nothing but deductive proof. Others later amplified the scope of reason to cover also induction, enumerative and hypothetical. Later still, it now seems plausible that both deduction and induction are only subsidiary strategies used in pursuit of reason's fundamental objective, to maximize the coherence and comprehensiveness of our body of beliefs: coherence in all its relevant modes, and thus not only deductive but also probabilistic and explanatory.

Epistemology itself indeed comes of the rational drive for coherence. When the far-reaching skepticism consequent on the demand for proof clashes with our confidence in the aptness of our many beliefs, some of us reject skepticism's demand for proof and retain confidence in the aptness of our beliefs, but some relinquish such confidence and embrace skepticism. In either case the need for coherence is manifest. And it is further manifest when those who reject absolute proof as the key to aptness and knowledge set out to develop an alternative account of aptness and knowledge. In time their work bears fruit in theories of aptness (cognitive justification, evidence, warrant, etc.) whose claim to credibility rests on how well they cohere with the body of beliefs into which they seek admission.[4]

L. IS COHERENCE FUNDAMENTAL FOR APTNESS?

It would of course be a crude mistake to think that just because coherence thus underlies the credibility of epistemic principles or theories, that therefore it also underlies the credibility of object-level propositions about ourselves and the world around us. But it is far from mistaken to carry coherence just as far as possible in our search for sources of knowledge or aptness, since we need it anyhow to account for the aptness of our views in epistemology. Coherence and comprehensiveness cannot be carried all the way, however, as is shown by the thought experiment of some pages ago.

Our earlier exchange with the coherentist concerning that thought experiment yielded the need for coherentism to require not only the

---

4 The outlook in this paragraph and the meta-epistemic angst of this essay come from Roderick Chisholm, in whose writings such questions stand out early and late. See "Knowing about Evidence," in his *Perceiving* (Ithaca, N.Y.: Cornell University Press, 1957), and "The Problem of the Criterion," both in the 1966 and in the 1977 editions of his *Theory of Knowledge* (Englewood Cliffs, N.J.: Prentice-Hall).

coherence and comprehensiveness of a world view but also that the subject who holds that view place himself within it at the time in question with awareness both of his own beliefs at the time and of his possible means of intellectual access to himself and the world around him at that time and in the past. For it seemed clear that the coherence and comprehensiveness of a world view violating these requirements would not suffice to make it a source of knowledge or even apt belief for the subject holding it. A good label for coherentism modified to include these requirements is *perspectival coherentism*, for it is coherentism requiring of an epistemically effectual world view that it make essential provision for a subjective and epistemic perspective by including both a view of the object-level beliefs held by the subject and a view of the sorts of reliable beliefs – about himself, his world, and his past – open to him.

What then of perspectival coherentism? Will it give us an adequate sketch of epistemology's most basic source of aptness or cognitive justification? If so, that relegates reliability to a subsidiary position, for in that case the reliability of faculties like introspection, perception, and memory lends aptness to the beliefs they emit only if their reliability is noted *within* the world view along with the sources of the various beliefs emitted. It is hence only the coherence of the reliability of a faculty whose reliability is noted within a world view that helps to make apt the beliefs attained by that faculty (or intellectual virtue).

For the perspectival coherentist, therefore, the reliability of a reliable source of beliefs is epistemically effectual only if such reliability is noted through a belief that coheres adequately with the adequately comprehensive world view of the subject. The reliabilist thus finds himself absorbed into the world of the coherentist and assigned an important but wholly subordinate position. Has he any recourse?

M. COHERENCE OR RELIABILITY: A QUESTION OF EPISTEMIC PRIORITY

In brief our question is one of epistemic priority. Which, if either, is prior – the coherence of reliability, or the reliability of coherence? And the reliabilist does have a powerful response, anticipated in our discussion of a coherent and comprehensive world view applied to a world that is (at best) largely random.

Could such a broad world view conceivably overlap with an entire much narrower view, such that only the overlap with the narrower is true? I see no conclusive reason to preclude such overlap, even *if* historically that is rarely or never the way it has turned out. Given such overlap, then, would those who hold the broader view have somehow better or sounder knowledge of the facts in the overlap? The perspectival coherentist must clearly answer in the affirmative but he is far from being clearly right. What if a world view is wholly or largely true and overlaps partially with a more comprehensive and also coherent world view the remainder of which is wholly false? (Not, suppose, that there is comprehensiveness in another direction, which persistent inquiry would reveal; rather suppose that the world is flat, narrowly limited.) Which of the two world views affords better, more sound knowledge of the facts in the overlap? Again the perspectival coherentist must opt for the larger view, even more implausibly in this case.

These most recent reflections suggest it is not the coherence of reliability but the reliability of coherence that bids fair to deserve the place of honor. Only by supposing the world coherent and comprehensive could we grant reason's claim to reliability. In fact, only stronger assumptions will ensure reason reliable – and I mean reason as we know it, with its thirst for comprehensive coherence – assumptions like the following:

(CC) There is a single fully coherent and comprehensive world view from the perspective of any given subject and time, and that is the true world view from that perspective; or at least there is a single most fully coherent and comprehensive such view, or at the very least, a narrow class of such views, and each of these gives the truth or at the very least approximates the truth.

(RR) Reason properly and persistently employed yields coherence and comprehensiveness in one's world view and eventually would yield a world view at the very least in the narrow class specified above in CC.

N. RELIABILITY AND RATIONALISM

Rationalism can be viewed as particularly strong reliabilism. What someone like Descartes requires for knowledge and requires of acceptable sources of knowledge or "routes to knowledge" is indeed *perfect* reliability. It is assumed that reason puts us directly and *infallibly* in touch with certain truths *from our particular perspective* and then enables us to reach many other truths, again infallibly, through deductive proof. For the rationalist, therefore, reason both intuitive and deductive is the only source of knowledge or "route to knowledge" and "the mind should admit no others."

In practice, of course, Descartes does make a concession to fallible memory with one of two sorts of deduction he in practice allows. If intrinsically fallible memory is nevertheless to be of help in attaining perfect knowledge through deduction, we must find circumstances in which use of such memory is after all perfectly reliable: perhaps the lap of a perfect God? If only we could prove there is such a God *even with the use of intrinsically fallible memory* we might of course have our desired result. But such proofs have proved at best controversial.

O. RELIABLE KNOWLEDGE

Reliabilism has yet some recourse: granting the narrow scope of perfect knowledge, and turning to imperfect but reliable knowledge. This would allow admitting sources of knowledge less than infallible. And among these might be found introspection, perception, and memory, thought of most abstractly as "one's way of arriving directly and noninferentially at beliefs respectively about: certain of one's own states at the time; certain features of one's surroundings; and certain aspects of one's past." But if reason is allowed as a further source of apt beliefs, it too must surely be assumed reliable (if *not* necessarily infallible).

What is reliable relative to one scope of application may be unreliable relative to another, however, which raises the question of the proper scope relative to which we ought to evaluate the likes of observation, memory, and reason. And this surely depends on whether we conceive of pursuit of knowledge as an endeavor whose most basic seat is the individual; his tribe; his historical epoch; humanity at large: past, present, and future; or rational beings generally (beings capable of knowledge). In any case, reason – no less than introspection, perception, or memory – can be highly reliable within its proper scope, even if it occasionally leads us astray. It is required only that it lead us (close) to the truth reliably, and more reliably than alternatives including random procedures.

P. A KIND OF PRAGMATISM

These last reflections recall Peircian themes about the relation between truth and inquiry and about the basic seat of inquiry. Even if the seat of inquiry is the most comprehensive community of rational inquirers past, present, and future, and even if to give knowledge rational inquiry must be reliable – at least in the sense that it would lead us reliably to the truth if followed far enough – even then it is not entailed that we need *define* the truth as the world view such inquiry would necessarily tend to if pursued far enough. For *ideally rational inquiry* may rather be defined as what would thus lead us to the truth. There is no infallible assurance that an appropriate community is realizable on earth, nor is it certain that, as presently constituted, we are fit to belong. It seems best to take a broad historical and evolutionary perspective, and to require only that we have cognitive faculties well suited to further the progress of rational inquiry beyond our present stage toward that future ideal stage in which we would have the whole truth, or at least the whole structural truth – abstracting from the infinite details of history, forecast, geography, cosmology, etc. – or at the very least in some sense a close approximation. If we have such faculties – doing their proper work at our historical stage – then the beliefs they engender are sound, even if in time they will prove to have been false. Humanity cannot flatter itself that reason gives infallible access to all reality (even in principle), but we still trust our drive for rational coherence along with perceptual probing. (Not that we have much choice, really.)

Q. THE RELATIVE PRIORITY OF RELIABILITY AND COHERENCE

But is there nothing that justifies such continued trust in our (supposed) rationality? Must this be a mere arational basic posit? Again the question is thus raised of whether coherence is epistemically prior to reliability or the converse. Which is epistemically prior, the coherence of reliability or the reliability of coherence?

Take the proposition *that reason, with its drive for explanatory coherence and comprehensiveness, is reliable* and call it R. Is our acceptance of R a mere posit with no other epistemically effectual feature? What if such acceptance turns out to further the explanatory coherence and comprehensiveness of our own world view? Surely if R is true, and if acceptance of R does further comprehensive coherence, and if reliable sources issue apt beliefs, then our belief of R does have an epistemically effectual basis, for then it is apt by virtue of (a) its origin in coherence-seeking reason, and (b) the reliability of such reason.

Note, however, that even if it were false that our belief of R coheres – e.g., *because we did not even believe R* – R might still be true nevertheless; and it might still be true, further, that sources of belief give knowledge iff reliable. By contrast, it seems absurd, as we have seen by examples, to suppose that even if coherence-seeking reason were thoroughly unreliable, such reason might still serve as a source of some measure of aptness, and even of knowledge if a coherent belief also happened to be true.

The coherence of reliability seems basic for the project of validation. We cannot strain by reason beyond making coherent place in our comprehensive world view for trust in our own procedures of rational inquiry *such as the pursuit of explanatory coherence and comprehensiveness.* That is validational bedrock. Unaided, our quest for validation goes no deeper.

213

The reliability of comprehensive coherence still seems basic for actual aptness, nevertheless, since the attainment of larger and larger increments of explanatory coherence and comprehensiveness would do nothing (or worse) for how well our world view enabled us to know the little that might be known in a largely random world. The relevant beliefs constituting what little knowledge there might be in such a world would be ostensibly better validated for being embedded in more comprehensively coherent systems, but there would be no reality behind such appearance.

The pursuit of comprehensive coherence is fundamental for our project of validation: there is nothing deeper that the employment of ostensible reason – of currently preferred intellectual procedure – enables us to *bring about unaided*. But there is something epistemically deeper, for we do not bring about the reliability of such reason: that lies beyond us. And if the world is ill disposed for discovery by such reason – if for instance it is largely random and not coherent, or narrowly restricted and not comprehensive – then even the deepest employment of reason as we know it will not enable increase of knowledge or aptness of belief.[5]

5 Thanks for helpful discussion to my audience at the Naturalistic Epistemology Conference held by the History and Philosophy of Science Department, University of Pittsburgh, May 1981.

12

Testimony and coherence

Testimony is important both practically and intellectually. We rely on it for our grasp of history, geography, science, and more. We stake our time and fortune, and even our lives, on our beliefs. Which plane to board, what to eat or drink, what instrument readings to accept – all decided through testimony.

If we are largely justified in accepting testimony, how so? We might appeal to a principle like this:

(T) Testimony is correct more often than not.

But how to justify acceptance of T? There is so much testimony, past, present, and future! There are so many cultures, and cultures so diverse! How can one be sure about anything so strong as T?

Perhaps nothing so strong as T is needed; maybe it's enough to accept this:

(T') From the sort of people I have dealt with in the sort of circumstances now present, testimony is normally correct.

Some have despaired of justifying any general claim about the correctness of testimony. H. H. Price, for example, prefers to postulate a *policy* of accepting testimony, in sharp contrast to any substantive belief in the likes of T or T'. Because policies need justification, moreover, for his testimonial policy Price offers the pragmatic justification that if we did not adopt it we would forfeit the rich supply of knowledge brought by testimony.[1] Try to suspend judgment on everything based on testimony, and see how much supposed knowledge you must then relinquish.

Such a pragmatic defense of testimony is dubious, however, since the whole question before us is whether or not testimony provides knowledge, and if so how. To argue that it does so through our policy of accepting it, a policy justified in turn through its alleged yield of knowledge, is unacceptably circular.

Let us look more closely into the requirements for knowledge by

1 Cf. H. H. Price, *Belief* (New York: Humanities Press, 1969), pp. 111–12.

testimony. According to Keith Lehrer, for one to be completely justified in believing that p, it is required not only (a) that this belief cohere with one's acceptance system of beliefs, including probability assignments, but also (b) that it cohere with one's acceptance system purged of all falsehood. And we are offered the following general restriction on testimony, the Justification Restriction (J):

> (J) Receiving information from another is no source of our own justification unless we attribute complete justification to the informant.

Lehrer provides an example along with some general comments:

When Ms. Oblate tells me that the sun is not round, then I must evaluate this information. I must evaluate whether Ms. Oblate is trustworthy in what she thus conveys. As a result, I am completely justified in believing that the sun is not round only if I am completely justified in accepting that Ms. Oblate is trustworthy in what she conveyed. The latter is true only if Ms. Oblate is completely justified in accepting that the sun is not round. The knowledge we acquire by the transfer of information from others is, therefore, intrinsically dependent on the others being completely justified in accepting what they convey.[2]

James Ross, in his detailed treatment of the subject, places an even stronger requirement on testimony, summarized in part as follows:

S comes to know that h on W's testimony iff: W knows that h, tells S, and his telling S brings it about that S believes that h and h is evident for S.[3]

Nevertheless, even J may be stronger than it should be. Lehrer has also written that "a child, like a recording device, may receive and convey knowledge, but also, like the recording device lacks the understanding to have knowledge."[4] I agree with Lehrer's later insight. It seems unnecessary to require complete justification on the part of the informant. The informant can be trustworthy in the way a child or a recording device can be trustworthy, which suffices to make the informant a possible source of our own justification. Indeed, one can even imagine circumstances in which the testifier is very unreliable and yet one arrives at knowledge through essential reliance on his testimony. And it is possible to generalize even further, as does Leibniz. "Rhetoricians," writes he, "distinguish two kinds of arguments: 'artful' ones which are developed from things by means

2 "Personal and Social Knowledge," *Synthese* 73 (1987): 87–107, 96–7.
3 "Testimonial Evidence," in Keith Lehrer, ed., *Analysis and Metaphysics: Essays in Honor of R. M. Chisholm* (Dordrecht: Reidel, 1975), p. 53. I focus here on a disagreement, but there is much to agree with in both Lehrer's and Ross's accounts, and I have learned from them both.
4 *Ibid.*, pp. 97–8.

of reasoning, and 'artless' ones which simply rest on the explicit testimony either of some man or even, perhaps, of the thing itself. But there are also 'mixed' ones, *since testimony can itself provide a fact which serves in the construction of an 'artful' argument.*"[5] Here are some examples:

(a) T testifies that p, S perceives that T testifies that p, and S knows thereby that someone testifies that p.

(b) T testifies that n times now has someone testified in place P, with no idea that hers is the nth such testimony or even that she is at place P. S witnesses the testimony and knows (i) that there had been n − 1 earlier instances of testimony at place P, and (ii) that this testimony of T's is at place P and unaccompanied by any other present testimony at P.

In both cases, S can come to know that p through essential reliance on T's testimony that p, but in neither case need T know that p, or be completely justified in believing that p, or even so much as be at all reliable on questions such as the question whether or not p.

Consider, however, the claim that one's informant is not only (i) reliable (like a child or recording device) but also (ii) completely justified. There are, of course, circumstances in which this claim may add a *further* measure of coherence to our belief system, and it may thus serve to make our acceptance of the information even bettter justified. But such a claim seems unnecessary for us to be completely justified in accepting the information. For we can be justified in accepting the information as when we accept information from a child, or when we accept testimony that we know to be self-verifying in the circumstances even if the testifier is wholly ignorant of this.

If we need not obey the Justification Restriction J, that makes it easier to acquire knowledge through testimony, but we still lack any very good explanation of how it might be done. Recall, for instance, our modest principle of testimony:

(T') From the sort of people I have dealt with in the sort of circumstances now present, testimony is normally correct.

What could possibly serve as our basis for believing a general claim such as T'? Call the sort of testimony referred to in T' "preferred testimony." How can we justify our acceptance of preferred testimony? Might we rely on an appeal to induction through perception and memory? Perhaps we have noted through perception many instances of the accuracy of preferred

---

5 *New Essays on Human Understanding*, trans. and ed. by P. Remnant and J. Bennett (Cambridge University Press, 1981), Bk. IV, Ch. xv, sec. 4; my emphasis.

testimony and have retained through memory a running record of such success, all of which now serve as an inductive basis for our continuing acceptance of preferred testimony, which is thereby justified. Maybe so, but questions arise:

(Q1) What is testimony? What are the conditions required for S to testify that p?

(Q2) Related to Q1, how can S' tell that S is testifying or has testified that p?

(Q3) Does one normally, through perception and memory, gather a large and diverse enough basis for an inductive inference to the conclusion that preferred testimony is generally correct?

(Q4) What sort of correlation would one need between preferred testimony and correctness for that correlation to serve as a good basis for the inductive inference of Q3? Would one need to postulate some sort of causal connection between the testimony and its correctness?

It may help to step back and compare testimony with more easily and widely recognized sources, such as perception, introspection, memory, and reason. Memory, for example, turns out to resemble testimony rather closely.

Retentive memory is a psychological mechanism that conveys beliefs across stages of a life. Testimony is a social mechanism that conveys beliefs across lives at a time. In a well-ordered mind, memory will tend to be selective and to be a function of attention and interest. If we remembered every detail, our minds would be swamped with clutter. In a well-ordered society, testimony must be selective. If everyone reported everything to their neighbors, the lines of communication would be clogged, and our heads full of a useless jumble.

Memory is, of course, not the only psychological mechanism relevant to epistemology. Perception and reason are often cited as well, with two varieties of perception (the inner and the outer) and two varieties of reason (the intuitive and the inferential). These three broad categories – memory, perception, and reason – are said to be fundamental, and none reducible to the others in epistemic value. Even the coherentist will need to appeal to all three in explaining the full variety of what we take ourselves to know, and the appeal will need to be fundamental, because perception won't be fully justifiable except by circular reasoning going back to perception again. If we wipe our tabula clean of all perceptual inscriptions, we shall never be able to legitimate their reinscription on the basis of any linear appeal to memory and reason alone. And similar reasoning will apply to each of these in turn. All three seem needed, and none is certifiable by unaided appeal to the others. What about testimony?

Returning to our four questions, let's say that one "testifies" that p if and only if one states one's belief that p. This is a broad sense of testimony that counts posthumous publications as examples. More commonly, testimony requires an object to whom it is directed, as in a court of law. Thus, for Ross, testimony is "any verbalized reporting of a purported state of affairs where the reporter intends that the hearer (reader, viewer, etc.) will take it on his report that the state of affairs is *as* reported."[6] But here we opt for a broader notion of testimony that requires only that it be a statement of someone's thoughts or beliefs, which they might direct to the world at large and to no one in particular. That will have to do for now in answer to our first question. As for the second question, it raises a difficult and complex problem in the epistemology of other minds, which I mention only to put it aside. Thus, we come to our two questions most properly on the epistemology of testimony: Q3 and Q4.

Hume offers a response to our questions as follows:

There is no species of reasoning more common, more useful, and even necessary to human life, than that which is derived from the testimony of men and the reports of eye-witnesses and spectators. . . . This species of reasoning, perhaps, one may deny to be founded on the relation of cause and effect. I shall not dispute about a word. It will be sufficient to observe that our assurance in any argument of this kind is derived from no other principle than our observation of the veracity of human testimony, and of the usual conformity of facts to the reports of witnesses. It being a general maxim, that no objects have any discoverable connexion together, and that all the inferences which we can draw from one to another, are founded merely on our experience of their constant and regular conjunction; it is evident that we ought not to make an exception to this maxim in favour of human testimony, whose connexion with any event seems, in itself, as little necessary as any other.[7]

And shortly thereafter he adds:

The reason why we place any credit in witnesses and historians, is not derived from any *connexion*, which we perceive *a priori*, between testimony and reality, but because we are accustomed to find a conformity between them.[8]

We are "accustomed," says Hume, "to find a conformity" between testimony and reality. And just how do we manage that? Can we have tested a large and varied enough sample of testimony? And are the

6 *Op. cit.*, p. 36.
7 David Hume, *An Inquiry Concerning Human Understanding*, ed. Charles W. Hendel (Indianapolis: The Library of Liberal Arts Press, 1955), p. 119.
8 *Ibid.*, pp. 120–1.

deliverances of testimony regularly enough the sorts of things that we can and do check by means other than testimony? Of course, much testimony we can and do check perceptually in a normal day. "Coffee," reads the can. We open it and smell the coffee. We drive to work and know the intentions of fellow motorists by their signals, verified perceptually. And so on, for the rest of the day. But most testimony is uncheckable by perceptual means, if only through lack of time and resources. Most of what I take myself to know about history, geography, and science, for example, is in one way or another perceptually inaccessible to me.

There is, moreover, the phenomenon of team research in contemporary science. A recent experiment in particle physics required 50 scientist-years to prepare and 50 scientist-years for data collection, which was just the beginning. Analysis and interpretation of the results then required even more time and effort on the part of even more people. The resulting publication in the *Physical Review Letters* was $3\frac{1}{2}$ pages long, with a list of 99 authors.[9] Granted, that was a somewhat unusual case, but it is not unusual for such articles to list more than ten authors, and occasionally as many as forty.

That suggests a pattern of cooperation whereby no one participant knows all the supporting data or reasoning. Instead, each specialist's contribution must be taken on trust by others. Only all the contributions put together yield the overall conclusions, but no one scientist has direct knowledge of the entire basis. Rather, each scientist works largely on testimony.

Hume seems insensitive to the true nature of our predicament. On this question, at least, Thomas Reid is more perceptive:

The wise and beneficent Author of Nature, who intended that we should be social creatures, and that we should perceive the greatest and most important part of our knowledge by the information of others, hath, for these purposes, implanted in our natures two principles that tally with each other.

The first of these principles is, a propensity to speak truth, and to use the signs of language so as to convey our real sentiments. . . . Another original principle implanted in us by the Supreme Being, is a disposition to confide in the veracity of others, and to believe what they tell us. This is the counterpart to the former; and, as that may be called *the principle of veracity*, we shall, for want of a more proper name, call this *the principle of credulity.* . . .

It is evident that, in the matter of testimony, the balance of human judgment is by nature inclined to the side of belief; and turns to that side of itself, when there is nothing put into the opposite scale. If it was not so, no proposition that is uttered in discourse would be believed, until it was examined and tried by reason;

9 For a discussion of this case, see pp. 346–8 of John Hardwig, "Epistemic Dependence," *Journal of Philosophy* 82 (1985): 335–50.

and most men would be unable to find reasons for believing the thousandth part of what is told them.[10]

If Reid is right, testimony is strikingly similar to memory. In each case, causal mechanisms operate in us to convey beliefs from source to recipient: from one's own past to one's present, or from one's neighbor to oneself. Through experience one gradually learns to override these mechanisms in special circumstances, but normally they operate without impediment.

However, Reid does not in that passage address the question of how to justify acquiescing in the operation of his divine principles of testimony. Have we any rational defense against a skeptical challenge to them? Clearly, much testimony can be tested only by appeal to other testimony. But is this not to test one copy of a newspaper by appeal to other copies? That caricature has a point, because our whole question is how to justify accepting *any* testimony. Is it not therefore a vicious circle to invoke any testimony at all in pursuit of that objective?

We are told that our knowledge can derive from memory, perception, and testimony. Each of these might be justified by appeal to the others, but none can be justified fully without such appeal. One thing seems clear: To support reflective knowledge, one's raft of theory needs central planks detailing one's ways to know. What persuades me of this is mostly an argument about the I/now point of origin for much of one's perceptual system. A vast framework of beliefs is organized around such an origin, and many other nodes of our system depend logically on it in one way or another.

Consider now a systematic replacement of one's "I" and "now" concepts by some other person and time concept pair: N and t. The replacement would look in part as depicted in the following table:

CONCEPTUAL ORIGIN TRANSFORMATION

I/now system	*N/t system*
I am standing now.	N is standing at t.
I am speaking now.	N is speaking at t.
I flew from Providence to Cleveland yesterday.	N flew from Providence to Cleveland a day before t.
I now remember a JFK speech.	N at t remembers a JFK speech.
And so on. . . .	

Remarkably, the conceptual origin transform centered on N/t is bound to be about as coherent and comprehensive as the I/now system, so long as we restrict ourselves to object-level beliefs such as those listed. Indeed,

10 Thomas Reid, *Inquiry and Essays*, ed. R. E. Beanblossom and K. Lehrer (Indianapolis: Hackett, 1983), pp. 93–5.

even an I/now system much more coherent and comprehensive than our own would still suffer the same fate. It would still have a conceptual origin transform centered on N/t with the following two features: (a) being about as coherent and comprehensive as the I/now original and (b) being *far* from justified for us.

A simple and attractive move will solve our problem: to require that if a system is to yield justification for its member beliefs, it must contain an "epistemic perspective" or a body of "meta-knowledge" about one's own faculties and their reliability. There are several reasons in its favor, but here I wish to highlight our problem of conceptual origin transformation. How would the requirement of an epistemic perspective make a difference? How would it help?

It would not be enough to require that one's I/now system include an epistemic perspective that details what sorts of beliefs one holds, on what basis, and how reliable is the basis. For that much can be transformed along with the rest, and will all have correlates in the N/t transform. The difference, however, is this: When one holds the original I/now system, one has an account of one's own faculties and of how they serve as reliable sources for what one believes about oneself now. When one makes the transformation to the N/t system and accepts that resulting system, however, one does so in the absence of such an epistemic perspective for one's newly acquired beliefs.

Compare, for example, the beliefs on the left side of our table with their correlates on the right. Through perception and introspection one knows that one is standing and speaking now, and through memory one knows about one's flight of yesterday, and the speeches of years ago. But how does one know that N stands or speaks at t, or that N flew a day earlier, or that N remembers such and such? The transformation deprives one of any epistemic perspective permitting an explanation of how one knows these things, and many others like them. It bears emphasis in this connection that N and t could be any person and any time one pleased, long ago or far away.

The requirement of an epistemic perspective seems an indispensable prerequisite for an apt system of beliefs. This epistemic perspective would be constituted by beliefs about one's basic sources of knowledge, none of which can be accepted justifiably as such except by appeal to the others as sources unquestioned for the sake of support in favor of the one. In this sense, testimony seems as basic a source of knowledge as the traditional perception, memory, introspection, and inference.[11]

11 This essay grew out of a symposium with Keith Lehrer at the 1988 Oberlin Collo-quium. Lehrer's paper, "Social Knowledge," was a helpful stimulus, as was the ensuing discussion.

PART IV

Intellectual virtue in perspective: the view developed

13

Knowledge and intellectual virtue

I

An intellectual virtue is a quality bound to help maximize one's surplus of truth over error; or so let us assume for now, though a more just conception may include as desiderata also generality, coherence, and explanatory power, unless the value of these is itself explained as derivative from the character of their contribution precisely to one's surplus of truth over error. This last is an issue I mention in order to lay it aside. Here we assume only a teleological conception of intellectual virtue, the relevant end being a proper relation to the truth, exact requirements of such propriety not here fully specified.

Whatever exactly the end may be, the virtue of a virtue derives not simply from leading us to it, perhaps accidentally, but from leading us to it reliably: e.g., "in a way *bound* to maximize one's surplus of truth over error." Rationalist intuition and deduction are thus prime candidates, since they would always lead us aright. But it is not so clearly virtuous to admit no other faculties, seeing the narrow limits beyond which intuition and deduction will never lead us. What other faculties might one admit?

II

There are faculties of two broad sorts: those that lead to beliefs from beliefs already formed, and those that lead to beliefs but not from beliefs. The first of these we call "transmission" faculties, the second "generation" faculties. Rationalist deduction is hence a transmission faculty and rationalist intuition a generation faculty. Supposing reason a single faculty with subfaculties of intuitive reason and inferential reason, reason itself is then both a transmission faculty and a generation faculty. The other most general faculties traditionally recognized are, of course, perception, introspection, and memory. Shall we simply admit these, so as to break the narrow limits of reason in our search for truth?

Memory would seem a transmission faculty.[1] If I remember that the

---

1 Actually this is true only of one sort of memory, "retention." For a notion of generative memory see Carl Ginet's *Knowledge, Perception, and Memory* (Dordrecht: D. Reidel, 1975), esp. ch. 7, sec. 2, pp. 148–53.

square of the hypotenuse is equal to the sum of the squares of the legs then my present belief to that effect derives in a certain way from my earlier belief to that same effect. If we think of memory thus it is then as little fallible as deductive reason. Given the truth of its input beliefs, there is no chance whatever for a false output, just as in deduction. Indeed memory then seems if anything more secure than deduction, since the object of the input belief is the very same as that of the output belief. We go from belief at time t in the Pythagorean Theorem to belief at a later time t' in that very same proposition. There should hence be no rationalist compunction about such transmission memory as a further faculty beside intuitive and deductive reason.

Possession of an excellent transmissive memory is yet compatible with frequent error in one's ostensible memories. Someone might have an excellent ability to retain beliefs once acquired, and yet suffer from a terrible propensity to believe new things out of the blue which come as apparent memories, as beliefs from the past.

Turn next to intuitive reason, a faculty of grasping relatively simple necessary truths, an ability or power by which one cannot consider without accepting any necessary truth that is simple enough. Someone might then be gifted with such a faculty, while all the same suffering from a terrible propensity to believe things out of the blue as apparent truths of intuitive reason, as apparently truths that he grasps just because of their simple and obvious necessity, while in fact (a) other operative causes suffice on their own to bring about the beliefs in question, and (b) the intrinsic character of the propositions believed – their simple necessity – would *not* alone call forth his assent upon consideration.

If the possibility of a propensity to error in one's ostensible intuitions does not rule out intuitive reason, then the similar potential for error in one's ostensible memories cannot alone rule out transmissive memory, even for strict rationalism.

Whereas memory is like deductive reason in being a transmission faculty, perception is rather like intuitive reason in being a generation faculty. Both the external perception of the senses and the internal perception of introspection generate beliefs out of states that are not beliefs. [More strictly: "out of states that are not beliefs at the same or at higher levels in the hierarchy of beliefs $B(P)$, $B(B(P))$, $B(B(B(P)))$, etc." This in order to allow for the introspection of $B(P)$ by $B(B(P))$.]

The perceptual faculty of sight, for example, generates beliefs about the colors and shapes of surfaces seen fully, within a certain range, and in adequate light. Such beliefs issue from visual impressions derived in turn from the seen objects. Here again we have the familiar possibility in a new form: now it is someone with excellent sight subject besides to frequent hallucinations. His ostensible visual perceptions are thus highly error-prone but that should not cancel the virtue of his faculty of sight so long as both erring intuition and erring memory retain their status. And similar reasoning applies to introspection as well.

If on the other hand perception as a faculty can ever conceivably lead us astray, then perhaps what makes a belief perceptual is its basis in experience as if P, leaving it open whether or not the belief derives from a perceptual process originating in a fact corresponding to the object of belief: namely, P. Such perception *can* of course lead us astray. It does so whenever a perceptual belief turns out to be in error. Such perception would then be *essentially* an experience-belief (input-output) device and it would seem a dubious virtue for any epistemic community so circumstanced that it nearly always would lead them astray.

That is a promising tack for external perception but dubious for other general faculties. Take for instance memory. Even if on occasion we accept P because of what seems phenomenologically a memory feeling or inclination to accept P, surely not every case of memory can be conceived thus. Here we run against the fact that nothing in the operation of memory need play experience's role as input for perception. One may simply find oneself believing that the square of the hypotenuse equals the sum of the squares of the legs with no separate memory feeling of any sort. Yet that might still be a perfectly acceptable case of remembering. And something similar holds good for reason, both intuitive and deductive.

III

What makes a faculty intellectually virtuous? *Its* performance or powers, surely? If so what is required in a faculty is that *it* not lead us astray in our quest for truth: that *it* outperform feasible competitors in its truth/error delivery differential. This even if one is often wrong, or nearly always wrong, in one's beliefs as to the outputs of that faculty. Someone may be gifted with comprehensive and accurate recall well above the average for his epistemic kind. What if in addition he is nearly always wrong when he both believes something and takes himself to believe it on the basis of memory – wrong both on the source of his belief, which in fact is not memory, and also wrong in the belief itself, which in fact is false? Would this invalidate the claim to knowledge of any deliverance of his excellent memory, even one about whose source he forms no further belief?

How to determine the truth/error delivery differential of a faculty will depend on whether it is generative or transmissive. For a generative faculty the relevant differential covers all deliverances of that faculty. But it can't be right to charge against a transmissive faculty errors that enter with its inputs, for which it bears no responsibility. The relevant differential for a transmissive faculty is accordingly the truth/error differential over outputs yielded by *true* inputs. Intuitive reason, deductive reason, and propositional memory all hence deliver a truth/error differential apparently undiminished by falsehood. But neither introspection nor perception may seem so favored.

Introspection may seem not so favored in general, if defined as acquisition or sustainment of belief about one's own mental state on the basis of one's own mental state. For one can look within and attribute n sides to a visual image that in fact has n + 1 sides. Dependent as it is on the favor of external conditions, outer perception is all the more prone to lead us astray. And it seems unavailing to plead that misleading perception is no true perception. Despite perfection *in the subject himself* outer perception can still go astray through unfavorable *external* conditions, a difference from inner perception whose consequences we need to explore.

Pure introspection, it may be argued, is not guessing or miscounting or any such error-prone process that may *build* on introspection but is not exhaustively introspection. Of course not just *any* belief about one's own mental state counts as pure introspection. Pure introspection requires a certain causal aetiology: it requires that one's belief about a mental state of one's own have its source in that very mental state. But not just in any way whatever may the mental state serve as source of one's belief: not when one miscounts the sides of one's image, for instance. Here it is not just *introspection* that plays a role, but also *counting* (a process with external application liable perhaps to lead us astray).

Pure introspection is a cognitive process that in normal conditions reflects the actual character of one's mental states and as such cannot normally cause error. Through greater attentiveness and circumspection one can normally improve the quality of one's introspection and thus enhance its accuracy. But except for rare special phenomena – excruciating pain, for example – it does seems plausible that abnormal conditions could always frustrate one's best attempts at accurate introspection. Such abnormality could derive from a variety of causes including hypnosis, brainwashing, and neural engineering.

Yet why call the source of a belief "introspection" when it derives wholly from the suggestion of a hypnotist? And if a belief is not after all a deliverance of introspection when a mere hypnotic suggestion, why call it pure introspection if it derives *even partly* from hypnosis and partly from a somewhat misdescribed internal phenomenon? If we follow this line, then pure introspection seems again no less infallible than rational intuition. In each case we have a faculty in the subject leading causally from given facts to the belief in them. The process can of course go wrong in various ways – haste, perhaps, or inattentiveness, or hypnosis – but when it goes wrong we are denied a *pure* exemplar of introspection or intuition, as the case may be.

If we do yield to such purism on reason both intuitive and deductive, on memory, and on introspection, with what right can we deny the same treatment to outer perception? When some abnormality dupes us through illusion or hallucination, we could absolve the faculty of perception by alleging that any such error cannot be charged to *pure* perception: "Pure perception requires normal conditions, internal *and* external, and hence precludes the presence of abnormalities responsible for such illusion or hallucination."

But it is hard to credit someone with good perception if he is frequently enough duped by illusion or hallucination: we need to reconsider purism in general.

IV

We are thus back to our question: If someone's ostensible intuitions, deductions, memories, introspections, and perceptions are mostly wrong, how can we credit him with intellectually virtuous faculties of reason, memory, and perception, when the virtue of such virtues would have to derive from their maximizing our differential of truth over error? There is, perhaps, a plausible response: "What makes something an *ostensible* x is that it *seems* an x, but a belief can *seem* a deliverance of reason, or of memory, or of perception, without really being such. Thus the fact that *ostensible* deliverances of X are nearly always wrong is quite compatible with *true* deliverances of X being nearly always right, and hence quite compatible with X's being an intellectually virtuous faculty." Yet it still seems absurd to credit someone with good perception if he is frequently duped by hallucination or illusion, even when such anomalies issue from a variety of sporadic causes. Most especially does that seem absurd if the responsible causes are intrinsic to the subject himself.

Someone prone to frequent illusions or hallucinations of mainly internal origin cannot be credited with good visual perception in an epistemically most relevant sense. This even if in normal external conditions he *does* reflect with unsurpassed accuracy the colors and shapes in his environment, by virtue of his excellent eyesight. Perhaps then such receptiveness is necessary for virtue but *not* sufficient. Perhaps one needs to mirror such properties not just in the sense of showing their impact when they are appropriately placed and mediated in one's environment,

229

but in the fuller sense that includes *also* a further requirement: that one show the characteristic trace of such impact *only* under the action of the correlated sensible properties, in normal conditions.

The key element of a specific perceptual faculty would then be some quality enabling the subject to reflect accurately the presence *or absence* of some correlated range of properties and relations. The presence of such properties would project characteristic images or traces in the subject, whose presence or absence could then guide his perceptual beliefs. Under this fuller conception of a virtuous perceptual faculty, then, to the extent one is prone to illusion or hallucination in certain conditions, to that extent is diminished whatever relevant faculty one might still retain: to that extent is it diminished in its ability to justify in such conditions.

Unfortunately, that analysis does not carry over easily to other traditional faculties. There is nothing that plays for them the role played by sensory images or "traces" for outer perception. Ostensible memories, it may be recalled, will not serve, since they amount not to pre-belief images (except for the very special cases in which personal memory does function via imagistic traces), but to the beliefs themselves believed retained in memory. And something similar holds good in each of the other cases: introspection, intuition, and deduction.

For faculties other than outer perception we are hence left with a question: is there nothing in them analogous to the hallucinations or illusions that make a subject's perception less virtuous than it might be? Must we say that such faculties are always error-free, since there is no way of understanding how their true operation could possibly lead to error? Our understanding of how belief can be *perceptual* though false depends on understanding perception as essentially an experience-belief mechanism fallible through the occasional failure of an experience to reflect what experience of that sort normally reflects. What can play the role of experience for any of the other faculties?

Is there any sort of belief-guiding pre-belief appearance in the operation of introspection, of memory, of intuition, or of deduction? In the absence of any such appearance, moreover, how can any belief be in error while yet an introspective, memory, intuitive or deductive belief?

Take memory. Shall we say that any belief about the past will count as a memory belief? Surely not: one can *infer* to new beliefs about the past, which do not then issue from memory. Shall we say that any belief is due to memory which is just there at a time with no inferential or experiential lineage? Surely not: a belief due to present subliminal suggestion is not a memory belief, nor is one implanted by advanced neural technology. How then can we conceive of a *memory* belief without involving its aetiology? There seems no way. But once we do involve such aetiology, how then do we understand the lineage required for legitimacy as memory while still allowing the possibility of error due to the misoperation of *memory* (and not to flaws in the original inputs)?

Suppose $B_t(P)$ can derive by memory from $B_{t'}(Q)$ where $t > t'$ and $P \neq Q$ (failing which it is hard to see how error could possibly arise from the operation of memory). This entails a hard question: How may P and Q be related for it to be possible that B(P) derive by memory from B(Q)? Can they differ to any width?

Everyone is of course familiar with the decay of information in memory. Thus one may ostensibly remember a friend's phone number as 245–6088 when really it is 245–9088. But here we must ask: Is the presence of the "6" due to the operation of *memory*? Or is it due to nothing more than guessing in the absence of true memory, or perhaps to an unfortunate disposition to switch the "6" and the "9"? "Well, it *feels* no different than any of the other six digits!" True, but can that be a good guide to when we do and when we do not have memory, if a hypnotist might have created that same feeling for all seven digits, *none* in that case being a deliverance of memory? The relevant feeling, so far as I can tell, might be just the feeling of confidence in the absence of reasons, and *that* hypnosis can provide. Therefore it cannot be such a feeling that *makes* a belief a memory belief, however well or ill it might serve as symptom or criterion. And we are thus left with our main questions: (a) What then *can* constitute the character of a belief of being a memory belief if not the causal aetiology of that belief? (b) If it *is* its causal aetiology that makes a belief of P a pure memory belief, what short of an earlier belief of P can serve as relevant cause? "Nothing" seems in each case a defensible answer. And until we are shown some flaw in this answer it will seem defensible to suppose memory infallible when pure.

Since the relevant considerations seem applicable not just to memory but equally to introspection, intuition, and deduction, each of these raises the same question of how it may be understood so as to allow error. The difficulties already encountered suggest a shift in the burden of proof: Why *not* conceive of such faculties as infallible?

V

There is one other subfaculty of reason beside intuitive reason and deductive reason, and that is of course ampliative reason, whether inductive or explanatory. This is just reason in its role as seeker of coherence and comprehensiveness, however, and granted the *possibility* that our most coherent and comprehensive account of a certain matter fails to accord with the brute facts, such ampliative reason must take a place next to external perception among fallible faculties. Just as with external perception, our most justified ampliative procedure may yet lead us into error. But there is nothing here to require revision of the view that intuition, deduction, introspection, and memory are all infallible.

Yet there is one remaining scruple. We made an exception by admitting the fallibility of perception for one main reason: because there can be perceptually justified yet false beliefs. And this fits with our notion that a belief's justification derives from the endowments and conduct that lie behind it. For the falsehood of a perceptually justified belief may go unreflected in the subject's perception because of external abnormalities that he could not possibly have grasped. In such circumstances his perceptual false belief shows no defect or misconduct in the subject, and may be perceptually justified. That is why we had to allow perception to be exceptional in being fallible. But is there not a similar reason to allow fallibility in each of the other faculties?

Take a student gifted with excellent memory who attributes *An Essay Concerning Human Understanding* to David Hume. Given his excellent memory proven right on countless occasions, is he not justified in accepting what he ostensibly remembers? And don't we then have as much reason to admit the fallibility of memory as that of perception?

Take again a logician gifted with excellent deductive powers who goes through a relatively simple proof and somehow fails for once to detect an invalidating flaw. Might he not be justified still in believing the (false) conclusion on the basis of his inference from the (true) premises? And are we not thereby forced to admit the (transmissive) fallibility of deduction?

Or take, finally, someone of normal sophistication and acumen who believes in the existence of a class of all classes that are not self-members. Given his normal ability to understand simple necessary truths and to grasp their truth, might he not be justified through intuition in accepting that untruth about classes at least until shown an opposing demonstration? And are we not thereby forced to admit the fallibility of intuition?

To the contrary, in none of these cases is there really no plausible alternative to admitting the fallibility of the relevant faculty: memory, deduction, or intuition. For in each of them it is at least equally plausible to insist that the false belief derives *not* from the operation of true memory, or true deduction, or true intuition, but from various other interfering causes. Thus, to take just one example, at the point where the logician makes his mistake he is *not* following any relevant rule of deduction. How then can that part of his procedure be true deduction as opposed to, say, blundering through inattention?

But if in no such case does the belief really have its source in the corresponding faculty, whence can it derive its justification? In each case the justification can plausibly be attributed to coherence-seeking amplia-tive reason, as follows. In each case, the subject (a) is aware of his gift, of his relevant faculty F and its reliability, (b) finds himself with a belief B which he justifiably attributes to his faculty F, and (c) on the basis of (a) and (b) justifiably sustains his belief B. And that is all compatible with the falsity of B. Hence the way in which ostensible memory, deduction, and intuition can lead one into error is roundabout, and compatible after all with the infallibility of the corresponding faculties. In each case, the source of the false belief is not the corresponding faculty F (memory itself, or deduction, or intuition) but rather ampliative, coherence-seeking reason. It is such reason which when provided with the assumptions: (a) that the subject's faculty F is normally reliable (as proved time and time again already), and (b) that present belief B derives from F, a reasonable assumption in the circumstances; reaches on that twofold basis the conclusion (c) that belief B must be true, which sustains the subject in upholding B. In each case, however, B turns out to be false, and – we may now reasonably add – turns out *not* to be a deliverance of F after all.

Thus may we after all explain the apparent fallibility of introspection, intuition, deduction, and memory as illusory reflections of the true fallibility of ampliative, explanatory reason, which may take a belief B for a deliverance of a faculty F when B is neither true *nor* a deliverance of F. (And the objection that no subject S is so reflective as is required by our explanation would receive a twofold response: (a) emphasis on the implicit character of the assumptions attributed to S; and (b) appeal to the distinction between animal knowledge and reflective knowledge in Sec-tion IX below.)

VI

The question does remain whether intuitive reason (for example) would be of any use to epistemology if ostensible intuitions could always fail to be real and the true ones were indistinguishable from the false ones. But what is it here to distinguish a true one if not to know that it is a true one? And if that's all it is, then why can't the rationalist respond that we *can* tell a true intuition after all, since we can intuit-cum-introspect that an intuition of ours is such, *even if not all ostensible intuition-cum-introspection is real.*

But surely that response would not be plausible if ostensible intuitions almost never turned out to be real. Exactly why not, however, if in any case where ostensible intuition turned out to be real the output belief *would* come out of an infallible process (not simply a reliable process, note, but an infallibly reliable process)? Why should it make a difference how many other cases seem cases of such a process without really being so or what ratio there is of real to false ostensible cases?

Besides, why should one's fallibility with regard to the source S of one's belief B and its justification impugn such justification if the justification derives from source S itself and not from one's knowledge of it. Requiring that one always know the source of one's justification, would seem to land us in a vicious regress.

Despite such doubts from the other side, however, it still seems absurd to allow that someone can know that p because his belief that p does derive from intuition even though his ostensible intuitions almost never turn out to be real.

VII

There is anyhow an alternative to explore before yielding to anything so implausible as human infallibility. According to our alternative, we first define a *faculty* of retentive memory, and only then define a retentive memory belief as a belief deriving causally from the exercise of that faculty. This provides an alternative answer to our question: "If it is its causal aetiology that makes a belief of P a pure memory belief, what short of an earlier belief of P can serve as relevant cause?" And this alternative answer leaves it open that retentive memory be fallible. Whether it is or is not fallible now depends on how we conceive of the faculty itself, on how we define it.

Consider first the notion of a faculty in general. The primary meaning attributed to "faculty" by my dictionary is: "ability, power." Faculties are therefore presumably in the general family of dispositions. Here are some simple examples of dispositional properties:

(a) Being an incline-roller: being a thing x such that were x placed at the top of an inclined plane in certain conditions (absence of obstacles, etc.), then x would roll down.

(b) Being a level-roller: being a thing x such that were x placed on a level plane surface and pushed in certain conditions, then x would roll.

(c) Being a round-snug-fitter: being a thing x such that were x placed with a certain orientation on a hole of a certain diameter, x would fit snugly.

Both a basketball and a bicycle tire would have dispositions or powers a, b, and c. And in each case of an ordinary object and an ordinary disposition something intrinsic to the object would ground its having the disposition in question: some intrinsic property or some set of intrinsic properties. Thus it's the roundness of a basketball that grounds its having each of the three dispositions or powers: a, b, and c. But it's rather the cylindrical intrinsic character of the tire that grounds its possession of each of a, b, and c. How now shall we think of faculties: as dispositions or as grounding intrinsic characters of dispositions? Faculties seem abilities to do certain sorts of things in certain sorts of circumstances rather than what *underlies* the possession of such abilities. Otherwise, since many different intrinsic characters or natures can underlie possession of the same ability (as happens with a ball and a tire *vis-à-vis* dispositions a, b, and c) we would have to speak of different faculties in the tire and the ball, which seems wrong. (It is of course somewhat forced to speak of faculties at all in something that is not an agent, but then similar examples could surely be contrived in which a human and an extraterrestrial would take the place of the basketball and the tire, respectively.)

If indeed cognitive faculties are viewed as abilities or powers, how more specifically is it done? Here is one possibility: To each faculty there corresponds a set of accomplishments of a distinctive sort. Indeed the faculty is *defined* as the ability to attain such accomplishments. Now of course an accomplishment attainable in given circumstances may be unattainable in other circumstances. Therefore, abilities correlate with accomplishments only relative to circumstances. There is for example our ability to tell (directly) the color and shape of a surface, so long as it is facing, "middle-sized," not too far, unscreened, and in enough light, and so long as one looks at it while sober, and so on. And similarly for other perceptual faculties. Compare also our ability to tell simple enough necessary truths, at least once having attained an age of reason and discernment; and our ability to retain simple enough beliefs in which we have sufficient interest. In each case our remarkably extensive species-wide accomplishments of a certain sort are explained by appeal to a corresponding ability, to a cognitive faculty; or at least we are thus provided the beginning of an explanation, an explanation sketch. But in none of these cases is there really any pretense to infallibility. All we're in a position to require is a good success ratio. Common sense is simply in no position to specify substantive circumstances in which the exercise of sight is bound to be infallible. (By substantive circumstances here is meant circumstances that are not vacuous or trivial in the way of "being such as to be right about the facing surface.") Of course that is not to say that there aren't underlying abilities which are in fact infallible: it's just to say that if there are such abilities common sense is at this point unable to formulate them. (Compare the fact that corresponding to common-sense generalizations about falling bodies and the like science did discover underlying principles with a good claim to being substantive and exceptionless.)

Any actuality involving an individual as essential constituent displays abilities or powers of that individual. The dance of a puppet displays not only abilities of the puppeteer but also powers of the puppet. The powers in the puppet that serve as partial source of its behavior are not however of the sort sufficient to make it an agent, much less a responsible agent. Similarly, someone hypnotized into 'believing something to his mind groundless would seem too much a puppet of external fate to count as knowing what he believes. His belief does of course display certain powers seated in him as well as certain abilities of the hypnotist. But the powers constituting susceptibility to hypnosis are hardly of the sort to give knowledge or epistemically justified belief. (At least that seems so if one is hypnotized unawares *in our world as it stands*. But it also seems plausible both (a) that we can embellish the example so that hypnosis does provide knowledge, at least in the way the reading of an encyclopedia may do so, and (b) that we can conceive of a world where even being hypnotized unawares does regularly enable people to know things by being hypnotized into believing them.)

What powers or abilities do then enable a subject to know or at least to acquire epistemic justification? They are presumably powers or abilities to distinguish the true from the false in a certain subject field, to attain truth and avoid error in that field. One's power or ability must presumably make one such that, normally at least, in one's ordinary habitat, or at least in one's ordinary circumstances when making such judgments, one *would* believe what is true and *not* believe what is false, concerning matters in that field.

Just how fields are to be defined is determined by the lay of interesting, illuminating generalizations about human cognition, which psychology and cognitive science are supposed in time to uncover. In any case, fields must not be narrowed arbitrarily so as to secure artificially a sort of pseudoreliability. Human intellectual virtues are abilities to attain cognitive accomplishments in "natural" fields, which would stand out by their place in useful, illuminating generalizations about human cognition.

Faculty F is a *more refined subfaculty* of faculty F′ iff the field f(F) of F includes but is not included by the field f(F′) of F′. Thus the visual faculties of an expert bird-watcher would presumably include many more refined subfaculties of the faculties of color and shape perception that he shares with ordinary people. Moreover, the visual faculties of a bird-watcher with 20–20 vision would presumably include many more refined subfaculties of the faculties that he shares with those who fall well short of his visual acuity.

Faculty F is *more reliable* than faculty F′ iff the likelihood with which

236

F would enable one to discriminate truth from falsehood in f(F) is higher than the likelihood with which F′ would enable one to make such discrimination in f(F′).

Thus may we explain why in certain conditions one is better justified in taking a surface (S) to be polygonal (P) than in taking it to be heptagonal (H): there may then be faculties F and F′ such that (a) F′ yields the belief that S is P; (b) F yields the belief that S is H; (c) F is a more refined subfaculty of F′; and (d) F′ is more reliable than F.

VIII

Infallible faculties are required by rationalism. But pure rationalism with its *perfectly* reliable certainty is a failed epistemology. A more realistic successor claims our attention today:

> *Reliabilism* is the view that a belief is epistemically justified if and only if it is produced or sustained by a cognitive process that reliably yields truth and avoids error.

There are two main sorts of objection to such reliabilism and they pull in opposite directions. One questions the sufficiency of such reliability for justification. The other questions its necessity.

Consider first someone gifted with a sort of clairvoyance or special sense who considers the deliverances of his gift to be inexplicable superstition, and has excellent reason for his dim view. How plausible would it be to suppose him justified in his clairvoyant beliefs?[2]

From the opposite direction, consider the victim of a Cartesian Evil Demon. If his experience and reasoning are indistinguishable from those of the best justified among us, can we in fairness deny him the justification that we still claim for ourselves? Yet if we do grant him such justification, then *unreliable* processes do yield him much belief that is in fact justified (given our hypothesis).

A response to the first sort of objection modifies radical reliabilism by requiring for justification not only that the belief in question be caused by a reliable process, but also that there be no equally reliable process in the subject's repertoire whose use by him in combination with the process that he actually does use would not have yielded that same belief. Such alternative methods would of course include the recall and use through reasoning of relevant evidence previously unused though stored

2 Cf. Laurence Bonjour, "Externalist Theories of Empirical Knowledge," *Midwest Studies in Philosophy* 5 (1980): 53–75. Cf. also William Alston, "What's Wrong with Immediate Knowledge?" *Synthese* 55 (1983): 73–97.

in memory, including evidence about the reliability of one's pertinent faculties.[3]

That revision will not deal with the problem from the other direction, however, the problem of the justified victim of the Evil Demon. And there is besides a further problem. For if a process is reliable but fallible, it can on occasion fail to operate properly. But that opens the possibility that a process can yield a belief B through *improper* operation where by lucky accident B turns out to be true anyhow. Take for example memory, and suppose it fallible. Suppose, in particular, that memory could take a belief that a friend's phone number is 245-9088 as input and yield as output later belief that it is 245-6088. Might not one's memory be such that on a given occasion it *would* in fact have that unfortunate result but for the effect of extremely rare and random inversion-preventing radiation? Would the (correct) output belief properly earn it status as epistemically justified? If so, since no reasoning via falsehood seems involved, would the belief also amount to knowledge? If these are good questions, parallel questions can obviously be raised about our various perceptual faculties.

What in brief is the problem? Apparently, though a belief is caused by a reliable but fallible cognitive process, that process may actually operate improperly and cause the true belief only through the intervention of some highly unusual factor whose presence is merely a lucky accident. Would the belief then fall short of sound epistemic justification, and not be a true instance of knowledge? What might be missing? Perhaps some closer connection between the belief and its truth? Perhaps these cannot be so independent as when they come together only by lucky accident, the way they do in our example of fallible memory.

Compare the Gettier case in which S acquires the belief that p in a highly reliable way and deduces from it that-(p ∨ q), where this last belief turns out to be true but only because it's true that q, since in fact it is false that p. If S has no reason to think it true that q, and no reason to think that-(p ∨ q) except his having inferred it deductively from his belief that p, then it seems clear his belief that-(p ∨ q) turns out to be true only by luck (in some appropriate sense) and is not a case of knowledge.[4]

Finally, compare also the case where we are out driving and spot a barn by its barnlike look from our perspective on the highway; where unknown to us it is the one true barn left standing in that vicinity, in the midst of barn facades all presenting equally realistic barnlike looks, and many such facsimiles may be found for miles in either direction. If visual perception remains a reliable process, then by reliabilism our belief would

---

3 Cf. Alvin Goldman, "What is Justified Belief?" in George S. Pappas, ed., *Justification and Knowledge* (Dordrecht: D. Reidel, 1979).

4 Cf. Edmund Gettier, "Is Justified True Belief Knowledge?" *Analysis* 23 (1963): 121–3.

seem justified; yet although it is true, it seems clearly no knowledge.[5]

These three examples pose a problem not so much for reliabilism as a theory of justification, as for the combination of such a theory of justification with a conception of knowledge as justified true belief.[6]

IX

Here is a short story. Superstitious S believes whatever he reads in the horoscope simply because one day in August it predicted no snow. Tricky T intends to offer S a lemon of a used car and plants the following in the horoscope under S's sign: "You will be offered a business proposition by T. The time is ripe for accepting business propositions." Does S know that T will offer him a deal? T planted the message and would have done so if he had been going to offer S a deal, and would not have done so if he had not been going to offer S a deal. So it is not *just* a lucky guess nor is it *just* a happy accident that S is right in thinking that a deal is forthcoming, given his daily use of the horoscope. In fact here S not only believes the truth that p; but also he would believe that p if it were true that p (in nearby possible worlds where it is true that p), and he would not believe that p if it were false that p (in nearby possible worlds where it is false that p). One thing seems clear: S does not know in such a case. What S lacks, I suggest, is *justification*. His reason for trusting the horoscope is not adequate – to put it kindly. What is such justification?

A being of epistemic kind K is prima facie justified in believing P if and only if his belief of P manifests what, relative to K beings, is an intellectual virtue, a faculty that enhances their differential of truth over error. But such prima facie justification may of course be overridden in special cases: e.g., through his learning that the conditions are not normal for the use of that faculty.[7]

It is of prudential importance to the subject himself to know how reliable and trustworthy his own judgments are in various categories. That is also moreover of prudential importance to his fellows and of social importance collectively to his epistemic kind. Testimony is of paramount importance to the *epistemic* weal and progress of any social, language-using species.

5 Cf. Alvin Goldman, "Discrimination and Perceptual Knowledge," *Journal of Philosophy* 73 (1976): 771–91.
6 For alternative reactions to our recent difficulties, see Robert Nozick, *Philosophical Explanations* (Cambridge, Mass.: Harvard University Press, 1981), ch. 3, esp. part I; and Peter Klein, "Real Knowledge," *Synthese* 55 (1983): 143–65.
7 That epistemic justification is prima facie and defeasible is argued already in Roderick M. Chisholm's *Theory of Knowledge* (Englewood Cliffs, N.J.: Prentice-Hall, 1966), p. 46.

That is why we take an interest not only in the truth of beliefs but also in their justification. What interests us in justification is essentially the trustworthiness and reliability of the subject with regard to the field of his judgment, in situations normal for judgments in that field. That explains also why what does matter for justification is how the subject performs with regard to factors internal to him, and why it does not matter for justification if external factors are abnormal and unfavorable so that despite his impeccable performance S does not know. What we care about in justification are the epistemic endowments and conduct of the subject, his intellectual virtues.

From this standpoint we may distinguish between two general varieties of knowledge as follows:

> One has *animal knowledge* about one's environment, one's past, and one's own experience if one's judgments and beliefs about these are direct responses to their impact – e.g., through perception or memory – with little or no benefit of reflection or understanding.

> One has *reflective knowledge* if one's judgment or belief manifests not only such direct response to the fact known but also understanding of its place in a wider whole that includes one's belief and knowledge of it and how these come about.[8]

Since a direct response supplemented by such understanding would in general have a better chance of being right, reflective knowledge is better justified than corresponding animal knowledge.

Note that no human blessed with reason has merely animal knowledge of the sort attainable by beasts. For even when perceptual belief derives as directly as it ever does from sensory stimuli, it is still relevant that one has *not* perceived the signs of contrary testimony. A reason-endowed being automatically monitors his background information and his sensory input for contrary evidence and automatically opts for the most coherent hypothesis even when he responds most directly to sensory stimuli. For even when response to stimuli is most direct, *if* one were also to hear or see the signs of credible contrary testimony that would change one's response. The beliefs of a *rational* animal hence would seem never to issue from *unaided* introspection, memory, or perception. For reason is always at least a silent partner on the watch for other relevant data, a silent partner whose very *silence* is a contributing cause of the belief outcome.

Both animal and reflective knowledge require a true belief whose

---

8 That the "wider whole" essentially involved in good reasoning is wider than might appear is argued by Gilbert Harman in "Reasoning and Evidence One Does Not Possess," *Midwest Studies in Philosophy* 5 (1980): 163–82.

justification by its source in intellectual virtue is prima facie but not overridden. Possible overriders of such justification would have to be wider intrinsic states of the subject diminishing significantly the probability that the belief in question be true. The probability that it be true since yielded by the intellectual virtue is then significantly greater than the probability that it be true given the wider intrinsic state.

Overriders come in two varieties: the opposing and the disabling. An overrider of prima facie justification for believing P is opposing iff it would provide prima facie justification for believing the opposite: not-P. Otherwise it is a disabling overrider.[9]

If one has visual experience as if there is a pink surface before one, the reception of good testimony that there is no pink surface in the room would provide an opposing overrider. But if the good testimony says only that there is a red light shining on the surface before one, that provides a disabling overrider. What is it in either of these cases that defeats one's prima facie justification when one accepts such testimony?

In our eyes anyone who still believes in a pink surface before him after accepting either testimony above would lack justification – this because we consider rational coherence the best overall guide. Even if the testimony is in each case false, given only adequate reason to accept it, one still loses one's justification to believe in the pink surface. Ironically that is so even for someone who does respond directly to the experience of pink with the corresponding belief and whose belief turns out true while the testimony is false. Here it would *seem* that the subject is at least as well off epistemically as his neighbor who also responds to pink experience while ignorant of the (misleading) testimony, and at least as well off as the nearby young child who could not have understood the testimony even had he heard it. But that is an illusion. Once having attained years of reason and discretion, and once in possession of the credible testimony, one errs not to give it due weight, which may betray a flawed epistemic character. This is important news to fellow members of one's epistemic kind, and even to one's own higher self, as is revealed in one's loss of "justification" for belief in the pink surface.

But not just *any* sort of incoherence would betray such a flaw. The author who sincerely takes responsibility in his preface for the "errors that surely remain" is not guilty of epistemic misconduct for continuing to accept individually the contents of his carefully wrought treatise, nor would he sin by accepting their conjunction could he somehow manage to conjoin them. The convinced skeptic with the reasoned conclusion that

9 Cf. John Pollock, *Knowledge and Justification* (Princeton, N.J.: Princeton University Press, 1974).

perceptual beliefs about one's environment are never justified does not lose all justification for his many such beliefs in the course of a normal day. Yet both the author and the skeptic are of course guilty of a sort of incoherence. But how can this be so? How can such incoherence differ relevantly from that of the victim of credible-hence-accepted but misleading testimony who arbitrarily retains what the testimony discredits?

According to our leading idea, the relevant difference must reside in a difference for one's prospects towards getting in the best relation to the truth. This is borne out by reflecting that anyone who lets skeptical arguments mislead him to the cynical extent of a massive withdrawal of doxastic commitment would save his coherence at enormous cost in truth. And the same goes for the honest and sincere author at work on his preface.

X

An intellectual virtue may be viewed as a subject-grounded ability to tell truth from error infallibly or at least reliably in a correlated field. To be epistemically justified in believing is to believe out of intellectual virtue. To know you need at least epistemic justification. But there are two prominently different sorts of knowledge: the animal and the reflective. Animal knowledge is yielded by reaction to the relevant field unaided by reflection on the place of one's belief and its object within one's wider view. Even for such knowledge it is not just the reliability of the cognitive process yielding the relevant belief that provides its justification. Nor is it enough to require further the absence of any equally reliable process in the subject's repertoire whose use by him combined with the process actually used would not have yielded that belief. For even that will not preclude a subject with excellent eyesight subject however to internal hallucinogenic interference 99% of the time, one deprived of any way to distinguish his cases of true vision from the hallucinations. Such a subject can hardly be granted even animal knowledge in his rare cases of true vision, surely, nor even warranted or justified belief. Though he has a reliable cognitive process of true vision, he yet does not have a relevant faculty in an epistemically most relevant sense: he does not have a faculty F correlated with a "natural" field $f(F)$ such that F is constituted by the ability to discern truth from error with high reliability over $f(F)$. Despite his occasionally operative true vision, our victim of frequent, stable, and long-standing hallucinogenic irregularities does not have the sort of ability constitutive of an epistemically relevant faculty.

Since justified belief seems anyhow insufficient for knowledge (see the objections early in Section VIII above), it is tempting to bypass justifica-

242

tion and try some wholly fresh approach.[10] Yet justification proves stubbornly required for knowledge. The next chapter argues for a split of epistemic justification into two concepts: justification proper and epistemic aptness. Each of these is needed for a full understanding of our knowledge.[11]

SUMMARY

I. A teleological conception of intellectual virtue.

II. Transmission faculties and generation faculties. Examples of each. What makes a belief of a certain sort a belief of that sort: e.g., what makes a memory belief a memory belief, and what makes a perceptual belief a perceptual belief?

III. What makes a faculty intellectually virtuous? Purity of faculties: pure reason, pure memory, pure introspection, and pure perception.

IV. Ostensible intuition (etc.) versus real intuition (etc.). The epistemological relevance of this distinction. The role of sensory experience in determining ostensible perception. The absence of any correlate of such experience for intuition, deduction, memory, or introspection.

V. Ampliative reason: as clearly fallible as external perception. How the fallibility of ampliative reason may help explain the apparent fallibility of introspection, intuition, deduction, and memory.

VI. Why should the high likelihood of error in *ostensible* deliverances of source S impugn the justification of beliefs that flow from S if S itself is highly error-free or even infallible? Yet somehow it seems very implausible to count as justified a belief B with source S and held by person X even though for X ostensible deliverances of S are nearly always wrong.

VII. What yielded the (implausible) infallibility of retentive memory (in Section II) was our view of a retentive-memory belief of proposition P on the part of person X as a belief of P caused by an earlier belief of P on the part of X himself (roughly). The faculty of retentive memory was then conceived as the ability to retain beliefs thus. And similarly for intuition, deduction, and

10 For example, Robert Nozick's in his *Philosophical Explanations, op. cit.* Compare Fred Dretske's *Knowledge and the Flow of Information* (Cambridge, Mass.: MIT Press/ Bradford Books, 1981). For Dretske's *précis* of his book, discussion by several commentators, and replies by the author, see *The Behavioral and Brain Sciences* 6 (1983): 55–90.

11 An earlier version of this essay was part of the Special Session on Knowledge and Justification at the Twelfth World Congress of Philosophy (Montreal, August 1983).

introspection. An alternative is examined here: to reverse the order of definition. Instead of defining the faculty of memory as what leads to memory beliefs, we first define the faculty of memory (in some other way) and then define memory beliefs as beliefs that flow from the faculty of memory. According to our alternative proposal, epistemically relevant faculties are abilities to distinguish reliably the true from the false in certain "natural" subject fields.

VIII. Infallible faculties comport with the perfect reliability required by rationalism. Contemporary reliabilism jibes better with our highly reliable but fallible faculties. Four examples are considered which pose as many problems for the combination of reliabilism as a theory of justification with a conception of knowledge as justified true belief.

IX. The chapter concludes with some general reflections on the nature of justification and two of its main varieties, which leads, in the following chapter, to a proposed split in our concept of epistemic justification.

14

Methodology and apt belief

The theory of knowledge has two sides – epistemology and methodology – and a bridge to join them: *that a belief is justified if and only if obtained by appropriate use of an adequate organon* – a principle of theoretical epistemology requiring an organon or manual of practical methodology. Such organon justification is internalist. (How could one ever miss one's source for it?) But it leads briskly to skepticism on pain of regress or circularity – or so it is argued in Section 1. In Section 2 we consider the epistemology embodied in the Socratic elenchus, which provides a new angle on how methodology relates to epistemology and to science and metaphysics. Thus are we made to face once again the organon account of justification: our internalist bridge principle. That account proves in Section 3 to be a special case of a more general *argumentative* account of justification, which in turn agrees with intuitions so powerful as to be enshrined already in our dictionaries. Good rhetoric suggests therefore that "justification" and its cognates be yielded to the argumentative account; in which case justification must likely fall from its status as principal concept of epistemology. Justification is hence unlikely to be all that is required in general for knowledge, nor is it likely to be what is always required in any premises of use to justify anything. That way, apparently, lies regress or circularity. Better to demote justification to the status of one way for a belief to be appropriate or apt for knowledge, while allowing other ways not dependent on already attained justification: perception, perhaps, or introspection, or memory.

1. METHODOLOGY AND EPISTEMOLOGY

The theory of knowledge has two branches: one practical and one theoretical. The first, *methodology*, is like engineering or like the lore of carpentry. Such learning or lore is directed at certain special ends or goals (other than that of knowing more in general), and a body of such learning is a set of specified means/ends relationships. To be real (useful) practical learning, however, such a body of learning must not rest with means/ends relationships totally detached from human goals and needs and from materials and skills accessible to human beings. (It seems best therefore to

245

think of practical learning as a relative notion: what is practical learning for one group, time, or place may not be practical learning for another.) Theoretical learning, by contrast, simply specifies facts, independently of whether they help attain any special goals. Theoretical *epistemology*, in particular, aims to develop a body of truths. It is hence in that respect to be classed with geometry, psychology, and American history. Practical learning is easily drawn from some bodies of theoretical learning – bodies of theoretical learning specifying cause/effect relationships, for example. Not just *any* body of theoretical learning will yield practical learning, however, since it must be theoretical learning connected in known ways with human needs or goals, and with skills and materials accessible to humans.

Each chapter of methodology is an organon directed at the attainment of some specific sort of knowledge. Such an organon is constituted by rules to further one's aim of attaining knowledge of that sort. Theoretical epistemology, by contrast, specifies facts about the nature, conditions, or extent of knowledge independently of whether those facts could yield any manual for the attainment of that whose nature, conditions, or extent they specify.

Descartes seeks epistemological learning of both sorts. The *Rules for the Direction of the Mind* is mainly about practical epistemology, as its title would suggest, and gives rules (strategies, heuristics) for attaining truth and avoiding error. But it does say something about the nature of knowledge: "Science in its entirety is true and evident cognition," as Haldane and Ross translate the first sentence under Rule II. And it also specifies conditions of knowledge: either intuition or deduction from the intuitive is required for real knowledge (see the comments under Rule III). Their placement in that manual, however, and even their wording suggest that Descartes conceived even these general reflections on the nature and conditions of knowledge as part of the practical learning suitable for the would-be knower. Thus he concludes his discussion of intuition and deduction as the conditions of true knowledge by saying: "These two *methods* are the most certain *routes* to knowledge, and the mind should admit no others" (my italics).

The first two *Meditations*, by contrast, are meant mainly to determine the true extent of our supposed knowledge, a project of theoretical epistemology. But in later meditations Descartes takes up yet a third project of epistemology, distinct both from developing a manual or organon and also from developing an account of the nature, conditions, and extent of knowledge. Having shown in the early meditations the narrow extent of true knowledge by comparison with the much greater width of supposed knowledge, Descartes tries in later meditations to regain territory lost to the skeptic. Since by then he takes himself to have shown that true knowledge requires intuition or deduction, it is clear what he must do. He must next intuit or deduce the bodies of common-sense belief to which he is so strongly drawn; or at least, more realistically, he must show how one could really do so with sufficient ingenuity and diligence.

Philosophers often waver in their conception of epistemology between the practical and the theoretical. A good example is the "Introduction" by Ernest Nagel and Richard Brandt to their excellent anthology, *Meaning and Knowledge*, whose second paragraph reads as follows:

As we read the history of theories of knowledge in Western philosophy, most of them were developed as generalized critiques of currently held notions of what constitutes knowledge [1], and can be interpreted as so many proposals of policies for obtaining reliable if not completely certain beliefs [2]. Such critiques were undertaken in some cases to locate and eliminate specific sources of error in perceptual and other judgments, in some cases to supply a comprehensive foundation for adjusting traditional beliefs to scientific and social innovations, and in many cases simply to satisfy theoretical curiosity concerning the power of human reason. But whatever the specific purposes of historic theories of knowledge may have been, we share the conception to which their authors in the main subscribed: the central task of epistemology is to provide a generalized critique of the grounds on which claims to knowledge are supported [3], by constructing a systematic account of the principles by which the truth of statements may be properly assessed [4], as well as of the rationale of these principles. A theory of knowledge so understood is indistinguishable from a theory of logic that is general enough to deal not only with the formal validity of arguments, but with the basis on which cognitive claims of any sort can be judged to be warranted, either as cases of knowledge or as instances of probable or reasonable belief [5].

That gives five distinct characterizations of epistemology, two of which seem practical, two theoretical, and one ambiguous.

A connection is made between methodology and epistemology by the following explication (the "organon" explication):

(O) A belief is justified (warranted, reasonable, . . .) iff it is obtained or supported by appropriate use of an adequate organon.

(According to my dictionary, an "organon" is "an instrument for acquiring knowledge; specifically, a body of principles of scientific or philosophic investigation": a *methodology*.)

What would the principles (policies, rules) in an organon look like? There could be principles of at least two general sorts: (a) *indirect rules*: those helpful in seeking knowledge or true belief but which do not say exactly what to believe in given circumstances; (b) *direct rules*: those that do say what to believe (or at least what is permissible) in given

247

circumstances. An indirect rule might be: "Stay sober!" A direct rule: if *P* is clear and distinct, then (one may) accept *P*. (Most of Descartes' rules in his *Rules for the Direction of the Mind* are indirect.) An adequate organon, one that can possibly serve for the explication of justification as in O above, will have not only indirect rules, but also direct rules. And the "appropriateness" required for justification demands that the rules in the organon used be followed with *acceptance*. One could hardly gain true knowledge merely by *conforming* to such rules just to spite someone or just as a joke. Moreover, to be "appropriate," to give knowledge, one's following such rules must not be wildly arbitrary or irrational, but must reflect justified acceptance of them.

The most general rule forms would seem to be:

(R) (1) In conditions *C*, one is to *X*.
    (2) In conditions *C*, one may *X*.

And conditions for following such a rule with justified acceptance on an occasion *t* would seem to include:

(a) Accepting R with relevant justification (i.e., accepting either R1 or R2 with relevant justification)
(b) Justifiedly taking oneself to be in conditions *C*
(c) *X*ing
(d) *X*ing because of (a) and (b).

(All, of course, on occasion *t*.)

Methodism is the view that combines: *(i) the organon conception of justification (O above)* with the claims *(ii) that R above are the general forms of the rules in an organon*, and *(iii) that (a)–(d) above are the conditions for following such a rule with justified acceptance.*

Methodism seems viciously regressive or circular, and this for two reasons. First, whence derives the justification for accepting the rules used? Second, one needs justified belief that one is in conditions *C*: What is the source of *that* justification?

One could perhaps apply a certain rule to itself. Thus perhaps the *practical rule* that one is to accept what is self-evidently right is itself self-evidently right and hence acceptable. And compare the *theoretical principle* that one is justified in accepting whatever is clear and distinct (obvious, intuitive). Might that not be clear and distinct, so that the principle would itself explain why its own acceptance is justified?

But in either case it is not *just* the fact that the rule or principle applies to itself that provides justification for it. For there are many rules or principles that apply to themselves with no semblance of justification. Thus consider:

(E) If a rule or principle contains the proposition that the earth is flat, then it is acceptable, as is the proposition that the earth is flat.

Rule or principle E is of course wrong, and that makes it a counterexample to the notion that *just* by applying to itself a rule or principle might justify itself. That, however, does not preclude a rule or principle which does apply to itself and which does justify itself. It precludes only that such a rule or principle justify itself *merely* by applying to itself. And if so, then possibly Descartes' principle that the intuitive is always acceptable is itself an acceptable principle for the reason that it is intuitive (i.e., by applying to itself though not *merely* by applying to itself).

If it is not just by applying to itself that a rule could derive justification, however, then suspicion remains about methodism (above). How could it avoid both vicious regress and circularity?

This is not to say that otherwise all suspicion would have been removed; for in applying the rules one needs justified belief that conditions are appropriate for such application, that the antecedents of the rules are justified. And could *all* such justification in turn derive from further applications of rules in the organon? According to methodism the only way one could acquire such justification is through a further appropriate application of an adequate organon. But that application in turn requires the appropriate following of rules, which in turn requires that one justifiedly consider oneself to be in the conditions required for the application of *these* rules. And so on.

Consider the super-radical skepticism that requires accepting only what is really apparent, what is present to the mind *per se*, with no need of extrinsic support. Not even super-radical skepticism is sufficiently radical to satisfy methodism. Only *total* skepticism is compatible with that doctrine. And total skepticism is pragmatically incoherent since there is no remote possibility of its correct and reasonable adoption. In order to retain for ourselves at least the possibility of rational coherence, therefore, we know how to treat total skepticism and by extension also how to treat methodism. Even the minimum of reasonable belief admitted by super-radical skepticism already requires a more liberal conception of reasonable belief. For such skepticism does allow that one is reasonable in believing at least what is present to one's mind as intrinsically obvious *per se*. And this presentation of something to one as intrinsically obvious *per se* need not result from one's application of any methodological manual or the like. When something thus presents itself to one, one's own role may be quite passive; one need not have taken any action, not even any intellectual action; one need not have reasoned in any way or checked anything. Justification in that case need not derive from any process of justifying that one or anyone need have carried out, but rather derives from one's satisfaction of certain conditions, and it is not necessary that one satisfy those conditions as a result of one's own volition, nor need one even be conscious of satisfying them. Hence the point of distinguishing as we have done between "methodology" and "epistemology," or between the practical and the theoretic branches of theory of knowledge. Hence also the importance of recognizing that epistemology *need not* be founded on methodology in the way proposed by methodism.[1]

2. METHODOLOGY AND THE ELENCHUS

Consistency is prized as a guide to truth in Plato's Socratic elenchus, which for Gregory Vlastos is a method whereby an interlocutor's belief that *p* is refuted by appeal to further beliefs on his part shown to entail the falsity of his belief that *p*. We consider this controversial method as a preface to a second view of how methodology relates to epistemology (and to science and metaphysics) – having rejected a first view above.

Vlastos suggests that Socrates' reasoning is based on an assumption:

(A) that anyone who ever has a false moral belief will always have at the same time true beliefs entailing the negation of that false belief.[2]

Donald Davidson has subsequently endorsed such a view of the Socratic elenchus, and has suggested the possibility of its extension by Plato to "... metaphysics more generally."[3] What is more, he has in his own right both endorsed the elenchus as a method of philosophy and endorsed the assumption on which it rests.

To his first assumption (A), Vlastos adds a second (B), which Socrates is said to accept on an inductive basis:

1 This section derives largely from my "'Circular' Coherence and 'Absurd' Foundations," in Ernest LePore, ed., *A Companion to Inquiries into Truth and Interpretation* (Oxford: Blackwell, 1986), where the argument takes a different direction. Section 3 below takes up again the question of vicious circularity or regress.
2 Gregory Vlastos, "The Socratic Elenchus," in *Oxford Studies in Ancient Philosophy* (Oxford: Clarendon Press, 1985), pp. 27–58, 52.
3 Donald Davidson, "Plato's Philosopher," *London Review of Books* (August 1, 1985), 16. And compare his "Coherence Theory of Truth and Knowledge," in Dieter Henrich, ed., *Kant oder Hegel?* (Stuttgart: Klett-Cotta, 1983), pp. 423–38, and "Empirical Content," *Grazer Philosophische Studien*, pp. 471–89, where he traces in detail some historical background of his theory of knowledge. Questions are raised about Davidson's arguments in my "'Circular' Coherence and 'Absurd' Foundations."

(B) The set of moral beliefs held by Socrates at any given time is consistent.[4]

Finally, Vlastos notes that from assumption A, combined with B, "Socrates would naturally infer [C] that his own set of moral beliefs is the true set."[5] To this claim by Vlastos, Richard Kraut responds:

I think it wrong to say that Socrates *inferred* the truth of his beliefs from A and B. For if Socrates adhered to A, he did so only because he was already confident of his ability to distinguish moral truths from falsehoods. As Professor Vlastos says, A is a methodological assumption that Socrates justifies inductively: whenever he meets people who have a false moral belief, he finds that they also have true beliefs which entail the negation of that false belief.[6]

From A and B there is in fact no way to infer that Socrates' own set of moral beliefs is *the* true set, and I propose to substitute the claim that Socrates' moral beliefs form *a* wholly true set (C'). C' *still* does not follow from A and B, since Socrates' *moral* beliefs may be consistent yet inconsistent with *other* beliefs of his.[7]

There are ways of patching up our logical difficulty, and let us assume that at least one of these will preserve Vlastos' basic point. For instance, perhaps it will do to replace B with

(B') The set of beliefs held by Socrates at any given time is consistent.

C' does follow from A and B', and I can see no reason why Socrates cannot *infer* C' from A and B'. Here I must side with Vlastos. Even if the inductive backing of A requires that Socrates discriminate true from false moral beliefs in many *particular* cases, that does not make it circular for Socrates to reason from A in turn (together with B) to the *general* C'. And Davidson may well be right: the elenchus might perhaps serve as a method of Platonic philosophy generally, not just of Platonic ethics or value theory.

But how plausible is it that such a method could be *fundamental* – either for Plato or for ourselves? And by that I mean again fundamental inferentially or evidentially. Suppose the method to be

(E) the method of searching for inconsistencies in a body of beliefs, on the assumption (A) that the presence of falsehood is always

---

4 Vlastos, "The Socratic Elenchus," p. 55.
5 Vlastos, abstract of "The Socratic Elenchus," *Journal of Philosophy* (1982): 714.
6 Richard Kraut, "Comments on Gregory Vlastos, 'The Socratic Elenchus'," *Oxford Studies in Ancient Philosophy* (Oxford: Clarendon Press, 1983), p. 68.
7 As was pointed out to me by Richard Lee.

betrayed by inconsistency, so that removing all inconsistency removes all falsehood.

Such a method E is a procedure, of course, an intellectual procedure, and it is less than obvious what inferential relation such a *procedure* can have to a body of substantive beliefs about ourselves and the world around us. Shall we say that the rational employment of the procedure requires no backing from our science or metaphysics? But according to Vlastos, Davidson, and Kraut, the proper use of method E does require assumption A or the like, and that is said by Davidson to hold good both as Platonic exegesis and in our own philosophy. How credible is it really that such an assumption be axiomatic and fundamental? For Vlastos and Kraut it of course is *not* axiomatic. Rather is it derived by a sort of inductive procedure from many specific instances.

What is more, assumption A might be plausibly connectable with Platonic metaphysics and epistemology via the following assumptions: first, that what is truly known is either intuited or proved deductively from the intuited; second, that all rational beings (even slave boys) intuit (dispositionally) the set of basic truths; and, third, that we can discover the answer to any question we can grasp. The argument is simple: if we believe a falsehood f, we can grasp the question whether f; if we can grasp the question whether f, we can discover whether f; if we can discover whether f, then since not-f, we can discover that not-f; if we can discover that not-f, then we can deduce that not-f from intuited truths; therefore not-f must follow from that basis (though slave boys need to be shown how); hence any falsehood one believes will always be inconsistent with one's intuitive basis of beliefs.

That way of defending assumption A on the basis of a rationalist epistemology would rule out the notion that our elenchus method is basic, however, since the method would then be based on epistemology. We might of course stop short of rationalism and appeal with Vlastos and Kraut only to a simple inductive procedure: "*This* false belief was found inconsistent with true beliefs by the same believer; *that* false belief again was found thus inconsistent; that *other* false belief . . . ; et cetera; and we have found no exception. So *every* false belief will be found inconsistent with true beliefs of the believer." And this last is thesis A (or its generalization, from which it follows). But here again method is not fundamental and is based rather on an assumption (A or the like) which itself is inferred inductively from a host of specific non-methodological data.

Exegesis aside, how shall we think of the relation between epistemology, science and metaphysics, and methodology? We need to distinguish between our philosophy and our total body of knowledge, though our total knowledge encompass our philosophy. "Starting points" of philosophy may then be distinguished from "starting points" of knowledge. We may start in philosophy from intuitions about issues of morality, of causation, of knowledge, of perception, et cetera, which does not imply that our knowledge starts with our philosophy. Starting points of our philosophy need not be starting points of our knowledge. Starting points of philosophical reflection need not be original sources of justification. Our attention may be drawn to beliefs about morality, causation, perception, knowledge, and the rest, as a way to begin philosophical reflection, and we may reach various conclusions and form various hypotheses on the basis of such beliefs. Such beliefs would then be psychological starting points of reflection, and even sources of justification for results of such reflection. Nevertheless, that does not deny them a source in turn of their own justification. Nor need the source of their own justification have been another inference or even reflection. For example, epistemological reflection *might* yield the conclusion that intuition, perception, memory, and coherence are ultimate sources of justification. And so our starting basis for philosophy might turn out to have a basis of its own in intuition, perception, memory, and coherence, without ever having been inferred from anything, not consciously anyhow. If so, then though they serve as starting points for philosophical reflection, such beliefs do have a source of their own justification.

3. APT BELIEF

According to my dictionary, *to justify* is "to prove or show to be just, right, or reasonable," in a way that implies "appeal to a standard or to precedent."[8]

Consider the following twofold account of justification (AJ):

(a) that for a belief to be justified is for the subject to justify it or to have justified it; and

(b) that for one to justify a belief (really, successfully) is for one correctly and seriously to use considerations or reasons in its favor.

This *argumentative* account of justification is in line with our dictionary definition, and the methodism also considered earlier is a special type of such argumentism. What is more, the threat of vicious circularity or regress for methodism is as large a threat to argumentism. That is to say, any view that only inference from the justified can serve as a source of

---

8 Here I've used my *Webster's*, but the much more extensive and detailed OED is essentially in agreement.

justification is faced with the questions raised above for methodism. For AJ the threat of circle or regress derives from the fact that seriously and correctly to use considerations or reasons in favor of a belief is to use (i) other things one believes with justification and (ii) their (justifiedly believed) appropriate connection with the belief targeted for justification.

Actually it is perhaps *not* methodism and AJ *per se* that are viciously regressive or circular. It seems possible to believe p because one believes q and believes that if q then one may believe p, while at the same time believing q partly because one believes p and believes that if p then one may believe q. Might not the rules themselves enter into such a system of mutually supportive beliefs, each accepted (in part at least) because of certain others? This seems no more absurd than does a raft each plank of which is kept in place by its relation to other planks. So the absurdity – the viciousness of the circle or regress – may not derive from methodism or AJ as formulated, but rather from the notion that such conceptions provide the basis for fully explaining all justification. Yet that is absurdity enough for those who see in methodism (or the like) the only possible explanation of justification. But why exactly *is* it absurd to suppose that such mutual buttressing could suffice to explain justification? Because we can easily find cases in which such mutual buttressing is clearly insufficient to explain justification. Thus one may believe (i) that X is guilty, (ii) that Y is guilty, and (iii) that X is guilty iff Y is guilty; and one may believe each of these in part because one believes the others. Suppose further that one in fact *is* justified in each of these beliefs. That would satisfy the argumentative conception of justification and yet surely that would not suffice to explain fully the justification that one has for any of (i), (ii), or (iii) – not if we think of justification as that positive epistemic status which a belief must have if it is to constitute knowledge. There has to be more by way of explanation of how one is thus justified in believing any of (i), (ii), or (iii) – more than just what is provided by the fact that the three buttress each other in the way specified.

A drastic way to deal with our threat of circle or regress is to reject the argumentative account of justification entirely, and to claim that one might be justified in a belief without one's justification deriving from any reasons adduced in favor of that belief. But this runs counter to our dictionary definition, which reflects an appealing view of what "justification" requires, or at least of what it is ordinarily taken to require. Good rhetoric and good sense may now call for yielding the word "justification" in favor of some other term to represent the positive epistemic status required for belief to be knowledge. The words "warranted" and "reasonable" seem subject to our doubts about the word "justified": they immediately suggest that warrants or reasons are present or in the offing.

Better terms are "appropriate" and "apt," and the latter is moreover brief. Apt then is perhaps what a belief must be to qualify as knowledge, in addition to being true (and un-Gettierized). *One* way a belief might be apt, moreover, is by being justified, which means that it has the support of reasons (implicit if not explicit). But it is left open that there be other ways for one to believe aptly: it is left open, for example, that some simple memory beliefs be apt though lacking any support by reasoning (and in that sense lacking *justification*). Rhetorical good sense may therefore prescribe the more indirect course of conceding the organon conception of epistemic justification (O), or at least the more general argumentative account (AJ), while demoting epistemic justification from its prominent position in recent epistemology. Gettier showed us long ago that justified true belief is not sufficient for knowledge. On the basis of either the organon or the argumentative conception of justification, it would now be clear that justified true belief is not so much as necessary for knowledge. And though justification is clearly internalist, and always accessible on reflection, it remains an open question whether aptness must be so as well.[9]

4. SUMMARY

We opened with a divide between epistemology and methodology, and a bridge to span it: *that a belief is justified if and only if obtained by appropriate use of an adequate organon*, a principle of theoretical epistemology requiring an organon or manual of practical methodology. Such organon justification is internalist, but it leads to skepticism on pain of regress or circularity – or so it was argued. We turned next to recent controversy about the epistemology in the Socratic elenchus, which led us to consider from a new angle how methodology relates to epistemology and to science and metaphysics. Thus were we made to face once again the organon account of justification provided by our internalist bridge principle. That account was shown to be a special case of a more general *argumentative* account of justification, which in turn agrees with intuitions so powerful as to be enshrined already in our dictionaries. Good rhetoric demands therefore that "justification" and its cognates be yielded to the argumentative account. Which requires in turn that justification be demoted from its position as principal concept of epistemology. Justification had better not be *all* that is required in general for knowledge, nor what is always required in any premises of use to justify

---

9 Further discussion of aptness and justification may be found in Chapter 16 in this volume.

anything. That way lies vicious regress or circularity – though exactly where it lies is not just obvious on causal inspection. Obvious it does become, anyhow, thanks to a bit of reasoning. Justification is best demoted, therefore, to the status of *one* way a belief may be apt for knowledge, while we allow other ways not dependent on already attained justification: e.g., perception, perhaps, or introspection, or memory. Such aptness may still be internalist but that remains here an open question.

15

Equilibrium in coherence?

The method of reflective equilibrium aims to maximize two factors in one's beliefs: harmonious coherence, and plausibility of content.[1] Analytic philosophy has long paid deference to these factors, for instance in its use of the counterexample, which attacks a principle as *incoherent with the plausible* (by one's lights). A critique of this tradition has recently appeared, and it shall be my main objective here to assess its merits. An appendix will apply our results to issues of moral relativism and rationality.

A. EPISTEMOLOGIES IN CONFLICT

Radical methodism is opposed to narrow reflective equilibrium. Karl Popper champions such methodism, Nelson Goodman such equilibrium. This opposition leads to a more moderate equilibrium, wide rather than narrow, in a sense to be explained.

1. Methodism

"Science is justified by means of induction on the basis of observation and experience." This has been widely accepted and is widely accepted today. According to Popper, nevertheless, to think thus is a grave error, for as Hume showed, no supposed inductive reasoning is of any value. Popper reasons that " . . . theories can never be inferred from observation statements, or rationally justified by them." For " . . . induction cannot be logically justified" (Popper, 42). That is to say, the fact that a theory T has been induced from certain data does not justify accepting T, since it does not ensure that T is true. Even if induced correctly from true data, it is still possible that the theory be false.

That is why Popper opposes induction and favors appeal to falsifica-

---

1 Comprehensiveness has occasionally been added as well, insightfully in my view, but we leave this aside in the present context. Reflective equilibrium has been adopted by John Rawls in ethics, and Roderick Chisholm has long defended a closely related view in epistemology: critical cognitivism, which answers the "problem of the criterion." See Rawls, *Theory of Justice*, esp. Section 4; also see Chisholm's *Theory of Knowledge*, the chapter entitled "The Problem of the Criterion."

257

tion. Unlike induction, falsification is a deductive process. A datum D falsifies a theory T only if it entails the negation or falsity of T. If the negation of a theory follows by deductive logic from certain data, then the theory must be false. For Popper, corroboration consists *not* in inducing a theory on the basis of experience but in submitting it to tests: i.e., in trying to falsify it by means of observational data. (And a statement is scientific only if it is at least falsifiable.)

But how do we respond to the Duhem-Quine objection? "No matter how experience turns out," says the objection, "it is always possible to retain any given commitment, even if this requires drastic changes in the rest of our beliefs." In other words, no statement is strictly falsifiable, scientific statements included, especially those which are highly theoretical.

Against this objection, Popper offers a twofold defense:

(a.) To derive a testable prediction from a scientific theory it is often necessary to make use of auxiliary suppositions which are numerous and complex, and many of them implicit. "If we do make auxiliary assumptions, then of course we cannot be certain whether one of them, rather than the theory under test, is responsible for any refutation. So we have to guess."[2]

(b.) We " . . . can always immunize a theory against refutation. There are many such evasive immunizing tactics; and if nothing better occurs to us, we can always deny the objectivity – or even the existence – of the refuting observation." But such evasion puts an end to any science worth pursuing.[3]

Popperian methodology is intricate when displayed fully, yet it seems incoherent for the following reasons.

First of all, it rejects induction *for not being deductively valid*, yet accepts a method of falsification no more valid than induction, since strictly speaking falsification takes us only so far; beyond that we cannot proceed except by guessing and by rejecting abhorrent immunizing tactics; but neither such guessing nor such rejection can be deduced from perceptual experience or observation.

One can of course immunize a scientific theory against all refutation, if only by denying the objectivity or even the existence of any contrary observation. But to immunize thus is a ridiculous evasion. About that Popper is clearly right. How ironic that he should scorn his message in his own practice! What motive could there be to deny that certain predictions and expectations are justified (as, for instance, that normally a pen held aloft will fall if released), or at least better justified than others (as it is

---

2 Karl Popper, "Replies to my Critics," in Paul Schilpp, ed., *The Philosophy of Karl Popper*, p. 998.
3 *Ibid.*, p. 983.

more reasonable to expect the pen's fall than its metamorphosis into an elephant)? Whatever may be Popper's motive, the effect of his practice is to immunize a certain theory derived from Hume. Apparently, for neither philosopher is any belief reasonable unless formed by an infallible process: no fallible form of reasoning can yield justified beliefs.

This Hume/Popper epistemology is incompatible with many data: its truth would preclude justification for the simplest and most common expectations that guide our daily lives. Consequently, only immunizing it can we sustain our belief in such a theory; only denying that our common expectations are a whit more reasonable than their respective denials, no matter how insensate or even insane.

In sum, Popper accepts an exclusively deductive methodology: only deductive proof can justify belief. It follows that almost nothing of what we believe ordinarily can be justified, which applies both to science and common sense. Popper defends his method by denying that we could possibly be justified in our beliefs of science or daily life. Ironically, this immunizes a theory of justification uncritically accepted from Hume and Descartes.

2. Narrow reflective equilibrium

These most recent observations are in close harmony with an influential methodology of philosophy expounded by Nelson Goodman as follows:

How do we justify a *deduction*? Plainly by showing that it conforms with the general rules of deductive inference. An argument that so conforms is justified or valid, even if its conclusion happens to be false. An argument that violates a rule is fallacious even if its conclusion happens to be true. . . . Analogously, the basic task in justifying an inductive inference is to show that it conforms to the general rules of induction. . . .

Yet, of course, the rules themselves must ultimately be justified. The validity of a deduction depends not upon conformity to any purely arbitrary rules we may contrive, but upon conformity with valid rules. When we speak of *the* rules of inference we mean the valid rules – or better, *some* valid rules, since there may be alternative sets of equally valid rules. But how is the validity of rules to be determined? Here . . . we encounter philosophers who insist that these rules follow from some self-evident axiom, and others who try to show that the rules are grounded in the very nature of the human mind. I think the answer lies much nearer to the surface. Principles of deductive inference are justified by their conformity with accepted deductive practice. Their validity depends upon accordance with the particular deductive inferences we actually make and sanction. If a rule yields unacceptable inferences, we drop it as invalid. Justification of general rules thus derives from judgments rejecting or accepting particular deductive inferences.

This looks flagrantly circular. I have said that deductive inferences are justified by their conformity to valid general rules, and that general rules are justified by their conformity to valid inferences. But this circle is a virtuous one. . . . *A rule is amended if it yields an inference we are unwilling to accept; an inference is rejected if it violates a rule we are unwilling to amend.* The process of justification is the delicate one of making mutual adjustments between rules and accepted inferences; and in the agreement thus achieved lies the only justification needed for either.

All this applies equally well to induction. An inductive inference, too, is justified by conformity to general rules, and a general rule by conformity to accepted inductive inferences. (Goodman 1973, 63–64)

Foundationism with regard to a certain domain is the project of legitimizing that domain by showing how it may be founded on a certain basis. Descartes's radical foundationism tries to show how all our beliefs, both the scientific and the quotidian, may be founded by means of deduction on a basis of intuitive reason. But ethical foundationism need not be so radical. Having adopted as basis some theory of practical reason, or about the meaning of moral language, ethical foundationism may then try to derive principles of ethics from the given basis. Recent foundationist projects have elicited less than universal agreement, however, and many have turned to the alternative method used for example by John Rawls in his *Theory of Justice*. It is not Rawls's objective to appeal beyond ethics in search of some external foundation. On the contrary, one may proceed in the way pointed out by Goodman. Specific moral judgments about actual or imaginary situations may be justified by means of moral principles or rules, and these in turn may be justified by their agreement with the specific judgments accepted. This is the method of *narrow reflective equilibrium*. But one may also appeal to a wider reflective equilibrium, as follows.

3. Wide reflective equilibrium

Let us distinguish our moral philosophy from our enclosing body of knowledge and wisdom. And let us distinguish further between (i) philosophical reflection aimed at formulating moral principles, (ii) philosophical reflection aimed at explicating how one justifies accepting particular moral views or principles, and (iii) the knowledge or wisdom in general possessed by one who reflects in either of the two ways just distinguished. Having drawn these distinctions, we turn next to the "starting points" of the knowledge or wisdom of the thinker who reflects. In such philosophical reflection we may begin with intuitions and beliefs about matters of morality, of causation, of knowledge, of perception, *et cetera*; which does not imply that our knowledge and wisdom must begin with our philosophical reflection.

Starting points of the process of philosophical reflection need not be original sources for the justification or aptness of the resulting beliefs. Our attention may be drawn to certain beliefs or attitudes about morality, causation, perception, knowledge, *et cetera*, as a way of launching philosophical reflection, and we may reach various conclusions and form various hypotheses on the basis of such beliefs or attitudes. Such beliefs or attitudes would then be psychological starting points of reflection and occasionally even grounds for the *results* of such reflection. However, that does not deny them a source in turn of their own aptness or justification. Nor need that source of their own justification have been some further inference or reflection. For example, epistemological reflection *might* give rise to the conclusion that perception and memory are ultimate sources of aptness or justification and our initial basis for philosophical reflection *might* have as its own basis some perception and memory. Thus, reflection might begin with things that one reads (perception) or remembers (memory). Yet this part of our initial basis of perception or memory for philosophical reflection might never have been inferred from anything, not by the subject who reflects. Accordingly, even though they serve as starting points for philosophical reflection, such beliefs might still have a source for their own aptness or justification through their origin in perception or memory.

The method of *narrow reflective equilibrium* in any domain is restricted to the end of securing harmony between specific judgments and general principles in that same domain. This is the method expounded and defended by Goodman. The method of *wide reflective equilibrium* seeks harmony between the beliefs and principles accepted in the given domain, but it seeks harmony also with beliefs and principles in any other pertinent domain. Clearly, the narrow method cannot be fundamental. Narrow reflection must be supplemented by wider reflection, at least to the point where we are satisfied that there is no other domain relevant to the topic under reflection.[4]

B. CRITIQUE OF REFLECTIVE EQUILIBRIUM

The use of reflective equilibrium has been attacked as serving only to organize and protect conservative orthodoxy. This objection has some weight when directed against the narrow equilibrium favored by Goodman, the sort of reflection that encloses itself in a particular ambit – say,

---

4 Rarely, if ever, could a domain lie in total epistemic isolation. Is there some citadel of reason hermetically sealed and protected from other theoretical and empirical concerns?

induction, or normative ethics – and aims for the best coherence of one's views *within* that ambit. More defensible is the method of wide equilibrium, however, since it does not isolate itself from any knowledge or wisdom, no matter how far afield, but takes into account *everything* that may seem pertinent.

Wide equilibrium seems equivalent to a pure coherentism which at any juncture would always opt for the most harmoniously and comprehensively coherent view available. If a conflict pits the intuitive pull of an example against the tug of a familiar principle, we seek to remove or revise one or the other, so as to remove the tension. Sometimes the particular intuition(s) will win, but sometimes the tug of the principle must prevail. In any case, our aim in dealing with the problem is to remove the tension and restore harmonious coherence while retaining as much as we can of our views (thus the comprehensiveness desideratum).

Equilibrium coherentism has been a target of repeated attacks. Most recently a spirited critique has been published by Stephen Stich,[5] who warns against supposing that mere reflective equilibrium, and the comprehensive coherence involved, can rationally justify one's beliefs and attitudes.

Actually, Stich takes aim at "the tradition of analytic epistemology," defined as " . . . any epistemological project that takes the choice between competing justificational rules or competing criteria of rightness to turn on conceptual or linguistic analysis" (405). But I doubt that there is any such tradition.

Not since Moore's "open question" attack on the "naturalistic fallacy" has normative ethics or epistemology been thought by many (if any) to turn on conceptual or linguistic analysis – except in an outlandish sense of "turn" which makes *every* choice among sentences "turn" on such "analysis" by "turning" on what the terms involved mean, on what concepts are thus involved.

Stich offers two exhibits as evidence for his conception of analytic epistemology: (A) some quotations from Alvin Goldman's *Epistemology and Cognition* (1986) and (B) a reference to Robert Shope's *The Analysis of Knowing* (1983).

Concerning exhibit A, Stich argues that much of what Goldman says

suggests that, on his view, *conceptual analysis* or *conceptual explication* is the proper way to decide among competing criteria of rightness. The correct criterion of rightness is the one that comports with the conception of justifiedness that is

---

5 Stich (1988). (Parenthetical page references will be made to this article.) Earlier work on reflective equilibrium in ethics includes, in addition to that already cited in footnote 1 above, Rawls (1974–5); Daniels (1979); and DePaul (1986).

"embraced by everyday thought or language" (58). To test a criterion we explore the judgments it would entail about specific cases, and we test these judgments against our "pretheoretic intuitions." "A criterion is supported to the extent that implied judgments accord with such intuitions, and weakened to the extent that they do not." (66)[6]

It is puzzling to argue thus when writers in normative ethics and epistemology have long distinguished emphatically between mere linguistic or conceptual analysis and substantive theorizing. To use exhibit A as above, in the teeth of that widely shared distinction, must depend on some such assumption as this: "Unless one has some pretty strange views about intuitions, it is hard to see what we could hope to gain from capturing them apart from some insight into the concepts that underlie them" (411). But the required views about intuitions are not strange in contemporary ethics and epistemology.

As for exhibit B, Shope's book is about the analysis of propositional knowledge or of "S knows that p", in response to the Gettier problem. *This* may well fall properly within the ambit of conceptual or linguistic analysis, and has widely been thought to do so. But theories of justification are quite another matter.

Besides, Stich's main point against so-called "analytic epistemology" can be disentangled from his unusual views about the place of linguistic or conceptual analysis. What he highlights in his whole discussion is, after all, the simple fact that the prevalence of certain "intuitions" is no sure guide to theory or practice, that such consensus cannot function as a fundamental criterion in epistemology or ethics. And *this* valuable point deserves emphasis. Agreement can still remain a relevant factor, moreover, with *some* proper weight in one's formation of ethical or epistemic views. If we find ourselves in *disagreement* with others, it would lend us plausibility and coherence to have a theory of error explaining why and how others go wrong – especially if our position turns out to be solitary.

There are hence *two* versions of reflective equilibrium and coherentism: (a) the individual version, which requires reflective equilibrium and coherence in one's own views, even if these turn out to disagree with those held by others, and (b) the social version, which requires reflective equilibrium and coherence *across* persons in a group, even for the justification of individual members in the group. The individual version seems more plausibly defensible, especially since it would still admit social considerations in the way already suggested – through the increment of coherence that may derive from knowing oneself in agreement with others.

Perhaps Stich's arguments could be applied even against our individual

---

6 Stich, *op. cit.*, p. 404. The references in parentheses are to *Epistemology and Cognition*.

version of reflective equilibrium. Stich himself does not do so, even in his claim about a " . . . guru who is as bonkers as he is charismatic," that " . . . we certainly don't want to say that the followers of such a guru would be rational to invoke whatever wild inferential principle might be in reflective equilibrium for their leader" (410). For there is here no *explicit* suggestion that the guru himself cannot be rational (though bonkers).

If the argument is *not* extended even implicitly to the individual version, however, then analytic epistemology can easily meet the critique, simply by opting for that individual version of reflective equilibrium. It seems to me that this is anyhow the best position open to analytic epistemology, and that the appeal to "common sense" or to "ordinary intuitions" should be considered accidental. As epistemologist (or moral philosopher) one is primordially concerned to elaborate one's *own* coherent view. One's primary project is thus first-person, though normally one takes one's own situation to be more or less widely shared in relevant respects, and one hence offers one's (first-person) results to others in the familiar style of Descartes. And if one's pertinent intuitions seem widely enough shared, they may then be labelled "common sense intuitions," though it is not their being common that really matters. For that is after all just an accidental feature which both relieves one from the burden of a theory of error and also makes one's results seem of interest to others.[7]

Again, Stich's arguments might be applied even against our individual version of reflective equilibrium; and here we must make a stand, or so I will argue. Nevertheless, even here Stich's reasoning retains the merit of highlighting the value of a distinction important for epistemology, that between rational justification and wider intellectual virtue.[8]

C. DEFENSE OF REFLECTIVE EQUILIBRIUM

Admonished to recall that by the test of equilibrium a coherent madman or fanatic would count as rational, we need to distinguish two forms of madness or fanaticism. On one side is the madness or fanaticism that weaves systems of impressive complexity, systems that satisfy the requirements of deductive logic, and even probability theory, statistics, and inductive logic. Such a madman or fanatic is willing to postulate hypoth-

---

7 Being thus relieved from a theory of error does not entail that one can ignore the question of how and why others know rather than err. But presumably this question can now be answered by appeal to the same theory of knowledge that one would apply to oneself.

8 That we must distinguish similarly between *justified* and *apt* belief is the main burden of my "Methodology and Apt Belief" (1988) – chapter 14 above.

eses heavy with epicycles, if they will only preserve the beliefs or attitudes favored by his madness or fanaticism.

But there is also a madness or fanaticism which needs no aid of epicycles. For it relies rather on selective or even illusory perception or memory. Whatever incoming data may clash with the favored beliefs are ignored or forgotten. And whatever suits the system – presto! – appears. Nor need that result from premeditated policy. Rather, it may simply express the subject's nature. Such an unfortunate can develop a coherence as perfect as that of the best scientist, philosopher, lawyer, or police detective. Having attained thereby a reflective equilibrium of the greatest width, must he not be granted rational justification?

It might be alleged that the perception or memory of such a madman or fanatic is too defective, that it gives him a view of things too unrepresentative of reality and that so large a cognitive defect is incompatible with rational justification. To test this hypothesis, we perform a thought experiment. Suppose yourself a victim of the Cartesian evil demon. Your inner life is then just as it has been in every nonrelational detail, yet you are in broad and deep error about your surroundings. But are you guilty of irrationality? Are you not on the contrary as rational and as rationally justified as you are now in actuality?

It might be responded, on the basis of an externalist account of the content of our thoughts and experiences, that the example is incoherent, since someone so detached from their external world could not so much as form beliefs or have experiences pertaining to it. One's access to propositional content may derive from a normal childhood and adolescence, however, if one becomes a victim of the demon only as an adult. I see no incoherence here, even granting the externalist account of content.

Our question was what to say of the madman or fanatic whose *data* are defective through some defect in his memory or perception. If he reasons admirably or even brilliantly on the basis of such data and achieves wide equilibrium, we have indeed no choice but to grant him rational justification. But such a concession is as correct in his case as it would be in ours were we now victims of a Cartesian demon.

And just how broad are the concepts of rationality and of rational justification? This seems in large measure a matter of terminology and convention. If only to fix ideas, let's give them the widest allowable breadth. Even so, we must still distinguish rationality and internal justification from a broader intellectual virtue which derives from pertinent cognitive faculties, perception and memory among them.

The most that philosophical reflection can give us is rational justification. Broader intellectual virtue is not attainable just by reflection, not even by the deepest, most wide-ranging and intense reflection. Broader virtue requires faculties other than reason, such as perception and memory. And this distinction between rational justification and broader intellectual virtue makes it possible to accept wide reflective equilibrium as a way to rational justification, without conceding that coherent madmen or fanatics are not only rational but also more broadly virtuous.

Conclusion: Philosophical reflection enhances rational justification through wide reflective equilibrium. But it is philosopher's arrogance to suppose mere reflection the source of all intellectual virtue. Perception, in particular, be it of nature or of values, is not derivable from reflection alone. It requires instead the formative influence of God, or evolution, or a good upbringing. What is more, such a virtue is virtuous only relative to appropriate surroundings, which are not the product of any reflection.[9]

D. APPENDIX: AN APPLICATION TO ISSUES OF
MORAL RELATIVISM

Relativism emerges through disagreement in deep conceptions or beliefs irresolvable through any shared procedure, as in Philippa Foot's example of two cultures or races that disagree on what it takes to be good-looking (Foot, 1970). In the spirit of that example, consider also disagreement as to what is good music, or a fine meal, or as to what does or does not taste good. On matters of taste, we should often just agree to disagree, since there is no such thing as the truth *period*. There is instead what is true for me and what is true for the other, or at most what is true for us and what is true for them.

What it is to be good-looking for us or to taste or sound good for us may not have a similar status for others. If there is such disagreement, then, who is in the right? This seems as bogus as asking who is in the right when the Pygmies disagree with the Watusi over what it takes to be tall. Such disagreement is only apparent and is removed by the introduction of a pertinent index. A Pygmy is equally tall *as a Pygmy* for the Watusi as for the Pygmies.

Real disagreement lies beyond preferences of facial appearance, taste, or music, for opinions on such matters are objectivized and absolutized more or less in the way of opinions on height, as above.

May we extend that train of thought to cover morality as well? That depends on what we include in morality, for "moral" and its cognates are a slippery crew. Parts of moral doctrines shared by large groups and even civilizations have aspects so subjective and relative as the phenomena of taste preference. Often it is the fact of *custom* that makes the correspond-

9 Compare Section II of Chapter 3 above.

ing conduct morally correct for the group involved, even though another group may have an incompatible custom.

The interesting question is whether *all* of morality is based thus fundamentally on the customs in force, *and nothing more*. And that is closely related to the question of whether there is any conduct that it would never be correct to permit, that is *impermissible*, even if the customs of some society in fact allow it. This would mean that some concept of the permissible is absolute and distinct from the concept of the *permitted* in a given society S. For such impermissible conduct would of course be "permitted-relative-to-S" if S does permit it. The more fundamentally interesting question is hence whether there are any such absolute moral concepts *in addition* to the relative ones, since the relative ones are there for all to see.

Absolute moral concepts are often alleged to be illusory and unacceptable as objective categories, given the absence of any rational procedure for the resolution of deep disagreements. But just what may be meant by such "rational procedure"? Suppose there is a disagreement as to whether a contradictory proposition could ever be true. If someone opts for the affirmative, there is no procedure to refute him which does not already presuppose the negative. Hence there is no noncircular logical procedure to defend elementary logic against such a dissenter.

It may be said that by definition of "rational," elementary logic cannot be rejected *rationally*, whereas even the most basic moral disagreement need not involve any failure of reason on either side. If the term "reason" is to be reserved so categorically, however, we would just need some other vocabulary for the objectivity of morality, perhaps the vocabulary of "intuition," or of "perception," or of "sensibility," or that of inferential or ampliative reason. The main point is anyhow this. Not only in fundamental morality, but also in basic epistemology, and in elementary logic, there will be a circle of principles each defensible only by appeal to itself and the others. In logic there is at least the principle of noncontradiction. In epistemology there would be principles of perception, perhaps, of memory, of intuitive reason, of inferential reason, of coherence, etc., none of which we could defend without leaning on itself or others. Is not morality subject to the same logical phenomenon? May there not be principles of justice and of general welfare defensible only circularly or at least through appeal to more particular moral intuitions? May it not be so even if the intuitions require coherence with moral principles for their own full justification? Of course anyone who rejects all principles and opinions to which one might appeal cannot be answered without *petitio*. But that would apply not only to morality but also to epistemology and logic. It remains to be seen, therefore, what idiosyncrasy of basic moral

267

principles may distinguish them from their epistemic or logical counterparts, subjecting them to a correspondingly idiosyncratic relativity.

What is distinctive of morality, it may be replied, is the extent and depth of actual disagreement. It is not enough that there be *some* disagreement: some disagreement there is in any ambit. More important is the question whether or not there is any fundamental disagreement which cannot possibly be resolved by any conceivable procedure yielding something more than *just* a third opinion. Many opposing preferences are thus irresoluble, of course, neither preference being superior to the other. Are all moral disagreements like that: opposing preferences, neither objectively superior?

It may be replied that the spread of history and the diversity of cultures must hold many disagreements of maximum depth. Supposing some at least of these turn out to constitute irreconcilable opposing preferences, just what procedure might we invoke to declare winners and losers?

In a way the problem is not so much the lack of procedures as their excess. Each party to a disagreement could appeal to their own deepest principles for a resolution, and would of course emerge victorious. Still, it is a popular error to think such circularity *necessarily* vicious. This error forces one to view even the most elementary logic as necessarily relative, for even its defense must in the end come full circle.[10] To give logic the prestige label of "rational" cannot conceal this fact.

The error of believing circularity irremediably vicious may simply overlook that criteria of rational thought for a person or group need not be criteria for correct and rational interpersonal dialogue – an oversight abetted by the ancient notion of thought as inner dialogue. Nevertheless, we have seen already how reflective equilibrium might lead to a circular coherence which yields rational justification – even if a circular *petitio* is always a fault in dialogue or debate (which seems less than obvious anyhow).

REFERENCES

Chisholm, Roderick. *Theory of Knowledge*. Englewood Cliffs: Prentice-Hall, 1st ed., 1966; 2nd ed., 1977; 3rd ed., 1989.

Daniels, Norman. "Wide Reflective Equilibrium and Theory Acceptance in Ethics," *Journal of Philosophy* 76 (1979): 256–82.

DePaul, Michael. "Reflective Equilibrium and Foundationalism," *American Philosophical Quarterly* 23 (1986): 59–69.

Foot, Philippa. "Morality and Art," Henrietta Hertz Lecture, *Proceedings of the British Academy* 56 (1970).

10 Its defense would be circular, or at least "spiral," in the sense given in Chapter 11 above.

Goldman, Alvin. *Epistemology and Cognition*. Cambridge, Mass.: Harvard University Press, 1986.

Goodman, Nelson. *Fact, Fiction, and Forecast*, 3rd ed. Indianapolis: Bobbs-Merrill, 1973.

Popper, Karl. *Conjectures and Refutations*. London: Routledge & Kegan Paul, 1969.
"Replies to my Critics," in *The Philosophy of Karl Popper*, Paul Schilpp, ed., Illinois: Open Court, 1974, Vol. II.

Rawls, John. *Theory of Justice*. Cambridge, Mass.: Harvard University Press, 1971.
"The Independence of Moral Theory," *Proceedings and Addresses of the American Philosophical Association* (1974–5): 5–22.

Shope, Robert. *The Analysis of Knowing*. Princeton University Press, 1983.

Sosa, Ernest. "Methodology and Apt Belief," *Synthese* 74 (1988).
"The Coherence of Virtue and the Virtue of Coherence," *Synthese* 71 (1985): 3–28.

Stich, Stephen. "Reflective Equilibrium, Analytic Epistemology and the Problem of Cognitive Diversity," *Synthese* 74 (1988): 391–413.

16

Intellectual virtue in perspective

A. INTELLECTUAL VIRTUES

Intellectual virtues might be viewed as ways of coping that are cognitively effective, a view however that would invite the question of just what might make a way of coping "cognitively effective." According to my dictionary, "cognition" means "the act or process of knowing . . . *also*: a product of this act." As for "effective," it is said to mean "producing or capable of producing a result," with an emphasis on "the actual production of or the power to produce an effect <effective thinking>." Putting all this together, what makes a way of coping "cognitively effective" is its power to produce effects relating to or involving knowledge. But now look where that leaves us:

> What is "knowledge"? True belief that is at least justified.
> And what makes a true belief "justified"? That it have its source in intellectual virtue.
> And what is "intellectual virtue"? A skill or ability that enables one to cope in a cognitively effective way.
> And what makes a way of coping "cognitively effective"? That it have the power to produce effects relating to or involving knowledge.

Thus we start with knowledge and return to it in a narrow circle.

For a more illuminating account we need to escape the circle. One way to do so understands intellectual virtue not as a "cognitively effective" skill or ability, but rather as one that is truth-conducive (or as the ground of such a disposition). This might elicit objections as follows.

"*First*, accepting such an account of intellectual virtue drives us back upon the question about the nature of justified belief – back, in short, to the foundationalist–coherentist dispute. For if we understand 'intellectual virtues' as truth-conducive dispositions or the like, then we will want to ask how we know which dispositions are virtues, how we know which are truth-conducive. But since, by wide agreement, our best access to truth is justified belief, this strategy leaves us with the primary notion of justification as that of justified beliefs; justified dispositions would remain secondary.

"*Second*, it is doubtful that the ordinary notion of justification can be captured by the idea of a reliable generating mechanism for beliefs. Just as there is presumably some way in which one has a say in the matter whether or not one is morally virtuous, so there should be also a way in which one has some say in the matter whether or not one is intellectually virtuous. But it is nonsense to attribute such 'say' to someone regarding his reliable belief-generating mechanisms or their exercise."

Taking the two objections in reverse order, I admit first a narrow Aristotelian conception of virtue according to which a virtue is a certain disposition to make appropriate deliberate choices. And this is of course much narrower than any simple notion of a truth-conducive belief-generating mechanism. For whether or not belief is *ever* a product of deliberate choice, it surely is not *always* a product of such choice. Thus perceptual and introspective beliefs are often acquired willy-nilly. And yet even where deliberate choice is thus absent, some mechanism may yet generate one's belief. For example, it may be one's faculty of sight operating in good light that generates one's belief in the whiteness and roundness of a facing snowball. Is possession of such a faculty a "virtue"? Not in the narrow Aristotelian sense, of course, since it is no disposition to make deliberate choices. But there is a broader sense of "virtue," still Greek, in which anything with a function – natural or artificial – does have virtues. The eye does, after all, have its virtues, and so does a knife.[1] And if we include grasping the truth about one's environment among the proper ends of a human being, then the faculty of sight would seem in a broad sense a virtue in human beings; and if grasping the truth is an intellectual matter then that virtue is also in a straightforward sense an intellectual virtue.

As for the first objection, it charged truth-conduciveness accounts of intellectual virtues with driving us "back upon the question about the nature of justified belief [and leaving] us with the primary notion of justification as that of justified beliefs." But when and how are we supposed to be thus driven back? When we try to determine the credentials of a candidate intellectual virtue, and when we ask more generally "how we know which dispositions are virtues, how we know which are truth-conducive." The problem is supposed to be that to determine whether a disposition is truth-conducive we must determine whether the beliefs that manifest that disposition are mostly true. And, since "our best access to truth is justified belief," in order to determine whether a belief is true we must determine whether it is a justified belief.

---

1 See Plato's *Republic*, Bk. I, 352.

If that is the problem, it is apparently captured by the following argument:

A1. To determine that a disposition of one's own is truth-conducive one must determine that beliefs manifesting it are mostly true. (Assumption)

A2. To determine that a belief of one's own is true one must determine that it is a justified belief. (Assumption)

A3. To determine that a disposition of one's own is truth-conducive one must determine that beliefs manifesting it are mostly justified. (From A1, A2)

Even if conclusion A3 is true, that does not immediately refute the account of justified belief as belief that manifests a truth-conducive intellectual virtue – not even if we take such an "account" to be a philosophical analysis. For how we must determine something is an epistemological question, whereas our philosophical analysis of justified belief would be something semantical or ontological, and there is no immediately obvious connection between the two. In particular, there is no manifest absurdity in the notion that X be analyzable (semantically or ontologically) as Y despite the fact that to determine whether Y applies in a certain situation you need to determine (first) whether X applies. Thus to be a cube may be analyzable as being a six-sided closed solid with sides all square but in a certain situation it may be easier to see that there is a cube before you than to determine that there is a closed solid that both has six sides and has sides all square. You may be able to see right away that it's a cube you are holding as you turn it in your hands, though you lack the time and patience to count the sides keeping track of which you have already counted; and hence you may conclude that it has six sides from your analysis of cubicity and from your perceptual knowledge that it is a cube.

For some sort of philosophical or semantical analysis, however, it may perhaps turn out that if X has Y as its analysis of that sort, then it cannot in consistency turn out that to determine whether Y applies you must determine whether X applies. That there is such a connection between meaning and justification is of course a familiar theme of recent decades.

But the argument before us still does not rule out the account of justified belief as belief issuing from an intellectual virtue, even if this account is understood as a meaning analysis requiring the mentioned connection between meaning and justification. My objection now pertains not to what the conclusion would show even if we accepted it, but pertains rather to the truth of the second premise. Consider the following argument:

272

B1. It rains.

B2. I (occurrently) believe that it rains.

B3. It rains and I believe that it rains. (From B1, B2)

B4. If it rains and I believe that it rains, then my belief that it rains is true. (Obvious)

B5. My belief that it rains is true. (From B3, B4)

It seems plain I can determine [B5] – that my belief that it rains is true – by means of this argument (where square brackets will function as nominalizers, so that [It rains] = that it rains). Since [B4] is obvious, since [B5] is deduced by modus ponens from [B3] and [B4], and since [B3] is deduced by conjunction from [B1] and [B2], it all goes back to the premises [B1] and [B2]. But I may just start from the following two bits of knowledge: (a) my knowledge of the fact [B1], which I have as a result (in part) of being outside and looking up and putting out my bare arms; and (b) my knowledge of the fact [B2] which I have by simple introspection. So it appears I can after all determine that a belief of my own is true without considering whether it is justified, and without considering in the course of that determination whether any particular belief of mine is or is not justified.

Accordingly, if it is true that "our best access to truth is justified belief," that is so only in a certain sense. For our best access to truth may be justified belief simply in the sense that in our search for truth we are better served by harboring beliefs that *are* justified rather than those that are unjustified. But it is not entailed that in order to determine that a belief of one's own is true, one must first *determine* it to *be* justified. Hence the sense in which indeed "our best access to truth is justified belief" is not after all one that dooms as viciously circular our account of what it is for a belief to be justified: namely, our account that for a belief to be justified is for it to manifest a truth-conducive faculty or intellectual virtue.

But what, again, is such a faculty or intellectual virtue? The primary meaning attributed to "faculty" by my dictionary is "ability, power." Faculties are abilities to do certain sorts of things in certain sorts of circumstances, but how more specifically should we conceive of them? One possibility is to *define* each faculty as the ability to attain certain accomplishments. But of course an accomplishment attainable in given circumstances may be unattainable in other circumstances. Abilities correlate with accomplishments only relative to circumstances. There is for example our ability to tell (directly) the color and shape of a surface, so long as it is facing, "middle-sized," not too far, unscreened, and in enough light, and so long as one looks at it while sober, and so on. And

273

similarly for other perceptual faculties. Compare also our ability to tell simple enough necessary truths, at least once having attained an age of reason and discernment; and our ability to retain simple enough beliefs in which we have sufficient interest. In each case our remarkably extensive species-wide accomplishments of a certain sort are explained by appeal to a corresponding ability, to a cognitive faculty; or at least we are thus provided the beginning of an explanation, an explanation sketch. But in none of these cases is there really any pretense to infallibility. All we're in a position to require is a good success ratio. Common sense is simply in no position to specify substantive circumstances in which the exercise of sight is bound to be infallible. Of course that is not to rule out underlying abilities which are in fact infallible in specifiable circumstances; it is only to imply that if there are such abilities common sense is at this point unable to formulate them.

What powers or abilities do then enable a subject to achieve knowledge or at least epistemic justification? They are presumably powers or abilities to distinguish the true from the false in a certain subject field, to attain truth and avoid error in the field. One's power or ability must presumably make one such that, normally at least, in one's ordinary habitat, or at least in one's ordinary circumstances when making such judgments, one *would* believe what is true and *not* believe what is false, concerning matters in that field.

A faculty is, again, an ability. An ability to do *what*? To *know*? That would be circular. To believe with justification? Still circular. To believe correctly propositions of a certain sort: perceptual ones, say, or mathematical ones? That can't be enough since *every* correct belief of a proposition of the sort involved will manifest *that* ability, i.e., that *mere* ability. To tell the true from the false with a good success ratio? A similar problem arises here, since one might just through a fantastic coincidence *actually* get mostly true beliefs in a certain field, and this would manifest *that* ability, i.e., that *mere* ability.

Indeed it is probably better to think of a faculty *not* as an ability but rather as a virtue or a *competence*. One has a faculty only if there is a field F and there is a set of circumstances C such that one *would* distinguish the true from the false in F in C. But of course whenever one *happens* to have a true belief B, that belief will manifest *many* such competences, for many field/circumstance pairs F/C will apply. How then can one rule out its turning out that just *any* true belief of one's own is automatically justified? To my mind the key is the requirement that the field F and the circumstances C must be accessible within one's epistemic perspective.[2]

2 This theme is developed in Section C.

(Note that this requires considering servomechanic and animal so-called "knowledge" a lesser grade of knowledge, or perhaps viewing the attribution of "knowledge" to such beings as metaphorical, unless we are willing to admit them as beings endowed with their own epistemic perspectives.)

B. A SOCIAL COMPONENT OF KNOWLEDGE

In earlier discussion above we took note of a certain contextual relativity in our attributions of knowledge. It seems that linguistic and/or epistemic communities conceive of knowledge and, more specifically, justification, by reference to community correlated standards. Why is that so? We can now suggest an answer as follows.

All kinds of justification are a matter of the cognitive or intellectual virtue of the subject. We care about justification because it indicates a state of the subject that is important and of interest to his community. And that holds good for all sorts of epistemic justification, from mere "animal" justification to its more sophisticated, reflective counterpart. In all cases we have a state of interest and importance to an information-sharing social species. What sort of state? Presumably, the state of being a dependable source of information over a certain field in certain circumstances. In order for this information to be obtainable and to be of later use, however, the sort of field F and the sort of circumstances C must be projectible, and must have some minimal objective likelihood of being repeated in the careers of normal members of the epistemic community. For it is through our cognizance of such relevant F and C that we grasp the relevant faculties whose possession by us and others makes us dependable informants and cognizers.

Recall now that we are in no position to require *infallibility* for possession of a cognitive faculty or virtue. All we are in a position to require is a good success ratio. But how good a success ratio might we agree on in order to have a commonly shared standard for knowledge? A concept of knowledge requiring a perfect success ratio would not be very discriminating, and would not help us to keep track of the facts regarding epistemic dependability, our own and others'. Nor would that concept of perfect knowledge aid intercommunication of such facts amongst members of the group. It seems a reasonable conjecture that a concept of knowledge tied to virtues of approximately normal attainment would be most useful to the group. But of course what is normal in one group may be far from it in another.

The foregoing has displayed a contextual relativity of knowledge attributions to an epistemic community; and we have sketched a sort of explanation for the implied social component of knowledge. Our explanation sketch may be summed up most briefly as follows: We are social animals. One's linguistic and conceptual repertoire is heavily influenced by one's society. The society will tend to adopt concepts useful to it. A concept of epistemic justification that measures the pertinent virtues or faculties of the subject relative to the normal for the community will be useful to the community. The community will hence tend to adopt such a concept.[3]

C. INTELLECTUAL VIRTUES IN CONTEXT

A further sort of contextual relativity is built into our concept of knowledge by the view that our faculties or virtues give us knowledge only if they work properly in an appropriate environment.[4] But what powers or abilities do thus enable a subject to achieve knowledge or at least epistemic justification? These presumably would be powers or abilities to distinguish the true from the false in a certain subject field, to attain truth and avoid error in that field. One's power or ability must presumably make one such that, normally at least, in one's ordinary habitat, or at least in one's ordinary circumstances when making such judgments, one *would* believe what is true and *not* believe what is false, concerning matters in that field. Consider for comparison a slicing golf swing in a unique complex of circumstances including a clump of trees obstructing the hole and a tree off to the side: the sliced ball bounces off the tree to the side for a hole in one. Relative to its highly specific set of circumstances it was of course an effective stroke to hit. Does that earn it any credit, however, as a stroke to learn, practice, and admire? Of course not, since the circumstances in question are unlikely to be repeated in any golfer's career. And even if they happen to be repeated in every game of someone's career, that is just a fantastic accident which one could not have expected with any reasonable assurance and which other golfers cannot expect in their own careers.

Something similar holds true with regard to cognitive faculties. A certain doxastic response to given stimuli may be successful in a very special complex of circumstances. Take a subject who believes in a large grey object nearby when he hears the cannonade in Tschaikovsky's *1812 Overture*, where by coincidence there happens to be an elephant nearby

---

3 For more on the concept of epistemic justification, along with doubt that it can serve all the purposes epistemology has assigned it, see Chapter 14 in this volume.

4 Cf. Chapter 13 in this volume. Also see Alvin Plantinga's "Epistemic Justification," *Nous* (1986): 3–19, and "Positive Epistemic Status and Proper Function," *Philosophical Perspectives: Epistemology* (1988): 1–51.

from whose neck there happens to hang a radio, which happens to be tuned to a classical station, one which happens to be playing the relevant passage of that *Overture*. Relative to that highly specific set of circumstances that is of course an excellent doxastic mechanism to have. Has it thereby earned much credit, however, as a faculty to have, develop, exercise, retain, and admire? Of course not, since the circumstances in question are unlikely to be repeated sufficiently often in anyone's life. And if they happen to be repeated often for someone, that is just a fantastic accident that he could not have expected with any reasonable assurance, and that others cannot expect for themselves.

Even if that doxastic mechanism happens to serve a particular subject well, moreover, its use in the community at large might be epistemically undesirable. What is more, even if the use of that mechanism by the community is a success, that is only luck, which does not turn it into a true cognitive faculty for that community. To become a faculty a mechanism needs more than merely accidental success. A doxastic mechanism leading from certain sorts of inputs I to certain sorts of beliefs B(I), is a cognitive faculty relative to an epistemic community K only if that community is so circumstanced that its members *would* not normally be caused a belief B(I) by an input I unless belief B(I) were true.

We have reached the view that knowledge is true belief out of intellectual virtue, belief that turns out right by reason of the virtue and not just by coincidence. For reflective knowledge you need moreover an epistemic perspective that licenses your belief by its source in some virtue or faculty of your own. You trust your own correctness, holding your belief to be right through its origin in a reliable faculty or virtue.

Virtues are either fundamental or derived. Fundamental virtues are involved already in the child's beliefs about its surrounding causal and spatio-temporal network of bodies and events. Even a child's mastery of its own body, its slowly evolving repertoire of physical skills, and its first acquisition of a public language may be viewed as requiring already the acquisition or activation of such fundamental virtues.

Many questions arise, and here we take up only some of the most prominent. One has an intellectual virtue or competence, we are told, if and only if one would most likely believe the truth and avoid error in a certain field F of propositions, in certain conditions C. But this is easy to trivialize absent restrictions on C or F. Thus for any proposition P, let F be just {P, Not-P}, and let C be the condition that: *one-believes-P iff P-is-true and one-believes-Not-P iff Not-P-is true*. The corresponding virtue will then impeccably yield truth and only truth, avoiding error without fail. As a result *every* true belief will derive from the exercise of an impeccable faculty.

Restrictions are hence required on C and F. At a minimum, for S to believe P at t out of intellectual virtue, there must be a field of propositions F such that P is in F, and there must be conditions C such that S is in C at t (with respect to P), and such that S is nomologically (but not tautologically) likely to be right if S believes a proposition in field F when in conditions C.

For reflective knowledge one not only must believe out of virtue. One must also be aware of doing so. Of course one need not know with precision and detail the exact character of the relevant C and F. Some grasp of them is required, however, even if it remains sketchy and generic. Thus it may appear to you that there is a round and red object before you and you may have reason to think that for middle-sized objects in daylight at roughly arm's length (C) you would be likely to turn out right about their shapes and colors (F) if guided by your perceptions; so long as conditions remained relevantly like those in the past when you had been guided by your perceptions, in daylight, about such matters; all on the assumption, allowable in the context, that such conditions *would* remain unless one had some sign to the contrary.

So much for the relatively fundamental virtues involved in perceptual knowledge of colors and shapes in good light, etc. *Derived* virtues are virtues acquired by use of the more fundamental as when one learns how to read and use an instrument through a friend's teaching or through reading a manual or through empirical trial and error methods. Derived virtues are correlated with field-(F)/condition-(C) pairs; in that respect they are akin to fundamental virtues. Indeed, an intellectual virtue is *defined* as a competence to pick out the truth and avoid error within a certain field F of propositions and in certain circumstances C.[5]

Truly fundamental virtues may be largely innate. In any case, more derivative virtues are derived through exercise of the more fundamental. Neither will yield reflective knowledge without appeal to one's epistemic perspective.

Derived virtues are based in one way or another on established correlations. Either the correlation is established by enumerative induction, as in primitive agriculture, or it is established by theoretical reasoning which assumes certain boundary conditions, as in the use of ordinary instruments. In either case, though once established it may be conveyed by word of mouth, the use of the correlation remains epistemically dependent on the presence of the conditions relative to which it was originally

---

5 So anyhow may one define the generative faculties: perception, for example, or introspection, or intuitive reason. Transmission faculties like memory are another matter.

established or later sustained. And these conditions, it is assumed, would be bound to continue in the absence of some sign to the contrary.[6]

Several problems still remain. Some will now be raised briefly for intuition and deduction, but in fact they apply also to memory and perhaps even to introspection.

First of all, suppose we are happily intuiting or deducing along, without a care and with little or no self-consciousness. And suppose some of the "intuitings" or "deducings" that we do along the way are only ostensible and not real (so that it is not really our logical faculty for detecting simple necessities that is at work, but rather some other mechanism which, no matter how closely related, is not quite the same). Propositions thus falsely "intuited" might include for example some about barbers or about heaps or about self-membership of classes. (Or perhaps it *is* after all the same logical intuition which both leads us correctly often enough but also misleads us on occasion, as with the paradoxes just cited? If so, take a case of ostensible deduction which is in fact – at a certain crucial juncture – not strictly deducing but rather blundering through inattention.)[7] Is it not plausible that our epistemic justification for the unreal intuitions and unreal deductive conclusions would seem about as good as that enjoyed by many of the real intuitions and real deductive conclusions? But since the unreal intuitions and deductions may be regarded as not yielded by rational intuition or rational deduction at all, the question remains of how we could possibly explain the epistemic justification of those unreal intuitions and deductions. One way in which we could *not* explain it is of course to attribute the unreal intuitions or deductions to any true faculty of rational intuition or rational deduction. For, by hypothesis, it is not these faculties that yield the false intuitions and deductions. Here then is a first problem we need to face.

A second problem involves the *real* intuitions and deductions· of someone whose ostensible intuitions and deductions from intuitions are nearly always shown to be ostensibly false. Can we plausibly attribute to his few real intuitions and real deductions from them any very high epistemic status? Can we even go so far as to attribute to him knowledge in the rare cases in which his ostensible intuitions and deductions from them turn out real and true?

6 This assumption of "normality" absent any sign to the contrary is a recurrent theme of empirical knowledge. Further variations appear in Chapter 4 of this volume. See also Castañeda's "Theory of Questions, Epistemic Powers, and the Indexical Theory of Knowledge," *Midwest Studies in Philosophy* 5 (1980): 193–230.
7 Chapter 13 takes up this issue.

D. EPISTEMIC PERSPECTIVISM

Our two problems lead again to a view of "epistemic perspectivism," according to which the deeper, reflective justification of the beliefs ostensibly yielded by a certain faculty derives from an explanatory inference that attributes those beliefs to the faculties from which they ostensibly derive. Since the products of such faculties are very likely true, this helps in turn to sustain our faith in the particular beliefs in question. And it helps to attach those beliefs coherently to a corpus that already includes belief in the reliability of the corresponding faculties. When one accepts an ostensible memory m, therefore, one's justification for accepting what one accepts cannot always derive from the operation of memory, for sometimes the ostensible memory is *merely* ostensible. What then accounts for one's justification in such cases? What justifies accepting one's ostensible memory m in such cases is, I suggest, a meta-belief in the virtue of one's memory which delivers m. So much with regard to our first problem, that of explaining how one becomes justified in believing something *ostensibly* a product of memory, say, or of intuition, but not really so. One is justified in believing the ostensible memory or intuition because one justifiedly attributes the belief in question to one's trustworthy memory or intuition. One's justification hence derives from an explanatory induction applied to oneself and one's pertinent faculties.

As for the second problem, here again we may appeal to the requirements of coherence for deeper, reflective justification. If the ostensible products of my ostensible faculty F turn out ostensibly false in the great majority of cases, I can' hardly sustain my confidence in the product beliefs by attributing them to such an ostensibly unreliable faculty. (Similar questions may be raised if most products of the faculty in question turn out *actually* false, whether ostensibly so or not, but these seem really problems for the thesis that one can attain *knowledge* by use of such a faculty, and not so much for the thesis that one can thereby attain justification.) An example of this second problem is how to explain someone's lack of justification for believing a particular perception if many of his ostensible perceptions turn out false, but only because they are not really perceptions at all, but derive rather from hypnotic suggestion or neurophysiological manipulation. A first explanation is now that in such circumstances one would be unable to accept one's own faculties of perception, and would hence be denied a coherent epistemic perspective from which to admit the deliverances of any such faculties. But there is also a further explanation: namely, that in such circumstances one would have no real faculties of perception, since these faculties if real must enable one to do *two* things reliably: first, to grasp the truth in the field proper to the faculty; and, second, to avoid error in that field. Our subject would qualify on the first count, but *not* on the second. (And indeed it may be questioned whether *ostensible* perceptions could coherently be ostensibly false with a high percentage. How could the subject attribute to himself *any* perception in such circumstances?)

Epistemic perspectivism is a view one is led to in response to certain problems with coherence theories of epistemic justification.[8] Now the development of faculty epistemology leads in the same direction. And the requirements of epistemic perspectivism may help also with the notorious generality problem, and with the new evil-demon problem, both of which let us now discuss (in reverse order) if only with preliminary tentativeness.[9]

The new evil-demon problem

Consider T, an "internal twin" of S's, externally situated in a world W(T). Whereas S's perceptual faculties are reliable in his own world W(S), let T's corresponding faculties be wildly unreliable in W(T). Clearly T does not have the knowledge of W(T) that S has of W(S). Yet it seems intuitively outrageous to deny that T in some sense does have justification for what he believes just as does S. The epistemology of virtues-cum-perspective yields the following assessment:

(i) Both the beliefs of S and those of T are justified (and reflectively apt), since they both fit equally coherently and comprehensively into their respective experience-plus-belief frameworks.

(ii) Whereas S's coherent framework is largely enough true to contain not only justification but much knowledge as well, T's equally coherent and comprehensive framework differs dramatically because it is pervaded by falsehood concerning the supposed virtues or faculties by appeal to which T explains his beliefs (and concerning much else besides). T therefore *depends* on some falsehood for justification of many particular beliefs therefore blocked from constituting knowledge. (Compare here the Gettier problem.)

The generality problem

All kinds of justification involve the cognitive or intellectual virtues, faculties, or aptitudes of the subject. We care about justification because it

---

8 In, e.g., Chapter 11 in this volume.
9 Concerning the generality problem, see Richard Feldman, "Reliability and Justification," *The Monist* (1985): 159–74. On the new evil-demon problem, see Keith Lehrer and Stewart Cohen, "Justification, Truth, and Coherence," *Synthese* 55 (1983): 191–207.

tends to indicate a state of the subject that is important and of interest to his community, a state of great interest and importance to an information-sharing social species. What sort of state? Presumably, the state of being a dependable source of information over a certain field in certain circumstances. In order for this information to be obtainable and to be of later use, however, the sort of field F and the sort of circumstances C must be projectible, and must have some minimal objective likelihood of being repeated in the careers of normal members of the epistemic community. For it is through our cognizance of such relevant F and C that we grasp the relevant faculties whose possession by us and others makes us dependable informants and cognizers. What is more, it is precisely by grasping how one does oneself have such animal aptitude over a certain field F in certain circumstances C that one bootstraps up to a higher level of reflective justification. For one is able to boost one's justification in favor of P if one can see one's belief of P as in a field F and in circumstances C, such that one has a faculty (a competence or aptitude) to believe correctly in field F when in conditions C. Moreover, to arrive at this true awareness of one's animal endowments one must have attained awareness of one's persistent tendency to be right in field F when in circumstances C. And one must have reasoned that such a tendency cannot have been just an accident, that in the prevailing conditions one must have been persistently right through some faculty or aptitude. One thereby attributes to oneself some intrinsic state such that when there arises a question in field F and one is in conditions C, that intrinsic state adjusts one's belief to the facts in that field so that one always or very generally believes correctly.

To arrive at true awareness of one's animal endowments one must have attained awareness of one's persistent tendency to be right in field F when in circumstances C. And one must have reasoned that such a tendency cannot have been just an accident. Or so I claim. But there is a problem: What is required for such a tendency to be an accident? Some might appeal here to the notion of design.[10] My own best bet of how to understand what it is to be right only by accident is however not in terms of design, but in terms of one's epistemic perspective and one's faculty of reason. What makes a new belief B of one's own in a certain field F only accidentally correct and *not* the outcome of a pertinent faculty? My conjecture is that this has to do with one's reflective awareness, implicit though it normally remains, as to the source of belief B in one's pertinent

---

10 Alvin Plantinga, for example, given the large role played already by that notion in his theory of knowledge. See his "Positive Epistemic Status and Proper Function," *Philosophical Perspectives: Epistemology* (1988): 1–51.

epistemic competence or intellectual virtue. Normally, it is possible for one to have such reflective awareness only if one *has been* persistently successful in a certain field F and circumstances C, and one is then able to make an explanatory induction or projection that one is the sort of being who *would* be successful in that field given the pertinent circumstances that have persistently prevailed. What then makes the new belief B only *accidentally* correct is the fact that those pertinent circumstances C continue only accidentally relative to their having held in the many earlier cases from which one made one's explanatory induction or projection about one's propensity to be right in the circumstances. And for circumstances C to continue only accidentally is a matter of their continuing for reasons importantly different from the reasons why they held in the cases from which one made one's induction.

For a simple example of the phenomenon, suppose you have established your credentials as a judge of the shape of certain objects reflected on a screen, but that the lenses in your eyes become distorted while, unbeknownst to anyone, the images on the screen coincidentally become distorted in a compensating way. In such circumstances your next judgment would of course be right only by accident and would represent no knowledge. Here your past success had been due to the stable development of each of two causal processes (one for your eyes, etc.; one for the screening device). Now each of these suffers a jerky change not smoothly integrable with its earlier development, the two yet coinciding, for no discernible deeper reason, in such a way that the basis for your success remains. The basis – contained in circumstances C – remains, but for reasons importantly different from the reasons why it held in the past cases of your success. And the reasons seem importantly different because they apparently do not flow from the operation of the same stable regularities, no matter how deep one probes. On this view, accidents which are mere coincidences derive from irregularities in causal processes (i.e., in at least one such), *irregularities which lack any accessible enough explanation by appeal to deeper regularities*. To bring in "explanation" is of course to suggest the relativity and context-dependence of our notion of an accident which is a mere coincidence. In the eyes of God there may be no such accidents. (And we are still left with something of a fudge: "accessible *enough*," which means presumably "accessible enough to the supposed knowers or to the attributors of knowledge, or perhaps to both.")

Concerning the generality problem, now, what should one say about the field F and the conditions C relative to which one can attain pertinent animal justification, through one's tendency to be right in F and C? What restrictions may appropriately be placed on F and C? Such restrictions must heed a twofold objective: *(a)* that F and C not be made so specific that one is always perfectly reliable and justified whenever one's belief is true; but also *(b)* that they not be made so generic that one cannot explain how a subject could have two beliefs both derived from the given faculty (e.g., from his sight, or, more generally yet, from his sensory perception), though one is justified while the other is not. The likely solution is to be sought, as I see it, in the requirements that F and C must fulfill if (i) F and C are to be usefully generalized upon by us as the epistemic community of the subject S (assuming he is one of us – and, if not, then knowledge attributions may need to be indexed or relativized to such communities); and if (ii) F and C are to be usefully generalized upon by the subject himself as he bootstraps up from animal to reflective knowledge. Such generalizing is itself an intellectual act which to be respectable must reflect intellectual virtue. This virtue moreover is bound to be overarching by standing upon our other virtues in doing its proper job. For its raw material is of two sorts: first of all, it uses deliverances of the subordinate virtues or faculties, for example, the specific observational beliefs delivered by our senses; and, secondly, it uses *also* the respective facts of successful operation of such subordinate virtues over various fields in various conditions. This overarching virtue is thus a faculty of faculties, a faculty that uses our brute animal endowments to raise us above that level and make of us the animal that is rational.

E. INTELLECTUAL VIRTUE DEFINED

One has an intellectual virtue or faculty relative to an environment E if and only if one has an inner nature I in virtue of which one would mostly attain the truth and avoid error in a certain field of propositions F, when in certain conditions C. The distinction between E and C is not sharp or important and amounts to a distinction between relatively stable background conditions and relatively episodic conditions. Consider:

(V) S has an intellectual virtue V(C, F) relative to environment E if and only if S has an inner nature I such that

if   (i) S is in E and has I,

         (ii) P is a proposition in field F,

         (iii) S is in conditions C with respect to P, and

         (iv) S believes or disbelieves P,

then   (v) S is very likely right with regard to P.

The distinction between E and C is closely allied to that between a capacity and a disposition. If (in the corresponding account of virtues generally) conditions C are allowed wide compass while the environment E is narrowly circumscribed, then, as a newborn, Chris Evert already had the virtues of a tennis player. But it is much more plausible to restrict the scope of conditions C in such a way that only after a period of maturation and learning does she come to be in an environment E with an inner state I (a *total* relevant epistemic state, including certain stable states of her brain and body) by virtue of which she *would* then perform stellarly when in the conditions C of a tennis match (on the surface of the earth, etc.).

F. INTERNAL APTNESS

Given our view of intellectual virtue, what makes one's belief that-p a result of enough virtue to make one internally apt in that belief?

> (IA) Subject S believes that-p out of sufficient virtue relative to environment E and epistemic group of subjects G if and only if S has an inner nature I such that
>
> *first,* the proposition that-p is in a field F, and S is in conditions C with respect to that proposition, such that S has an intellectual virtue V(C, F) relative to E, and
>
> *second,* by comparison with epistemic group G, S is not grossly deficient in ability to detect thus the truth in field F.

IA presupposes the following:

> (GD) By comparison with epistemic group G, S is grossly deficient in ability to detect the truth in field F if and only if, by comparison with G, S has a grossly deficient range relative to F, C, or E.

This requirement is meant to rule out a sort of Magoo case, a case of someone extremely nearsighted but totally unaware of his condition. Accordingly, his visual judgments just inside his visual range are in some relevant sense a matter of luck, since he would continue to pass confident visual judgments well beyond that range. The preceding account tries to preclude such a case by ruling Magoo grossly deficient as follows: Even if *within* his visual range he has a high enough probability of success in his visual judgments, the maximum broadening of that range wherein Magoo remains proficient is grossly deficient in its breadth relative to the epistemic group G of humans generally – which is to say simply that humans generally are not nearly so limited in their visual range, and their judgments even just within Magoo's range are not right just by luck, since they would still tend to be right well beyond that range.

Although it rules out the Magoo case, that requirement is unacceptable: It rules out too much else. For example, it rules out someone myopic but, unlike Magoo, well aware of his limits: thus, he passes judgment on the scene before his nose but never on that beyond his window. Can't he read his newspaper headlines even if he cannot read highway signs from a distance, or even house numbers from the curb? Similarly, someone color-blind is still able to tell what is white and what is black. The myopic can know much about the shapes of environing things, as can the color-blind about their colors, even though each is grossly deficient, relative to the average human, in the breadth of the relevant maximum conservative broadenings. Once you extend the field/conditions/ environment complex to include middle-sized objects beyond arm's length, the myopic fall far below the average. And once you include the red and the green as well as the white and the black, the color-blind also reveal their gross deficiencies. Despite this they clearly still retain their ability to know about shapes and colors within certain restricted parameters of distance and hue.

The big difference between Magoo and the ordinary myopic is a difference in self-knowledge with a corresponding difference in self-imposed limits for the use of one's eyes. The ordinary myopic and Magoo are equally deficient beyond arm's length, but the former knows his limits and proceeds accordingly.

These recent reflections suggest a problem for the earlier account V of intellectual virtue. On that account the completely blind have the same intellectual virtue as the most acutely sighted, so long as the blind naturally would refrain from making relevant judgments about the colors, shapes, and so forth, of facing surfaces even in good light. Let's try again:

(V') S has an intellectual virtue V(C, F) relative to environment E if and only if S has an inner nature I such that

if   (i) S is in E and has I,

      (ii) P is a proposition in field F, and

      (iii) S is in conditions C with respect to P,

then (iv) S is very likely to believe correctly with respect to P.

It is clearly in accord with V' that the sighted have intellectual virtues lacked by the blind. And it is clear that the ordinary myopic has his more limited virtues as well, as does someone who is color-blind. V' is still problematic, however, since Magoo also is judged virtuous by account V', and in the absence of any further resource we must say that Magoo's beliefs within the range of his myopia are no less virtuous than those of an ordinary myopic. (If the latter's beliefs can amount to knowledge, therefore, V' provides no way to explain how Magoo's beliefs can fail to constitute knowledge as well.) We need to try again.

First, a preliminary definition:

(B) X1 is a broadening of X2 iff X2 is an allowable subfield of field of propositions X1, or X2 is an allowable restriction of condition X1, or X2 is an allowable subenvironment of environment X1 – where in each case X1 is a limiting case of a broadening of X1 itself.

(The conditions imposed in Section D on allowable C and F should be extended now to E as well, and these conditions also determine what is an "allowable" subfield, or restriction, or subenvironment.) Our concept of a "broadening" enables a new proposal:

(V'') S has an intellectual virtue V(C, F) relative to environment E iff S has an inner nature I such that

(a) if (i) S is in E and has I,
   (ii) P is a proposition in field F, and
   (iii) S is in conditions C with respect to P,

then (iv) S is very likely to believe correctly with respect to P, and

(b) for no broadening E' of E, C' of C, or F' of F is it the case that S is in E' and has I, P is in F', and S is in C' with respect to P, *and*, moreover, *if* (i) S is in E' and has I, (ii) P is a proposition in field F', and (iii) S is in conditions C' with respect to X, *then* (iv) S is likely to believe with respect to P, but S is not likely to believe *correctly* with respect to P.

Finally, we can say what it is to believe out of intellectual virtue:

(BIV) S believes P out of intellectual virtue V(C, F) iff

(a) S is in an environment E such that S has intellectual virtue V(C, F) relative to E,
(b) P is a proposition in F,
(c) S is in C with respect to P, and
(d) S believes P.

And we can add an account of what it is to believe out of sufficient virtue that one is internally apt in so believing.

(IA') S believes proposition P out of sufficient virtue relative to epistemic group G iff

287

    (a) S believes P out of intellectual virtue V(C, F), and

    (b) the likelihood that S believes *correctly* when S believes out of virtue V(C, F) is at least up near the average for group G.

(For restrictions on the sort of C or F that can appropriately figure in any of V″, BIV, or IA′, see again Section D.)

G. THE VIEW OF INTERNAL JUSTIFICATION IN TERMS OF INTELLECTUAL VIRTUE APPLIED TO OUR PROBLEMS

Consider again the new evil-demon problem. What makes the subject epistemically blameless and even admirable seems not just a matter of his internal "justification" so much as a matter of the intellectual virtue and total internal aptitude of that subject relative to an assumed group G and environment E, which absent any sign to the contrary one would take to be the group of humans in a normal human environment for the sort of question under consideration. Given these assumptions, the victim of the evil demon is virtuous and internally apt in every relevant respect, not just in respect of enjoying internal justification, for the victim is supposed to be just like an arbitrarily selected normal human in all cognitively relevant respects. Therefore, the internal structure and goings-on in the victim must be at least up to par, in respect of how virtuous that internal nature makes the victim, relative to a normal one of us in our usual environment for considering whether or not we have a fire before us or the like. For those inclined toward mentalism or toward some broadly Cartesian view of the self and one's mental life, this means at a minimum that the experience-belief mechanisms must not be random but, rather, must be systematically truth-conducive, and that the subject must attain some minimum of coherent perspective on his own situation in the relevant environment and on his modes of reliable access to information about that environment. Consider next those inclined toward naturalism who hold the person to be either just a physical organism or some physical part of an organism, or to be anyhow constituted essentially by some such physical entity; for these it would be required that the relevant physical being identical with, or constitutive of, the subject in the situation in question must not be defective in cognitively relevant internal respects, which would mean, among other things, that the subject would acquire beliefs about the colors or shapes of facing surfaces only under appropriate prompting at the relevant surfaces of the relevant visual organs (and not, e.g., through direct manipulation of the brain by some randomizing demon).

We have appealed to an intuitive distinction between what is intrinsic or internal to a subject or being and what is extrinsic or external. Now, when a subject receives certain inputs and emits as output a certain belief or a certain choice, that belief or choice can be defective either because of an internal factor or because of an external factor (or, of course, both). That is to say, it may be that everything inner, intrinsic, or internal to the subject operates flawlessly, and indeed brilliantly, but that something goes awry – with the belief, which turns out to be false, or with the choice, which turns out to be disastrous – because of some factor that, with respect to that subject, is outer, extrinsic, or external.

On the present proposal, aptness is relative to environment. Relative to our actual environment A, our automatic experience-belief mechanisms count as virtues that yield much truth and justification and aptness. Of course, relative to the demonic environment D, such mechanisms are not virtuous and yield neither truth nor aptness. It follows that relative to D the demon's victims are not apt, and yet *relative to A their beliefs are apt.* This fits our surface intuitions about such victims: that they lack knowledge but that internally they are blameless and, indeed, virtuous.

Finally, we may now see the victims of the evil demon to be internally "apt," relative to our actual environment E, just as internally apt as we are. Equivalently, we may see the victims to be "intellectually virtuous," or at least as intellectually virtuous as we are.

Distinguish now between "justification" and "aptness"[11] as follows:

(a) The "justification" of a belief B requires that B have a basis in its inference or coherence relations to other beliefs in the believer's mind – as in the "justification" of a belief derived from deeper principles, and thus "justified," or the "justification" of a belief adopted through cognizance of its according with the subject's principles, including principles as to what beliefs are permissible in the circumstances as viewed by that subject.

(b) The "aptness" of a belief B relative to an environment E requires that B derive from what relative to E is an intellectual virtue, i.e., a way of arriving at belief that yields an appropriate preponderance of truth over error (in the field of propositions in question, in the sort of context defined by C).

Clearly, then, "justification" amounts to a sort of inner coherence, something that the demon's victims can have despite their cognitively hostile environment, but also something that will earn them praise

---

11 For this sort of distinction, see, e.g., "Methodology and Apt Belief," Chapter 14 of this volume. The more generic distinction between external and internal justification may be found in Chapter 1 of this volume.

relative to that environment only if it is not just an inner drive for greater and greater explanatory comprehensiveness, a drive that leads nowhere but to a more and more complex tissue of falsehoods. If we believe our world not to be such a world, then we can say that, relative to our actual environment A, "justification" as inner coherence earns its honorific status and is an intellectual virtue, dear to the scientist, the philosopher, and the detective. Relative to the demon's D, therefore, the victims's belief may be inapt and even unjustified – if "justification" is essentially honorific – or, if "justified" simply because coherent, then, relative to D, that justification may yet have little or no cognitive worth. Even so, relative to our environment A, the beliefs of the demon's victim may still be both apt and valuably justified through their inner coherence.

H. SUMMARY SKETCH OF VIRTUE PERSPECTIVISM

(i) Let us distinguish between animal (and even servomechanic) knowledge and reflective knowledge. A belief that p constitutes reflective knowledge that p only if one has a perspective on the source of that belief in a faculty or intellectual virtue of one's own. Otherwise it is unreflective. (Of course human reflective knowledge is most likely to depend ultimately on unreflective knowledge, since we cannot climb infinite ladders of reflection.)

(ii) Let us distinguish also between aptness of belief and justification of belief. Justification of belief that p requires the (implicit or explicit) use of reasons in favor of P. A belief can be apt, however, without being thus justified: if it is a memory belief, for example. Animal knowledge will generally be apt belief but rarely if ever justified belief.

(iii) The aptness required for a belief to qualify as animal knowledge is best explained by the truth-conduciveness of that belief's generating faculty, though we still need to face the generality problem. (Animal knowledge encompasses some special cases of unreflective knowledge: perceptual knowledge, for example, and certain types of procedural knowledge, such as the procedural knowledge involved in certain physical skills or abilities.)

(iv) Virtue perspectivism solves our generality problem by viewing attributions of animal knowledge as indexically context-bound. If S attributes animal knowledge that p to A, then S implies that A's belief of P is apt by deriving from the exercise of a faculty that detects truth well enough in a field of propositions F in circumstances C, where P is in F and A is now in C. But, as we have seen, not just any F and C will do. And since lower brutes are unable to use hypothetical or explanatory induction, we cannot restrict the relevant Fs and Cs in their cases of Fs and Cs thus usable by *them*. Our best recourse, in keeping with perspectivism, is hence to restrict such Fs and Cs to those appropriately usable by the *attributor*.

(v) Virtue perspectivism therefore accepts a sort of reliabilism with respect to animal knowledge, and with respect to unreflective knowledge generally. To the extent that reflective knowledge ultimately depends on unreflective knowledge (see (i) above), moreover, there follows a substantial element of reliabilism for reflective knowledge as well. Human reflective knowledge depends on a level of unreflective knowledge, where one *conforms* to virtuous intellectual procedure: *conforms not just by accident, however, but out of one's intellectually virtuous nature*. But even here we must restrict the relevant F and C, on pain of disaster, and even here for perspectivism the likely solution lies in allowing only Fs and Cs appropriately usable by us for reasonable generalizations about our intellectual aptitudes. Unreflective meta-knowledge requires, moreover, that the pertinent F and C be accessible and appropriately usable by the *knower* and not just by the attributor.

(vi) Reflective justification, our best reflective intellectual procedure, is a matter of perspectival coherence – and necessarily so. Hence even a Cartesian demon could not give us an unjustified though appropriately coherent view of things – no matter how many others of our supposed faculties (besides coherence-seeking reason) turn out to be pseudo-faculties that lead us astray more often than not. Does it not seem conceivable, however, that even coherence-seeking reason could in some possible world more often lead us astray than aright? What then shall we say of the beliefs of the rational in such a world? Rational beliefs would be *inapt* in such a world. But might they still be *justified*? If justification by definition derives from the "application" (rational, logical, coherential) of our deepest logical and intellectual standards and procedures (which would need to be specified for more substance in our definition), then even in such a world rational subjects would by our lights be justified. Might their beliefs still be *inapt* though justified? Well, might not their *ampliative* coherence-seeking reason be *for the most part* a source of error? Because this is hard to deny, we are led to consider the possibility that a rational subject might be led by the exercise of rationality to mostly erroneous beliefs and that *ampliative*, coherence-seeking reason itself be inapt in some possible world.

(vii) Justification is therefore by our view *internal* – and not even an evil demon could deprive us of it merely by tampering with our external context. For justification is *defined* as the correct "application" (by our logic, naturally) of our deepest intellectual procedures (which makes justification relativist and indexical).

(viii) Aptness is nevertheless *external*. For a belief is apt iff it derives from the proper exercise of virtue – which means that the proposition believed must be of the right sort, in field F of propositions, and the circumstances C must be right (external circumstances often included).[12]

(ix) Note the interesting circularity. Apt belief is defined as virtue-derived belief. Virtue is a matter of non-accidental truth-conduciveness of one's beliefs in a field F (of propositions) in circumstances C (possibly external). But there is a restriction for appropriate Fs and Cs; for they must be Fs and Cs usable by us in attaining a *coherent* view of our own intellectual economy. Coherence therefore helps define not only justification but also aptness. Might not coherence-seeking reason itself be *inapt*, however; is this not at least conceivable? Yes, conceivable it does seem to be; but, though conceivable, coherence itself requires that we regard it as *false*. There is no aptness without coherence, or without at least our potential for coherence, as things stand; for aptness is *defined* in terms of Fs and Cs that ensure such potential. Yet even coherence-seeking reason *might conceivably* turn out *inapt*, in which case even our best justified true beliefs might be no knowledge – since they would inaptly derive from very low intellectual aptitudes, and would be right only by accident.[13]

(x) What in sum is required for knowledge and what are the roles of intellectual virtue and perspective? For the exercise of virtue to yield knowledge, one must have some awareness of one's belief and its source, and of the virtue of that source both in general and in the specific instance. Hence it must be that in the circumstances one would believe P iff P were true. And this must be so in virtue of a field of propositions F and conditions C, such that P is in F and one is in C (with respect to P), where one would be very likely to be right whenever one believed a proposition in F while in conditions C with respect to that proposition. And, finally, one must grasp that one's belief non-accidentally reflects the truth of P through the exercise of such a virtue.

(xi) That much seems right for object-level beliefs, but we need to go beyond it for doxastic ascent. It would be absurd to require at *every* level that one must ascend to the next higher level in search of justification (recall the problems for Bonjour's coherentism), and it seems equally

---

12 For definitions of what it is to believe out of intellectual virtue and out of *sufficient* intellectual virtue, see Section E of Chapter 8.

13 I discuss the issues raised by (vi)–(ix) in Chapter 11 in this volume. For related issues, see James Van Cleve's "Foundationalism, Epistemic Principles, and the Cartesian Circle," *Philosophical Review* (1979): 55–91, and "Reliability, Justification, and the Problem of Induction," *Midwest Studies in Philosophy* 9 (1984): 555–67, and William Alston's "Epistemic Circularity," *Philosophy and Phenomenological Research* 147 (1986): 1–30.

absurd to suppose that a meta-belief MB can help justify an object belief B, even though MB is itself unjustified and no knowledge. The solution is to require the comprehensive coherence of a body of beliefs for the justification of its members, a coherence comprehensive enough to include meta-beliefs concerning object-level beliefs and the faculties that give rise to them and the reliability of these faculties; but to allow that, at some level of ascent, justification is acquired by a belief as a belief that is non-accidentally true because of its virtuous source, and through its place in such an interlocking system of beliefs, without any requirement that it in turn must be the object of higher-yet beliefs directed upon it.

Index

a priori truth, 20
abduction, 45, 48, 79–83
    defined, 81
Ackerman, F., 199n
Alston, W. P., 68n, 130n, 237n, 292n
analyticity, 73–4
aptness, 144, 255, 285, 289
    and coherence, 209
    and validation, 208
Aristotle, 187, 271
Armstrong, D., 36, 131
Audi, R., 68n
Aune, B., 68n, 179
authority, epistemic, 91, 110
Ayer, A. J., 15

Barnes, G., 123n
basic propositions, 17
Beanblossom, R. E., 221n
behaviorism, epistemological, 92
belief
    aptness of, 144, 255, 290
    nature of, 135
Bennett, J., 217n
Bonjour, L., 68n, 94n, 113, 115–20, 132n,
    170n, 181n, 237n
Brandt, R., 247
Brentano, F., 84n

Castañeda, H., 279n
causation, 36, 90, 187, 194, 221
charity principle, 122
Chisholm, R. M., 15, 19n, 20, 65, 66n,
    67n, 81n, 84n, 90n, 112n, 127, 128n,
    149n, 158, 209n, 216n, 239n, 257n
clairvoyance, 94, 132, 237
classification, 44, 56
cognitive equipment
    defective, 26, 48, 285
Cohen, S., 132n, 281n
coherence
    and aptness, 209
    defined, 114, 124
    and justification, 184–5
    priority of, 210–11

and reflective equilibrium, 262
    and validation, 209
coherentism
    and consistency, 96
    explanatory, 209
    and formal foundationalism, 180
    logical, 96
    non-linearity of, 68
    personal and verific justification in, 124
    perspectival, 97, 206
    and present abstraction, 94, 221
    probabilistic, 124
    and self-abstraction, 203–7, 221
    and truth, 211
Conee, E., 127, 149n
confirmation, 127
contextualism, 195
criteriology, 128

Dancy, J., 12n, 128n
Daniels, N., 262n
Davidson, D., 8n, 9n, 108, 120–3, 250
deduction, 166, 258–9
DePaul, M., 262n
Descartes, R., 20, 88, 115, 166, 211, 246
Dewey, J., 89
dispositions
    and epistemic virtues, 140, 189
    see also virtue, intellectual
doxastic ascent
    and foundationalism, 94, 181–2, 292
    and internalism, 126
    and justification, 125–6
    and supervenience, 183
doxastic presumption, 115–20
Dretske, F., 36, 131
Duhem, P., 258

elenchus, 250–3
empiricism and phenomenalism, 65, 88
epistemology
    evolutionary, 105
    naturalized, 78, 100, 106
    normative, 78
    as psychology, 100, 105

see also justification; knowledge
evidence
  defeasibility of, 72, 80
  and self-evidence, 20, 40
  sociality of, 28
  see also justification
evidentialism, 127
evil-demon problem, 157, 237, 265
  and new evil-demon problem, 132, 135, 143, 281
experience, sensory, 83, 128, 136, 185–8
  and ostensible perception, 227, 229
externalism
  and induction, 196–7
  and justification, 139, 193
  and reliabilism, 131
  see also reliabilism

faculty, intellectual, 234
  generation, 225–6
  transmission, 225–6
  virtuousness of, 227, 235
  see also virtue, intellectual
Feldman, R., 127, 128n, 132n, 281n
Firth, R., 67n, 106n
Foley, R., 71n, 175n
Foot, P., 266
foundationalism
  absurdity of, 108
  confrontational, 108
  conventionalist, 93
  and doxastic ascent, 94, 181–2, 292
  epistemic, 157, 173
  and epistemic principles, 67, 187
  formal, 151, 178
  and intellectual virtue, 189
  internalist, 127, 128, 157
  justification in, 90
  meta-epistemic, 157
  rationalist, 88
  regress in, 109–10, 149–50, 173
  relativity of, 28
  reliabilist, 94, 189
  substantive, 151, 178, 184
Frege, G., 21
French, P., 94n, 103n, 132n
full validation, 30
Fumerton, R., 67n

Gettier, E. L., 15n, 24n, 25n, 238n
Ginet, C., 225n
given, 108
Goldman, A., 10n, 35n, 36n, 131, 133n, 135n, 189n, 238n, 239n, 262

Goodman, N., 259
Greco, J., 12n
grounding, epistemic
  and evidence, 21, 30
  and self-evidence, 22
  see also justification
Guttenplan, S., 5n, 101n

Hardwig, J., 220n
Harman, G., 26, 27n, 45n, 68n, 113n, 240n
Hendel, C. W., 219n
Henrich, D., 108n, 250n
Hume, D., 20, 166, 219, 257

individuators, 69
induction, 196, 257
infallibility
  and justification, 84, 170, 185
  and rationalism, 194, 211
inference
  and justification, 113, 171
  sociality of, 91–2
infinite regress, 112, 121, 149, 155, 173–7
internalism
  and Cartesianism, 194, 246
  and contextualism, 195
  and doxastic ascent, 126
  and justification, 193, 245, 291
  and sensory experience, 128, 136
  and skepticism, 249
  see also foundationalism, internalist
introspection, 128, 228
intuition
  ostensive, 226, 279
  real, 279

justification
  and aptness, 144, 255, 290
  argumentative, 90, 109, 171, 195, 253
  and causation, 89, 187, 194
  and cognitive equipment, 26, 48
  communal relativity of, 142, 239, 287–8
  defeasibility of, 72, 80, 241
  environmental relativity of, 140, 144, 240, 276
  and epistemic perspectives, 97, 207, 222, 277
  inferential, 113, 171
  and intellectual virtue, 139, 142–4
  internal, 139, 142–4, 265
  normativity of, 86, 165
  not closed under deduction, 24, 71, 80
  objective, 16
  and overdetermination, 22

personal, 124
practical, 86, 165
regress of, 112, 121, 149, 155, 173–7
sociality of, 275
and standard conditions, 38, 43, 56, 59
strong and weak, 133
supervenience of, 86
universalizability of, 87
and validation, 21
verific, 124
see also grounding, epistemic;
    meta-justification; perspectivism,
    epistemic; validation

Kierkegaard, S., 198
Klein, P., 239n
knowledge
  causal factors in, 36, 221
  of coexemplification, 69
  collative, 70
  and evidence, 20, 40
  and Gettier problem, 15, 24, 40
  human and animal, 95, 240, 282
  illative, 70
  introspective, 185
  intuitive, 65
  of kinds, 44
  and looks, 45, 47, 51, 55
  observational, 186–7
  sociality of, 27, 275
  see also justification
Kraut, R., 251

Lee, R., 251n
Lehrer, K., 24, 25n, 32n, 68n, 123–6, 132n,
    216n, 221n, 222n, 281n
Leibniz, G. W., 216
LePore, E., 250n
Lewis, C. I., 65, 66n
logicism, 88
looks
  natural, 51
  normal, 52, 55

Machamer, P., 123n
Malcolm, N., 20n, 29n
memory, 35, 94
  fallibility of, 226, 230
  retentive, 218, 225
meta-incoherence, 132, 134
meta-justification, 134–5
methodism, 158, 166, 257
  circularity of, 248, 254
  and principles, 158
methodology, 245, 250

Mill, J. S., 156
Montefiore, A., 112n
Moore, G. E., 155, 262
Moser, P., 130n

Nagel, E., 247
naturalism, 136, 288
Nozick, R., 10n, 131, 239n, 243n

Oakley, I. T., 181n
observation, 186–7
overdetermination, epistemic, 22

Pappas, G., 131n, 189n, 199n, 238n
particularism, 158–61, 166
Pastin, M., 68n
Peirce, C. S., 45, 79
Pendlebury, M., 127n
perception, 65, 83, 125, 128, 136, 185–8
persons, identification of, 51, 55
perspectivism, epistemic
  and coherentism, 97, 206–7
  and foundationalism, 28
  and generality problem, 236, 278, 281–4
  and intellectual virtue, 274, 277
  and new evil-demon problem, 135–6,
    143, 281
  and reliabilism, 221–2
  see also virtue, intellectual
phenomenalism, 65, 88, 100
Plantinga, A., 7n, 276n, 282n
Plato, 19, 250, 271n
Pollock, J., 68n, 71n, 73n, 80n, 128, 129n,
    241n
Popper, K., 45n, 257, 258n
Post, J., 176n
pragmatism, 212
Price, H. H., 215
principle of charity, 122
principles, epistemic
  and coherentism, 68
  and foundationalism, 20, 40, 67, 73, 163,
    187
  and methodism, 158
probability, 65
  conditional, 124–5
"problem of the criterion," 158, 257n
projectibility, 127, 275, 282
pyramids, epistemic, 22, 167–8

Quine, W. V., 6n, 45n, 68n, 91–2, 100–4,
    179, 258
Quinton, A., 67n, 68n, 73n, 112n

Ramsey, F., 10n, 131n

rationalism, epistemic
  and infallibility, 88, 233, 252
  and reliabilism, 89, 211
rationality
  ampliative, 231, 233
  internal, 265
  social, 91–2
Rawls, J., 257n, 260, 262n
realism, fictional, 104
reason
  ampliative, 213, 231, 233
  deductive, 225
  intuitive, 226, 233
  and memory, 225
reasons
  and causes, 90
  conclusive, 36–8
recognition, 47, 51–5, 69
reflective equilibrium
  and coherence, 262
  and conceptual analysis, 263
  narrow and wide, 259–61
  social, 263
Reid, T., 220, 221n
relativism
  environmental, 140, 144, 240, 276
  moral, 266
reliabilism
  and circularity problem, 196–8, 271–2
  and evil-demon problem, 132, 135, 143,
    237, 281
  and foundationalism, 94
  and generality problem, 131, 236, 272,
    281–4
  historical, 132
  and meta-incoherence problem, 132,
    134, 144, 237
  and naturalized epistemology, 106
  priority of, 210, 213–14
  and rationalism, 89, 211
  see also externalism
Remnant, P., 217n
Rescher, N., 68n, 113n, 179
resemblance, 70–2
Rorty, R., 8n, 9n, 89–92, 108, 121
Ross, J., 216, 219
Ross, W. D., 156
Russell, B., 29, 102

S-epistemic propositions, 30
Sacks, O., 3n, 4n
Schilpp, P., 258n
science, 82, 102
Sellars, W., 20, 68n, 82n, 113n, 179, 181n,
  199

sensible characteristics, 188
Shope, R., 262
skepticism, 159, 168, 193, 249
Skyrms, B., 35n, 36n, 42n
Socrates, 250
standard conditions, 38, 43, 56, 59
Stich, S., 262–3
Stroud, B., 103n
supervenience
  and formal foundationalism, 152, 179
  and justification, 78, 87, 110, 156, 192
  see also full validation
Swain, M., 10n, 131, 189n
Swartz, R. J., 112n

testimony
  conditions for, 219
  epistemology of, 215–16, 219–20
  and memory, 218, 221
  and perception, 220, 241
trees, epistemic, 32–3, 40

Uehling, T. E., Jr., 94n, 103n, 132n

validation
  and aptness, 208
  and coherence, 209, 213
  full, 30
  and justification, 21
  and understanding, 87
  see also grounding, epistemic;
    justification
Van Cleve, J., 68n, 149n, 166n, 292n
virtue, intellectual
  and choice, 271
  and coherence, 123
  contextuality of, 276
  defined, 138, 140, 287
  derived, 278
  as disposition, 140, 189, 271
  environmental relativity of, 139, 140
  fundamental, 277
  as intellectual faculty, 236
  and internal justification, 139, 142–4,
    288
  as power, 235, 273
  social aspects of, 142
  and truth, 84, 189, 270
Vlastos, G., 250n, 251

Wettstein, H. K., 94n, 103n
Williams, B., 112n
Williams, M., 170n
Wittgenstein, L., 20, 89, 112, 149

WIDENER UNIVERSITY
WOLFGRAM
LIBRARY
CHESTER, PA.

D